SO
GOINGS
ON!

ISABEL PICKERING

Enjoy!   *Isabel Pickering*

**A selection of newspaper articles
about Fowey, Polruan and Lanteglos districts
from 1800-1899.**

Copyright 1995 by Isabel Pickering

ISBN 0 9521980 2 9
British Library Cataloguing-in-Publication Data
A Catalogue record for this book is available from the British Library

First Published 1995

Published by ISABEL PICKERING
Lescrow Farm, Passage Lane, Fowey, Cornwall PL23 1JS

Designed and Produced by John Thomlinson, Polruan, Cornwall

Printed and bound by Paperturn Print Ltd.

To my dear husband
Bob Pickering
who always encouraged
my research into
Lanteglos and Fowey history.

ACKNOWLEDGEMENTS

I wish to thank all the people who were so generous in pointing me towards interesting news articles and in giving me advice and encouragement, without whom this book would never have been completed. The Courteney Library at the Royal Institute of Cornwall was invaluable in giving me access to the original newspapers, as my eyesight would probably not have stood up to reading those issues on microfilm. Angela Broome and Mr. H.L. Douch were always welcoming and tolerant of my perusing the volumes of newspapers until the very last minute of each session. Mr. Rex Hall, a regular visitor to the Library, introduced me over a period of years to many splendid articles in the West Britain, which he often copied out for me most generously. Veronica Cheshire and Barbara Guernier, as well as the Fowey History Group gave me much valuable advice on collecting the articles I had gathered over a period of years into a book for the people of Lanteglos and Fowey parishes to enjoy. And finally, John Thomlinson, as always, was invaluable in guiding me through the intricacies of setting out the material in book form. My deep gratitude to you all.

CONTENTS

INTRODUCTION

One of the most interesting sources for local history which I have found have been the local 19th century newspapers. Just as we enjoy reading news stories today, we are similarly entertained by accounts of festivities, stories of drama and poignancy, announcements of inventions and progress in past years. In scanning these weekly reports we can catch a glimpse of how people were thinking and experiencing the events of their time.

We have a colourful picture of how the century unfolds - the excitement of the beginning years when threat of invasion and smuggling were rife, when captured ships were being brought into the harbour almost weekly; followed by more sober times, and periods of austerity which led people to look further afield to make new lives abroad. Those who stayed behind struggled and worked to improve their situation and surroundings; this is reflected in the admirable progress made in politics, education, housing, sanitation, and transport.

We also get a wonderful picture of how people sought to enjoy themselves, and enjoy themselves they certainly did. Regattas were indulged in with great zest. Anniversaries of chapel openings, jubilees of Royalty and of vicars were enthusiastically observed.

There were innumerable concerts and fetes or bazaars organized to raise money for all kinds of ventures, a most enjoyable method for achieving their ends.

We see how people did care about the miserable lives of those in need. Benevolences of the wealthy, Friendly Societies, the Foresters, Band of Hope, the building of the Fowey Cottage hospital, the Seamen's Rest, and the Working Men's Institute, the innumerable letters to the editor pleading for alleviation of hunger, better housing for agricultural labourers, better working conditions for women, etc. all show a widespread concern for the less fortunate.

In compiling this book I have scanned some 4000 issues of the Sherbourne Mercury, the Royal Cornwall Gazette, and the West Britain from 1800 to 1899 to extract some of the more interesting articles which have relevance for the Fowey-Lanteglos area. I have indicated at the beginning of each article the newspaper from which has come, in order to direct the more avid reader to read further. I have used the spelling and punctuation as found in each article; this sometimes varies from today's usage. One particular instance is the sign for Sterling pound - often it is £ and often *l*. Some articles have necessarily been shortened, as indicated by ..., and space would not permit me to include all the relevant articles I found. Those who wish to pursue a particular property or family can always contact me for further information. In a few instances I have also deleted names of those concerned because of the sensitive nature of the account. I trust that those who read these papers, now about a hundred or more years in the past will not be offended if they come across the name of an ancestor involved in some escapade, but that they will recognise that human history is always made up of misdemeanours as well as lofty deeds. I do humbly apologise if any are disappointed. What I feel these newspapers show overwhelmingly is the vigour of the nineteenth century, the colour and variety of every day living, the difficulties and the jollities of the lives they led.

ISABEL PICKERING

CHAPTER 1
1800-1809

1800

14 July (SM) To be SOLD by PUBLIC AUCTION,....All that large and Commodious Dwelling-house, situate in the town of Polruan, within the pleasant harbour of Fowey, commonly called YOUNG'S HOUSE, with extensive and Kitchen Gardens, Orchard, Stable, and small Meadow behind; together with 2 small Meadows called Castle and Little Meadow, about 1 acre and half. The house is delightfully situated,....commanding a prospect of Fowey and its harbour; was formerly the residence of the Young family, and has since been occupied by several genteel families; for a few years has been unoccupied and gone out of repair, but from its very beautiful situation would be a most desirable residence for a genteel family, and particularly for any gentleman fond of the sea, as a pleasure boat may be kept close to the house. (Perhaps Dolphins, Hockens Lane?)

Also, the Freehold and Possession of and in a very large and extensive FISH CELLAR, SALT CELLARS, and QUAYS, with the convenient Apparatus for curing Pilchards, more than sufficient in any prosperous year to cure a sean's fish;.... with water for a very large vessel to lay alongside; well adapted for a merchant, particularly to store salt in, as the cellars are extensive, and very dry; now let at £21 per annum to the proprietors of the *Lanteglos sean*, as tenants at will, together with 3/16th Parts in said Sean, Sean boats, Salt, and Materials.... A Public Auction will be held at the house of Richard Woon, innkeeper, in the town of Polruin,....the 25th day of Jul next..... The premises may be viewed by applying to Samuel Sanders of Polruin; for further particulars....to the Rev Philip Mayow, Plympton, Devon.... (Perhaps Vaughn's or Dunn's Yard?)

11 August (SM) FOWEY BOAT-RACE. On Friday, the 12th of September, will be ROWED FOR, at eleven o'clock in the forenoon, FOUR, TWO and ONE GUINEAS, for the Best, Second and Third Two-oared BOATS, not exceeding fourteen feet in length.- After which the Pilchard Sean-Boats will row.... John Hearle Tremayne, Esq. and Rev. Darell Stephens, Stewards. N.B. An Ordinary at four o'clock, at the Ship Inn; and a Ball in the evening.

6 October (SM) PORT of FOWEY. By order of the Honourable the Commissioners of his Majesty's Customs, on Thursday the 23rd day of October, 1800, by ten o'clock in the forenoon, will be exposed to PUBLIC SALE, at the Custom-House, in this port, The under-mentioned GOODS, viz.
Brandy, 5845 gallons; Rum, 190 Gallons
Geneva, 3214 Gallons; White Salt, 195 Weight
Which will be set up in lots for the accommodation of small families,

Also the *British Constitution* Sloop, burthen 15 tons, with her materials. The Broken Hull of the *Little Nett* Sloop.

The Pieces of two open Boats and their Materials.
N.B. The above goods may be viewed, and tasted, three days before the day of sale.
10 November (SM) MISSING from FOWEY, on Wednesday the 22nd of this instant October, from the house of George Thomas, an innkeeper, in the above place. A MAN, lately a DANISH CAPTAIN, about 5ft 8in high; having on when he left Fowey a blue jacket and trowsers, a light coloured wig, and more particularly had on the elbows of the jacket cloth of an inferior quality to that of the jacket; supposed to be in a delirious state when he left Fowey. Whosoever will give an account of a man of the above description, so as to prove to be the same, to Gabriel Brays, Esq, at Fowey, or to the above mentioned George Thomas, shall receive a REWARD of 1 gn...., and any reasonable expense paid.

1801

26 January (SM) WHEREAS a BOAT belonging to Captain Henry Jane, of the port of Fowey....was taken from her moorings on Saturday night, or early on Sunday morning last, (supposed by Frenchmen who had escaped from prison), - her dimensions were, in length 22 feet 10 inches, her breadth 7 feet 10 inches; had in her a mast with proper rigging, a fore sail, a main sail, some iron ballast, and a trawl net; copper nailed, and marked on the stern "Henry Jane, Fowey". If such boat should by accident, or by recapture, be in the possession of any person or persons who may peruse this, Captain Jane will allow the full salvage according to law, upon information that the`said boat is in safe possession, and will be delivered up in proper condition.

23 March (SM) A considerable number of Traders in Linen-Drapery and Pottery have been detected in various parts of England travelling without either Horse or Foot Licenses, and many with three Horses, by virtue of only a One Horse License: notice is hereby given, that such offenders will not be suffered to impose upon the revenue in future. Several hawkers have been detected and brought to conviction; others are now closely pursued....

18 April (RCG) A MEETING AT TRURO OF THE HIGH SHERIFF AND MAGISTRATES. On Wednesday the 15th, The following resolutions....(1) that the Magistrates will use their best endeavours to alleviate the Distress arising from the present Scarcity. (2) That it be recommended as a general Plan of Relief that the Earnings of every Person properly industrious, should be made adequate to the purchase of 6 Quarts Barley, or 1 Gallon Wheat, with 6d per Head per Week, for other Accessories to each Individual of the Family, besides such occasional Relief as extraordinary Circumstances may require.....

To the FARMERS of CORNWALL.... THE RIOTS THAT HAVE PREVAILED IN THIS fortnight past, and still continue, are not the fruit of....sedition; but the imperious calls of craving hunger. It is in your power, and yours only, to save the lives of many hundreds of your fellow creatures, who ware not only pining with want themselves, but whose distress is heightened by the agonizing cries of their starving children...You know the price of labour; and you know the price of Corn. You know then how inadequate the former is, to purchase a sufficiency of the latter for the support of a family of children. You cannot say the last harvest was a scanty one....in Cornwall at least the crop was abundant....a reduction of the price, should it increase the consumption, will lessen the present *destruction*. for every gallon of flour that is now *saved*, by placing it beyond the reach of the poor, there is a bushel destroyed, by shipping and cellaring it, till it heats, sours, and rots. It rests with you to....restore peace and content....In London....warehouses....are so choked with corn that "the quantities utterly destroyed, and thrown into the Thames, are astonishing.

Riot and disorder during the last and present week, have so generally prevailed through the county, that we might fill our paper...with their particulars. Scarcely a town in the county has escaped...but in the markets, it has been chiefly confined to the lower order of women only....In the mining districts, however, large bodies of tinners have assembled; particularly in the neighbourhood of *St Austle,* where they went around to the farmers, carrying a written paper in one hand, and a rope in the other. If the farmers hesitated to sign this paper,(which contained a declaration that they should sell their corn, etc. at a reduced price) the rope was fastened about their necks, and they were terrified and tortured into compliance.

2 May (RCG) The price of grain...is now falling more rapidly than it rose.... Four thousand five hundred barrels of American flour were sold by auction....on Thursday last.... Several cargoes are now on their passage from America...., some of which are hourly expected.

The decline in the price of grain, has been accompanied by a similar reduction in that of butcher's meat. The best cuts of beef and mutton are now sold throughout the county at 7d. Veal, lamb, and Pork, proportionably lower.

Fresh pilchards have been sold this week in Falmouth, at a penny a dozen - mackarel one shilling a dozen.

9 May (RCG)-Orders....are now circulating from the War-Office to the Army and Yeomanry along the coasts: - they direct, that in the event of an invasion, all cattle and horses be immediately driven into the interior, with a view to impede the progress of the enemy, who cannot be supposed, from our superiority at sea, to be able to bring with them a proportionate number of draught and other horses.

9 May (RCG)The Providence Chapel, at Fowey, will be opened by the Methodists on Holy Thursday next.

11 July (RCG) Fowey. To be sold by Auction on Tuesday, the 16th day of July next by 4 o'clock in the afternoon at the Ship Inn.... All that ELEGANT NEW-BUILT COTTAGE, with the offices, gardens and outhouse, now the Property, and in the Occupation of Gabriel Bray Esq, comprising on the 1st Floor a Dining Parlour, Breakfast ditto, and Drawing-Room, China Closets, Dressing Room and Pantry; on the 2nd floor 3 Bed-Rooms, a servant's ditto, and Dressing ditto; together with a Kitchen, Scullery, Laundry, Wash-House, and 2 Servants' Rooms, in detached Wings, and Cellars under the House. Is most delightfully situated adjoining the Borough of

Fowey....commanding an extensive View of the English Channel, and the Harbour of Fowey...., and would be a most desirable situation for....a small genteel Family, particularly where Sea Bathing, Fishing, and excursions on the Water are Objects;.... The Premises are held under the Grant from the Corporation of Fowey, for 21 years, renewable every 11 years, on Payment of a Fine of Twenty-two Pounds on the rent Day by 10 o'clock in the Forenoon. Will be sold also by Auction, on the above Premises all the neat and genuine HOUSEHOLD FURNITURE now therein, consisting of the Choicest Goods of every description. For Particulars, apply....to Wm. Brown, Attorney-at-Law, Fowey. (Perhaps 42-43 Esplanade?).

12 September (RCG) Great quantities of pilchards have been lost to the county, for want of salt to cure them.

3 October (RCG) To JOURNEYMEN SHIPWRIGHTS. IMMEDIATELY wanted, Two MEN who understands their business, to whom constant employ and good wages will be given. Apply Mr Richard Collom, Fowey.

3 October (RCG) The cargo of Indian corn imported....by the *Hero* from North Carolina and advertised in our last, was sold yesterday at from 23/-37/6 a quarter.- From this grain is made an excellent flour, which, when mixed with wheaten flour, renders the bread extremely wholesome and moist. This grain is much used in the Southern climates. Several heads of it has been grown in this county; and we have no doubt.... this grain might be raised at much less expense than wheat, or even barley - the head being so very large, and of course prolific.

1802

16 January (RCG) FOWEY The season for exportation of pilchards is over, there have been shipped in this port 8,500 hogsheads.

5 April (SM) FOR SALE by PUBLIC AUCTION, at the Ring of Bells Tavern, in the borough of Fowey, on Thursday the 20th of May next, at two o'clock in the afternoon, the SCOT and LOT PILCHARD SEINE, in complete repair; together with a great Quantity of FRENCH SALT....apply to Mr. Nicholas Olver, carpenter, Fowey.

22 May (RCG) NEW WINDOW TAX -.... Total sum to be paid for any number of windows from six to forty-four.- This duty commenced on the 5th April. For *six* windows, if the rent of the house is under £5 per year, 6s per year. Seven windows £.0.18.6. Nine windows £1.18.0. Ten windows £2.10.0. Eleven windows, £3.6.0. Twelve windows, £4. Thirteen windows, £4.15.0. Fourteen windows £5.10.0. Fifteen windows £6.5.0. New house duty commenced the same day. Houses of 5*l.* rent and under 20*l.* pay 1s 4d in the pound.

22 May (RCG) John Beard begs to inform Nobility, Gentry, and others that he has taken the Ship Inn which he has fitted up in a genteel style and for their accommodation, at the request of his friends, he has erected a commodious bathing machine on a pleasant beach near the entrance of the harbour. Fowey is a most delightful and healthy situation, distant from Plymouth about 24 miles and the harbour for sea bathing, fishing, and excursions on the water cannot be excelled.

Those who may honour J. Beard with their favours may depend on his utmost endeavours and exertions to merit a continuance.

3 July (RCG) FOR SALE BY PUBLIC AUCTION. On Monday, the 2nd of August next, by Three o'clock in the Afternoon, at the SHIP INN, Fowey. The Handsome fast-sailing Cutter *SWIFT*, now lying in Fowey Harbour, late in his Majesty's service; she then carried fourteen twelve-pound carronades, and two stern chases. Length from stem to stern, 72 Feet; Extreme Breadth 24 Feet 6 Inches;.... And admeasures 163 Tons per Register. The above vessel is only three Years old, a prime sailer, copper-bottomed, is a beautiful model, remarkably strong Built, and highly finished. She is well provided with stores and sails, the greater part new. For Inventories....apply to....Captain Walter Colmer, Fowey.

3 July (RCG) The venerable Philip Rashleigh, Esq., of Menabilly, who has for several years past been the father of the House of Commons, and nearly forty years represented the borough of Fowey, retires from public life. Reginald Pole Carew, Esq., of East Anthony in this county, and E. Golding, Esq., are expected to sit for that borough in the next Parliament.

31 July (RCG) FOWEY. Yesterday morning, about two o'clock the *Shillalagh* of Belfast, James Chambers master, from London to Belfast, with a valuable cargo of groceries, etc. was run on shore on Par Sand, near this place. The captain thought he was got to the Lands-end, and proceeding up St. George's Channel! She will be got off without damage.

7 August (RCG) By a late regulation of the Customs and Excise, the limits for capturing smuggling vessels, of all descriptions, laden with contraband goods, are now extended to eight leagues from the nearest headland, instead of the old limits prescribed in 1783, which were only four leagues; this will give a great advantage to the Cruisers and Revenue vessels in the channel.

28 August (RCG) EXCISE-OFFICE Jul 27 - WHEREAS, on the 29th of December last, a Shot was fired, from amongst a number of Men unknown, at GEORGE HAINS, Officer of Excise at Fowey...., which passed very near him: - and Whereas the said GEORGE HAINS was also attacked on the Evening of the 22nd ultimo, when in the execution of his Duty, and was knocked off his Horse, by Stones thrown out of a Ditch, near St. Blazey,....the Commissioners of Excise, in order to bring to Justice the Persons guilty of these atrocious Offences, do hereby offer a Reward of FIFTY POUNDS for the discovery of any one or more of them, so that he or they may be apprehended and convicted, to be paid...., upon the Conviction.

4 September (RCG) Arrived in Fowey the *"Expectation"* excise Cutter, Wren, to receive the *Joseph* sloop, and her cargo of salt, which had been collusively seized in January last, by John Foot, for which offence he was dismissed, and cast in 500*l.* and the seizure restored to Captain Adams, of the *"Eagle"* excise cutter.

29 November (SM) TO be LET, for a term of years, from Ladyday next, A Large and Commodious DWELLING-HOUSE, situated in the centre of the borough of Fowey; consisting of a large and well-accustomed Shop, in which an extensive business has been carried on for many years; a kitchen, dining-room, two parlours, five lodging-rooms on the second floor; four ditto on the attic storey; a wash-house, pantry, and scullery; six cellars; and a neat little pleasure-house that commands the entrance and harbour of Fowey. The premises are exceedingly well situated for carrying on an extensive foreign trade, as vessels of 200 tons burthen may discharge their cargoes lying alongside the premises. Further particulars....to Mr. P. Lukey, the present occupier.

1803

9 May (SM) TO be LET for a term of 14 years, from Michaelmas next, the BARTON and FARM of LAWHIRE, with several tenements adjoining, and now occupied therewith, by Thomas Graham, Esq. comprizing a good farm-house, with every requisite outhouse and about 115 acres of remarkably rich land, in a high state of cultivation, situate... within half a mile of the town of Fowey. The greater part of the estate is free of great tythes and land-tax. - For viewing the estate apply to the hind thereon.... a Survey will be holden in the Ship Inn, in the borough of Fowey....

16 July (RCG) The two companies of Fowey Volunteer Artillery, under the command of Thomas Orchard, Esq. paraded on Wednesday last, and mounted the guns on the batteries; after which they escorted the French prisoners to Mill prison.

16 July (RCG) FOWEY. Arrived, *Le Nairac*, from Martinique bound to Bourdeaux, taken the 29th ult. by the *Resolution* privateer of this port, in sight of the *Active* of Guernsey, and *Mary* of Jersey, with coffee, sugar, and hides, valued at 25,000*l*.; *Le Malouin*, French brig schooner privateer, commanded by Capt. Lauriol, taken by the *Speedwell* privateer, Capt. Colmer; the *Malouin* had taken and sent for Spain, the *Princess-of-Wales*, Gregg, of London, from Jamaica, with 1000 hogsheads of sugar, and other goods, valued at 100,000*l*.; the *Little Jane*, Koyle, of London, with sugar, coffee and wood. The captains and many of their crews were on board the privateer when taken, as were the prize-masters of two ships taken by two of our frigates, and retaken by *Le Malouin*.

Passed by a French West-Indianman, prize to the *Brothers* privateer, of Plymouth, valued at 15,000*l*.

23 July (RCG) East Looe Ladies Boarding School has opened....in a most desirable healthy situation.... English instruction, Board (washing included) Sixteen guineas per annum. One guinea entrance. Writing, French, Dancing, Drawing by approved Masters.

5 August (RCG) The Admiralty Court have appointed Mr. Brown of Fowey, (attorney-at-law, public notary, and a master extraordinary in Chancery) to be an Actuary at that port, for the condemnation of prizes. And we hope the "*gallants of Fowey*", once so celebrated for their maritime powers, will furnish him with plenty of prizes to condemn.

27 August (RCG) PROTECTION OF THE COAST - A regular establishment for the inrollment of seafaring persons, under the denomination of Sea Fencibles, having been formed by the Board of Admiralty, upon the line of coast more immediately opposed to the enemy, it is thought advisable that measures should be taken for a further extension of that system, and ...for the purpose of manning the batteries upon the coast....With this view, it is....recommended....to co-operate with the Board of Admiralty, in obtaining the enrolment of all seafaring men, not applicable to the service of the navy, upon their respective coasts....- Secondly, that it be recommended to the principal sea port towns to equip, at their own expense, a certain number of armed vessels and hulks,....for the better....protection of such ports, and to be.... manned by Sea Fencibles, who shall take charge of them and be exercised on board at the guns as often as may be required. Thirdly, that where the proportion of Sea Fencibles, which any place can furnish, is greater than such place can find shipping to employ;....vessels shall be furnished by Government Fourthly, that as colliers and coasting vessels are well adapted to be armed as gunboats, it be recommended to the principal Merchants and Owners in every port....to fit (the expense of such fitting has been calculated under 54*l.*) their vessels of that description with slides between decks, and loop-holes in the combings of their hatchways, for close quarters; these vessels to carry two guns forward and two aft, to fight on either side, as well as fore and aft. Fifthly, that when the vessels are reported ready, guns and ammunition shall be put on board by Government, free of expence to the owners; the masters giving a receipt and voucher to return them when demanded, and to keep a regular account of the expenditure of the Stores. Sixthly, that these vessels be fitted with ring and eye-bolts for guns, and that small vessels be prepared to receive large oars, that they may be able to act in a calm, if necessary. Seventhly that the said vessels be under orders to.... obey....the Commanders of his Majesty's ships, or....the signal stations on the shore, and when detained, that they be entitled to demurrage according to their regular tonnage, at the same rate as common transports;.... Eighthly, that the said vessels, on arriving at and sailing from port, be subject to be visited by the Commanding Officer of the Sea Fencibles of the district.

17 September (RCG) LOSTWITHIEL *Sept.* 8. A few days ago, a party, consisting of three ladies and three gentlemen, in a small boat, sailed from Lostwithiel to Fowey; and the weather being extremely pleasant, they proposed going out to sea, and had nearly reached Mevagissey, when the wind which had on the morning been very light began to blow stronger, and caused a gentle roll in the water, which was a signal for them to tack about. The wind increasing, and the sea becoming much agitated, the party began to be alarmed. It still blew harder and harder; and the waves which were very high, broke over them very much, which produced feelings which my pen would in vain attempt to describe. You may suppose their situation was truly distressing when they discovered it was impossible, by sailing, to reach land, as the wind had shifted so much north. Having a pair of small oars, they, by great exertions, got within a mile of the shore, when for want of refreshment and through great fatigue, the rowers were exhausted, and could keep the boat a-head no longer. The boat was left to the mercy of the waves, and when every hope had nearly fled, to their great joy, a vessel, which had seen their distress, was perceived at a great distance coming towards them. Providentially she came down just in time to rescue them from a watery grave, as her Captain, Charles Rowett, declared, that the boat would not have kept above water ten minutes longer. They were all taken up safe, and happily landed at Polperro; a circumstance that reflects the highest honour on the humanity of Captain Rowett and his crew, and which the party thus providentially preserved will ever gratefully remember.

8 October (RCG) FEMALE FASHIONS. Head dresses. A white lace veil placed on the head to form a cap; the right side hanging carelessly over the face, and ornamented with a row of beads, and a medallion; the left side drawn close over the hair, with a wreath of roses. - A large straw bonnet turned up in front and lined with blue. Cap of lace or muslin ornamented with a green wreath. - White beaver hat, turned up in front, and ornamented with roses. - The hair dressed with a black velvet band and gem clasp. - A Chinese hat, trimmed round the edge with white lace, and ornamented with a wreath of flowers....

8 October (RCG) On the 3rd instant was launched at Mr Nickels's yard, at this place, a fine ship, called the *Twins of London*, admeasuring between three and four hundred tons, but will carry about five hundred: perhaps the largest ever built in Cornwall.

29 October (RCG) The Truro Volunteer Infantry....were....assembled....to ask them whether, if His Majesty were to call on them to garrison Plymouth....for two or three months, they would volunteer.... The whole corps immediately proclaimed their cordial assent, by repeated huzzas, and (to Cornishmen) the inspiring cry of ONE AND ALL.... We understand the brave Fowey Volunteers have made a similar offer. The offer of the free use of the Fowey sean-boats, has been accepted by the Admiralty.

26 November (RCG) FOR SALE, And now Landing at Fowey. Two Cargoes of the best Norway TIMBER, DEALS, LATHWOOD, PALING BOARDS, and SPARS; calculated for Luggers, Cutters, &c. Also on Sale, a Quantity of very valuable MASTS and Square BALK. Apply to Mr John Kelly Graham, at Fowey.

10 December (RCG) FEMALE FASHIONS. The dresses are made very short waisted, and very low in the back, and in almost every part of them there is lace. For full dress, crape is much worn. Ostrich feathers of all colours are universal. Pelisse and spencers of velvet and cloth are much worn. The most favourite colours for them are dark green, sky-blue, and black: the military fronts are generally adopted. For undress, silver bear muffs and tippets are worn; - for dress swansdown.

24 December (RCG) A list of Fire-Beacons, in the Western District, on the Firing of which, the Forces are to assemble at the places of rendezvous. CORNWALL.... Fire-Beacon at Castle Doer, near Fowey,....Padderbery Top near Liskeard....

31 December (RCG) One third of the two companies of Fowey Volunteer Artillery, commanded by Thomas Orchard, esq. are exercised twice a day at the batteries that command the entrance of Fowey harbour.

1804

18 February (RCG) TO BE SOLD.... For the Remainder of a Term of 99 years, determined on the health of three healthy young lives, of the ages of 14, 4, and 3. All those new built Premises situate in the borough of Fowey,....comprising a Dwelling-house and Bakehouse, with a large patent Oven therein, 9 feet by 10 feet, together with an unfinished Dwelling-house adjoining, consisting of two Parlours and Breakfast ditto, kitchen, and 6 Bedrooms; also a Malt-house, Grannary, Drying Kiln, and large Courtlage behind... The above Premises are extensive, and well worth the attention of any gentleman who wishes to carry on an extensive Baking, Flour, and Corn Trade, or any other business where large premises are required, as vessels may lay alongside and discharge cargoes....a Public Auction will be held at the SHIP INN.

23 June (RCG) Fisher's company of Comedians leave Bodmin next week, on a short excursion to Lostwithiel and Fowey; and return again to Bodmin to perform in the assize week.

21 July (RCG) BOROUGH OF FOWEY. AT LEASE, FOR YEARS, DETERMINABLE ON LIVES. The Bell Inn, conveniently situated at the W. entrance of Fowey; consisting of a large House, 10-stall Stable, Courtlage, and other convenient Offices. Tenant - J. Eastlake.... Yearly rent 8s. (Perhaps Gullicks - it was an inn once).

28 July (RCG) Our pilchard season has commenced, and a few maunds of fish have been caught on different parts of the southern coast; but no shoal of consequence yet, that we have heard of, though the prospect is said to be encouraging.

28 July (RCG) It would, perhaps, be well if the firing of cannon in the neighbourhood of the several fishing bays, were suspended during the pilchard season, which lasts but about two months; at the noise of the cannon, as at that of thunder, pilchards immediately disappear, and are very shy of approaching the coast afterwards.

28 July (RCG) Among the many premiums offered by the Cornwall Agricultural Society for the ensuing year, is 5 guineas for the best specimen of cheese made in this county, between this time and June next; the quantity made not to be less than 112 *lbs*. There is but little cheese eaten in Cornwall, nor will it perhaps come into general use, till beer, as a beverage, shall be substituted for *grog*.

30 Jul (SM) EDWARD HINGSTON respectfully acquaints the public, that he is removed from FOWEY to MEVAGISSEY, where he intends to carry on the business of a BLOCKMAKER, in all its branches, and on the most reasonable terms; and he also begs leave to inform them, that he intends still to carry on his trade in the same shop at Fowey. - He takes this opportunity to return his sincere thanks to those who have favoured him with their orders, and to assure his friends, that he hopes by his good conduct to merit a continuance of their custom.

8 September (RCG) As some children were diverting themselves in Fowey, on Tuesday last, swinging on a board, one of them unfortunately slipped off, and, falling on his head, was killed upon the spot.

17 November (RCG) Some little uneasiness having appeared among the poorer people of Fowey and its neighbourhood, at the shipping of corn from that port, the town-crier of the borough, a few days ago, at the instigation of some impertinent person, proceeded to call an assembly of the populace to consider of the subject! The Magistrates very properly interposed, dismissed Mr. O-Yes from his office, and bound over Mr Busy-body to answer for his conduct at the next quarter sessions for the borough.

17 November (RCG) TO BE SOLD, The FEE-SIMPLE and INHERITANCE of all that capital Messuage and Farm, called HILLHAY, situate....within half a mile of the Borough of Fowey....; consisting of a good Farm House, Planch Barn, and all other necessary Offices, and about 100 Acres (be it more or less) of rich arable Meadow, and Orchard Land, now in the occupation of Mr. Thomas Littleton. The premises being so near the Borough and River of Fowey, where Pilchard Chaff, Lime, and rich Sand, for Manure may be had at a moderate expence, render them a very desirable purchase.

29 December (RCG) A brown cow stolen or strayed from Mickstow, in Lanteglos by Fowey - a vere old cow, of a bright brown colour, a white spot in her forehead, white legs and belly. Whoever will bring or give information of said cow to John Couch at Mickstow shall be handsomely rewarded and all reasonable expenses.

1805

9 Mar (RCG) Last week a Danish vessel, laden with timber and salt entered the port of Fowey. An excise officer happening to be on board while she was unloading a part of her cargo, discovered twenty hogsheads of wine, and two puncheons of brandy, concealed under the salt; upon which, he immediately seized the ship and her cargo.

30 March -(RCG) TO BE LET, For the Term of seven years from Michaelmas next, THOSE FARMS, situate within the parish of Lantegloss, by Fowey,....called TREDUDWELL, and GREGON; comprising the Farm part of Tredudwell House, Two Barns, and other Outhouses, and about One Hundred acres of Arable, Meadow, and Pasture Land, exclusive of 12 acres of Tredudwell, reserved by the proprietor; now in the occupation of Mr. Abraham Nastell, and Damaris Joli, widow. The Estates are in a high state of cultivation, most eligibly situated for procuring sea sand, and other manure, and for the disposal of its produce, being within half a mile of a navigable branch of the Fowey Harbour, two miles and a half of Fowey, ten of St Austle, twelve of Liskeard, and eight of Looe....

4 May (RCG) FOR SALE BY AUCTION.....THE good SHIP *RAPHAELA*, burthen per register 295 Tons, a prime sailer, and calculated for any trade, with her Provisions, Stores, and Materials (amongst which are eight very handsome Carriage Guns) and all of which are in the best condition. The Vessel was built in Spanish America, and her timbers and planks in most excellent order, and now re-fastened, and having lately been fitted out for a voyage to the Bay of Honduras, may be sent to sea at a trifling expense. *Immediately after the Sale of the above, will also be Sold,* The following GOODS, part of the said Ship's Cargo,

For Exportation.

1 Pipe, 1 Butt, 2 Jars in Baskets of GENEVA
3 Cases, 6 ditto BRANDY
6 Jars of OIL of OLIVES
35 Baskets of Tobacco PIPES
1 Bag containing about 40 lbs. THREAD

For Home Consumption

33 Tierces of PORTER in Bottles
6 Hogshead of PORTER
20 Cases of Cherry and Raspberry BRANDY
1 Cask with Children's TOYS

....apply to Mr Richard Dugger, at Fowey

8 June (RCG) His Majesty's birth-day was ushered in at Fowey by ringing of bells, &c., the ships in the harbour were decorated with colours, and at noon, the guns of the fort, &c., fired. Captain Commandant Brown and Captain Bennet's companies of Fowey Volunteers fired a *feu de joie* with great precision; and after the fatigues of the field, the officers of the corps with the principal inhabitants of the respectable and loyal borough of Fowey, partook of an excellent dinner, and toasted our good King and his friends till a late hour.

22 June (RCG) On Thursday se'nnight, as Mr Richard Thriscutt, of Fowey, went to fish from the rocks near that place, he accidently fell into the sea, and was drowned.

6 July (RCG) FOWEY Jul 3. Arrived,.... *Ann and Susan*, Collins(?) from Llanelly, seized by the *Hind* and sent in a boat with 55 casks spirits; *Cormorant* Revenue cutter, with two boats laden with spiritous liquor.... (*Ann and Susan* was built and owned locally).

13 July (RCG) It has long been a matter of regret that the vessels which are occasionally taken from the smugglers, should be broken up and destroyed. These vessels are in general *chef d'ouvres* in marine architecture. It is now said that Government intends to appropriate a number of them to the use of the sea-fencibles; and that several are already fitted up....on the coasts of Kent and Sussex. A correspondent observes, that when cutters and luggers (which are the class principally used by smugglers) are taken into the navy, they generally lose their chief excellence, that of swiftness. Naval officers, bred on the quarter-deck of square-rigged vessels, acquire a partiality for bulwarks below, and standing topmasts, cross-trees and yards above - all of which tend to stiffen, encumber, and retard that free motion, which constitutes the chief excellence of cutters and luggers. The cutters employed in the navy, (continues our correspondent) resemble the ladies of the last reign, with their toupees and fardingales; while a cutter in the hands of smugglers, who first built them, and who best know their use, is as unincumbered as a modern belle, and as fleet as the half-naked nymph who out-ran Apollo.

27 July (RCG) PORT OF FOWEY. *By Order of the Honourable Commissioners of His Majesty's Customs;* On Thursday the 8th day of August, 1805, by Two o'Clock in the Afternoon, will be exposed to PUBLIC SALE, at the CUSTOM-HOUSE, in this Port, The undermentioned GOODS, viz. - BRANDY...5610 Gallons, RUM...974 ditto GENEVA...1770 ditto, WINE...66 Gallons, PEPPER...564 pounds, SALT...690 ditto. Which will be sat up in small lots for the accommodation of the Purchasers. *Also* Three open BOATS, one ANCHOR, and some CORDAGE.... The above Goods may be viewed and tasted three days before the day of Sale.

3 August (RCG) FOWEY July 30.-.... Passed by for Plymouth, the English man of war, of 90 guns, with the loss of her foremast, and two English frigates, each towing a captured Spanish line of battle ship.

7 September (RCG) *To keep Crows from Corn.*- Take a quart of train oil, as much turpentine, and bruised gun powder; boil them together, and, when hot, dip pieces of rags in the mixture, and then fix them on sticks in the fields. About four are sufficient for an acre.

7 September (RCG) Rats and Mice will immediately quit barns, granaries, &c. wherein you shall place the field plant called Dog's Tongue (Cuneglossom Officinale Lianaeus), gathered when full in sap, and bruised with a hammer.

14 September (RCG) DIED. Supposed of eating the berries of the deadly nightshade, the son of Mr. Welman, of the Custom-house, Fowey, a fine boy of about six years of age.

21 September (RCG) FOWEY. *By order of the Assignees of* John Kelly Graham, *a Bankrupt.* TO BE SOLD BY PUBLIC AUCTION, on Thursday, the 26th day of September instant, at the house of John Beard, Innkeeper, in the borough of *Fowey.* THE FOLLOWING GOODS, part of the said Bankrupt's Estate, viz. About 500 pieces Dram and other BALK, 124 Dram SPARS, from 46 to 56 feet in length, and from 8 to 12 inches diameter, 9 Dram MASTS, 2 Large Round ditto, 1 four-oared BOAT and Materials, 1 LIGHTER and ditto, 90 dozen CREASE, 70 Bundles LATHS, 3 dozen Long OARS, 2 dozen Small SPARS, 40 Short ditto, With various other Articles. Also, now lying at Lostwithiel, and to be delivered there, 39 Quarters Sunderland COALS.

1806

18 January (RCG) FOWEY - Put back by contrary wind the *Hope,* Rowe, for St. Ives, having sailed four times and as often returned....

10 May (RCG) The veteran satirist Peter Pindar is courting the muses at his favourite retreat at Fowey. We are told he is composing a congratulatory address to the Princess of Wales on her visit to the West.

10 May (RCG) The Hon. Mr. Eardley, Mr. Edward Holland, and three ladies, detained in France since the commencement of the war, landed a few days ago at Fowey.

26 July (RCG) The fish adventurers of this county have suffered considerable loss by the seizure made by King Joseph Bonaparte, of all the money and effects found in the hands of his Neapolitan subjects, belonging to England. The pilchards of the last season, which reached the market, had sold pretty well; but the proceeds had not been remitted home in time to escape the rapacity of the Usurper of Naples.

27 September (RCG) SALE AT FOWEY By virtue of directions from the Commissioners for the care and disposal of Prussian property condemned to his Majesty, on Thursday the 23rd day of October, 1806, at Ten o'clock in the forenoon, will be exposed to PUBLIC SALE, at the Ship Inn, in Fowey, about 145 TONS of FRENCH SALT; the entire cargo of the Galliass *Johanna Charlotta,* ....taken on her voyage from Vannes, by the Revenue cutter *Cormorant,*, Robert Hearle, esq., commander, and condemned as lawful prize to his Majesty
After which will be Sold, the said GALLIASS, *JOHANNA CHARLOTTA,*.... Length 77 feet 3inches, breadth 21 feet 10 inches, and admeasures about 144 tons. The above-mentioned vessel and salt may be viewed, and an inventory of the materials belonging to the said vessel had, three days preceding the sale, on application to John Kimber, esq. Collector of the Customs, Fowey, or to John Welman, his Clerk. (A Galliass was like a Galley, but larger and heavier.)

25 October (RCG) The want of a market for our pilchards, has been this season so dispiriting to the fishing adventurers....indifference....seems to have pervaded some of the fishermen....whether they should even catch the shoals that fell in their way....the same spirit prevented the timely laying in of salt, for the preservation of such as were caught....Good fish....hitherto sold at about 20s. per hogshead to the merchant, exclusive of the bounty....relaxations lately announced....at Leghorne, which will admit our fish there in neutral vessels, will shortly produce a rise in the price.

8 November (RCG) On Saturday last came the election for the borough of *Fowey.* The Candidates were the Right Honourable Reginald Pole Carew and Robt. Wigram, Esq. on the interest of Philip Rashleigh, Esq. and Admiral Cochrane and Mr John Teed merchant of Plymouth, on the Treffry interest. The two latter gentlemen demanded a poll; on the termination of which the numbers were, for

Reginald Pole Carew, Esq..... 68
Robert Wigram, Esq............. 60
John Teed, Esq..................... 16
Admiral Cochrane................. 6

whereupon the two former were declared duly elected.- Mr Teed was doubly unfortunate in his electioneering trip. He started from Plymouth for Fowey, in his own vessel, the *Trafalgar* privateer, but mistaking Lantivet cove for the harbour, ran on shore, where his vessel was completely wrecked.

8 November (RCG) To the WORTHY ELECTORS of the ancient Borough of FOWEY. Gentlemen, PERMIT me in this manner to renew to you the tender of my most cordial thanks, for the honour which you have conferred on me by electing me, for the third time, one of your Representatives in Parliament; and allow me to assure you, that while I live, a just sense of the weight of the obligation cannot cease to be felt, by Gentlemen. Your devoted humble Servant. REGINALD POLE CAREW.

8 November (RCG) The losing parties at Liskeard and Fowey are regaling themselves with oxen roasted whole, and nut-brown ale, which they very wisely prefer to fiddling and dancing.

13 December (RCG) FOWEY- Arrived....His Majesty's brig *Cockatrice*....with the loss of fore-topmast and main-top-gallantmast, &c. in the late gales, in 36 hours procured new and ready for sea...

1807

3 January (RCG) FOWEY. Dec. 31.Arrived, the *Lively* privateer, Capt. Cock, with the *Gode Habb*, J. Bal, master, from Bordeaux for Copenhagen, with Brandy and Wine. Sailed the *Fran Metta*, Frederic Addicks, master, for Tonningen having been liberated after two months detention. Notwithstanding the many gales lately experienced no damage has happened to any British or Foreign vessel in this harbour altho' they are moored in tiers.

10 January (RCG) FOWEY Jan 6. Arrived....*Habet*, E.J. Scholle, master, from Rochfort, with brandy &c. pretended to be Norway property and bound for Christiansand. It is reported this brig was built at Grenoak in Scotland: the master has no lastage, brief, or register. She was taken by the *Snapdragon* privateer, J. Lawton, commander.

17 January (RCG) FOR SALE, At the Ship Inn,....on the 3rd day of February next.... For Exportation or Home Consumption, on payment of the duties, 40 PUNCHEONS and 10 Tierces of PRUNES, 3 Cases of ditto, 12 Cases of PRESERVES and PICKLES in bottles, About 12 Bottles in a Case, 1 Case, containing 1 dozen small Casks ANCHOVIES. Being part of the Cargo of the Danish Brig *Holom*, detained on her voyage from Bourdeaux to Rostock by the private ship of war *Lively*, Hender Cotton Cock, Commander. For....information apply to.... Walter Colmer, Broker, Fowey.

24 January (RCG) The trade of this county has sunk to a most deplorable state. The want of a market for our fish, induced many many fishing adventurers in the last season, to let loose vast quantities of pilchards, after they had enclosed them, rather than incur the expense of saving for an uncertain sale; and of those that were landed, a considerable part was sold at 6d. to 10d. per bushel, for manuring the land. But....this....has been followed by an evil of still greater magnitude and more extended influence, in the failure of our mines. The fall in the price of copper has already compelled the adventurers to stop several mines, and others which were lately

1807

distinguished among the most profitable in the county, are now become, some of them wholly unprofitable, and others working at a considerable loss....

7 February (RCG) FOWEY Feb 4. .... sent in by the *Snapdragon* privateer, the *Dispatch*, of and from Dongarvon, Nicholas Cantwell late master, bound for Weymouth, with pork, butter and barley, taken by a French privateer, who took out the master and all the ships papers, this vessel was retaken by the *Snapdragon*.

7 February (RCG) Died on Saturday, Samuel Higgs, of Fowey, formerly one of the best wrestlers in this county. He won the silver cup at Boconnoc, at the christening of the late Lord Camelford.

23 May (RCG) FOR SALE BY AUCTION, At the SHIP INN, in FOWEY...the entire cargo of the gallias *Carl Henrick*, Hans Jurges, master, taken on her voyage from Bourdeaux to Rostock, by the private ship of war *Lively*, Hender Cotton Cock, commander, and condemned in his Majesty's High Court of Admiralty of England.... Immediately after the sale,....will be sold....the entire cargo of the brig *Resolution*, C. Hohorst, master, taken on her voyage from Bourdeaux to Lubec, by the private ship of war *Lively*, Hender Cotton Cock, commander, and condemned in his Majesty's High court of Admiralty of England. (Cargoes included wine, vinegar, brandy, turpentine, argol, verdigrease, molasses, perfumery, colouring, corks, prunes).

13 June (RCG) FOWEY. TO BE SOLD BY AUCTION....On Tuesday, the 23rd of this instant June, and following days until all are sold. ALL that Neat and Genuine HOUSE-HOLD FURNITURE, belonging to GABRIEL BRAY, Esq. at his Dwelling-house in the borough of Fowey....; comprising handsome fancy-painted and other chairs, sofas, mahogany circular and other Dining Tables, Card, Pembroke, and Tea ditto, Pier and Swing Glasses, Floor and Bed carpets, neat mahogany and other Bedsteads with handsome Furniture, Feather Beds, mahogany commode, Chest of Drawers, ditto Wardrobes, Receptacles, and Wash-stands, Romford and other Stove Grates, commode, Fenders and Fire-irons, useful and ornamental China and Glass Wares, Tea and Table sets, handsome plated Candlesticks, Snuffers, Stands, &c.,.... Kitchen Utensils, a choice collection of valuable Paintings, of the Venetian, Flemish, and French Masters, a brilliant-toned Piano-Forte, a Patent Mangle, with a variety of other articles, too tedious to mention, as Stacks of Hay, &c. the whole comprising six hundred lots.

N.B. Each days sale to begin precisely at ten o'clock in the forenoon, end at one, begin again at half past two, and end at eight in the evening. Catalogues may be had, five days before the sale, at....Bodmin,....Lostwithiel,....St. Austle, Ship Inn, Fowey, on the premises, ...at 6d each. (ESPLANADE OR WATERLOO HOUSE?).

11 July (RCG) Died on the 8th instant at Fowey, of a dropsy, after having been tapped seven times, Mrs. Chapman, wife of Mr. John Chapman of that place.

18 July (RCG) *To SHIP and BOAT BUILDERS.* By order of the Assignees of THOMAS NICKELLS, the younger, a Bankrupt, *TO BE SOLD BY PUBLIC AUCTION* on Tuesday the eleventh of August next, at two in the Afternoon, at the house of GEORGE THOMAS, Innkeeper in the borough of Fowey,....in Lots, ABOUT 60 Loads of OAK TIMBER, a great quantity of Slabs, and Offals of Oak and other Timber, Edging of Planks, Shores, and Staying, sett and ring Bolts for working Plank, Moulds for a Ship's frame, with a quantity of other Shipwrights Stores and Materials. The Slabs and Offals being left from the construction of a large Brigantine for Government, will be found worth the attention of Shipwrights having smaller vessels to build.... Apply to Wm. Brown, Solicitor, Fowey.

18 July (RCG) The season is now almost gone, when it was usual to commence our great pilchard fishery.... Scarcely a single pilchard has appeared.... Ten or a dozen seans will, we are informed, be the outside of what will be put to sea this year, and those to provide only for our own markets, and the trivial demands of the West Indes. The mackerel fishery of the present year also, as in the last, has been most unprofitable. In some seasons these fish have confined their visits almost entirely to the coasts of Cornwall and Devon. But of late, while very few indeed have been caught here, we find they abound in vast shoals on the coast of Norfolk!

8 August (RCG) FOWEY. On the 5th instant was launched amidst a numerous concourse of spectators, his Majesty's sloop *Primrose*, supposed to be the most complete vessel ever built in this county; finished by Messrs Thomas and Colmer, securities for Nickells, jun. who is a bankrupt.

15 August (RCG) There have been several small catches of pilchards on our coasts during the present week, which are in general of good size and quality; and, though little expectation is formed of commercial advantages from them at present, they will prove a great relief to the poorer classes of the inhabitants.

1808

2 January (RCG) TO BE SOLD. The CUTTER *ECHO*, of *Fowey*, which admeasures 112 tons, now lies at Polperro, within the port of Looe, was built at Fowey, about twelve months since, and has been invariably been allowed by the best judges who have witnessed her sailing, to be as fast a sailer as any cutter out of England. She is exceedingly well found, and may be equipped for sea in a few days, is a remarkably fine vessel, and in all respects calculated for privateering, being pierced for twelve guns.

An inventory of her materials may be seen at Mr. REAN'S at Trevarder, near Fowey, or at Mr. JOB'S, Polperro, either of whom will treat for disposal of said vessel, by Private Contract: but if not so sold, A PUBLIC AUCTION will be held....

23 January (RCG) The Rochefort squadron, which has been understood to be ready for sea for some time past with a number of troops on board, has escaped the vigilance of the blockading squadron, and put to sea. Sir Richard Strachan soon got informed of this movement, and immediately went off in pursuit of the enemy. The high character of Sir Richard is a pledge that every exertion will be made to give a good account of the fugitives, and encourages the hope that we shall soon have to congratulate the public on another glorious naval victory. We are indebted for the above intelligence to captain Rawling, of the *Matchless* privateer of Fowey, who received it on Wednesday last from the *Ann* hired armed brig, which he spoke at sea and was desired to communicate it to all the cruizers he might meet with. *(Ann, perhaps of Mevagissey, within the Port of Fowey).*

2 April.(RCG) Saturday was exhibited for sale in Fowey market the finest heifer Beef ever seen in that neighbourhood, fed and slaughtered by Mr. W. Tregaskes of Tywardreath. The carcase weighed 9cwt. 1 qr. 26 lbs, besides 197 lbs. tallow, 81 lbs. hide; and was only five years old.

16 April (RCG) WANTED. A PAVIER, to new pave the streets of the Borough of Fowey. For terms, &c. apply, by letter post paid, to Mr. Brown, Solicitor, at Fowey.

23 April (RCG) MARRIED at Fowey, Mr William Bennett, to Mrs. Julia Gill, after a tedious widowhood of three weeks.

7 May (RCG) FOR SALE BY AUCTION. At the Ship Inn, Fowey, Thursday the 26th day of May...., at eleven o'clock.... That beautiful, fast-sailing, copper-bottomed Brig, *ANTELOPE*,....Length aloft - 89 ft. 9 in. Breadth - 23 ft.....Depth- 10 ft. 11 in. Admeasures 178, 44-94 tons. Condemned as a Prize to the private ship of war *Matchless*, A.M. Rolling, esq. commander, this vessel being fitted at an extraordinary expence, for the speedy conveyance of the mail and dispatches from Spain to Buenos Ayres and Lima, is abundantly found in stores of every description, mostly new; the properties of this vessel for burthen and dispatch are unrivalled, she is admirably adapted for a private ship of war, hired service, or any trade where unusual dispatch is required; *Immediately after the sale of the brig Antelope,* Will be SOLD her entire CARGO, consisting of about 3650 Reams of Writing Paper,
143 Cases Red Wine
200 Barrels of Tar
100 Spanish Leather Trunk Beds
4 Bales of Silk
1 Case of Ribbons
1 ditto containing 40 Engravings
1 Bale of Superfine Cloaths, Cassimeres, and Swandowns
13 Cases of Plowshare Moulds
15 ditto of Shovel ditto
29 Casks of Nails of different sizes
8 Ships Anchors from 2 to 9 Cwt. weight
300 Iron Sledges
213 Bars of Iron
108 ditto of Steel
1 Box containing a Diamond Necklace, and Bracelets,
1 Box containing a quantity of Spangled Veils, Mantles, etc.
1 Ditto Ditto five Gentlemen's Cloaks
1 Ditto of silk Stockings, Gloves, Pieces of Silks, &c.

1 Case containing a Bishop's Vestment, Scarlet, Silk, embroidered with Gold and spangled.

1 Ditto of Purple Silk both intended as a present from the King of Spain to the Bishop of Buenos Ayres, accompanied by a letter of thanks for his Holy conduct, and the Religion he had propagated, by which they had obtained the assistance of the Almighty to overcome General Whitelock, and the British Army, in that quarter.

Immediately after the Sale of the above Cargo Will be Sold the Ships PROVISIONS, consisting of a quantity of Beef, Pork, Peas, Beans, Bread, Oil, etc. For viewing apply James Sleeman or Peter Smith, of Mevagissey, or to Richard Dugger, Broker, Fowey.

28 May (RCG) The Spanish packet *Antelope* and her cargo, sold high on Thursday last at Fowey. The vessel fetched £1505. One lot of red wine sold at £77 5s. per ton exclusive of the duty. Tar, about 25 gals. to the cask, at 32s. to 34s.6d. per barrel. Bar iron £20 per ton; steel £31.- One of the bishop's state dresses, £53 11s.- Necklace, ear-rings and bracelets £105.

30 July (RCG) FRENCH PRIVATEERS. - The *Cormorant* revenue cutter, Captain Hearle, has captured and brought into Fowey, a French lugger privateer, which he discovered off the Lizard, and took after a chase of nine hours. By this vessel was learnt that no less than eleven other privateers were lying ready for sea at St. Maloes, when she left that port. The above vessel had made no captures; but one of a similar description took two brigs on the 22nd instant, within sight of Marazion.... Since writing the above we are informed that one of the brigs captured on the 22nd, was the *Mary Ann*, Maxfield, with wheat, malt, &c. from Yarmouth to Liverpool; the crew of which assisted by some fishermen, rose upon the Frenchmen, re-took their vessel and carried her into Newlyn.

30 July (RCG) DIED at Fowey, Miss Charlotte Polgrean, Miss Philippa Johns, and Miss Ann James; all very respectable young women, in the bloom of life; neither of them exceeding 20 years of age.

10 September (RCG) *PARISH...OF...LANTEGLOS*....TO BE SOLD BY AUCTION at the Ship Inn,....Fowey, on Saturday the 24th....the following ESTATES;.... Lot 2.- An Overland TENEMENT, situate at Polruen, in the parish of Lanteglos; consisting of 5 closes of rich Land, (together about 5 acres) with a Barn on the same, let from year to year to Mr. Thomas Arthur. This Tenement is well situated for building upon, opposite the town of Fowey....commanding extensive and picturesque views,....with the advantage of good markets, and a respectable neighbourhood.(now area where Greenbank is)

Lot 3 - A TENEMENT, called TREVIC, situate also in....Lanteglos, consisting of a Dwelling-house, Stable, moiety of a Barn, and 11 acres or thereabouts, of excellent Land, now in the occupation of Joseph Thomas, as tenant from year to year....

Should either of the Lots remain unsold, the same will, immediately after the Auction, be offered....to be Let for a term of years.

10 September (RCG) RAN AWAY from his Master, (Mr. W. Millet, of Tresare in the parish of Fowey, the 25th August last,) THOMAS TESTICK, his Apprentice, 17 years of age, about five feet high slight made, fresh complexion, brown hair, wore off a fustian jacket and canvas trowsers. Whoever will give information where the said Apprentice is, shall be handsomely rewarded; and whoever harbours or employs the said Apprentice after this public notice, will be prosecuted.

10 September (RCG) FARMS NEAR FOWEY *TO BE LET,* For a term of fourteen years and entered upon Michaelmas next, THE capital BARTON and FARM of TRENANT, situate in the parish of Fowey, within two miles of the harbour; consisting of an excellent newly-erected Dwelling-House, with all necessary and convenient Farm-Buildings, and 279 acres or thereabouts of excellent arable, pasture, meadow and orchard Ground, *free of all tithe*, very compact, capable of great improvement, and now in the occupation of Mr. Walter Eads, whose term will expire at Michaelmas next.

Also to be LET, for a term of 14 years, and may be entered upon at Michaelmas next, a FARM called PENVENTINEW, situate in the parish of Fowey, consisting of a Dwelling-House, with Farm-Buildings, and 67 acres or thereabouts, of arable, pasture, meadow, and orchard Land, now in the occupation of Mr William Hockin....

Also for a term of 99 years, determinable on the deaths of three persons of the purchaser's nomination. A PLAT OF GROUND at POLRUEN, in the parish of Lanteglos, for the purpose of building upon...a SURVEY will be holden at the SHIP INN...., Fowey, on Saturday the 24th instant, by three o'clock in the afternoon. To view the Premises apply to the respective Tenants, or at Place House....

22 October (RCG) DIED at Fowey, John Harvey, mason, whose death was occasioned by a fall from the roof of a house.

26 November (RCG) To PAPER-MAKERS. *TO BE SOLD BY AUCTION,* At the GENERAL WOLFE Inn, in St Austell... the remainder of a Term of 99 years determinable on the dropping of Three Lives, aged respectively about 62, 22, and 24, in ALL that well-accustomed PAPER-MILL, situate in the parish of Lanteglos by Fowey, with a newly-built Dwelling-house, Garden, Willow Garden of about half an acre, and a small Field thereunto adjoining and belonging, now in the occupation of Wm. Hawkins.

1809

11 February (RCG) *BOROUGH or other INTEREST.* ANY Lady or Gentleman who will procure for a respectable Young Man, A LIEUTENANT'S COMMISSION in the ROYAL MARINES, shall receive a HANDSOME PREMIUM.... The most impenetrable secrecy may be relied on.

4 March (RCG) DIED on Sunday last, aged 61, Mr. John Beard, of the Ship Inn, Fowey, of the effects of a compound fracture of his leg; lamented by a numerous acquaintance.

11 March (RCG) FOWEY....FOR SALE by PUBLIC AUCTION, at the SHIP INN.... on Thursday the 6th of April next....

1200 Pieces CASSAVELLOS, or half Pieces
superfine Bleached Platillas in Rolls
50 Pieces TICKING
24 ditto Sleeked DOWLAS
304 Dozen LOOKING GLASSES
27 Reams Stained PAPER
26 ditto Figured Gilt ditto
4 ditto Plain Tinsed ditto
518 Copper Plate PRINTS

Ex the *Lizette*,....detained on her voyage from Tonningen to Spain. The above goods may be viewed three days prior to the time of sale, and catalogues had, by applying to Mr. Charles Thriscutt, Fowey....

18 March (RCG) DIED on the 12th inst. Mrs. Beard of the Ship Inn, Fowey, supposed of grief for the loss of her late husband.

18 March (RCG) TIMBER FOR SALE.... At the Ship Inn, in Fowey, on Thursday the 30th day of March next, at four o'clock in the afternoon....OAK....ELM.... BEECH....SYCAMORE....Cherry, Chestnut & Wallnut, 72 POLES, marked with a Cross, all standing at Lanheriot, parish of Fowey.... The above Timber Trees are within half a mile of Water Carriage,- A deposit at the Rate of 20*l*. per Cent. will be expected at the time of the sale. Mr William Hicks will shew the Timber on Lanheriot....

18 March (RCG) FOWEY. In pursuance of a Commission of Appraisement and Sale addressed to Nevil Norway and Andrew Young, Esqrs. FOR SALE by PUBLIC AUCTION at the SHIP INN, Fowey, on Thursday the 6th day of April next, at eleven o'clock in the forenoon.

12 CHESTS of LINEN
2 CHESTS of WOOLEN STOCKINGS
2 CHESTS of CHECK
3 CHESTS of WAX CLOTH
1 CHEST of CAMBRIC
10 CHESTS of WINDOW GLASS
1 CHEST of WAX CLOTH and TABLE GLASS
1 CHEST of WOOLEN NIGHTCAPS, and
2 CHESTS of TOYS

part of the Cargo of the *Fortuna*....captured by the private ship of war *MARS*, on her voyage from Tonningen to Oporto.

15 April (RCG) Died at Polruan near Fowey, aged 83, Mrs. Mitchell, sixty years schoolmistress in that neighbourhood; having taught three generations reading, writing and arithmetic, among whom are many masters of vessels, who owe their nautical arithmetic to her.

5 August (RCG) The Assizes for this County commence on Monday next at Bodmin.... It is gratifying to observe that the Calendar contains only eight culprits-viz....John Connelly, for stealing coffee out of a ship at Fowey....

19 August (RCG) TO be LET, for the Term of 14 years from Michaelmas next, all that FARM and Premises, situate in the parish of Fowey, called LISCROW, now in the occupation of Joseph Thomas Austen, esq. comprising a large and convenient Dwelling-house and Out-houses, Horse Cyder-pound, and near 100 Acres of Land, a large portion of which is Meadow, is in a high state of cultivation, including upwards of 2 Acres of Orchard now coming into full bearing. The above is a most desirable Farm, inclosed within a ring fence, conveniently situated for manure, being within a mile of the borough and harbour of Fowey, where sea sand, broken fish, lime, and other manure may be procured in any quantity. For which purpose, a SURVEY, will be held at the SHIP INN, in....*Fowey*, on....the 7th day of September next, at four o'clock in the afternoon.

14 October (RCG) The *Hind*, revenue cutter, Bawden (acting), arrived at Fowey, has driven a French lugger privateer on shore on the French coast.

4 November (RCG) JUBILLEE FESTIVITIES - In Fowey the morning was ushered in by the ringing of bells, the roaring of cannon, and a display of colours of all nations. At eleven o'clock the Mayor and Corporation....(two Aldermen) walked to the Church, which was also attended by all the gentlemen, merchants, the company of Volunteer Artillery under the command of Captain Bennett, and the naval and military Officers resident in and near Fowey. An excellent sermon was preached by the Rev. Thomas Nankivell....and two beautiful hymns composed and set to music by Mr. Donnelly, music-master, of this town,....were sung in good style, by the choristers of Fowey. At one o'clock the Volunteer artillery fired fifty guns from the batteries, in honour of his Majesty's entering the 50th year of his reign. The interval between one and three, was occupied in charitable purposes. The collection made by the Mayor, &c. prior to the day which was not very considerable (as the principal merchants and tradesmen thought the Mayor should have taken the sense of a general meeting) was distributed to the poor, in cloathing, coals, &c. by a committee of ladies. The gentlemen, merchants, &c. not belonging to the Corporation, distributed their alms to the poor, and highly gratified themselves, with entertaining all their labourers and domestics, with roast beef, plum-pudding, and brown stout, at their houses; and then met at the Ship Inn, where a most excellent dinner and choice wines, were furnished by the Miss Hoals, for their entertainment.....Several loyal toasts were then drank....when the Chairman gave "*the Mayor and Corporation of Fowey*". The Vice-President then rose, and said "it was impossible for him to let that toast pass, without making a few observations on their recent conduct, particularly in not calling a meeting, prior to this day, and taking the sense of the inhabitants on the occasion, as every other corporate body had done; how highly so ever says he, I esteem their characters individually as gentlemen, I cannot but think it reprehensible on this occasion, that three individuals should arrogate to themselves the disposal of the bountiful subscriptions of their fellow townsmen, without asking a subscriber to point out an object charity; such a partial proceeding, it was notorious, had already retarded the public subscription; and I am convinced (said he) that many of the present company, seeing how the business was conducted, had with true christian charity, visited the cottages of the poor, supplied their wants, cheered their hearts, renovated their spirits, and made them bless this happy day, (*Loud applause*). As my sentiments on this occasion, appears to meet the unanimous opinion of the gentlemen present; with due submission to the Chair, I beg leave to substitute in its stead *"Prosperity to the Trade and Town of Fowey"*, which was drank with universal applause..... Before ten o'clock all the company had retired, highly gratified with their entertainment.

CHAPTER 2
1810-1819

1810

27 January (RCG) On the morning of the 23rd inst. three Frenchmen, who had been brought into Fowey in the *Phoebe* privateer, and were to have been sent to prison, escaped, and stealing a large sloop-sail boat, belonging to Mr. Salt, a pilot of Portruan (worth 80*l*.) sailed about 2 o'clock in the morning for France. Their escape being known about three hours after, an officer of a revenue cutter was informed of it, and several seamen offered him their assistance, to go in pursuit of them; from some cause, of which we are uninformed, he declined to do so, and the Frenchmen escaped with their prize.

28 April (RCG) CAPT. LAKE AND THE UNFORTUNATE JEFFERY. Observing in a London paper of last week the statement of an American ship having "taken poor Jeffery from the island of Sombrero - that he retained his senses, but had ate off his own flesh as far as he could reach, and died a day or two after he was taken on board the ship", we thought it our duty to make inquiry into the truth of the horrid story, before we gave it a place in our paper, and have accordingly received the following letter on the subject from a very respectable friend at Fowey.

28 April (RCG) Dear Sir - In consequence of your letter, I have had a conversation with Ann Line (sister to Nathaniel Jeffery's father) who informs me that her nephew, Nathaniel Jeffery, a native of Fowey, being on board the *Recruit* sloop of war, commanded by Captain Lake; at a time when the people wanted water in the West Indes, Jeffery got at and drank some spruice beer belonging to the captain, for which he was to suffer punishment. Mr. Richard Mould (also a native of Fowey) second lieutenant, was ordered by the captain to put Jeffery on shore. The lieutenant remonstrated, but could not prevail on the captain to adopt any other mode of punishment. Some of the boats' crew had a few biscuits and a piece of beef. Jeffery, when in the boat rowing on shore, desired them to drown him, but they could not, and must obey the captain's order. When the boat was on shore he clung to the boat. At last, the men forced him on the barren rock. They gave him the biscuit and beef. Lieutenant Mould would have given him money; but he replied, it was of no use to him; he then gave him the boat-hook and staff, and three handkerchiefs, to hoist as signals; after which they left him. This was related to her by ---Libby and ---Johns, two seamen of Polperro, then belonging to the ship (soon after they were discharged;) but these men will not say anything about it now, as this woman says. She heard Lieutenant Mould say, that on their arrival in England (Capt. Lake and Lieutenant Mould returning in hope of promotion, Libby and Johns being discharged) Captain Lake said "I hope when I have another ship, we shall sail together," Lieutenant Mould replied, "No, never. Recollect Jeffery." The captain said "I wish I had never done it." Mr. Mould is now in the East Indes....our worthy correspondent adds....

Sir John Sinclair said in the House of Commons, he had good authority for asserting that Jeffery was then alive in America....a vessel has sailed with commissioners charged to investigate the truth...we earnestly hope and trust that ample justice will fall upon the head of the perpetrator of such abominable inhumanity.

5 May (RCG) HARBOUR OF FOWEY. WHEREAS, WE, the undersigned, being employed as labourers, did ignorantly on the 31st of March, 1810, throw out Limestone from a Lighter in the maritime river of Fowey, below the Horse-Ferry on the Fowey shore, to the danger and prejudice of Navigation, for which offence, the Mayor and Corporation of Lostwithiel, as proprietors and conservators of the said maritime river, had commenced prosecutions against us; but on account of our extreme poverty and compasionating our families, have been pleased to drop the proceedings, on condition of our never being guilty of the like offence in future, which we hereby promise; and also the expense of this notice, which lenity we are grateful for; and hope it may caution to others, not to commit a similar offence. Witness our hands, THOMAS DIXON, JOHN CHAPMAN, jun., The sign X and mark of RICH. ROWE, WM. FACEY
Witness hereto. R.P. FLAMANK

19 May (RCG) *FOR SALE BY PUBLIC AUCTION* At the Ship Inn, in the borough of *Fowey, on Thursday* the 7th of June next, the American SCHOONER, *JULIET* with all her materials.... Immediately after, will be sold, her entire CARGO, consisting of about
81 Bales of New Orleans COTTON
20 Hogsheads of Kentucky TOBACCO
18 Tons of FUSTIC (YELLOW DYE)
17 Tons of LOGWOOD

2 June (RCG) The declining state of the Tin trade of this county, for some years past, has....been highly injurious to the mining, landed, and commercial interests of Cornwall.... Among the primary causes of the decline complained of, may be reckoned that of the pewter trade, which formerly exported vast quantities to America &c. exclusive of what was made use of in this country. This has been superseded by the general use of earthenware abroad and at home....

9 June (RCG) PILCHARD FISHERY.- This once important branch of Cornish commerce, promises to revive again a little. Preparations are making round our coasts, for setting a pretty many seans on float. The demand for the West India market increases as experience teaches a mode of curing, better adapted to the climate and taste of its inhabitants: and the high price of every article of provision at home, will heighten their consumption among us.- Mackerel have been rather plentiful with us of late.

16 June (RCG) ....respecting poor Jeffery, who was left on the Island of Sombrero....John Dennis, Master of the American schooner *Adams*, belonging to Marblehead, in the State of Massachusetts, ...voluntarily made oath, that in the month of December, in the year 1807, he did, while passing the island of Sombrero, in the Sombrero passage, in the West Indes, discover from his vessel a man waving his hand on the said Island, whereupon the said deponent hove his vessel to, and sent his boat on shore with the mate, who found a man on the said Island, extremely reduced and exhausted, so as not to be able to speak.- That the man having been brought on board the schooner, and somewhat recovered, declared that his name was Robert Jeffery, a seaman belonging to his Britannic Majesty's brig of war *Recruit*, commanded by Captain Warwick Lake, and that he had been eight days on the said Island....the said Robert Jeffery became quite recovered, and went to Beverly, where he resided, working at his trade of a blacksmith when this deponent last saw him.

23 June (RCG) CAPITAL FARM. TO BE LET, situated in the parish of Lanteglos, near Fowey,....known by the names of HIGHER and LOWER TRIGGANBROWNE, with a FIELD adjoining thereto called the WARREN, containing 243 Acres with a Farm-house, Barns, Stables and Cow-houses. This Farm within a ring fence, is capable of great improvement, possessing particular advantages as to Manure, it adjoins Lantic Bay, from whence it is abundantly supplied with sea-sand, and is within a mile of the market town of Fowey, and about 8 miles from those of St. Austell, Lostwithiel and Looe. A PUBLIC SURVEY will be holden at the Ship Inn, in Fowey,....the 18th day of July next,....where a plan of the Farm, will be produced ....further particulars may be known of Mr Sharman of Boconnoc....

4 July (SM) The Fowey Bank, said to have stopped, has been restored to credit and stability. A failure attended with circumstances peculiarly distressing is said to have happened in Falmouth ....

7 July (RCG) At the SHIP INN, in Fowey, on Thursday the 19th of July instant, at four, to be LET, during the life of John Foot, all that FARM and PREMISES, situate in the parish of Fowey, called HIGHER PENVENTINUE, comprising a neat and pleasantly situated Dwelling-house, Barn, and other Outhouses, and about 42 acres of very good Land, now and for some time past in the occupation of Captain Tetley. The above is a desirable situation for the residence of any small genteel family, as well as for a farmer,....

1 September (RCG) As Vevers Robinson, Esq., and his lady were taking an airing in their gig, on Monday last, near Fowey, the horse became restive, plunged, and threw them out, by which Mrs. Robinson was so injured, that for some time apprehensions were entertained that she would not recover, but it is now hoped she is out of danger.

13 October (RCG) Arrived the *O.P.* privateer, H.C. Cock, commander, with a brig called the *Dragon*, of London, Colin Buchanan, late master, from Valencia in Spain, laden with 20 bales of silk, 135 bags of wool, 68 bales of barilla, &c., and put under quarantine. The *Dragon* was captured the 4th instant, at 9 AM....by *Le Countess Montelivet*, French privateer, of 14 guns,....from Granville, who took out Capt. Buchanan, and all hands, except John Jones, mate; the *Dragon* was retaken the same day by the *O.P.* privateer.... One of the French prisoners says, that he was at the Isle

33

of Bas the 2d of Oct., when *La Junon*, a French privateer schooner of 14 guns, belonging to St. Maloes, arrived; she had two men killed and ten wounded in engaging the *Marlborough* near Falmouth. (NB The French ship was double the strength of the *Marlborough*).

27 October (RCG) FOR SALE by PUBLIC AUCTION, on Thursday the 8th of November next, at Four o'clock in the afternoon, at Thomas's the ROSE AND CROWN Inn, Fowey. The beautiful fast-sailing CUTTER, *ROVER*. Admeasures 128 Tons, or thereabouts, with her Materials. The Vessel is about three years old, her Sails and Stores principally new, has lately had a complete Repair, is admirably calculated for a Private Ship of War, or any employ where dispatch is an object, and may be sent to sea in a few days. For viewing....apply to Mr. W. Brokensha, Ship-Builder, Fowey.

24 November (RCG) FOWEY BANK CO. REQUEST whoever holds any Promissory Notes, either Local or payable in London, they may be sent to Fowey for payment or any other Demand...

22 December (RCG) THE PACKETS. Fowey Harbour has been surveyed, by order of Government, with the view, we are told, of sending the packets there. St. Mawes has also been spoken of. Government is sensible, that Plymouth, as we said is "too full".

29 December (RCG) TO SCHOOLMASTERS. ANY Usher of a School, or Qualified Person, wishing to engage in that line may, by applying, to MR. G. DANNELEY, Fowey, be put into immediate possession of one, with Desks, Forms, and every other requisite. N.B. School Re-Commences on January 7, 1811. (Usher = second Master)

1811

2 March (RCG) In announcing Mrs. Mary Truscott's death last week, instead of saying she had been blind 30 years, it should have been said, 50 years, she having a son 50 years of age, who had lived all his life with her, but whom she never saw.(NB Died at Bodinnick).

8 June (RCG) On Friday morning last, the tide in the harbours of Plymouth, Fowey, Falmouth, and all along the southern shores of Cornwall, was observed to be agitated in a most extraordinary manner; the rapid and successive influx and effluxes rising and falling from four to eight perpendicular feet in the short space of a few minutes, agitated the shipping and produced general consternation. As a like phenomenon was observed at the time of the great earthquake that destroyed Lisbon, it is feared that a similar commotion of the elements has happened somewhere on this occasion.

28 September (RCG) THE COMET - The tail of this sublime phenomena of late appeared to be about twelve degrees in length, and in breadth, at the farthest extremity, near six degrees. It is considerably nearer the earth than it was when it first appeared to us. No serious consequences need, however, be apprehended, as its path not only makes a very considerable angle with the ecliptic in which the earth moves, but its situation is now greatly above the plane of that circle...We should like to know with what thoughts Bonaparte views the Comet; knowing, as he must, that the only one that ever remained so long visible as this will, appeared in the time of the monster, Nero,..his only equal, perhaps, in atrocity....and who was assassinated soon after its disappearance....

30 November (RCG) MURDER. A Jew, called Israel Valentine, has been murdered at Fowey. This unfortunate man, (who usually resided, we apprehend, at Plymouth or Dock), arrived at Fowey on the evening of the 25th instant; and as it afterwards appeared, brought 260*l*. with him in bank notes. It is understood that he had been invited down, and desired to bring the money with him, by _ _ Wyat, (who had lately taken a public house in Fowey) on the pretence of his having guineas to sell. - Between nine and ten o'clock, Wyat and the Jew walked out of the house together; and, soon afterwards, a sailor on board a vessel in the harbour, heard a voice exclaim, "O! Mr. Wyat! Mr. Wyat!" - Wyat was seen soon after, walking through the streets and church-yard, beyond his house, to his stables, and observed to return and enter his house in a wet condition. He then went upstairs, without speaking of the *accident*, to any one of the company who were in his house, and put on dry clothes. Soon after this, the alarm was spread, of a man being found drowned. It proved to be the Jew. A respectable surgeon attended immediately, and tried the methods for resuscitating prescribed in such cases, without effect. The Mayor (who is also Coroner....) on the 26th, sent his constables to take Wyat into custody;....- and an inquest of no less than 23 persons having been assembled, a most minute and circumstantial investigation followed.... The result was, a verdict which fixed the charge of drowning the Jew upon Wyat, who was accordingly committed to the county prison at Bodmin to take his trial.... On the morning of the 27th, search was made in Wyat's stables, where notes to the amount of 260*l*. were found.- It is supposed that Wyat first pushed the Jew into the water, and that he got wet by going in himself afterwards, to take the money out of his pocket.

30 November (RCG) A few days ago a young man called Crago, belonging to the *Peggy*, Captain Cooper, was struck from the mast-head by the topsail-gaff, fell upon the deck, fractured his skull, and after languishing some days died at Fowey. (Cooper was of Fowey).

7 December (RCG) The murder of Valentine the Jew, at Fowey, reported in our last week's paper, has excited a great sensation. He was a youth of about three-and-twenty; of parents highly respectable among the Jewish order in Breslaw;- had studied at one of the Hebrew Universities on the Continent; and came over to England about twelve months ago, to be a Reader in the Jewish Synagogue in London. He was of small stature, thin and weakly. He had resided some time at Dock, where he became intimate with Wyat, who kept a public-house; and upon being cautioned lately by another Jew against the consequences of his intimacy with Wyat, answered, that *Wyat and he were as brothers*! It seems, he was not merely drowned;

35

for when found, there appeared on his forehead and jaw two deep wounds, which appear to have been inflicted by strokes of a piece of iron. Another young Jew named Levi, had been at Fowey about the same time with a large quantity of Cash Bills, negotiating with Wyat for guineas. This young man, we are told, has had his mind so impressed with a notion of his own narrow escape from the fate of his friend, that he has been scarcely capable of business since....

14 December (RCG) On the 10th instant, in the Night, as the *Peggy,* Cooper, coming into the harbour from Plymouth, got her rudder entangled in Fishing nets, which some injudicious fishermen had laid at the harbour's mouth, whereby the vessel became unmanageable and run on shore and sank. The crew were providentially saved.

1812

28 March (RCG) CORNWALL ASSIZES AT LAUNCESTON. William Wyatt, aged 40, for the murder of Isaiah Folack Valentine, by drowning him in Fowey Harbour, was found guilty, and received sentence of death. His trial lasted the whole of Thursday, from nine in the morning till after seven at night.- He will be executed at Launceston, next Monday morning.

4 April (RCG) The execution of *Wyatt,* for the murder of Valentine the Jew, did not take place at Launceston on Monday last, as expected. Some mistake is understood to have happened, with respect to dates, in passing of the sentence, &c.... It is now said, he will be executed at Bodmin on the 1st of May. The unhappy man is said to be sunk into a state of despondency bordering upon stupefaction. His wife (a respectable woman) visits him daily in prison; and the zealous attention of the Reverend Mr. Plummer, the chaplain, does him infinite credit

4 April (RCG) SUSTENANCE OF THE POOR. The Gentleman to whom we were indebted last week for an explanation of the benefits that may be derived from the use of Rice, has favoured us this week with the following: I find, by well boiling the Rice, that four pounds (at 3 1/2d. per lb. the price it is now selling at in Marazion) and 3/4 *lbs* of raw Sugar boiled in a gallon of milk, will satisfy fifty children of various ages. I have fed above sixty with the same quantity.- ....baked into Cakes, with a few seeds, &c, is a considerable saving, as but little butter in that case is required. .... We understand also that the medical gentlemen of the Cornwall Infirmary, convinced of its wholesome and nutritious qualities, are introducing Rice among their patients.- The upper and middling classes, with laudable consideration for the poor, are everywhere reducing their consumption of bread, and otherways contributing all in their power to their relief..... We would caution the poor, *not to injure themselves,* by indulging mistaken resentment against those who may be supposed to keep back their corn, potatoes, &c. from market.

4 April (RCG) On the 30th ult. was launched in Fowey harbour three vessels, two of which were upward of 100 tons each, and the other upwards of 200.

25 April (RCG) Names of Cornish Prisoners in France, who have been partakers of the sum of £625 0 8, raised in Cornwall in 1811, for their relief, at £2 5 11 1/2 per man; being all those whose confinement there could be ascertained.

Depot of Arras;.... Richard Pill, James Hooper, and Joseph Woolcock, of Fowey (N.B.all possibly Lanteglos by Fowey)

Depot at Cambray;.... Wm. Williams, Richard Collings, Jas. Barnes, of Fowey

Depot at Givet;.... Christopher Coombs of Lanteglos

Depot at Sarre Libre;.... John Hambly, Fowey....William Roach, Fowey;.... John Giles, Fowey.

2 May (RCG) Wyatt, who was found guilty at the last Launceston assizes of the murder of Isaiah Folack Valentine, a German Jew, by drowning him in Fowey, suffered the awful sentence of the law today at Bodmin.... The miserable man ascended the scaffold accompanied by the Rev. Messrs. Plummer and Feyrer, where unremitted and zealous attention to their spiritual duty throughout the whole of his long confinement, equally evinced their religion and humanity. He appeared greatly emaciated. A paper was read by the latter of these gentlemen, in which he had acknowledged the justness of his sentence. His first deviations from the paths of rectitude, he said, were those of smuggling. From that he had proceeded to worse, till he committed the dreadful act for which he suffered. He evinced deep contrition, with hope for pardon from an offended but merciful God; and was launched into eternity. An immense concourse of people attended, who appeared to be deeply impressed with the awfulness of the scene.

27 June (RCG) GALLANT ACTION. The *Hind* Revenue Cutter, of Fowey, cruising last week under the command of Mr. Bawden, the mate, fell in with a French lugger privateer of 14 guns and 56 men, which had just captured the brig *Mary of Sunderland*, off St. Austell-Bay, from Wales for London with iron. The nine Frenchmen who had been put on board the brig, endeavoured to get back to the lugger to assist in her defence, but were driven on shore in Talland Bay, and made prisoners. The Frenchmen on board the lugger, profiting of their very superior numbers, attempted to carry the *Hind* by boarding, but were beat back, with great slaughter; and the lugger soon after she had struck, sunk, from the shot-holes she had received, with twelve of the Frenchmen on board her. We are happy to add that not one of the gallant fellows of the *Hind* was killed. The Cutter arrived at Fowey on the 21st, to refit.

4 July (RCG) Mary, the wife of William Foot of Fowey, fell from a high cliff there, into the sea, and was unfortunately drowned.

22 August (RCG) HINT TO FARMERS - It is well known, that when black cattle are feeding on clover grass at this season, particularly when there is dew on the grass, they are often lost by wind in the stomach. A few gills of whale oil, with an equal quantity of whiskey, poured down their throats, is an immediate cure.

5 September (RCG) FASHIONS - Walking Dress. A Parisian wrapping dress of plain jaconet muslin, or fine cambric, trimmed on each side, round the neck and wrists, with double borders of fine mull muslin. The sleeves very full, confined at the wrist with gold bracelets and drop snap. A Wellington hat, composed of blended straw and white satin; confined under the chin with white ribbon, and decorated with a wreath of flowers round the crown. A small lace cap beneath, with a flower on the right side. A small palerine of blue satin, trimmed with broad black lace. A long sash, or bracer, of blue figured ribbon, passed over the shoulders, and tied in front of the waist. Roman shoes of buff coloured kid or jean....gloves the same colour. Parasol of blue shot silk, with deep Chinese fringe.

10 October (RCG) TO THE FREE AND INDEPENDENT ELECTORS OF THE BOROUGH OF FOWEY. Gentlemen. In returning you my sincere thanks, for the honour you have this day conferred on me, by selecting me one of your representatives in Parliament, be assured it shall be my earnest study, by a faithful discharge of the duties of so important a trust, to merit your future approbation. I have the honour to be, with every Sentiment of Respect your grateful and obedient humble servant, WILLIAM RASHLEIGH.

7 November (RCG) We have been favoured with the following *Cornish* names, extracted from the Report of the Committee for the Relief of British Prisoners in France:-
John Giles, seaman, " *Arthur*", Fowey, in Sarre Louis prison.
William Roach, seaman, "*Arthur*", Fowey,   "
John Williams, seaman, "*Resolution*", Fowey   " N.B. Lanteglos?).
Joseph Woolcock, seaman, *"Nassau"*, Fowey, "   (N.B. if Joseph Willcock, then Lanteglos).
Richard Pill, Master, *"Four Sisters*", Fowey   " (N.B. Lanteglos, captured 1810).
James Conner, seaman, *"Pheasant*", Fowey   "
14 November (RCG) CORNISHMEN, PRISONERS IN FRANCE
James Pearce, seaman, "*Pheasant"*, Fowey, in Cambray prison.
William Williams, apprentice, *"Four Sisters"*, Fowey   "
James Johns, seaman, *"Inveterate"*, Fowey, in Bescancon prison.

1813
16 January (RCG) On the 8th inst. a lad belonging to the *Amity,* of Fowey, was in the act of discharging a pistol on the beach, when it burst, and a large piece of the barrel entering his breast, wounded him so severely as to occasion his death within two hours.

10 April (RCG) On Saturday night last, about nine o'clock, as Mr. Williams of Fowey, Pork-Merchant, was walking on the town quay at that place, owing to the extreme darkness of the evening, he fell over the wharf, and was taken up dead.

17 April (RCG) Died at Looe, on Friday last, in consequence of a fall from the bowsprit of a Vessel, Mr. Richard Culm, Ship-Builder, of Fowey.

1 May (RCG) FOWEY - TO be SOLD by SEALED TENDER for the remainder of a Term of 99 years, determinable on the death of one good healthy Life, aged 52 years, all that capital and well accustomed SHOP, DWELLING-HOUSE and PREMISES, situate in the centre of the Town of Fowey, and now in the occupation of Mr. Petherick Lukey, Merchant, whose term thereon expires at Michaelmas, 1814. The House consists of a large and convenient Shop, with an Office attached, two Parlours, a Drawing-Room, Kitchen, Pantry, &c. ten Lodging Rooms, and three good Closets; together with a Wash-House, Scullery, Shoe-Room, and other conveniences. There is also a desirable Quay on the Premises, where Ships may discharge their Cargoes, with commodious Cellars thereon. Adjoining the House is a pleasant walk and Pleasure-House, commanding a beautiful view of the Harbour and River of Fowey and the surrounding Country. The whole forming the most desirable Purchase, either for the purpose of carrying on an extensive business, or for the residence of a Genteel Family.

15 May (RCG) BOROUGH OF FOWEY. At a meeting of the resident Burghers and other Inhabitants of Fowey held at the Town-Hall, on Thursday the 13th of May....JOSEPH THOMAS AUSTEN, Esq. in the Chair; *It was unanimously Resolved,*

That the address to Her Royal Highness the Princess of Wales, proposed by Mr. Dugger, and now read, be adopted....

That Joseph May Ward, esq., our deputy Mayor, in refusing to comply with the request of the Requisition, has acted....diametrically opposite to the views of the Inhabitants of Fowey.

ADDRESS

..... *May it please your Royal Highness.* WE, the resident prescriptive Burghers, and Inhabitants of the ancient Borough of Fowey, animated with the same spirit that, in a less civilised age, first drew our fathers into a social compact, for the maintenance and distribution of Justice, being legally assembled, with hearts full of duty and affection, assure your Royal Highness, that our unfeigned for the cruel and unmerited treatment which you have so long endured, is absorbed in our admiration of the unparalleled fortitude and dignity of mind,....which supported your Royal Highness, when prevented from entering that circle in which you were accustomed to move, you were assailed by false and disgraceful paragraphs in the public prints, and beset with spies, in the character of friends or domestics. But our admiration is still heightened by the noble, firm, and undaunted manner in which your Royal Highness....at length demanded of the Commons House of Parliament, that you should be 'proved to be guilty, or acknowledged to be innocent'.....we are unanimously agreed, that though your Royal Highness has been unable to bring to legal punishment your suborned and perjured traducers, yet as the innocence of your Royal Highness is acknowledged by the whole British Nation, which with one heart and voice do homage to your virtues; that acknowledgement is a more severe punishment than any the law could inflict.... we trust, that under the sway of your illustrious and affectionate daughter, the Princess Charlotte, whom God long preserve, the people will enjoy that portion of real power which alone can confer dignity on the Crown, and ensure the stability of the Empire.

Accept most illustrious Princess, our warmest wishes for your future welfare and happiness....

3 July (RCG) THE POTTERY at Fowey has just commenced manufacturing COARSE EARTHENWARE, And the shopkeepers, who retail the Article, in the adjoining towns of Looe, Polperro, Leskeard, Lostwithiel, Bodmin, Charlestown, St. Austell, Mevagissey, &c. and all the intermediate Villages, will find it SELLING on very advantageous terms. Application may be made to Messrs. Eyre and Co., at Fowey.

14 August (RCG) FOWEY HARBOUR. WHEREAS, a CLAIM has been set up by LOSTWITHIEL BOROUGH to the WHOLE RIVER of FOWEY, and to as much of the soil adjacent as is EVER covered by the TIDE;....on behalf of RICHARD READ, of Lostwithiel, against whom I commenced a prosecution for taking a BARGE load of Sand from a part of Fowey Beach, which, from the 22nd year of Elizabeth, I can prove by the counter-parts of Leases, to have been regularly Leased by my family....from time immemorial, ...I DO HEREBY GIVE NOTICE to the Magistrates of Lostwithiel, that I have built a Quay on Fowey Beach, since they made the Claim, and that I am ready to defend any action which may be brought against me for building the said Quay.   Joseph Thomas Austen.

1814

12 March (RCG) DIED at Fowey, aged 30, Mrs. Moody, having only five days before, been delivered of twins, who are both living. What gives additional colouring to the very melancholy event, is, that the father of those poor unprotected babes, is at present on the coast of France, under Admiral Penrose.

21 May (RCG) A CAUTION. I, RICHARD PILL, of POLRUEN, ...Mariner, *DO HEREBY GIVE NOTICE,* That, I will not be answerable or accountable for any Debt or Debts, that may after this notice be contracted, by LUCY, my WIFE, who has for some years past kept a Grocer's Shop, in Polruen aforesaid either for Debts to be contracted on account of the said, Shop, or otherwise. And all Persons now having claim on the said LUCY PILL, are to send the Particulars thereof to me immediately, that the same may be adjusted and settled.

21 May (RCG) RAN AWAY from his Master Mr. Thomas Nickels, Jun. of the schooner *AMITY,* belonging to Fowey. WILLIAM WELLINGTON, his Apprentice - The said Young Man is about 21 years of age, 5 feet 3 inches in height, dark complexion, had on when he absconded a blue jacket and trowsers. Whoever harbours or employs the said Apprentice after this Public Notice, will be prosecuted with the utmost rigour of the law.

25 June (RCG) In consequence of the re-establishment of Peace the Inhabitants of Fowey were at an early hour on Monday the 13th Instant, busily employed in decorating their houses with laurel, &c. and forming arches in the streets, variegated with flowers and emblematical representations, and 38 well-formed arches soon graced the Town. To regale the Poor a fine Bullock and two Sheep, each weighing 100 lbs. which, together with the Beef, made up an aggregate of one thousand pounds weight of excellent meat, also eight hundred two-penny loaves, with a great quantity of strong Beer and Porter, the gift of William Rashleigh Esq. were distributed in the Market-house and Town-Hall, by the Mayor and Gentlemen of the Town. It could not be otherwise than highly gratifying to see so many people with that joy painted on their countenances, which plainly indicated the delight of their hearts. To crown the day, a great number of respectable people drank Tea at Mrs. Redding's, after which, they adjourned to the Town-Hall and commenced dancing, which was kept up with great spirit and regularity. *Tuesday* morning was ushered in with ringing of bells &c. and a great number of people were assembled in the forenoon, before the Ship Inn, to dance, during which the Ladies were busily engaged in ornamenting with flowers, laurel, &c. two boats placed on wheel sledges in order to be drawn through the Town by the Populace. At three o'clock the Mayor and a very respectable Company sat down to an excellent dinner, prepared by Miss Hoal of the Ship Inn. During Dinner, the Band played many grand national tunes in an adjacent room; several excellent Toasts were drank by the Company. This repast finished three Royal Salutes were fired from the Battery in compliment to the Allied Sovereigns. The attention of the Spectators was called to a party of spirited young men, who personated a troop of Cossacks, properly accoutred, and who, on horseback, were in pursuit of Buonaparte, who was supposed to have taken flight out of the Town. He was soon driven back by the party, and taken prisoner. A personage representing a Miller, was then seated behind Buonaparte on his horse, and after heartily embracing him, bid him take consolation in the thought that if he had lost his honour, he had at least preserved his life. An interesting procession now took place, in which the two Boats which we have mentioned were highly decorated, and formed a conspicuous part. In the bow of the first was the figure of a Dove fixed on a pole, with its wings extended, and bearing in its mouth an olive branch. The Boat was filled with Ladies, splendidly dressed, and profusely decorated with Garlands of flowers, bearing in their hands appropriate symbols of Peace. The second boat was filled by a party of Musicians, who played a variety of national airs. The procession closed with an immense concourse of the Inhabitants of the Town and Neighbourhood exhibiting every demonstration of Joy. This day, like the preceding, was concluded by a Dance at the Town-Hall.

Early on *Wednesday* morning, the Boats were again decorated by the Ladies, on the beach, in order to join their friends on the opposite side of the harbour, who were assembled in great numbers on the heights of Saint Saviour's. A procession of Boats preceded by one filled with Musicians, proceeded across the harbour, and were received by the Inhabitants of *Polruan* with loud cheering. Lord Wellington was again mounted on horseback, with General Platoff, and a Cossack party, and after several skirmaches with Buonaparte and his followers, they compelled the sham Emperor to make towards the shore, where, accompanied by a few of his Satellites, he embarked, pursued by a number of other Boats filled with Cossacks, &c. who having overtaken the fugitive, proceeded with him to a small Island near the shore, where he was landed, and a board immediately fixed to a pole, on which was inscribed, "Elba".In the evening of this day, a grand display of fireworks took place on the Town Quay of Fowey, under the management of the Magistrates, and which highly gratified the spectators. On *Thursday* tables were placed in an eligible spot adjoining the street, where many large parties partook of Tea, who afterward adjourned to the Town-Hall, and finished the Festivities of the day with a Dance. On *Friday* and *Saturday* there were Dinners and Dances at the Crown and Anchor and Ship Inns, and Beer was liberally given away on the Quay. It is needless to add, that every Inhabitant feelingly entered into the spirit of rejoicing, and that at the close of a long week of continual Festivities, every one regretted that it had been so short. Great praise is justly due to the worthy Magistrates of the Borough for their indefatigable endeavours to give satisfaction and to promote harmony in the various arrangements of the week. The exertions of the Musicians were also highly praiseworthy, and ensured to them the lasting gratitude of their fellow townsmen.

20 August (RCG) TO QUARRY MEN. WANTED, several SLATE-CLEAVERS. Apply (if by letter post paid) to THOMAS DIXON, Mason, Fowey, where a Slate Rock has lately been discovered of nearly the same quality as Delabole.

22 October (RCG) The "*LITTLE JOHN*" (an open vessel) Joseph Michael, Master, from Fowey to Mevagissey, with 70 hogsheads of salted pilchards on board, shipped a sea in the course of her passage (on Tuesday last) by which she almost filled and went down. The master and two other persons, we regret to state, were drowned. One man (a passenger) was saved.

5 November (RCG) TO be SOLD for the Remainder of a Term of 99 years, determinable on three lives 19, 17 and 13. *All that eligibly situated and extensive* MALT-HOUSE, GRANARY, LIME-KILN, and PREMISES. Situate in the parish of Lanteglos, by Fowey, and on a navigable Branch of the Harbour of Fowey. Comprising three floors, 100 feet by 14 each, with every convenience for carrying on an extensive Business either as a Malt-House, or Granary, and for which, from its being so situated as for Vessels to load and unload alongside, but few situations are so well adapted. The Premises have been recently built by and are now in the occupation of Mr Robert Rean....a PUBLIC AUCTION will be held at the SHIP INN,....*Fowey*, on Monday the Seventh day of November.... Premises may be viewed on application to Robert Rean of *Trevarder*.....

And on the Tenth day of November next, the Interest of the said Robert Rean, in the ESTATES of TREVARDER Together with all the FARMING STOCK, CORN, IMPLEMENTS of HUSBANDRY and HOUSEHOLD FURNITURE, on the said Estates of *Trevarder*, will be SOLD by PUBLIC AUCTION. The Sale to begin precisely at Two o'clock.... and continue each day until the whole are disposed of.

12 November (RCG) TIMBER AND DEALS. JUST ARRIVED, and FOR SALE BY PUBLIC AUCTION, at the SHIP INN, *Fowey*, on Tuesday the 15th instant, at

Eleven o'clock in the Forenoon, a prime Cargo of TIMBER, BATTENS, and DEALS, direct from Dram in Norway, and now landing out of the Brig *Odin*, Capt. P.Pay.... The Timber used for Mining purposes will be allowed the drawback of the Duties....apply to Messrs. Norway and Dugger, Merchants, Fowey.

1815

4 February (RCG) A small vessel belonging to Plymouth, but supposed last from a French Port, having on board 118 ankers of Brandy and Geneva, was seized in the port of Fowey, on Monday last, by the Tide Surveyors and other Officers of the Customs. The Crew had deserted the vessel before the Revenue Officers obtained possession of her.

29 April (RCG) A barge belonging to Lostwithiel was swamped in Lantick Bay, on Wednesday last, in consequence of a sudden gale of wind. Two men who were on board were rescued from their perilous situation, after remaining a considerable time in the water.

13 May (RCG) CAPITAL FARM. TO be LET, for a Term of Ten Years, from Michaelmas next, a most eligible FARM, comprising the Three Estates, called GREAT TREVARDER, *TREREED, And LITTLE TREVARDER,* Situate in the Parish of Lanteglos, by Fowey....Consisting of a very commodious Dwelling-house, convenient Barns and Outhouses, Wall Gardens, and Three Acres of Orchard, and about 100 Acres of excellent Meadow and Corn Land, now in the occupation of Mr. Robert Rean.

These Estates are extremely well watered; lie within a ring fence, bounded on the south by the sea; and possess every advantage of situation for manure, and market, having the best Sea Sand and Weed constantly washing in on part of the Premises, and being only two miles distant from the Harbour and Town of Fowey, and seven miles from Looe.

For LETTING the above a SURVEY will be held, at the *Ship Inn*, within the Borough of *East Looe*, on Monday the 29th day of May....

10 June (RCG) CAPITAL *BARTON AND MANSION HOUSE.* Nearly contiguous to, and commanding, a most beautiful View of the South Channel and Neighbourhood, with Possession at Michaelmas next. TO be SOLD, the FEE-SIMPLE of all that compact and truly- desirable MANSION, BARTON and FARM, called TREDUDWELL, *In the Parish of Lanteglos, by Fowey:* Comprising a good Mansion-House, containing a Lobby, Breakfast-Room, Dining-Room, and Drawing-Room, six Bed-Rooms on the second floor, two Kitchens, with two Back-Kitchens, two Dairies, two Cellars, three Pantries, and other suitable Offices,; part of which is occupied by a Farmer, and divided; Stables, Barns, and other necessary Farm Outbuildings, and about 119 A. 33 P. of exceedingly good Arable, Meadow, Pasture, and Orchard Land, of which about two are Lawn.

The Estate is most eligible, and forms a most desirable residence for a Gentlemen or Farmer; and its situation is salubrious and universally admired; lying within two miles of the Post and Market Town of Fowey, and close to a beautiful Cove, where Sea Sand and Weed may be had in any quantity, and within a short distance of several good Market Towns.

*ALSO,*For the Remainder of a Term of 99 Years,....all that TENEMENT *called* HIGHER GRAGON, *In Lanteglos,*....Adjoining Tredudwell; consisting of a Barn and Ox-house, and about 20A. 3R. 8P. of good Arable, Meadow, and Pasture Land....an AUCTION will be held at the KING'S ARMS INN, in *Liskeard*, on Tuesday the 27th day of June instant.... The Estate may be viewed by applying to Tredudwell House....

10 June (RCG) RUNAWAY APPRENTICE   From his Master, WILLIAM HOCKEN, of Comb, in the parish of Fowey, Farmer, JOHN VANSON, his apprentice, aged 17, five feet 2 inches high, light hair, grey eyes, and fresh complexion; wore away a short brown coat, Corduroy Pantaloons, and a white and yellow striped plush waistcoat. Any person employing the above apprentice after this notice will be prosecuted.

24 June (RCG) DELIGHTFUL SITUATION IN CORNWALL. To be LET, for the Term of Three or Five Years, all that newly-erected DWELLING-HOUSE And SPACIOUS GARDENS, Either with or without Two Acres and Half of excellent Meadow Land, situate adjoining the Town of Polruen, within the Parish of Lanteglos by Fowey, on the Banks and near the entrance of the beautiful Harbour of Fowey, and immediately opposite the Borough of Fowey, lately erected and occupied by Capt. Pearce. The Harbour of Fowey and its Vicinity, for Persons fond of marine excursions, is not to be equalled; the Sea Views near the House are extensive, and the situation now advertised, for a small Genteel Family, is such as seldom offers.... A PUBLIC SURVEY will be held at the Hart Inn, in the town of Polruen, on Friday the 14th day of July next, at Four....(Dolphins?).

8 July (RCG) Advert for female fashions for July. Walking dress - high dress, short walking length of French cambric or jaconet muslin, trimmed at the feet with treble flounces of French work gathered into a rich bead heading, laid upon the dress at a suitable distance one above the other. Body made with open front worn with full ruff of French work. Long sleeve drawn alternately cross the arm ending in braid wristband. French bonnett of white satin with rich plume of white feathers. French mantle of twilled silk richly embroidered in shades of silks - roses or Lily of the Valley. Patent silk stockings. Slippers or half boots of blue kid or primrose, matching gloves.

26 August (RCG) *HORWOOD's* OXFORD WATER CLOSETS, *and* WELLINGTON WATERLOO CLOSETS, *For Ladies Only.*THESE CLOSETS are offered as a challenge to all England, for simplicity and cheapness, 40 per cent is also saved in fixing....The price of a Waterloo Closet is 8 Guineas; the others, from £3 to £4, packing, &c. compleat. Forcing Pumps, compleat, 4 Guineas; Floating Balls 1 Guinea;- These Balls indicate whether the cistern is full or empty, if within 100 yards of the pump, no object.

2 September (RCG) On Sunday last, about three o'clock in the morning, a fire broke out at Menabilly House and raged furiously for some time; but before the early arrival of the fishermen of Polkerris. Mr. Rashleigh's tenantry, with the engines from Fowey, and a great many of the inhabitants of Fowey, the flames were got under, after consuming the kitchen, and about all the servants' apartments up stairs. The fire was discovered in a dark closet adjoining the housekeeper's room and is supposed to have originated from a spark falling into the flue of the chimney communicating with that closet, the fire place of which had been closed up with lath and plaster.

30 December (RCG) The *ANN and ELIZABETH* Moyse, master, from Fowey to London, was driven on shore on the Isle of Shippey, during the late tremendous gales, when a great part of the cargo was lost, and almost all the moveable timber, iron-work, and cordage, were taken away by the people on shore, as were the clothes and provisions belonging to the sailors. The hull of the vessel has since been floated off, and hopes are entertained of recovering a part of the plundered property. (N.B.Fowey Ship, all Fowey masters).

1816

27 January (RCG) *TWO HUNDRED POUNDS* REWARD. WHEREAS it hath been represented to the Commissioners of His Majesty's Customs, that on the 30th Day of November last, about Nine o'clock in the Morning, JOHN HORNER, and JOHN CHUBB, Riding Officers in the Service of the Customs, at the Port of Fowey, in the County of Cornwall, being on Duty near Polgooth, in the Parish of   St. Mewan, ...met a numerous gang of Smugglers unknown, armed with Fire-arms and other offensive weapons, conveying on Horses a large Quantity of Smuggled Spirits, in small Casks, and upon the said Officers attempting to make a Seizure thereof, they were feloniously attacked by the said Smugglers, who assaulted and obstructed the said Officers, and dangerously wounded the said JOHN HORNER, and feloniously took, and carried away, his Sword and Pistol. The Commissioners,....in order to bring the said offenders to Justice, are hereby pleased to offer A REWARD OF TWO HUNDRED POUNDS, To any Person or Persons who shall discover and apprehend, or shall cause to be discovered and apprehended, any one or more of the said Offenders, to be paid by the Collector of His Majesty's Customs, at the port of Fowey, upon Conviction.

17 February (RCG) By Order of the COURT for the Relief of INSOLVENT DEBTORS. The Petition of WILLIAM KENT, late of the town of Fowey, Farmer, but now a Prisoner for Debt, confined in His Majesty's Gaol of Bodmin,...will be heard before his Majesty's Justice of the Peace...at a General Session of the Peace,...a list of the Creditors of the said Prisoner, is filed at the office of the said Court.

17 February (RCG) WINDOW-TAX. To the SHOPKEEPERS.... The Dimensions of Windows are generally limited by the Act of Parliament for laying Duties thereon; but the Legislature deemed it right to exempt Shop Windows....these may be of any *size* or *shape*, and are severally chargeable as one only, provided the divisions between the Lights be within Twelve Inches.

30 March (RCG) *FOWEY.* FOR SALE by PUBLIC AUCTION at the *Ship Inn,* on Friday the 3d day of May next by Eleven o'clock in the Forenoon, *The fast-sailing and handsome Copper-bottomed BRIG* TRITON, burthens 278 52-94ths Tons,. Pierced for 18 Guns, two mounted. This fast-sailing and well-equipped Brig is nearly new, having been at sea but a few days when she was captured by His Majesty's Schooner *Bramble,* T.W. Nicholls Esq. Commander, from Bordeaux, and bound to Guadeloupe; and as she will be Sold with all her Stores complete as when she arrived, she may be sent to sea at a very trifling expense.... Length 96 ft. Breadth 26 ft. 3 in. Depth 11ft. 10 in. This very desirable Vessel is faithfully built, and adapted to any trade wherein expedition is required.

Immediately after will be Sold her CARGO, *consisting of* 274 Hogsheads of CLARET WINE, 140 Cases Ditto Ditto, 7 Casks WHITE WINE, 7 Cases Ditto Ditto, 6 Tierces VINEGAR, 6 Cases CORDIAL, 27 Baskets Ditto, 5 Casks, containing 202 HAMS, 14 Cases of PICKLES, 22 cases of PRESERVED FRUITS, 16 Cases of CHEESE, 197 Baskets Fine OIL, 16 Bales COFFEE BAGS, 6 Bales LINEN, 79 Kegs PRESERVED MEAT, 2 Bales of highly-coloured PAPER and fit for a Nobleman's House. For viewing....and further particulars, apply to *Petherick Lukey,* Prize Agent, Fowey.

18 May (RCG) On the 13th inst., as Mr. Lamb (a respectable farmer) of Trefrawl, was driving his cart, laden with corn, down a hill, in the parish of Lanteglos by Fowey, the breeching of the shaft horse broke; and in attempting to keep the cart back, Mr. Lamb fell; the wheel went over his body and caused instant death. He was in the prime of life, and has left a wife and a large circle of friends and relatives to lament his loss.

25 May (RCG) To be LET by SEALED TENDER, for a Term of 14 Years from Michaelmas.... *All those Tenements and Farms of* TRETHAKE and part of *TREDUDWELL and GRAGON....* Consisting of a good Farm-house, good Barns, and all the necessary Out-buildings, and about Two Hundred Acres (customary measure) of exceeding good Arable Meadow and Pasture Land. These Estates, which adjoin, and form a most desirable Farm, are situated very near a Lime Kiln, and a Sanding Cove, and about Two miles from the Towns of Fowey and Polruan. The Taker will have liberty to sow Turnips and prepare for Wheat, and may be accommodated with all the Corn, crops of Wheat, Barley and Oats, on Trethake, and possessions of the Grass Land, except one field on Trethake immediately.

Tenders in writing stating the upmost Rent, clear of Rates, Taxes, and Repairs (except Walls and Slate Roofs) to be made to Arthur Puckey, Esq....on or before 27th May Instant....

22 June (RCG) TUITION. The officiating CLERGYMAN at Fowey will be happy to receive a few young GENTLEMEN under his care, for the purpose of instructing them in the LATIN and GREEK Languages. Boarders, 100 Guineas per annum; Day-Boarders, 50 Guineas; Day-Scholars, 25 Guineas; Admission 5 Guineas.

6 July (RCG) To be SOLD by AUCTION, at the House of Mr. George Beer, Innkeeper, in the Borough of Fowey, on Saturday the 20th Day of July instant, at   4 o'clock in the Afternoon. The Remainder of a Term of 99 years, Determinable on the Deaths of 2 healthy Lives, of and all those well-accustomed GRIST MILLS, known by the name of HIGHER CAFFA MILLS. With the DWELLING-HOUSE, OUT-HOUSES AND GARDEN Thereto Belonging; Situated.... no more than a Quarter of a Mile from the Borough of *Fowey*, now in the Occupation of Mr. George Isbell. For View, apply to Mr. George Isbell, on the Premises, or to Mr. Robert Puckey, Blacksmith....

13 July (RCG) During the tremendous gale of Monday last, the outward-bound East India ship *Cornwallis*, mistaking the Parr sands for the entrance of Falmouth harbour, approached so near those dangerous shoals, that had she continued her course a few minutes longer, her destruction would have been inevitable. Fortunately she was hailed by the master of the barge *KITTY*, of Fowey, into which port she was with great exertion, happily conveyed. About twenty small vessels have put into Fowey for shelter, several of which have received considerable damage from the storm.

26 October (RCG) On Wednesday last, the *Drake*, revenue cutter, sent in to Fowey, a smuggling boat with 25 kegs of spirits and three men on board.

14 December (RCG) By Order of the COURT for the Relief of Insolvent Debtors, the Petition of ROBERT REAN, late of Lanteglos,.... Farmer, now Prisoner for Debt in the King's Bench Prison,.... Surrey, will be heard at the Guild-hall....Westminster on the 4th day of January, 1817....

21 December (RCG) The *James Harris*, Captain Callew, from Liverpool, bound to Jamaica, has put into Fowey, having sustained considerable damage in the late gales. Her sails are all split, and her main-boom and rudder are lost.

1817

10 January (RCG) *By Order of the Assignees of PETHERICK LUKEY, a Bankrupt.* TO be SOLD by PUBLIC AUCTION, at the SHIP INN, in the Borough of Fowey, on MONDAY, the 20th day of January instant, at Four o'clock in the afternoon, for the remainder of a term of 99 years, determinable on the deaths of Three healthy Lives, aged 42, 15, and 12, all that NEW BUILT DWELLING-HOUSE AND PREMISES *Situate near the Market, in the Borough of Fowey,* Late in the occupation of the said Petherick Lukey....a large and commodious Shop, extensive Warehouses, and Lofts, a Chandle-house with all necessary apparatus for carrying on a business of a Tallow Chandler, Kitchen, Scullery, Two Parlours, Four Bedrooms and extensive Garrets. These Premises adjoin the harbour....and are eligibly situated and well adapted for carrying on an extensive trade as a general Shopkeeper, and Tallow Chandler.

For the like Term determinable on Three Lives aged 43, 16, and 19, all that NEWLY ERECTED STABLE Situate near West St, in Fowey, and formerly a Slaughter House. And this in the occupation of William Tregaskis....

25 January (RCG) *Fowey, January 23.* Last Sunday night we had a violent storm or hurricane, and an extraordinary rise of the sea on Monday morning, about four or five o'clock, which greatly damaged the quays, also many of the houses into which it broke, dashing the cupboards and their contents to pieces. The sea washed off a vessel from the stocks, and beat down a pleasure house, kitchen, and stables with a horse in it; the animal swam a half-a-mile before it landed. The injury done to the various premises, goods and merchandise in Fowey, is supposed to amount to some thousands of pounds. Though some individuals were in imminent danger, happily no lives were lost. Polruan, Polkerris, and Polperro, have likewise sustained considerable damage. Such a swell and tempest has never been known here since the memory of man. (WB 24 Jan.)- A sloop was driven against the gable of a house which it carried away. The damages will be at least £2000 - happily no lives were lost.

7 February (WB).... July last we inserted a disclaimer of the Office of Mayor of Fowey sent to Mr. Austen.... Fox's Act prevents any man's title to a Franchise from being impeached, after having been in exercise of it....six years, those who had held the Office as Mayor during the last five years, by the advice of some....formally renounced office.... By the aid of such a Mayor, the Corporate Body was soon filled up with, no doubt, some of the most virtuous of the inhabitants - one of whom unfortunately, soon after decamped with a considerable sum of trust-money, and is.... an outlawed bankrupt.... Thus then we may hail people of Fowey as free-men, considering that the Charter has run its course - and as this Charter was granted at the prayer of the INHABITANTS, no other can ever become valid which THEY *refuse to accept....* If *they* do not *protest* against every attempt to obtain one we shall think THEM FIT SUBJECTS FOR THE DIVAN!

7 June (RCG) *Borough of Fowey....*To be SOLD by PUBLIC AUCTION, at the SHIP INN....on FRIDAY, the Fourth day of July next, at Six o'clock in the evening, the Fee-Simple and Inheritance of and in all that *DWELLING HOUSE and PREMISES,* Situate near the Market Place within the said Borough, *Formerly the Dolphin Inn;* Together with a Garden, eligibly situated, the whole of which adjoin the Harbour of Fowey, and were lately in the occupation of Mr Walter Colmer. This House is one of the Prince's Tenements, and as such the Owner is entitled to vote as a Prince's Tenant in the Election of Members of Parliament for the Borough of Fowey; and the Occupier also entitled to vote as a Scot and Lot Vote for the same borough....

20 June (RCG) MISS MOORE, (late of Truro),in consequence of the request and advice of her Friends in Cornwall, intends, immediately after the ensuing vacation, to OPEN a BOARDING-SCHOOL, at LOSTWITHIEL for the reception of YOUNG LADIES.

In this seminary they will be taught every useful part of Female Education; a particular regard will be shewn to their improvement in general Literature, and religious principles will be seriously inculcated. The utmost attention will also be exerted by Miss Moore, to render *the morals* of the young Ladies entrusted to her care *pure,* and their *manners correct.*

Terms. Board, instruction in English Grammar, Geography and History, twenty-three guineas per annum. Entrance, one guinea. Washing, three guineas.

The French Language, Writing and Arithmetic, Drawing, and other accomplishments, will be charged separately, but on very moderate terms.

25 July (WB) At the information of Joseph Ham and Susannah Austen against the Mayor and Corporation of Fowey....praying the Court to grant an injunction to restrain them from acting regarding some charitable estates, and that a Receiver might be appointed. Some of those estates had been vested in trustees for charitable purposes in the reign of Henry VI.... In 1690 some of the trustees were appointed Members of the Corporation since when the Corporation had acted as if the charity had been vested in them, and....had let the property, which was worth £250 per annum for a rent of 8*l.* 1s, which certainly was so low that it required no comment, for it shewed an abuse of their usurped power.... Had they been let as they should have been done, the poor-rates would not have been so heavily imposed on the other parishioners. Much waste had also been committed.... The Members now wished a new Corporation.... Judgement - that the prayer of the plaintiffs be granted....

22 November (RCG) DEATH OF PRINCESS CHARLOTTE - (following birth of a still born child.) The day appointed for the interment of the late Princess Charlotte, was observed at Fowey with great solemnity. In the forenoon the bells tolled a funeral knell for an hour before the church service, when the psalms and lesson for the burial were read in a most solemn manner, and an edifying sermon preached to a respectable congregation, by the Rev. G. Nankivell.... The shops were shut all day, and the ships hoisted their colours half mast high. In the evening an appropriate and excellent sermon was preached at the methodist chapel....

6 December (RCG).... *Fowey, Saturday evening, Nov.22....*a numerous and respectable Meeting of the Inhabitants took place.... Mr. Richard Hewett....read the Address, as follows; To JOSEPH THOMAS AUSTEN, Esq. We the Inhabitants of the Borough and Parish of Fowey....beg to offer to you our most cordial and sincere congratulations and thanks, for your extraordinary and never ceasing exertions in restoring to us the Rights, Revenues and Privileges of our forefathers; and returning us from the slavery and oppression which ever will be inseparable from a local jurisdiction, where the Magistrates are not independent of the People.... We consider ourselves particularly happy that the gifts of fortune have so happily fallen upon one who not only possesses the head but the heart to annihilate the shameful and horrid corruptions that have existed in this Borough for upwards of one hundred years, fostered under an oligarchy, which has not only deprived the Town and Harbour of their local advantages, and the people of their just rights; but tended to demoralize their minds, by holding them to believe, that competence and wealth, instead of being the rewards of honest industry, are the attendants on bribery and corruption....

We beg again to repeat to you, our warm and sincere thanks....for destroying the power of those men who, by their undue influence over the local management of this Borough and Parish plunged us into numerous vexatious law suits - who misapplied the proceeds of considerable charity Estates, and a great deal of public money, raised in the shape of Parish Rates....

We also thank you for the exertions that you have always made to restore our Trade, in which, from present appearances, we have reason to hope that your efforts will be crowned with the same success as they have been in destroying our late Charter....we hereby resolve and determine, that every man who shall attempt to subject us again to the power of a Charter, will prove himself an enemy to the true interests of Fowey; that we will avoid all intercourse with him, as one bringing to us pestilence....and, that we would oppose him ...by all lawful means in our power.

Joseph Thomas Austen, Esq,....returned the following answer. "....I long since determined on emancipating you from the power of your late persecutors.... I once more beg to repeat, that if you are true to yourselves, never again will you be enslaved, and to add....that no injury can ever befall this place without my participating in your sufferings....

1818

31 January (RCG) TO be SOLD, by Order of the Assignees of PETHERICK LUKEY, a Bankrupt, One undivided eighth part of the SCHOONER *"FLY"*, of the port of Fowey ---SALT, Master; British built, length aloft 54 ft. breadth 18 ft 4in depth 8 ft, and admeasures 70 19.94 Tons. This vessel is well found, and ready for Sea at a moment's notice, has shifts without ballast, and has every qualification for the Coasting or Coal Trade, in which she has been particularly successful....a public Auction will be held....for viewing, apply to Mr. Philip Pill, at Polrenn,....where the said vessel now lies....

13 June (RCG) DISSOLUTION OF PARLIAMENT. The borough of Fowey received a visit on Thursday last, from Lord Valletort and Mr. Glyn Campbell....accompanied by Mr. Colman Rashleigh. He delivered an address to the people, who had assembled in great numbers to behold the two candidates and their *patriotic* supporter. After the surrounding populace had listened a short time with a degree of complacency to the usual strains of this popular orator, respecting *corruption, tyranny, oppression*, &c. they began to perceive some degree of inconsistency in his protestations; and the rhetorical flourishes, which for a while misled the audience, were at length opposed by the dictates of common sense. A murmur circulated through the crowd, that the champion of Reform, had something more in view than his professions indicated. When they heard him eulogize a noble Lord, so contrary to the expectation of the whole town, the honest crowd were no longer to be imposed upon.... They were aware that the Honourable candidate was no adherent to the principles of *resisting tyranny and oppression* - the Reformers' translation for opposing the Administration and the laws. Under these impressions a commotion was excited; one of the auditors procured a speaking trumpet, and sounded the *base* notes of his discordant instrument; to which the swan-like strains of the *flourishing* orator responded in delightful unison, to the no small merriment of the assembly. The *farce* being thus obstructed, the *actors* wisely made their *exit*, lest a general *cupping* should ensue.

27 June (RCG) *STATEMENT OF FACTS.* The right of election at Fowey is in such Prince's-tenants....on the rent rolls of the manor of the Borough....and such inhabitants as pay scot and lot. - During the existence of the late charter, the Borough Magistrates being the sole judges of all appeals against the poor's-rates; having the appointment of all the Overseers' and usurping that of one Churchwarden, great numbers of people hostile to their interest, were always left out of the rates; and every attempt to put them on was fruitless.

The last poors'-rate made whilst the Charter existed, was on the 17th of March, 1817.... The whole of the late Magistrates were soon afterwards turned out of office, by a decision of the Court of King's Bench. Previously to this, they had re-appointed their creatures as parish officers,- not for the purpose of making rates, but to prevent any from being made.- During last Michaelmas term, an application was made to the Court of King's Bench for a Mandamus, to compel the Overseers to make a rate.... their Agent in town (London), to gain time, made an affidavit that he verily believed they could shew good cause if time were allowed them! - and that from the distance of London to Fowey, he found it impossible that he could by post have an answer from his correspondent there. The Overseers' Agent by this affidavit succeeded in postponing shewing cause till Hiliary Term.... The defence set up at St. Hiliary Term was, that if the arrears of rates, which amounted to £110, were paid; that they should not only want no money then, but none for a considerable time to come. - Notwithstanding this, it appears by their own accounts, that at the Christmas before, they had expended upwards of £318, above the money raised; and in the April following they published a rate for above £477!! However,....a mandamus was granted to compel them to make a rate, which they delayed complying with until after the Sessions, lest it should be appealed against. Knowing that this rate could be investigated at the County Sessions, these Gentlemen parish officers discovered that, instead of being only 152 persons, which is the greatest number that they ever before rated, there actually were 279 persons properly qualified to be put on the poors'-rates,.... This rate having a retrospective operation....to cover the Parish expenses from Lady-day, 1817, it was presumed that the Portreeve would have used it...to decide on the qualifications of voters; particularly as there had been a great change of occupation in some of the best premises in Fowey within the last fifteen months. But he refused....as it was not dated six months previous to the election.- A Church rate was then offered to him, made subsequent to the Poors' rate of March, 1817;....in evidence of the rateability of the persons who had paid it. This rate was also refused, and the Portreeve called for the Poors'-rate of March, 1817; which was produced, to the astonishment of every one not in the secret; as whenever the parishioners demanded this rate to pay it, or a copy of it, the parish officers declared that it was lost!....

The Portreeve, after learning how the rate had been kept back and reported as lost, to prevent it being paid, decided those that had not paid it should not be allowed to vote, - Amongst these was Mr. Austen, although he offered to prove....that he had demanded this rate....for the purpose of paying it, and that their answer was, that they could not tell what had become of it!- Mr. Austen whose vote was thus rejected on the right of paying scot and lot, actually stands charged upon this rate, in considerably more money, for the property he occupies in the Borough only, than the whole of the persons, taken together, who voted for Mr. Lucy and Mr. Stanhope!!- Even on this rate, notwithstanding the numbers cut off, the Ex-corporation were beaten. To counteract this, they brought forward one freeholder or Prince's Tenant, and forty Fagots from London, Hammersmith, Plymouth Dock yard, and the "Lord knows where". Their opponents then brought forward forty five Freeholders out of more than double that number, being prepared to beat them at their own weapons;- but the Portreeve, who, by the way, is himself a Fagot, and against whom a rule of *Quo Warranto* has been made absolute in the Court of King's Bench, preparatory to his being turned out of office, admitted all the Freeholders in the interest of one party to vote,- though only one of them was so entitled....and rejected all those of the other party except five old ones,- But such means after cutting off forty Freeholders and one *hundred and twenty five* electors on the right of paying scot and lot, who tendered their votes against his friends, he pronounced the numbers to be as follows; Lucy...78, Stanhope... 77, Lord Valletort... 44, Mr. Campbell... 44....

Lord Valletort and Mr. Campbell are fully assured of final success.- At the commencement of the poll, the Portreeve was requested to read a notice warning all who intended to vote for Mr. Lucy and Mr. Stanhope, that they would throw away their votes, as their candidates had been guilty of *bribery*. The Portreeve refusing to do this, Mr. Adam, Counsel for Lord Valletort and Mr. Campbell, read it to each of these persons as he came to the poll.- The Attorney and Agent employed by Mr. Lucy, were served with writs, on charges of bribery, on the second day of the election.

15 August (RCG) CORNWALL ASSIZES. NISI PRIUS Tuesday, August 4. THE KING *versus* GILES. James Bice Giles, an inhabitant of Fowey, was charged by indictment with an assault upon Elizabeth Jacket, a girl about eighteen years of age, wounding her on the forehead with a stone on the 10th of December last.

Elizabeth Jacket stated that on the day of the assault she was servant to the late Mr. Colmer of Fowey. On that day, the two electioneering parties distinguished by the appellations of the *Blues* and the *Greys*, held processions in that town. The Greys of which her late master belonged, paraded in the early part of the day, and the Blues in the evening. When they approached her master's house, she was standing at the window on the first floor which was open. In front of the house the crowd cheered and went forward, except one man, whom she saw by the light of a candle which a neighbour had in her hand, in passing to her own house, and had no doubt it was the defendant. He stopped, raised his arm, as if in the act of throwing, and she was immediately struck by a large stone above the left eye; such was the violence of the blow that she fell back and fainted. It was between nine and ten o'clock at night. She was confined to her bed a week, in consequence of the injury, and attended by two surgeons.

Joseph Tedley, a boy of 13, grandson of the late Mr. Colmer, was standing at the window with the preceding witness when the stone was thrown. He was quite sure that the person who threw it was the defendant, whom he knew, and whom he saw at the time by the light of the candle before described.

Augustus Sellers saw the defendant pass his home towards Mr. Colmer's between 9 and 10 o'clock on the night in question.

Elizabeth Crew, who keeps a public house at Fowey, stated that the defendant was brought to her house in custody on the 12th of December, when she asked him, how he could be so cruel as to throw a large stone at the poor girl - to which he replied with a laugh that "it was not a large stone".

John Hallett surgeon, attended Elizabeth Jacket. The wound on her forehead was so severe, as to produce the following day symptoms of a concussion of the brain, when he thought it right to call in assistance.

Several witnesses appeared on the part of the defendant, to prove that the party of the Blues had dispersed on the quay just before the clock struck nine; and one of them, Peter Crapp swore, to his having thrown a stone at Mr. Colmer's window in return for dirt thrown from it at him.

Mr. Serjeant Pell in his reply animadverted with much severity on the evidence of Crapp. Mr. Justice Burrough, in summing up, observed, that the defence did not meet the charge, as the evidence for the defendant did not relate to the time when the assault took place, but to a prior period. The defendant was found guilty, and will receive sentence in the Court of King's Bench.

15 August (RCG) Lane *versus* Sowell. This was an action brought by the plaintiff, the Rev. Newton Charles Lane, against the defendant, for defamation.- This cause....arose out of the electioneering disputes at Fowey....- Mr. Serjeant Pell stated the case for the plaintiff, whom he represented as a respectable Clergyman....and uncle to Mr. Lucy.... The defendant, formerly a ship-master, is at present a malster, residing at Penryn, and took a warm interest in the contests which have for some time agitated the borough of Fowey. The learned Sergeant was free to admit, that in cases of disputed election some latitude should be allowed for the heat of party.... But....all the bounds of moderation had been exceeded. It would be proved, that on two different occasions the defendant had....charged the plaintiff, with being guilty of acts so horrible, as to render him wholly unfit for society,.... The cause of this atrocious attack was the interference of the plaintiff in the....Fowey election, for the purpose of promoting the interest of his nephew....

James Tool resides at Fowey. On the 23rd of March last, he was in Mr. Lamb's shop in that place, in company with Lieutenant Nicholls. Mr. Lamb was reading a

53

written paper containing questions and answers which were at that time circulated at Fowey. The paper imputed a detestable offence to the plaintiff. Witness and Mr. Lamb said they believed the statement to be true. The defendant came into the shop and heard them commenting on the paper;- he asked if they doubted the truth of the charge made in the paper. Some of them said they hoped it was not true. The defendant replied, that they need not doubt it; they might rely on it as a fact, and if they wanted any further information they might go to the house of a gentleman he named, where they would obtain a confirmation of the truth. The defendant further stated, that the plaintiff had lost his gown in consequence of the affair in question, that he was disowned by his connexions in London, and that whoever applied to them for information respecting him, was told he had been dead for five years. The same morning, the witness heard the defendant repeat the same observations....in the shop of a person named Lukey.... A daughter of Lukey's was present, and witness desired her to leave the shop, that she might not hear the observations of the defendant. At this time defendant said that a few days before Mr. Lane's nephew came to Fowey; but as soon as he found his uncle was there, he left the place, as he would have no intercourse with him.... Mr. Adam made an able appeal to the Jury on behalf of the defendant....it should be recollected that at the time party heat was great at Fowey, and this disposed persons to lend a ready ear to any charges made against their opponents....it did not appear that the defendant was the person who first propagated the report... nor....had anything to do with the written paper.... The offence....was, that he had found the report in circulation, and had, most imprudently, he admitted, propagated it in two instances. Under these circumstances, the Jury would recollect that it was the vindication of his character and not a pecuniary compensation that the plaintiff avowed as his object....

Mr. Justice Burrough summed up....and observed that....the plaintiff was entitled to what would heal his character, which nominal damages would not do - The Jury, after a short deliberation, found for the plaintiff,- £400 damages.

1819

2 January (RCG) Four men, named Carvorro, Jasper, Cary, and Blewett, found on board a smuggling boat at Fowey, were last week transferred to the naval service.

13 February (RCG) On Wednesday last, was launched in fine style from the yard of Mr. W. Brokenshaw, shipwright, Fowey, a handsome new schooner, called the *William*. She has been built for Mr. William T. Chappel, merchant, of this town, who intends her to sail as a regular trader to and from the Ports of Liverpool and Truro.

24 April (RCG) On the night of Thursday week, two men, named Lee and Jolly, with a boy, all belonging to Mevagissey, returning in an open boat from Plymouth, were driven into Lanivet Bay and drowned.

8 May (RCG) Timber is rapidly advancing in price; a proof that house and ship building is in a thriving state....

12 June (RCG) CIRCUS. MR. POWELL (from Astley's, London,....most respectfully announces to the Public, that....he shall visit....Fowey, St Austell, and Liskeard, where his select TROOP of EQUESTRIANS *and beautiful stud of horses,* (being indisputably the best Troop out of London.) Will go through their Equestrian Exercises.

THE FLYING PHENOMENON YOUNG CHAPMAN'S astonishing Performances on the SLACK ROPE.

Pleasing FEATS on HORSEBACK By the Celebrated Miss POWELL, Being most incontrovertibly the first Female Performer in the World.

The ANTIPODEAN YOUNG HORSEMAN, Master BUSAN, *Will, while his HORSE is in FULL SPEED,* Dance a Hornpipe Standing on his Head.

The Grand Act of RUNNING VAULTING, Shewing the method of Mounting and Dismounting, without the aid of a Stirrup, in full speed.

WONDERFUL FEATS, By MASTER EMIDY, of TRURO

A Grand Entree, by the BEAUTIFUL STUD of WELL-BROKE SPANISH and ARABIAN HORSES, in which they will represent themselves as DYING and DEAD - and place themselves in various positions. After which the SPANISH HORSE will dance to the Tunes of Nancy Dawson and Paddy Carey.

Performance on Horseback, By Master CHAPMAN, the Equestrian Hero, who will take some surprising Leaps over Whips, Handkerchiefs, Garters, &c.....

Boxes 2s.   Pit 1s.   Standing Places 6d.

16 July (WB) The annual Regatta of Lostwithiel, took place on Friday last. As usual, the band of the Royal Cornwall Militia attended. The assemblage of beauty and fashion was perhaps the gayest that ever graced the waters of Fowey. The numerous pleasure boats (upwards of sixty) in which the party embarked, decorated in the most tasteful manner, as they seemed to lead the dance through the winding and romantic scenery of the river; the standards and streamers floating in the air, and the delightful melody of music, as it trembled over the water, seemed to carry the imagination back to the imposing descriptions of Asiatic luxury, and presented an exact delineation of a grand spectacle of Oriental magnificence. On arriving at Fowey the party were most agreeably surprized by the appearance of several King's cutters in the harbour, decorated with colours, each of them firing a salute as the boats in procession rowed around....

16 July (WB)   MOON'S *Royal, Wonderful, and Pleasing* EXHIBITION. Mr. Moon returns his heartfelt thanks to the inhabitants of Penzance, St. Ives, and vicinity for the very flattering reception he has uniformly experienced from them, having been honoured with the presence of many hundreds each night and most respectfully informs the Ladies and Gentlemen of Helston....that he again intends displaying.... THAUMATURGIS, MATHEMATICAL OPERATIONS, AND MAGICAL DECEPTIONS. He also performs with GOLD AND SILVER APPARATUS, and far surpasses any other performer in the Kingdom. Also TACHYGRAPHY, and UNCOMMON DECEPTIONS with various other astonishing feats. His performances are universally acknowledged to be unrivalled and need only to be seen to excite the highest degree of astonishment and admiration, his unequalled skill having elicited the unqualified approbation of the Royal Family, and the Nobility and Gentry in every part of the United Kingdom. Before he leaves the County Mr. Moon intends to visit Falmouth ....Fowey....&c.

11 September (RCG) On Tuesday, as a young man, named Joshua Ede, was working in a saw pit at Pont, near Lanteglos, by Fowey, the bearer unfortunately broke, and the piece of timber falling on him occasioned his instant death.

18 September (RCG) TO be SOLD by PUBLIC AUCTION, on the BARTON of TRETHAKE, in the Parish of Lanteglos by Fowey, all the FARM STOCK, The Property of Mr. John B. Bate; *consisting of*

10 Capital Working OXEN; 6 Milch COWS three of which are nearly ready to calve; 2 Fat COWS; 21 Prime young BULLOCKS of different descriptions; 100 EWES, selected from the first breeders in the County; 30 Fat ditto; 30 Fat WETHERS; 70 Prime LAMBS; 2 Capital RAMS; 12 Capital HORSES and COLTS; 30 PIGS.

23 October (RCG) On Monday, the ploughing-match for the premiums offered by Mr. Rodd drew together a numerous assemblage of agriculturalists at Bodmin. Twenty-four ploughs were entered, and eighteen started for the premiums, their being a greater number than has ever appeared at a former Ploughing Match of the Society, and of these seven were drawn by horses in pairs without a driver....To the best Ploughman without a Driver, Wm. Dunn, of Fowey...£4....

30 October (RCG) Three vessels have been laid down at Fowey, to be engaged in the Newfoundland fishery from that place.

CHAPTER 3
1820-1829

1820

15 January (RCG) LOSTWITHIEL QUARTER SESSIONS William Crews and Peter Hambly, of Fowey, for unlawful fishing, were sentenced to one month's imprisonment, and a fine of twelve pounds.

15 January (RCG) On Wednesday last as Mr. Phillip Sings, butcher, was returning from Charlestown to his home near Fowey, passing under Par cliff when the tide was high, he was unfortunately drowned. This unhappy incident is supposed to have been occasioned by the stumbling of his horse against a rock, by which he was precipitated into the water; and the discovery was made by some persons who were returning from Mr. Cory's funeral, and saw the horse wandering about the sand without his rider. Mr. Sings' corpse was removed to a neighbouring house, and means made use of for his restoration to life, but also in vain.

22 July (RCG) A pleasure yacht, the *"GAZELLE"*, belonging to Mr. William Owen, Esq. M.P. is arrived at Fowey. She is fitted upon a new plan the invention of the proprietor, and is so singularly constructed, that if the vessel has a great heel to starboard or larboard, the cabin floor with table and chairs, and also the beds, preserve on even or level position.

28 July (WB) On Friday last, a mackerel sean belonging to Fowey inclosed part of a shoal of pilchards, but the whole escaped through the meshes, except about 200 of a very large size. On Saturday three pilchard seans were put to sea from Fowey when one of them took about five hogsheads.

29 July (RCG) TO BE LET BY TENDER. FOR a Term of 7 or 14 years from Lady-day last, all those excellent Pilchard Cellars called ST. CATHERINE'S CELLARS, with Salt Store-houses, Lofts, and every conveniency for the Pilchard Fishery....at Ready Money Beach in....Fowey. These Cellars are most commodiously situated, and Boats may be taken up under cover at any time.

29 July (RCG) DIED at Fowey last Monday, in the 80th year of her age, after a long illness, which she bore with Christian patience, Miss Anne Wolcot, (only surviving sister of the late John Wolcot, M.D., well known from his poetical compositions by the name of Peter Pindar). She was one who feared God and honoured the King; and was deservedly respected in life, and lamented in death; the poor, to whom she was a liberal benefactress, will especially regret her loss.- The eight bearers, who carried her to the grave, are old servants and other poor women, who besides ribbons and gloves are to receive a guinea each by her desire.

4 August (WB) On Tuesday, the body of Mr. Petherick Lukey, lately a respectable shopkeeper of Fowey, was discovered in the river near that place. An inquest had been summoned, but had not sat, when our correspondent wrote. It is supposed the deceased threw himself into the river, during the prevalence of a fit of despondency.

19 August (RCG) CORNWALL ASSIZES. *Austen* versus *Couch*.- This case arose out of the electioneering squabbles at Fowey.- The Plaintiff was the head of the *Blue* party there; the Defendant is a tailor, and....was engaged by the Plaintiff as a man of considerable oratorical powers to contest against the *Greys*.... The Defendant wishing to obtain pecuniary assistance, applied to the Plaintiff for a sum of money, and £150 was procured for him.... A compromise having taken place between the Plaintiff and his opponent, Mr. Lucy, to the exclusion of the Corporation of Fowey, the Defendant became his opponent, and joined the *Greys*. In consequence of this, the Plaintiff demanded payment of the money borrowed with interest, and also of other sums of money advanced to him, amounting in the whole of £204.- The Defendant resisted his demand on the grounds that the £150 was given to him by the Plaintiff, as a remuneration for services rendered during the election, and that the other sums were paid for ribbons furnished to the *Blues* at the time of the election.- He called witnesses but failed to prove these allegations; when the Plaintiff offered to take a verdict for £167.... The Defendant ....reluctantly acceded to the terms proposal. *Verdict for the Plaintiff, £167, and costs.*

1 September (WB) STRAYED, from a field near *Fowey,* about a Fortnight since, a Hackney Mare and Gelding, *Both Dark Bay, and between Fourteen and Fifteen Hands High.* The MARE has some Warts round her off ear and one under her near flank with a cropped tail. The horse is young, slight made, and has a switch tail, both are good looking horses and in high condition. They were seen on the road from Bodmin to Launceston a day or so after they strayed. Information to Mr. Illingworth of Fowey so they may be recovered, shall be handsomely rewarded.

9 September (RCG) NOTICE - GAME. ANY Person who shall ....be found hunting or shooting or in any other manner procuring or destroying Game, Woodcocks, Snipes or Rabbits, on any of the Manors or Estates the property of WILLIAM RASHLEIGH, Esq. of Menabilly lying in the several parishes of Fowey....Lanteglos....unless by written permission of the Proprietor, will be prosecuted for wilful damage and trespass.

9 December (RCG) On the 1st instant Mr. John Brickel, sitter of the Mevagissey preventative boat, and six of his boatmen came to the Custom-house, Fowey, to receive their last month's pay, and being about to return in the afternoon, Mrs. Mary Webb requested they would give her a passage home, which they consented to do. They went from Fowey after four o'clock, but Mr. Brickel having heard Lieut. Wise was arrived as sitter, at his new station at Polkerris, when they were a little west of the Gribbon, steered towards Polkerris, to communicate with Mr. Wise, they had not proceeded above a mile, and keeping too near the land, a swell of the sea upset the boat, which was soon dashed to pieces, and awful to relate Mr. Brickel, Peter Coulem, Edward Bickerlegs, Thomas Dillon, and Mary Webb were drowned. Benjamin Quick, Wm. Cloke and Reginald Langmaid were providentially saved though much bruised.

23 December (RCG) *Fame* of Guernsey,....from Jamaica, last from Halifax, Nova Scotia, is arrived at Fowey. Among the passengers by her is a Mr. George Hart, of

Cumberland, in that province, who has invented and brought with him a longitudinal quadrant, and is going to the Board of Longitude to obtain the premium. He has employed twelve years in the undertaking and calculation of tables.

1821

6 January (RCG) To render water particularly wholesome and palatable, it should, after being boiled and filtered, be put in a common barrel churn, where it may be agitated to any degree that may be wished, and then bottled, with a couple of dry raisins to each bottle. This will give it a sufficient quantity of fixed air, and if then used, it becomes truly delicious.

6 January (RCG) *Family Oven for making Bread.* - The family oven is usually erected on one side of the kitchen fire-place, and heated by a flue that passes from the fire-grate under the bottom of the oven. Although this is in many respects a convenient and neat way of heating the oven, yet the manner of managing the fire renders it only economical in families where a large fire is always kept up in the kitchen grate. In small families it is far more economical to heat the oven by means of a separate fire-place built underneath it. A fire-place 6 inches wide, 9 inches long, and 6 deep is sufficient to heat an oven 18 inches wide, 24 inches long, and from 12 to 15 inches high, which is a convenient size for the breaking of bread. The grate should be placed at least 12 inches below the bottom of the oven when the fuel employed is pit coal; and in order to prevent the fire from operating with too much violence on any part of the oven, the brickwork should be sloped outwards and upwards on every side, from the top of the burning fuel, to the ends and side of the bottom of the oven, that the whole may be exposed to the direct rays of the fire. If built in this manner, it is almost incredible how a small quantity of fuel will answer for heating the oven, and keeping it hot.... I have baked two loaves, each weighing 5lbs. and fifteen rolls weighing 2lbs. by means of half a peck (10lbs.) of coals.

20 January (RCG) A vagrant, calling himself Evan Evans, having applied to one of the Magistrates of Fowey for pecuniary assistance, to proceed to his parish at Redruth, and appearing to have lost his right hand, was accordingly furnished with an order to Lieut. Nicholls, the Overseer, for relief. The Lieutenant said before he relieved, he should examine him, on which the fellow attempted to run off, but by the activity of the last mentioned Gentleman, who procured immediate assistance, he was secured. On examination it was found that the fingers of his right hand were compressed with a bandage, and put into a leather case, so as to resemble the stump of an arm. In his knapsack were two purses, one containing £2 17s. 6d. in silver, and another upwards of four shillings in copper. He declared on oath that his real parish was in Carnarvonshire. This impostor was deservedly whipped on Wednesday at noon, in the public market place, in the presence of hundreds of spectators.

3 February (RCG) We are sorry to see that Smuggling has revived in Cornwall, since the peace, as well as in Devonshire, and most other maritime counties. It is a practice, destructive of prudent habits in young men, and leads to premature death, or impoverished age. Thirty to forty years ago, smuggling and intoxication were at their height in that county, going hand in hand, as they ever will do.... About two years ago, we were told, by an observing and sensible man, "I have lived almost to three score, in my native county of Cornwall. I have seen the jollity of a smuggler's life. Poor men have got comparatively rich, in a short time by smuggling; but the money seldom or never wore well; and I could recount the names of many, whose days it shortened, and many more who are suffering in old age, from the improvident habits which smuggling never fails to inspire. Smuggling has now been suspended in Cornwall for some years; and the consequence is, that you scarcely ever see a young man tipsy." The return of the practice of smuggling then, as far as it prevails, is calculated to throw young men backward again into poverty, vice and disgrace; and destroy those good habits which alone can lead to comfort and respectability in old age.

3 February (RCG) *A Cheap Fuel.* One bushel of small coal, or saw-dust, or both mixed together, two bushels of sand, one bushel and a half of clay. Let these be mixed together with water like mortar; the more they are stirred and mixed together the better; then make them into balls, or with a small mould, make them in the shape of bricks; pile them in a dry place, and when they are hard and sufficiently dried, they may be used. A fire cannot be lighted with them; but when the fire is quite lighted put them on behind, with a coal or two in front, and they will be found to keep up a stronger fire than any fuel of the common kind.

24 February (RCG) Wednesday the undersigned FREEHOLDERS and INHABITANTS of CORNWALL, request....a MEETING of the COUNTY, to consider....Petitioning the House of Commons....that they will institute a full and thorough inquiry into the causes of the present Distresses of the Nation, and especially of those by which the Agricultural Population and interest are depressed;- that they will adopt the most speedy and effectual measures for their Relief...E.J.Glynn, David Howell, J.C.Rashleigh, J.B.Trevanion, John Honney, N.Kendall. To the High Sheriff of the County of Cornwall.

GENTLEMEN, I am of the opinion that any interference, by convening a COUNTY MEETING....would tend only to increase that unsettled and feverish state of mind which has for some time existed in this Country, and under these circumstances prove hostile to the true interests of the state....

With great respect....High-Sheriff for Cornwall

In consequence of the refusal of the High-Sheriff to call a County Meeting....we the under-signed Magistrates....do hereby request the FREEHOLDERS, COPYHOLDERS, HOUSEHOLDERS, and INHABITANTS, residing in the County of Cornwall, to attend a MEETING to be holden within the ASSIZE-HALL; at BODMIN, to consider the steps necessary.....

24 February (RCG) *PILCHARD SEINES AND VESSEL.* TO BE SOLD by AUCTION to the best bidder at the SHIP INN, in the borough of Fowey,.... THREE

SIXTEENTH PARTS or SHARES and ONE THIRTY-SECOND PART or SHARE of and in the PILCHARD SEAN, called *THE UNION SEAN OF FOWEY.*

And ONE SIXTEENTH PART or SHARE in the PILCHARD SEAN, called THE VALLETORT OF FOWEY.

And also, ONE SIXTEENTH PART or SHARE in the PILCHARD SEAN, called THE LIBERTY SEAN OF FOWEY.

With the like Parts or Shares of the BOATS, NETS, SALT, and MATERIALS to the said Shares respectively belonging.

And also the HULL or VESSEL now on the Stocks, building, at Pill in the Parish of Fowey.... Apply to Mr. Borlase, of the Ship Inn, Fowey....

10 March (RCG) Several lambs belonging to J. Austen, Esq. of Fowey, having lately been destroyed, watch was set for the depredator, and a breeding sow was caught in the act of seizing a lamb from the side of the mother.

7 April (RCG) Two licensed Hawkers and Pedlars were last week fined at Fowey £10 each, for not having their packs marked according to law.

16 June (RCG) WHEAL PROVIDENCE COPPER MINE. *IN LANTEGLOS, BY FOWEY.* NOTICE IS HEREBY GIVEN, that a MEETING of the ADVENTURERS will be held at the Ship Inn, in Fowey, on Tuesday the 19th June Instant, at One o'clock precisely, for the purpose of making arrangements for the immediate working of the said Mine. And all Persons having any Demands on the said Mine, or claiming any Shares therein, are desired to deliver in accounts of their respective Claims either to the said Meeting, or in the mean time to Mr. Penrose, Attorney, Liskeard.

28 July (RCG) Last Thursday being the day of His Majesty's Coronation, was ushered in at Fowey with the ringing of bells and other demonstrations of loyalty: flags were hoisted on the different vessels, guns fired &c. A number of gentlemen dined together at the Ship Inn to celebrate the joyful events. The children belonging to the Sunday Schools were regaled with tea and supper, and the day concluded with great festivity.

4 August (RCG) Wednesday being the day appointed for the Fowey annual Regatta, several of the gentry of Fowey and its vicinity went to meet those of Lostwithiel, who came in yachts and pleasure boats to do honor to the day. The morning was unfavorable but the weather cleared up, and five hundred persons accompanied by the Cornwall Militia band to Fowey, the music of which, in the fine strains of our favourite national airs, sounded most melodiously on the water. The boats were very gaily decorated with flags, and the whole presented a most beautiful appearance. On their approach to the harbour, some of the vessels (which with the numerous boats displayed the Royal Standard, and colors of various nations, Neptune and his trident, and other appropriate emblems) fired a salute, and all parties seemed ready to renew those rejoicings that were so recently and heartily manifested on the day of the Coronation. The ball in the evening was attended by 130 persons; dancing commenced at 10 with 38 couples, and was continued in great spirit until near four in the morning. Quadrilles and lancers were danced alternately with country dances.

The unremitting attention of the three stewards gave universal satisfaction, and the room was tastefully decorated with laurel and flowers.

25 August (RCG) CORNWALL SUMMER ASSIZE. *Bodmin. Lean* v. *Nicholls.* The plaintiff is an inhabitant of Fowey, at which place the defendant was overseer of the Poor in March last....the management of the poors' rate has become a matter of importance. The plaintiff and others having, as they supposed, cause to suspect foul play, declined paying the rate, until they were allowed to compare the copy from which the collection was made, with the original rate;....the plaintiff went to the house of the defendant, on two successive days in the early part of March last, and having tendered him a shilling as his fee, demanded to inspect the rate. This the defendant refused to allow him to do, and the plaintiff brought an action under the statute, to recover a penalty of £20, to which the defendant had rendered himself liable by his refusal.... Mr Sergeant Pell, for the defendant, contended that this was a most vexatious action, brought from mere revenge....and produced Mr Ephraim Robins, who was in the defendant's house when the first demand....was made, and who it was supposed would prove that no refusal had been given; but he said that the defendant had told the plaintiff that he did not consider him (plaintiff) a proper person to come under his (defendant's) roof: but if his master, Austen, sent a respectable person to inspect the rate, he would shew it.- The Learned Judge said, the last witness had fully proved the case, and directed the jury to find for the plaintiff, which they did, for the amount of the penalty.

1 September (RCG) PILCHARDS APPROACHING THE COAST On Thursday a drift boat arrived at Fowey containing 10,000 pilchards....

1822

18 January (WB) TO be SOLD by AUCTION, at the SHIP INN, *Fowey,* on Wednesday, the 23rd instant January, at Eleven o'clock in the Forenoon, The well-known SCHOONER, *MARY KITTY, Of Fowey,* Registers 88 13-94ths Tons. This Ship was built in Plymouth in 1819, is in complete order, and may be sent to sea with a trifling expense. This Vessel is particularly adapted for the Fruit Trade. ....apply to Mr Robert Rean....

23 March (RCG) On Wednesday last, Mr. Colliver, of Lewhire, in the parish of Fowey, had a hog killed, which measured seven and a half feet in length, three feet deep, and weighed 777 lbs. This surprising animal was not more than two years old.

14 June (WB and Cornwall Advertiser) FOR CORK and will SAIL, on or before the 15th of July next, the good SLOOP, *"ELIZABETH AND JANE",* of *Fowey,* John Cooper jun. Master; Will take in Passengers for that Port, (having a number of Passengers already engaged.)....

20 July (RCG) *TO BE SOLD* a very fine SCHOONER of 66 Tons Register, three years old, *also* A FINE NEW SMACK *of* 64 *Tons Register.* Both these vessels are now in the Coal Trade, and are well adapted for the Fruit, Mediterranean, London, and Coasting Trades; burthen well, and sail fast; are well found and in excellent condition. For particulars, apply to Mr. George Nickels, shipwright, who has also for sale a SLOOP of 55 Tons Register.

27 July (RCG) LOSTWITHIEL REGATTA The annual Regatta at Lostwithiel, which took place on Monday last, was notwithstanding the unfavorable state of the weather remarkably gay. At nine o'clock in the morning about 50 boats, decorated with awnings, shewing all coloured flags, and preceded by the band of the Cornwall Militia in a barge playing favourite national airs, left Lostwithiel and proceeded in a gallant style down the river to Fowey. On their arrival in the harbour, they had the very unexpected pleasure of meeting his Grace the Duke of Buckingham, who was there at anchor in his yacht. The pleasure of the company was now considerably heightened, and the boats rowed twice round the yacht, the band playing the while; a compliment which his Grace politely returned by firing a salute of thirteen guns. He was then waited upon by the Stewards, Capt. Mitchell, R.N. Lieut. Donnellan, R.N. and Nicholas Kendall, Esq. who requested the honour of his Grace's company to the Ball in the evening; an invitation which he reluctantly declined, both from indisposition, and because there would be no tide to return to Fowey in the evening. His Grace however joined the party, and sailed with them up the river for some time. The Ball in the evening was very well attended, joy and good humour prevailed, dancing was kept up with spirit until daylight, when the company retired, highly delighted with the pleasure they had enjoyed, which was unalloyed by the occurrence of any untoward accident. To add to the gaiety of the scene, a sailing and a rowing match were appointed for that day at Fowey. The sailing match which took place, was well contested, and afforded much amusement; but the rowing match was obliged to be postponed, owing to one of the station boats having broke adrift in the harbour.

10 August (RCG) CORNWALL ASSIZE. *Congdon* versus *Nicholls.* The defendant, who is a Lieutenant in the Navy, residing at Fowey, some time since purchased a tenement there called the Old Killing House, which adjoined a small garden belonging to the plaintiff. This tenement he pulled down, leaving the rubbish in the narrow road or lane leading to the garden, he thereby rendered it impassable. The nuisance was continued for several months, notwithstanding the defendant's promise to Mr. Austin, the agent for Mr. Lucie's property at Fowey, to remove it; nor was it entirely cleared away up to the time of the Assize. The yearly value of the garden was stated to be about 30 shillings, and the value of the fruit and vegetables that had perished was estimated at £3.- The Jury gave the plaintiff 40 shillings damages.

22 November (WB) A few days since a lad named Adams was unfortunately killed in a shipwright's yard at Fowey, where he was at work, by a piece of oak timber which fell from a height on his head, and completely cleft his skull.

20 December (WB) A smuggling boat, with two men and 70 kegs of spirits on board, was captured near Fowey by the boat employed in the preventative service, on Monday.

27 December (WB) The *Arrow,* a vessel in the preventative service, has brought into Fowey an open boat containing 165 tubs of spirits, which she captured near the Deadman, with four men on board.

The *Greyhound,* another vessel in the same service, has also brought into Fowey an open boat belonging to Cawsand, which she captured on the 19th instant, whilst endeavouring to make the shores with 80 tubs of spirits and three men and a boy.

1823

18 January (RCG) In England and Scotland many meetings have been held, and requisitions are in preparation for assembling no less than *Sixteen Counties* to consider the causes and remedies for Agricultural Distress.... The table of the House of Commons will soon be covered with the petitions of the Agriculturalists....but what can Parliament do for them in the actual state of things? It cannot alter the condition of the markets: it cannot alter the superabundant supply of corn and cattle, the great cause of the decline in prices....

The reduction of the price of salt is felt as a most substantial benefit, by the poor, more especially in these maritime counties, where fish make up with pork, the bulk of their animal food.- Many of our cottagers deferred the killing of their annual pig, till the 5th of January arrived and *killed* the tax. Pork has risen in all our markets from this cause.

1 February (RCG) On Wednesday last, about 8 o'clock, a French ship from the Brazils bound for Havre, in distress, having been beating about the channel for the last twenty days with her rudder unhung and otherwise damaged, ran on shore near the pier head at Charlestown, having mistaken that place for Fowey harbour. By the assistance of the masters and sailors belonging to the vessel lying there, she was fortunately got off, and safely carried into Fowey harbour.

13 September (RCG) The fishermen employed in driving for pilchards, now find the advantages resulting from the repeal of the salt duty. The public are now enabled to buy more freely; and in proportion to the demand, so the price of fish advances,- in consequence, pilchards maintain a price nearly 50 per cent higher than last season. Before the duty was taken off, the salt used in curing pilchards cost from 25 to 50 per cent *more than the fish.*

1824

13 March (RCG) On Wednesday petitions to both Houses of Parliament, praying for the amelioration and gradual abolition of Slavery, were signed by the Mayor and principal inhabitants of the borough of Fowey.

13 March (RCG) THE PUBLIC are respectfully informed, that for the BETTER REGULATION of the TRADE from LONDON, the three following strong-built SCHOONERS, will be constantly employed in the said Trade, the *"ANN & ELIZABETH"*, Job Moyse, Master; the *"FOWEY"*, Moses Bone, Master; and *"CHARLES RASHLEIGH"*, John Pearse, Master TO LOAD AT GRIFFIN

WHARF,....and which in future will be known by the name of "Fowey, Bodmin, Lostwithiel, St. Austell, and Mevagissey Shipping Co.". *No vessel will remain longer at the Wharf than eighteen days, and regularly follow each other....* (Moyse and Bone were Fowey Master Mariners).

20 March (RCG) *Caution.* - A correspondent states that a tall black man, calling himself William Luboya, has been singing hymns and preaching in the streets in several towns in this county, and pretending to have been converted by means of the Methodist missionaries in Gibralter: and requests us to inform the public that he is not recognized by the Methodists in Cornwall, not having produced any credentials of his belonging to that body, nor is his conduct consistent with their rules; he having been found drunk in a public house at Fowey.

12 June (RCG) The ROYAL CAMBRIA STEAM PACKET, sails regularly from Stonehouse Pool, PLYMOUTH to FALMOUTH every Monday Morning at Eight o'Clock, calling at FOWEY in her passage each way. Fares.... To or from Fowey, after-cabin, 6s.; fore-cabin, 3s.6d. *Children under twelve years of age half price.*

31 July (RCG) The French cutter *"L'UNION",*....from Brest for Bordeaux, has been seized by the officers of the Customs at Fowey. Suspicions it seems were entertained, and on rummaging the vessel four pieces of silk were found, on which she was immediately seized. An individual we understand, of Considerable respectability in Fowey, has been implicated in the transaction, and his house has been searched. The offence has caused no small sensation in that town, but we forebear to state particulars until we receive them through an authentic channel.

30 October (RCG) On Tuesday last two boatmen having been hired by Lieutenant Thomas, R.N., to convey him to Lostwithiel on their return from thence they took on board two men and a woman to bring them to Fowey. They had reached to within a mile of that place, when one of the boatmen said he would not row any more, but would hoist the sails. The other boatman strongly objected to this and desired him not to do it. His companion however obstinately persisted, and just as the sails were up a squall of wind upset the boat, when James Stephens, one of the boatmen, with a passenger named Robert Keast, of Lanlivery were unfortunately drowned, and have each left a widow and three children to lament their unhappy fate.-neither of the bodies have been taken up.

13 November (RCG) The bodies of two men who were drowned a few weeks since between Lostwithiel and Fowey have since been taken up.

27 November (RCG) Last Monday the wind blew strong at S.S.E. all night and increased to a tremendous storm on Tuesday morning, when about 4 o'clock the tide rose to an unparalleled height, though the proper time of high water was not till seven. The sea came up in the streets, and entered several dwelling-houses, for it *burst open* some of the fore-doors, inundated the lower stories, completely washed away the potatoes, groceries, and coals belonging to the inhabitants, broke all their earthenware, and injured their other furniture. The quay belonging to Miss Puckey, Mr. Wilcock's shipwright's yard, Mr. Congdon's smith's shop, Mr. Richard Nicholl's, and Mr. Hill's quays and gardens were washed down. The back windows of several houses were dashed in pieces. A small fish was taken *alive* in the middle of the street. The Broadslip was so *broken up* by the violence of the waves that on Tuesday a plank was laid across to render the street passable, till it can be rebuilt. Several dwelling-houses, cellars, quays, &c. besides those abovementioned were injured, and gardens therein washed away or damaged - and some persons were in imminent danger; yet no life was lost - nor did the shipping in the harbour sustain any injury. Large quantities of fishery salt has been destroyed. The *"SCEPTRE"* of this port, Capt. Thomas Nickels, is unfortunately lost at Plymouth, but it gives us pleasure to hear that all hands are saved. A vessel is lost between Polperro and Talland, she is supposed to be the *"THREE FRIENDS"*, of London;....from the circumstance of a stern board so marked being washed on shore, as were the bodies of two fine young men near the spot.

1825

22 January (RCG) The Quarter Sessions (at Lostwithiel)....was occupied nearly two days, by an appeal from Fowey, for the purpose of having the names of several persons removed from the rates, on which it was asserted they were placed for election purposes. The Court ordered the names of the following persons to be taken off the rates:- John Isbell; John Nickels; John Crouch; George Bate; Henry Kingcombe; Richard Noell; James Payne, jun.; and Joseph Walter.

12 February (RCG) On Wednesday last the inhabitants of Fowey were gratified by a public exhibition of the inimitable performances of Mr. Powell's celebrated Troop. A very fine Air Balloon was also sent up as part of the amusements of the day, which altogether gave universal satisfaction to upwards of 4000 persons supposed to be present on this occasion....

2 April (RCG) Last Friday the *Lively,* a limestone vessel belonging to Fowey, sailed from that port for Plymouth, (as usual, without ballast,) but the wind being contrary and very violent she was unfortunately overturned off Wrinkle, and the three men on board were drowned; one of them whose name was Olford, and took the command of the vessel, has left a wife and six children to lament his loss. Captain Geach having business which prevented his going the voyage, was thereby in all probability preserved from a watery grave. (Might refer to CAPT. JAMES GEACH- of Polruan).

30 April (RCG) During the last week the coast between Polperro and Fowey has been kept in a state of disorder in consequence of a quantity of smuggled liquor found on the shore. It has been particularly annoying to the agents of Wheal Howell Mine, a little to the eastward of Fowey, the miners having been in a continued state of drunkenness. On Wednesday last the whole of the men belonging to the Mine had assembled, and by stratagem, in pairs, succeeded in getting underground where they had concealed part of a keg of brandy, and drank to unusual intoxication - so much so that it was with extreme difficulty several of them were brought to grass. In the evening a strong party of seamen of the Preventative service, with their officers arrived - it being apprehended (a great many tubs having been seized by them in a small cove near the Mine) that the miners had concealed some under ground, a diligent search was made by the preventative men, through all the workings conducted by the Captain, but it did not appear that more than one keg, that nearly empty, had been taken under ground. Too much credit cannot be given to the humanity with which the officers and crew of the coast guard stationed at Polperro, performed their duty and it may safely be stated that but for them several of the miners would have lost their lives. A great many idle and disorderly persons had assembled, particularly a miner named Thomas Sincock, who said he belonged to a mine called Wheal Sally, near Bodmin; he refused to go until one of the Preventative officers drew his sabre and compelled him. Notwithstanding the inconvenience and loss it occasioned the adventurers, it has been judged advisable to discharge the whole of the men, and every endeavour will be made to discover the man who first brought the spirit into the mine.

14 May (RCG) TO BE LET BY TENDER, for a Term of 14 years....all that capital BARTON and FARM called CARNEGGAN, *Situate in the Parish of Lanteglos by Fowey*; containing ninety-five acres of excellent Land, together with a commodious Dwelling- House, suited to the residence of a genteel Family, having a fine view of the British Channel, with Barns, Stables and all convenient Out Houses, and a Thrashing Machine worked by water, within a short distance of Sea Sand and of Limekilns.

The Taker to pay the Land-tax and all parochial assessments, and to keep the Premises in repair, except the Walls, Slate roofs and Timbers, and to enter into the usual covenants of good husbandry....

14 May FOWEY COURT OF CHANCERY May 6. - *In Re Bennett, Mayor of Fowey*,.... Petition to supersede the commission of bankruptcy sued out against Mr. Bennett;.... It is alleged that individual to be not only solvent, but a person of property; that the debt due to....Mr. Trefusis Smith, solicitor and Town Clerk of Fowey was the amount of a bill of costs for business of the Corporation; that the proceeding arose from a party feeling, growing out of election... the debt was a joint and not a separate debt.... Mr. Montague read the account headed - "John Bennet, John Masseh, Robert Hearl, and Robert Flamank, Esqrs. Dr. to J.T. Smith".... The account....showed that the business done was on account of the Corporation....and he commented with some severity upon the behaviour of Mr. Smith, whom he considered to be assisting the views of Mr. Austin.... He contended that the debt was in fact no debt; that no act of bankruptcy had been committed, that it was entirely a manoeuvre to injure the character of Mr. Bennett and the party he espoused.The person to whom Mr. Bennett was denied was an attorney, who represented himself as a traveller. The affidavits stated that Mr. Bennett was a most respectable person, worth £40,000; and this was not denied by the other party....

The petitioning creditor disclaimed any electioneering projects in this transaction. He observed that many acts of bankruptcy had been committed by Mr. Bennett. He complained of the imutations thrown out against Mr. Smith, who, if he deserved what had been said of him, ought to be struck off the rolls. His bill of costs remained two years unpaid. He offered to refer his claim to arbitration; the Mayor and his colleagues refused. His only remedy then was an action; but when he tried to serve Mr. Bennett with....the writ, the latter secreted himself; he was denied; and though he was seen in his garden looking at some feats of horsemanship, when the person on the watch went to his house the servant said he was not at home.... As to Mr. Bennett's respectability....if the Attorney-General's avocations threw part of his duty upon him, he would perhaps have to prosecute this very Mr. Bennett in a court of justice for smuggling. Contraband goods were found secreted on his premises, and were seized by the Custom-house officers, as the affidavits shewed;....prosecutions are still pending, though Mr Bennett has made ineffectual attempts to compromise.... *The Lord Chancellor*....intimated that he would hear the case further, if necessary, but as....documents....clearly stated that it was a joint debt, the commission was decidedly bad. The Lord Chancellor on Wednesday set aside the commission of bankruptcy.

4 June (RCG) Notice has been given of an application to Parliament for a Bill, to enable a Company to cut a ship Canal from Padstow to Fowey, a distance of only twelve miles, and whereby upwards of one hundred miles of dangerous coast would be saved. Mr. Brunel is the engineer.

20 August (RCG) On the 12th inst. three barges laden with sand in Lantivet Bay coming towards Fowey harbour with a N.W. wind, suddenly shifting to the south, it brought such a swell of sea as filled one of them which sunk, and Thomas Philp, the master, was unfortunately drowned, leaving a widow and nine children to lament his loss; the other two men belonging to the barge were happily rescued from a watery grave, by the prompt exertions of the *Lion* cutter, under the command of Lieut. Dicken, who also took the other two barges in tow, and thereby preserved the lives of their crews.

10 September (RCG)The Fowey seines have also taken fish every night this week: and the driving boats have been very successful, in both channels, where large shoals of fish are constantly seen in deep water.

26 November (RCG) On Friday the 18th instant, was heard at Fowey, before John Bennet, Esquire, Mayor, and Robert Parker Flamank, Esquire, Justice, certain informations against eight persons, for breach of the Customs laws, they having been in custody from the 6th instant (when a French sloop and her cargo, consisting of 377 casks, containing 1300 gallons of brandy, and 469 of Geneva were seized near Charlestown) who if found guilty, would have been liable to the full penalties, viz. the five Englishmen to serve in his Majesty's navy, and the three aliens to pay a fine of £100 each; when after six hours attendance, examining evidences on both sides, and the pleading of advocates pro and con, they were found not guilty.

1826

11 February (RCG) INFALLIBLE SAGACITY AND LUCK OF FORTUNE-TELLERS!! A party of Gypsies, not being permitted to come into Fowey, recently pitched their tent in the vicinity.... Among the numbers who resorted to them for information of future events, was a lad of Polruan who paid them a Mevagissey one pound note of Mr. Ball's, and received nineteen shillings in change for their telling his fortune. (Mr. Ball, banker, bankrupt in 1824; notes worthless).

1 April (RCG) Last Monday some children were sailing their little ships on a pool in a meadow near Fowey. One of them, a son of Lieut. Davis of that place, about eight years of age, unfortunately fell in. On information thereof being given by the affrighted playmates to two men, he was taken up and carried to his father's house and medical assistance procured, but we regret to say that all means for resusitation proved ineffectual.

9 June (WB) FOWEY. Some demonstrations indicative of opposition to the late candidates have been made by the Corporators here, but it is very much doubted whether they will venture to take the field against the united interests of Mr. Austen and Mr. Lucie or rather whether they can get any persons able to raise the ways and means to enter on so desperate a pressure.

10 June (RCG) On Wednesday a fine ship upwards of 300 tons burthen, named the *George*, (with a band of music on board playing God save the King,) was launched from the yard of Mr. George Nickels, at Fowey. She went off in fine style, amidst the cheering of the joyous spectators. Though the beauty of the weather had attracted a very numerous assemblage both on sea and land, we are happy to say that no accident occurred. This large vessel is built for Baillie and Co. of Bristol, and is intended for the West India trade.

1 July (RCG) SUPERIORITY OF STEAM. On Sunday morning last the *Sir Francis Drake* Steam Packet arrived at Plymouth, on her return from Guernsey at half past seven in the morning, after a fine passage of eleven hours and a half. It is generally supposed that with a fresh and fair breeze vessels navigating by steam possess no superior advantages over sailing vessels; the reverse however appears in the present instance to be decidedly the case, as, notwithstanding all the advantages of a fresh, fair, and steady breeze, the *Drake* arrived in Stonehouse Pool at least four hours before a fast sailing schooner which started from St. Peter's Port, Guernsey *an hour and a half* before the *Drake*.

29 July (RCG) DIED at Fowey, after a lingering illness, aged 39, Mr Borlase, innkeeper. He was so much respected that nineteen boats with people accompanied his remains to burial ground at Lanteglos.

16 September (RCG) NOTICE IS HEREBY GIVEN, that the Partnership lately carried on in the Borough of Fowey....between JOSEPH and SARAH HAM, of the said Borough, Grocers, Ironmongers, Drapers, and Druggists, being this day dissolved by mutual consent; All debts due to the said Firm will be received and settled by the said Joseph and Sarah Ham.

JOSEPH HAM, takes this opportunity of thanking his numerous Friends for all past favours and begs respectfully to inform them and the Public in general, that the whole of the above business will be continued by him in the same Premises where it has been carried on for many years past, and he trusts that by a strict attention to business, and the sale of goods on moderate terms, he will ensure a continuation of that support which he has so liberally received from the public for upwards of twenty years.

30 December (RCG) On the 22nd inst. John Sweet, a Butcher of Fowey killed three Ewes, in which were ten Lambs about the size of small rats, viz: four lambs in one of the sheep, and three in each of the others.

30 December (RCG) TO DRUGGISTS, &c. TO BE DISPOSED OF, by PRIVATE CONTRACT, the STOCK IN TRADE, *Of Mr. John Snell, late of Fowey.* Any person desirous of commencing Business as a Druggist would find the above worthy of attention. And if inclined to carry on business in Fowey, may be accommodated with the SHOP and PREMISES lately occupied by the said Mr. Snell, which are well situated and every way fitted up for carrying on the above Business....apply personally only to James Hill, Esq. of Fowey.

1827

18 August (RCG) Last Thursday night the house of B. Lamb, Esq. of Fowey, was robbed of several silver spoons, a silver milk cup, and some articles of wearing apparel. Three strange men, who had been lurking near the house the preceding evening, were pursued to Torpoint, and taken in crossing that Ferry, with the stolen goods in their possession. The fellows were secured, and it is hoped will meet with due punishment. (N.B. *Edward Reiley, 21, Richard Rowe, 21 and a lad, Nesbit,* travelling around the country were later sentenced to death).

1828

12 January (RCG) NEW SCHOONER FOR SALE....by William Geach and Son, a fine NEW SCHOONER, of the following dimensions, viz: Length aloft about 52 ft, Breadth 18 ft, Depth 9 ft 4 inch. and Registered about 67 tons - *Ready to Launch at a day's notice.* To appearance she will burthen and sail well, and is particularly adapted for the Coasting Trade, being of easy draught of water. Dated Polruan by Fowey.

19 January (RCG) FOWEY. The weather here has been extremely tempestuous. In the height of the violent gale last Saturday night, the *"Hero"*, Hester, drove ashore on the rocks and turned over. Her cargo, consisting of iron and coals, is taking out, and it is hoped the vessel will be re-placed by tomorrow. Had she not reached this port she would probably have foundered.

15 February (WB) On Saturday, at Fowey, a female child about four years of age, fell from the window of a room at which the poor infant was amusing itself, into the yard, a height of twenty feet, and was killed on the spot.

25 April (WB) The Sloop *Amity,* of Fowey, William Longmaid, master, and the Schooner *Charles* of Fowey, Charles Olver, master, sailed together from Falmouth on Sunday morning last, laden with copper ore; the former for Swansea and the latter for Neath. At about midnight they had both rounded the Longships, and in about an hour afterwards, the weather being extremely dark and both vessels on opposite tacks, the *Charles* ran foul of the *Amity,* taking her with the stem, abreast of her companion;- the shock was so violent that the *Amity* sunk almost instantly; whilst the damage to the *Charles* was confined to her rigging, sails, and light spars. Happily the crew of the *Amity* succeeded in saving themselves on board the Schooner, which has since put into Penzance to repair her damage.- We understand that the accident was solely owing to the extreme darkness of the night, as neither vessel was observed by the other, until close on board. The crew of the *Amity* all belong to Charlestown, and have since proceeded to that place.

20 June (WB) The hay harvest in this county has been much impeded since last week by very heavy storms of rain, accompanied by thunder and lightning.- We beg to remind agriculturalists, and others, of the acknowledged utility of salt in improving the quality of hay, more particularly if made in a "dropping season" . When the ricks are formed, or the hay housed, the salt should be equally sprinkled on each layer, in the proportion of from 25*lbs.* to 30*lbs.* per ton. It will prevent mow-burn or mouldiness, and improve nutritious quality of the hay.

2 August (RCG) DIED lately, at Trinidad, of the West Indian fever, aged 20, Mr. Daniel Palmer, of the merchant ship *Achilles,* son of Mr. Palmer, mercer &c. of Fowey. As the deceased was an interesting, active, steady youth, of more than ordinary promise, his loss is the more deeply felt by his parents and friends.

23 August (RCG) Immense bodies of fish are still seen off the coast, of which the driving- boats continue to secure great quantities; but they are as yet too distant from the shore for the seiners to operate with full success upon them.... The various seines in the bays within the port of Fowey, on Tuesday night, caught about 400 hhds. of pilchards.

13 September (RCG) The few seans belonging to Fowey harbour have been successful in securing about 1550 hogsheads of pilchards, of good quality, and the drift boats 50 hogsheads.

13 September (RCG) The *Abeona,* Sadler, sailed from Fowey a few days ago for Wales. At nine o'clock in the evening William Lobb, an expert seaman, took the helm of the vessel, after having been ordered by the master (who with a boy went below to sleep) to call him at midnight. This order, from some unknown cause, was not complied with; the master did not awaken until three o'clock in the morning; and when he came on deck he found that Lobb was missing!- It is supposed that he fell overboard and was drowned before midnight. He has left a widow and family to lament his loss.

20 September (RCG) DIED at Fowey, Mrs. Dormer, relict of the late Mr. Dormer, formerly master of a vessel in the Turkey trade, and who formed one of a party of

English sailors, who contrived to raise a ladder of ropes to the top of Pompey's pillar, near Alexandria, by means of a kite, when the party ascended to the top where they dined.

4 October (RCG) A few evenings ago, at Fowey, a woman put her child to bed, which having examined with a candle, she went out of the house. Some neighbours hearing the child shriek, went in and found it very much scorched, and the bed on fire; they extinguished the flames, but not till the bed was consumed. The child was rescued from *immediate* death, but died of the effects of the accident on Tuesday last. If the neighbours had not exerted themselves on the occasion the house probably would also have been burnt.

20 December (RCG) The *Dickens*, Swan, master, of London, from St. Ives, with pilchards for the Mediterranean,. met with a gale off Scilly, which greatly injured her rigging, and washed some of her men overboard, who however happily regained the vessel. The poor fellows were much fatigued and weather-beaten, all their clothes and bedding being completely saturated with the wash of the sea, and they were glad to reach this safe harbour (Fowey); they will remain here till the vessel is refitted.

1829

3 January (RCG) DELETERIOUS EFFECTS OF LEAD. Lead, taken in any quantity, soon produces great uneasiness in the stomach, obstinate and often bloody vomitings, excruciating colic,....convulsions and death. In smaller portions....it gives rise to colic, tremors, palsies, permanent contractions of the limbs....often irremediable....where water is to be drawn for drinking and culinary purposes, the first water, as much as may be supposed to be in the pipe, should be allowed to escape before receiving it for use....leaden cisterns, in which the water must, necessarily, stand some time....never can be safe.... As medicines, though powerful, the preparations of lead, are now deservedly rejected for internal use....in extensive burns....the free and continued use of the stronger lead ointment....are known to have brought on all the evils consequent to the internal use of lead. The popular cosmetics likewise, whether in the form of lotions, creamy powders, or paints, are unhappily made chiefly from the salts and oxides of this metal.

9 May (RCG) DIED at Fowey on Wednesday se'nnight, (after our letter announcing the birth of his twin daughters was sent to the post,) Captain James Courts, of the schooner *John,* of Fowey, leaving a widow and seven children, one of whom was born the day he died, and the twins were baptized last Saturday afternoon, immediately after his interment. Deceased was carried to the grave by eight masters of vessels. (se'nnight for seven night, i.e. a week ago).

16 May (RCG) The state of the country at the present moment is truly appalling, and....there is stagnation in every branch of trade;- the shipping interest send their vessels to sea without profit.... Complaints are pouring in from all parts of the country....

In Cornwall the distress is less severely felt....the price of copper has not fallen in such a manner as to give immediate alarm to persons who are interested in copper mines,....the increased consumption of copper in the place of iron is favourable to our mines in Cornwall, and....there is not that pressing distress that weighs so heavily upon persons employed in iron or lead mines elsewhere.

There is....another reason why the people of Cornwall are less affected by the state of general depression....the circulation of one pound notes has not been diminised in so violent a way as it has been in other counties;....our farmers and tradesmen are aware of the advantages which a plentiful and secure small note currency afford them; they have confidence in their bankers; they know that these gentlemen can pay their notes in gold....

5 September (RCG) LOSTWITHIEL REGATTA. *To the Editor*.... I came here on Tuesday last, to attend the Regatta. What it may have been at this place in past days, I cannot tell; its spirit and attractions were, however, I should think on this occasion unabated. The band of Cornwall Militia, and the company embarked here yesterday morning at eight o'clock, in their gaily dressed little boats, the band occasionally playing, as they quitted the Lostwithiel quay, the national airs of "God Save the King" and "Rule Brittania" with a very lively composition called "*The Belles of Lostwithiel.*" The weather proved exceedingly fine, and it therefore gave to the party all those real enjoyments of pleasure, which a fine summer's day, the pastoral beauties of a lovely river, and the soft and winning charms of music are so well adapted to afford. The ball at the Rooms in the evening, commenced about ten o'clock, when there appeared around the Stewards a very large assemblage of the most respectable families of the County; and too, of its youth and beauty, as might have challenged almost any other County in the kingdom. Sir, I could not help moralizing on the scene before me; and viewing with high delight the proud defiance which those charms of my young countrywomen (that shone around me like a brilliant summer's rainbow) seemed to bid to the voluptuous and the profligate, whilst they were courting alliance only with their kindred spirits of Innocence and Youth.... After a dance which continued to a very late hour, closed one of the most delightful days I have for along time passed.   A Rambler.

19 September (RCG) Mrs. Stribly, of Fowey, whose death we mentioned last week, had been married half a century. She has left 28 grandchildren; and no death had occurred in the family, or in any of her children's families, for 40 years before. One of her daughters (Mrs Lane) was churched, and the child christened, at the time of the funeral.

7 November (RCG) A friend to morality assures us, that of late years the principles of the juvenile classes have been much improved at Fowey, through the assiduous exertions of the Rev. John Kempe, in the Church of England Sunday School instituted by him at that place.

21 November (RCG) Last week, as Lt. Nicholls, of Fowey, was fishing at some distance from that harbour, he observed a number of sea-fowl hovering over his boat.

Having thrown out his line, baited by a sand-eel, one of the birds instantly seized it, and was hauled alongside, but escaped before it could be secured. Again the line was thrown out and again the bird (a muir) pounced on the bait, but it got free again. On the line being a third time committed to the water, the same bird eagerly darted at the bait, and so effectively swallowed the hook as to be taken. After this successful haul, the bait was refitted and the line again thrown, when a gull seized the tempting morsel and was secured; both birds were brought alive to Fowey.

28 November (RCG) Last week at Fowey a girl named Longmaid about 16 years of age, going for water fell into the well, and was unfortunately drowned - as she made no outcry it is supposed she must have fallen in head foremost.

5 December (RCG) Mr. Adams, grocer, of Fowey, we understand, purchased at a sale a few days since, an old book for two-pence; and on examining it, previous to its being torn up as waste paper, it is said he discovered in the lining of the cover, several gold coins of the reigns of James I. and Charles I.

12 December (RCG) Mangel-wurzel is coming into use in many kennels as a common food for hounds, with whom it is found to agree remarkably well. It is never used except with flesh, and then in the proportion of two bushel baskets of the roots to two bukets of oatmeal. It is then boiled to a pulp and mashed up with the food.

CHAPTER 4
1830-1839

1830

10 April (RCG) On Monday last at noon, as Captain Nickels, of the brig *THOMAS*, his little son, a man and boy who sailed with him, and two young men, passengers to Devonport, were going in the jollyboat to board the vessel outside Fowey Harbour, just as they got alongside, the sea rebounding caused the boat to veer off and upset, which precipitated them all immediately into the water. We regret to say that two sank and were unfortunately drowned, viz. first the mariner, named Giles, whose distressed widow has been in fits almost ever since. The other sufferer was Mr. Henry Pye, of London, who had been on a visit to his relation, Mr. Thomas, ropemaker of Fowey, intending to go to Devonport, to commence business as a mathematical instrument maker. A rope was thrown from the vessel to their assistance, by which the sailor boy presently got on board; and soon after, the boat being righted, some of them laid hold of Captain Nickels with a boat-hook, and lifted him into the boat by the hair of his head, to appearance lifeless. Mr. William Puckey, of Fowey, the surviving passenger, being able to swim, nobly refused assistance till the others were relieved; he supported Captain Nickel's little boy in the water till an oar was procured for him to hold fast by, and when they had regained the boat, shook and rubbed the child's stomach, if possible to restore animation. When they arrived at Fowey Mr. Illingworth of that place was called in, and a physician who happened to be in the town; and, by the blessing of the Almighty on their indefatigable exertions, both Captain Nickels and the lad were restored, to the great comfort of their friends.

15 May (RCG) The body of Mr. Henry Pye, one of the men who was unfortunately drowned....on the 5th ult....was taken up on Thursday the 6th inst. and brought to Fowey, having been in the sea four weeks and three days....the deceased was conveyed to the house of his kind relative Mr. Thomas, and by his direction from thence to the Church by eight creditable tradesmen--the interment was attended by numbers of the respectable inhabitants of Fowey, who seemed to regret the untimely end of this young Londoner.

3 July (RCG) On Tuesday a new Independent Chapel was opened at Polruan by the Rev. Timothy Wildbore, of Penryn, and several other ministers. (The old chapel, corner of West St. and St. Saviour's).

3 July (RCG) On Monday, when the news of his Majesty's death was received at Fowey, the colours of all the shipping in the harbour were hoisted half mast high; and the minute bell tolled its solemn knell in testimony of the public sorrow. (George IV).

10 July (RCG) On Tuesday morning a meeting of the principal inhabitants of Fowey, was convened at the Town-hall, for the purpose of forming a procession for proclaiming King William the Fourth, which was immediately done by the Rev. John Kempe, Vicar, in that building; and (as the multitude was too numerous to enter;)

afterwards on the Town-hall steps, on the Custom House Quay, and in several other of the most public parts of the town. The Proclamation was audibly and ably read, and the Herald loudly cheered at each conclusion of it. The Fowey Arms, and other Colours were carried through the town, and the procession all in black, headed by Messrs. Austen and Kempe, County Magistrates,....the Officers both of the Navy and Customs took an active part in the joyous proceedings of the day; indeed the Band of Music which played most melodiously was provided by the Collector of Customs, William G. Hemsworth, Esq. who also had the honour to serve his King and Country in the Navy from his early youth.

17 July (RCG) Charles Ambrose, 37, was indicted for stealing cider belonging to J. T. Austen, Esq. at Fowey, on the night of the 16th of May last. It appeared from the evidence, that Mr. Austen having a considerable quantity of cider last year, five pipes of it were put in an empty house at Fowey. On the 10th of May it was discovered that a quantity of this cider had been drawn off, and that one of the pipes was almost empty....a watch was set, and on the night of the 16th of May, a person who proved to be the prisoner, was heard to enter the house by a window, and to commence drawing off cider, having bored one of the pipes with a gimblet for that purpose. The persons watching rushed on him, and he was secured.- Guilty. (Four months at hard labour).

23 October (RCG) We learn that a great number of children, at Fowey and its neighbourhood, have lately been inoculated for the small-pox, by a medical practitioner, and that in consequence the greatest alarm is felt lest that frightful disorder should become prevalent in the town, and extend its ravages throughout the county.

6 November (RCG) MELANCHOLY ACCIDENT.- On Sunday evening last about half-past nine o'clock, as two young men named Bartlett and Hambly, both aged about nineteen years, with two other young men their companions, were proceeding in a boat from Fowey to Polruan, (built says one of our correspondents for racing rather than safety) symptoms of quarrelling - it is presumed from the party being in a state of intoxication - were heard on board, when by some unfortunate accident the boat was upset, and the four men precipitated into the water. Two of them being good swimmers, reached the shore in safety - Bartlett and Hambly were unfortunately drowned. Their bodies were found on Monday morning. (John Bartlett).

27 November (RCG) We understand some miners in the vicinity of St. Austell assembled this week with a view to prevent a shipment of wheat at Fowey. They were met by some neighbouring gentlemen, who reasoned with them on the gross impropriety and wickedness of their conduct, when the men returned to their work.

4 December (RCG) The people of Cornwall are not such fools, as to destroy the produce of the fields, which enables the farmer to pay wages, or the landlord to spend his money among them. The little disturbance at Mevagissey arose out of an opposite - a better although a *mistaken* feeling - a desire to hinder the County from being exposed to a want of corn. Our Miners are a religious people, and the Clergymen as well as the dissenting Preachers, have an influence over their flocks, which they will exert for good....not....evil.

11 December (RCG) It has often been a matter of surprise to us, living in a county....bounded on three sides by the sea and divided from its only neighbour Devonshire, by a considerable river....that so many.....trampers and sturdy beggars, are allowed to find their way to the towns in the West. These vagrants are in the habit of going to farmers' houses, more especially when the men of the family are known or supposed to be absent, and of frightening the women into forced charity.... A vigorous administration of the law....would be the effect of making the county too hot for them....

11 December (RCG) It often happens that masters of vessels when first they make land in coming up channel are apt to mistake head lands, particularly in bad weather, and perhaps no head land on the south coast of Cornwall has been more mistaken than the Greeben, of Gribben head, between Fowey and Par, which, from its resemblance to St. Anthony's Point east of Falmouth harbour, has induced many masters of vessels to run for Par bay, immediately abreast of the Gribbin, under an idea that they were running into Falmouth harbour. On Monday last, just at the height of the gale, a schooner was observed from Fowey and Polruan hills in very great distress, and as she neared the land a vast number of people lined the coast between Fowey and the Gribbon, under an impression that it was impossible for her to clear that point; she did so however; and the master thinking that he was entering Falmouth Harbour, had very nearly run her on the western part of the Spit rocks, when a man in the rigging not only discovered that they were fast approaching the breakers, but that they were too far embayed to escape by weathering either of the headlands; at that moment he caught sight of Mr Austin's new pier, placed at the eastern extremity of the Spit Rocks in Tywardreath bay,....and he was fortunate enough just to weather the pier head, and instantly found himself from a most tempestuous sea in comparatively smooth water; she proves to be the schooner *Pulteray* from Exeter,....bound to St. Michaels, but after having been out 23 days in very bad weather, she was obliged to put back in consequence of springing a leak, and just on entering the Channel was overtaken by the hurricane on Sunday. The master saw two lights in the night, which he took to be the Lizard Lights, and after losing all his fore canvas, the first land he made was....the Gribbin.

18 December (RCG) There are few observations which more forcibly strike the Cornishman, on returning from the Eastern Counties....than the inferiority and hilliness of our roads....he is naturally led into the unwilling admission, that we are still far behind the rest of the kingdom. It is with pleasure, therefore, that we have witnessed of late many decided indications of a better order of things, springing up throughout the county. Gentlemen in almost all quarters have been forwarding the work of improvement, and we do not despair of seeing the roads of Cornwall, within a few years, fully equal to those of other counties, fair allowance being made for our more uneven surface.

If Cornishmen cannot reasonably hope for the introduction of coaches propelled by steam, and travelling 20 miles an hour; they may still effect much on their own roads to secure easy and expeditious travelling than the county can yet boast of;....they must come forward, one and all, and shew a little more generosity and public spirit,....the improvement of our roads is deserving of support on many grounds...but especially on that of furnishing abundant employ for labourers, in these times of difficulty....

25 December (RCG) CHEAP AND EXCELLENT FUEL. (Letter to the Editor)....recommending to the poor and all persons who study economy, the use of Coke as fuel.... One great objection to Coke, that of its not producing a cheerful blaze, may be entirely and easily removed. Mix the coke with a little small coal, which is exceedingly cheap, and by which a cheerful fire might be produced, of much greater and more lasting warmth than that of a coal fire.... In some of our Northern Counties....small coals admixed with a large portion of common clay, has been in general use among the lower orders,....it produces a fire equally lasting, and emitting more warmth than a coal fire, and has the additional advantage of being even cheaper than the admixture of Coke and small coal.

25 December (RCG) On Thursday last, owing to the very sudden change of wind from North to East, three vessels named *Hero, Venus,* and *Hydra*, the property of J.T. Austen, Esq. were very considerably damaged on rocks near Pentewan, in St Austle bay, whilst loading stones for the breakwater at Parr; they have since been buoyed off and been taken into Fowey harbour, where the vessels, if practicable, will be repaired.

1831

1 January (RCG) Coal, especially at the present season, is so very dear as to be unattainable to the lower orders of people.

1 January (RCG) At Fowey on Wednesday last, a brig called the *Providence* of Cork, Hayes master, from Cork, and bound to Jamaica, laden with provisions, was this day brought into the Harbour dismasted, having thrown part of her cargo overboard. She was deserted by her mate, five mariners and two passengers. - Much credit is due to the master and the remaining part of the crew, for their great exertions.

26 February (RCG) Early on Tuesday morning last a great number of men collected at Fowey Consols and Lanescot mines, and attempted to seize two men who had refused to enter into any combination, and who from the threat of summary punishment being inflicted on them, had been compelled to take refuge in the Counting House.... The Agents....were obliged to appeal to the magistrates, who, after entreating them, without effect, to disperse....reading the riot act....without effect.... the magistrates....N. Kendall,....and Jos. Thos. Austen, Esqrs. ordered the Constables to take seven of the rioters into custody. On their being put into chaises for conveyance to prison, a violent attempt to rescue the prisoners was made by several hundred persons present, but by the temperate and firm conduct of the civil power, they were enabled after a conflict of more than an hour to forward the prisoners to Bodmin.... As a matter of precaution, the High Sheriff....swore in between 30 and 40 special constables.... On Thursday evening intelligence was received that a body of miners was approaching Bodmin.... Militia Staff were got under arms at the gaol and the Special Constables assembled....about six o'clock, a motley crowd mostly composed of women and children, entered the town, and sent a deputation....of six or seven persons to the High Sheriff.... The sheriff, J.H. Tremayne, Esq. received these poor people mildly but firmly....and sent them back....accompanied by some gentlemen who kindly reasoned with the mob and....at length induced them to depart.

5 March (RCG) We have great pleasure in stating that the late disturbance amongst the miners has entirely subsided, and that the men in all parts of the County have quietly returned to their work, and continue to conduct themselves in a peaceable and orderly manner.

Some soldiers of the 73rd regiment arrived on Friday at Fowey by a steamer from Plymouth, but their services were not required. They are, however, quartered at Bodmin.

5 March (RCG) The Coal-duty ceased on Tuesday last - a great boon to the poor, as that indispensable article is now lowered 2d. per bushel in price....coals are now retailed at 8d. per bushel.

5 March (RCG) FOWEY We understand that Messrs. Crawcour, Surgeon Dentists, in consequence of the numerous applications that have been daily made for their professional services during their residence in this town, have been induced to delay their departure for one week longer.

9 April (RCG) CORNWALL QUARTER SESSIONS. *John Goins*, 30, was indicted for stealing a quantity of wheat and a sack, the property of John Colliver.- John Colliver, farmer, lives near Fowey; on the 28th of December last, a quantity of wheat was left in his barn in a sack, which was removed on the following morning - suspicion falling on the prisoner, a servant in the employ of Mr. Colliver, he went to a person's house named Dyer, with whom prisoner lodged, and there found the sack. He was told by Dyer that prisoner had brought with him about half a bushel of ground wheat. A warrant was obtained but prisoner absconded, and was not taken until a fortnight after, when he confessed the theft. *-Guilty.-* To be imprisoned nine months at hard labour.

18 June (RCG) EXPOSURE OF AN INFANT. On Saturday morning the 11th inst. was found at the door of Mr. Illingworth, Surgeon of Fowey, a basket containing an infant, supposed to be but a few days old, which had been left there by its unnatural mother....of Chacewater, near Truro. By what motive the wretched mother could have been induced there to abandon her innocent offspring, we have yet to learn, - she has however been taken up and carried before the Magistrates, and still remains in custody.

18 June (RCG) CAUTION.- The public cannot be too much on their guard against the tricks of travelling impostors, who hawk their useless wares about the County to the great injury of the regular tradesmen who have heavy rents and taxes to pay. On Friday last two men and a woman of this description, names unknown, were taken before the magistrates at Fowey, for having sold several bottles which they said contained distilled water, but on examination they were found to contain only a small quantity of oil of peppermint mixed with water. The Magistrates caused the same to be destroyed, and the parties to refund the money - they were then discharged.

20 August (RCG) PILCHARD FISHERY. We have much pleasure in noticing the successful commencement of this Fishery, so important in every point of view to this County.... About 60 hhds. have been landed at Fowey....and about 140 hhds. at Looe. These are pleasing beginnings, and with the prospect of fish on the coast, we hope only an earnest of future success. The driving boats also continue to secure large quantities of fish, with which our markets are plentifully supplied.

27 August (RCG) On Friday night, the 19th inst. about 12 o'clock, as the *Parr Pier,* of Fowey, Wm. May master, having taken in a cargo of stone about a quarter of a mile to the eastward of Fowey Harbour for the Breakwater at Parr, was attempting to get off, a heavy sea broke on board, which separated the hatches, and the vessel immediately sunk. A labourer who was on board, named John Hambly, took to the boat which was fastened close to the stern, but before he had power to cut the painter the boat was drawn under water by the vessel, and the poor unfortunate man drowned. The captain and one man saved themselves by climbing to the mast-head, where they remained until taken off by a fishing boat. The ill-fated Hambly has left a wife and three small children to deplore their loss. The body has not been found.

3 September (RCG) On Saturday last the body of John Hambley....was taken up. It floated on the 9th day, and was seen to rise by his mother and brother who had been constantly watching the place where they supposed the body lay.

26 November (RCG) NOTICE *TO SEAN OWNERS, AGENTS,* &c. - TO be SOLD by PRIVATE CONTRACT between this time and 20th day of January, 1832, a TUCK and STOP SEAN complete with one Lurker and one Sean Boat, and a quantity of other Sean Materials, such as Warps, Mooring Ropes, Grapnells, Capsons, Masts, Yards, Sails, Tarpaulings, and many other articles, with some Slings of New Knitting Twine, &c. If not Sold by the above date, the Seans will be then cut up and sold in different Lots.... Apply....Messrs Jos. Ham, Thos. Harvey, and John Thomas of Fowey.

17 December (RCG) News lately received from Italy we are sorry to learn is rather of a discouraging nature for the exporters of fish; the cholera regulations established in the port of Naples preventing the entrance of vessels from England, until after the due performance of a tedious quarantine.

31 December (RCG) CHOLERA MORBUS. In the present excited state of the public mind respecting the approach of that disease with which we are now threatened, it may not be uninteresting or unimportant to our readers to be informed that it is the opinion of one who has paid some attention to the subject that (next to a suitable regimen of diet), the regular use of a simple remedy....is, of all medical means, the best calculated to prepare and fortify the system against its influence. The remedy referred to is the white mustard seed taken whole....the best mode of taking it....is one, or two, or three tea-spoonfuls, according to the age, state, and circumstances of the individual, with, or immediately before, each of the three meals....taken in the course of the day.

1832

5 May (RCG) On the 30th ult. was laid the foundation stone of a beacon tower about 90 feet high, on the Gribbon Head, near Fowey Harbour, directed to be built by the Honourable Corporation of Trinity House, London, for the purpose of not only distinguishing that headland from the very similar one at St. Ann's Head at the Eastern entrance of Falmouth Harbour; but as a landing mark for vessels wind bound up or down Channel in the Harbour of Fowey, unquestionably one of the easiest of access, and safest harbours of its size in the whole Channel; as well as to serve as a leading mark to the commodiously safe made harbours laying between the Gribbon Head and the Dodman, viz. Par, Charlestown, Pentewan, and Mevagissey....if duly noted by Foreign and British masters of vessels, will doubtless prevent similar fatal catastrophes as occurred in December 1830, when three foreign vessels with valuable cargoes were wrecked by the Dodman, for want of knowing that there was perfect safety under their lee....

28 July (RCG) A lad, about eleven years of age, son of Mr. J. Frood, of Fowey, fell from a cliff near that place about 30 feet high, and is so seriously injured that no hope whatever of his recovery is entertained.

1 December (RCG) Thursday last was observed at Fowey as a day of thanksgiving to Almighty God for his merciful exemption of that town and the surrounding country from the cholera. The shops were closed and all business and labours were suspended as on a Sunday. Divine service was performed at the church, and in all the schools.

1833

9 February (RCG) ACCIDENT.- At Fowey last week Mrs R. Jago unfortunately left her infant (about 13 months old) in the kitchen by itself while she went into her neighbour's house; meanwhile the poor child got to the fire and was so much burnt that it died the next day.- This surely will be a caution to parents who have any regard for their helpless little children.

6 April (RCG) On the morning of the 30th ult. one hundred and fourteen tubs of foreign brandy were lodged in the Custom-house at Fowey. The brandy had been sunk by smugglers off Black-head, and was crept up by Lieutenant Best of the Coast Guard Station at Mevagissey, assisted by the crew of the Fox revenue cutter.

20 July (RCG) On Thursday last a fine schooner, named *"THE CATHERINE"*, John Rowett master and principal owner, was launched from Mr George Nickel's yard at Fowey. The weather being remarkably fine, a great concourse of people assembled from the adjacent towns and country to witness the launch, and were much gratified on seeing the vessel glide gently into the water. (This took place at a shipyard at Readymoney Cove).

7 September (RCG) The schooner *"AMITY"* of this port, Capt. S.S. Nickels (of Fowey), was lost on Saturday last on the sands at the entrance of the River Humber. Mr. William Prynn, passenger (son of...comptroller of this port) and George Williams, one of the crew, were drowned. The Captain, one seaman, and a boy were saved by clinging to the topmasts for upwards of six hours before they were released from their perilous situation.

14 September (RCG) TO BE SOLD BY AUCTION, by Mr. BROWNE, at the Ship Inn, *Fowey*, on Monday the 23rd day of September....a newly-erected and commodious DWELLING-HOUSE, *The residence of James Hill, Esq.* Situate in the town and commanding a beautiful view of the Harbour of Fowey; comprising Dining Room 14 feet by 22; Drawing Room 14 by 17; Breakfast Room 14 by 18; Kitchen and other Offices; three best Bed Rooms, and four Attics, with large underground Cellars, and a Garden, which has the advantage of adjoining the Harbour and communicating with the best part of the Town....Also a large newly-erected DWELLING-HOUSE and SHOP adjoining now occupied by Mrs. Lukey, and NINE DWELLING-HOUSES at the back thereof...Also, the old established and respectable SHIP INN, at Fowey,.... now and for many years past occupied by Mrs. Borlase,....with the Stables and Appurtenances thereto belonging....Also a well-built DWELLING-HOUSE and SHOP, in Fowey,....occupied by Mr. William Lane, Printer; a DWELLING-HOUSE adjoining, occupied by Mr. Ezekiel Collins, with the Premises behind the same and adjoining the Harbour called SOMERSET COURT, and containing Seven Dwellings, all held on one lease....

And on the 24th, and following days,....all the HOUSEHOLD FURNITURE of Mr. Hill, which has been selected with great taste and is equal to new....elegant mahogany sideboard....dining tables....chairs, Brussels carpet....beautiful rosewood furniture ....handsome carved mahogany pillar bedsteads....china,....glass of the best quality....

16 November (RCG) On Wednesday last four casks of smuggled brandy were picked up off Fowey harbour by the coast guard boat, and deposited in his Majesty's warehouse at Fowey.

23 November (RCG) On Thursday last a man named Thomas Jeffers was committed to the county gaol by J.T. Austen, Esq. for stealing on the previous night a great quantity of shirts, &c. &c. from different persons, who had left the linen in their gardens to dry. He appears to be a thief by wholesale, having made a complete sweep from one end of the town of Fowey, to the other, and then made off. He was pursued next morning, and by the active and praiseworthy conduct of Mr. John Bate, constable of Fowey, taken into custody at St. Austell. (He was tried on two indictments, sentenced to be transported for 7 years on each offence.)

1834

10 January (WB) MELANCHOLY ACCIDENT On new-year's-day two brothers named Hicks - the one 18 and the other 12 years of age - sons of Mrs. Hicks of Polruan, near Fowey, went from home with the intention of shooting rabbits on the cliffs near that place; they had but one gun which was carried by Nicholas, the elder brother, who is supposed to have approached too near the edge of the cliff in pursuit of game, when slipping, he fell over. The younger lad did not observe the accident, but suddenly missing his brother, he peeped over the edge of the cliff, and saw him lying at the bottom, a depth of 150 feet. The poor boy ran to obtain assistance and a boat being speedily procured, the unfortunate youth was taken up and carried home, still living. Medical aid was speedily procured, and it was found that both legs and both arms were fractured, and the head was so severely injured as to render recovery hopeless; the sufferer expired in a few hours, from a concussion of the brain. The deceased, who was highly respected, had just embarked in business, in consequence of the recent death of his father, and was the chief support of a widowed mother and a large family.

10 January (RCG) CORNWALL QUARTER SESSIONS. SENTENCES. Thomas Jeffers, for stealing shirts belonging to Capt. Pullen, of Fowey, whilst they were hanging out to dry; and also for stealing a shirt and pair of stockings belonging to John Collins, of the same place. There were five indictments against the prisoner.... He was only tried on the two.... He was convicted. - To be transported for seven years for each offence.

10 January (WB) CORNWALL EPIPHANY SESSIONS. SENTENCES. Richard Gower, a boy 11 years of age, for stealing raisins from the shop of David Couch, at Fowey - one week, from his commitment, 29th December.

11 January (RCG) On Friday evening the 3rd instant, about six o'clock, Robert Thomas, of Fowey, aged 83 years, fell over a very high wall, or *hoist* whilst walking from his daughter's house to his son's, a distance of about 30 yards, and was so seriously injured that he expired on the following day. (Note; aged 89 in obituary)

22 March (RCG) A lofty stone-bridge, eighteen feet wide, has been built over the river at Par, between St. Austell and Fowey, by that public-spirited Gentleman, Joseph Thomas Austen, Esq. of Place, at his sole expense. The stream was formerly passed by a narrow wooden bridge, which has thus been eligibly replaced. The new bridge is now passable, and will afford great facility of communication between the towns of St. Austell and Fowey.

10 May (RCG) On Saturday last commenced working at the Fowey Consol and Lanescot Mines, a new splendid steam engine of 700 horse power.- The shaft sinking immediately under the engine will bisect the principal lode of these mines at 290 fathoms below the base of the engine house, and it is calculated that the engine is of sufficient power to unwater these mines at a still greater depth.... When Mr. Austin, eleven years ago, determined on working these mines by water power, below their 30 fathom level, a great outcry was raised against him for attempting, even by the cheapest of all means, to sink them below that level which from their nature it was reported....would never pay for working deeper or on a more extensive scale. Happily for this neighbourhood he persevered, and so mistaken were the opinions of those who opposed him, that these mines, which have ever since been profitably working, are now returning more ores than any other under one direction in Cornwall, with one only exception, the richest level in them being exactly 100 fathoms deeper than the one at which they were so condemned in 1823.

5 July (RCG) For want of the usual quantity of snow during the winter, and rain since to swell the rivers on the coast of America, a considerable part of timber fell'd has not been removed from the interior to the harbours on the coast; many of the ships will therefore be obliged to leave without their cargoes, and timber has advanced there from 50 to 100 per cent, in consequence.

5 July (RCG) FOWEY BOAT RACE.- On Tuesday last, the 1st inst. the Fowey Boat Race took place, and from the remarkably fine weather, the hills, banks of the harbour, yachts, and ships, in short every place commanding a view of the race were crowded with spectators, it being estimated that upwards of five thousand were present.- The day was ushered in with a merry peal of the bells, and ringing was continued during the whole day. The town was gaily decorated with arches of laurel, flowers, &c. and flags were displayed in all parts which had a very pleasing effect; batteries were fixed and guns firing in various parts of the harbour, commanding the race. An excellent band of music was on the river the whole day, and at the close of the amusements paraded though the town, accompanied with the committee and a multitude of spectators walking in procession. A grand display of fireworks ended the day's sport, which was fully enjoyed.

On the following day the Cricket Club met on the usual place of meeting at Fowey when hundreds of persons were assembled; a band of music was on the ground and flags displayed round the field.

16 August (RCG) On the 6th inst. the new line of road from Par to Fowey over the cliff was opened for the accommodation of the public. Some years since by the liberality of the landowner, Lord De Dunstanville, the first cut was made by that public spirited gentleman J. T. Austen, Esq. of Fowey, at an expense of nearly 300*l.*, and who has also given all the stones to finish it, and which were brought from the extensive granite hills at the head of that gentleman's canal in boats, a distance of nearly three miles. - Through the liberal donations of Lord Dunstanville, William Rashleigh, Esq. Sir J.C. Rashleigh, Bart., Captain Collins, R.N., and other gentlemen in the neighbourhood, besides the yeomanry who have also contributed largely by giving their carts free of hire, this most desirable object is now completed, thus facilitating travelling between the towns of St. Austell and Fowey, over the new bridge and through the works at Par and picturesque scenery, marine views and mining districts, forming one of the most pleasant drives in the southern part of the County.

1834

6 September (RCG) So great is the improvement in travelling upon the southern lines of road in Cornwall, that on letting the tolls last week belonging to the Liskeard Turnpike Trust, an advance of £194 was made in the rental of gates on the direct line of road between Liskeard and Torpoint; and above 50 per cent. on the more southern line towards Looe, Fowey, &c. owing to the convenience of the new Steam Ferry Bridge which plies between Torpoint and Devonport- leaving more gates to be let.

13 September (RCG) On Saturday last, the 6th instant, the sloop *"SPEEDWELL,"* about 70 Tons, J. Finch, master, and E. Hocken, of Bideford, owner, was launched from Mr. G. Nickel's yard at Fowey, completely rigged for sea. She went off in fine style in the presence of a great assembly of persons.

The large schooner called the *"THOMAS PROTHEROE"*, about 150 Tons, was also launched the same evening from another of Mr. Nickel's yards, E. Nickels, master. This launch was a very interesting sight. The vessel was built a distance of upwards of 200 feet from the water, in a stone quarry, from whence she had to pass the main road before she descended into the water, and from the steady and good management of the builder she started immediately the doghorses were gone, and glided off on her ways in a most magnificent style, to the great satisfaction of a vast concourse of spectators, it being estimated that upwards of two thousand were present. - The Fowey amateur band was also in attendance, which added much to the gaiety and pleasure of the evening.

27 September (RCG) On Monday the 22nd inst. a match was played between two elevens of the Fowey Cricket Club, the sides being divided in alphabetical order: the playing on both sides was very creditable to so infant a club.... The game being concluded earlier than was expected, the two parties agreed to play another game with the same sides as before.... The *fielding* by both sides was considered very superior. The attendance on the field was very numerous and very respectable, the day being remarkably fine. At the commencement of the game, to the astonishment of all parties, a hare made its appearance on the ground and passed across the wickets and round the field several times. Everyone present was immediately in chase, which lasted upwards of ten minutes, and at last puss evaded its pursuers by breaking over a hedge.- The excellent performances of the Fowey Amateur Band added gaiety to the scene. At six o'clock the cricketers adjourned to the *Town-Hall,* where they partook of an excellent dinner provided by Mr. Hicks, landlord of the King of Prussia Inn. The conviviality and harmony of the evening was prolonged with toasts and songs to an early hour of the next morning.

1835

28 March (RCG) DIED at Fowey, on Thursday, in consequence of injuries received by being thrown from his horse when hunting, Mr. W. Couche, youngest son of the late H.J.W. Couche, Comptroller of the Customs of the Port of Fowey, aged 26 years; he is deeply lamented by a large circle of friends and acquaintances.

11 April (RCG) CORNWALL EASTER SESSIONS. The trials of the prisoners of felony commenced on Wednesday, when *Henry Sprague* and *Wm. Tucker*, charged with having stolen an iron chain, the property of J. T. Austen, Esq. were put to the bar. Sprague against whom the evidence was inconclusive, was acquitted - Tucker was found guilty, and sentenced to - *Three months imprisonment at hard labour.*

Jonathan Hawke was found *guilty* of a charge for stealing a bag of wheat belonging to Mr. W. Harris, of Lanteglos by Fowey, and sentenced *to be transported for seven years.*

18 April (RCG) HIGHWAY ROBBERY.- On Monday night last, as Mr. Edward Strike of Fowey was returning on horseback from Lostwithiel, and when about a mile and a half from that place, in the high road near Castle lane, he was attacked by three men, one of whom struck him a blow which knocked him off his horse, in almost a senseless state, and he was kept for some minutes on the ground by one of the villains kneeling on his back and severely kicking him, whilst the others rifled his pockets and robbed him of two sovereigns.- They would have also robbed him of his watch and other articles, which they were in the act of doing, when Mr. Strike called loudly upon the name of some friend, who he stated was approaching; -on this the robbers made their escape, one by riding off Mr. Strike's horse at full speed on the road for Fowey, and the others by breaking over the hedge. They were dressed as sailors in blue jackets, one having light trousers on and the others dark ones. The public will do well to be on their guard when such characters make their appearance on the high roads.

19 June (WB) CHARLESTOWN REGATTA.-The annual regatta which was held`at this`place on Monday last was attended by a concourse of spectators, the weather proved exceedingly fine and the arrangements for the day were admirably conducted, the prizes were adjudged in the following order,....Rowing-Gigs first prize £1 10s. to Mr. Kingcombe, of Fowey; second, £1, to Mr. J. Jewell, of Polruan; third, 10s. to Mr. Nicholls, of Fowey....

7 August (WB) CORNWALL LAMMAS ASSIZES. *Edward Pearne (39), Thomas Olver Walls (37), Joshua Heath (36), William Austen (24),* and *Thomas Husband Carpenter (51),* were indicted for having feloniously assembled, in the parish of Lanteglos, by Fowey, in order to aid in landing, running, and carrying away a quantity of foreign brandy, on which the duty had not been paid; three or more of the persons concerned being armed with offensive weapons. Mr. Selwyn opened the case for the prosecution, by stating the facts,....afterwards proved; he read extracts from the Act of Parliament....that if any party shall assemble for the purpose of landing, or carrying away contraband goods, three or more of such party being armed with offensive weapons, the whole of the persons concerned shall be deemed guilty of felony....

Richard Stevens, belonged to the coastguard stationed at Fowey. On the night of the 28th of March last, was at Lantic-hill, in....Lanteglos,....he was accompanied by Walter Harper, on the look out; they concealed themselves amongst furze near

Pencannon Point, and over the beach. About half-past eleven o'clock, a party of men amounting to 100 and upwards, and some of them, perhaps 20 or more armed with clubs, passed within 10 or 15 yards of witness and Harper; they passed out of sight, and witness afterwards heard them walking on the beach, on which he sent Harper to Polruan for assistance; shortly after witness saw three men carrying four tubs of spirits; he went up and demanded the tubs, which they dropped and made off towards the large party. Having hid away the tubs, witness fired a pistol as a signal, which was answered by five men who were coming to his assistance. As soon as they joined him they went in pursuit of the large party of smugglers, with whom they came up. Witness and his five companions required the smugglers to surrender the tubs they carried, on which they declared that if they (the preventative guard) touched a man or tub, they would murder the whole of them. Many of the smugglers had sticks in their hands. Witness and two others of his party, named Tolloway and Hamley, each seized a smuggler; the man witness laid hold on, struck at him with his stick, which witness returned with the flat of his cutlass; the man then escaped, and witness laid hold on another of the party, who struck him with a stick on the left side of his head, this blow knocked witness down, and he lay insensible on the ground; when he recovered he found his party had taken three prisoners, two of whom were Pearne and Carpenter, then at the bar, he does not know who the third was. Witness was ill for a considerable time in consequence of the blow he received, and was attended by a surgeon. On his cross-examination witness said the smugglers did not carry the tubs on their sticks, they carried the tubs slung across their shoulders with a rope, some carried two tubs, one before and the other behind.

Walter Harper, John Tolloway, William Hockin, John Slade, and Richard Climo, who, with the last witness, formed the party of the coast guard mentioned by him, were severally examined, and corroborated his evidence.

Lieut. Ciddell, commander of the *Fox*, revenue cutter, stated that in consequence of information received by him, he sent a party of men to Lantic-hill; that shortly after he went to the spot himself and found the five prisoners at the bar in custody with 118 tubs of smuggled brandy, and a number of sticks, which the smugglers had left on their flight. He sent the prisoners on board the cutter, and delivered the tubs and sticks, which were now produced, to Mr. Strike, who was clerk at the Custom-house, Fowey.

Mr. William Strike....received from the last witness about 484 gallons of foreign brandy on the morning of the 29th of March last.-.... He stated that he has been in his present situation for 12 years, that he can distinguish between Foreign and British brandy, and believes the brandy in question to be Foreign.

Mr. Edward Illingworth, surgeon of Fowey, stated he had attended the first witness, Stevens, in consequence of the blow he had received on the side of his head, and which caused a slight concussion of the brain; Stevens was confined to bed for three weeks, and his life was certainly in danger, from the blow. - The case for the prosecution closed here.

The Rev. Richard Buller, chaplain to the Sheriff, being called by the Counsel for the prisoners, stated that he had known the prisoner Pearne, for 7 years, as an honest, sober, industrious man, and that he has a wife and 6 or 7 children to maintain by his labour.

A number of farmers from the parishes of Lanreath, St. Germans, &c. were called to the character of the prisoners, whom they stated to be honest and industrious men, against whom they had never heard any charge previous to this affair.

The Learned Judge, in summing up....said this was a most lamentable affair, injurious to the state, injurious to the community at large, and especially injurious to the fair trader.... He said it was for the Jury to consider, whether they belonged to a party who riotously assembled to defraud the revenue, and whether the sticks produced, in court, and which had been left in the field by the party, were or were not offensive weapons. Had the man Stevens died of the injury he received, every man assembled in defiance of the law would have been legally guilty of murder, thereby involving 100 or more families in one common ruin and degradation. The Jury, after a short consultation returned a verdict of Not Guilty, on the ground that the sticks produced could not be considered offensive weapons.

22 August (RCG) About 500 hhds. of pilchards have been landed by the Fowey seine boats; the seines are still in the water, and it is estimated that the fish in them will be about 500 hhds. more.

11 September (RCG) On Wednesday the 2nd instant, a well contested match at cricket was played by eleven *married* against eleven *single* members of the Fowey club, which was won by the latter. A return match was played on Wednesday last.

25 September (RCG) On Saturday last, James, the son of Lt. Kiddle, of the *Fox* cutter, aged 10 years, whilst at play with other lads on the Castle Hill at the entrance of Fowey Harbour unfortunately slipped off a bank and fell on the rocks (about 14 feet in height), he is very seriously injured in the head. He was taken up speechless and remained in that state for many hours, there now appears to be some hope of recovery.

2 October (RCG) On Sunday last were seized by the Fox Revenue cruiser Lieut. Kiddle, and delivered into the Custom-house warehouse, at the port of Fowey, eighty-nine casks containing foreign brandy and geneva, picked up at sea floating; they were thrown overboard in a chase of two hours from an open boat named the *"Industry"* of Plymouth, which boat was captured with three men and brought into Fowey with the tubs.

2 October (RCG) FOWEY. *By Order of the Honourable the Commissioners of His Majesty's Customs.* ON FRIDAY the 9th of October, 1835, at 11 o'Clock in the Forenoon, will be exposed to Public Sale at the Custom- House, at this Port, the broken-up Hull of the Sloop *"DANIEL and WILLIAM"* of Southampton and her Boat, seized and condemned for having been employed in Smuggling, together with the Sails, Ropes, Masts, Yards, and all other Materials belonging to the said Vessel. Also a seized Boat condemned and broken-up, together with a quantity of broken-up Ankers, and some condemned Coast Guard Stores &c.

16 October (RCG) Great quantities of pilchards were seen on the sands on Wednesday morning at the entrance of the harbour of Fowey. The seines are gone out and it is expected fine shoals will be enclosed. The past two days Monday and Tuesday it having blown a gale of wind the seines were prevented shooting, the fish being on the coast in abundance as far East as Looe.

23 October (RCG) The Amity Sean, Mr. George Nickels, master, seaner, last night shot to the Eastward of the harbour of Fowey, and enclosed a fine shoal of pilchards; she tucked last night and brought into Fowey about 70 hhds. leaving the stop sean in the water with good prospect. The Valletort sean also shot, but unfortunately from the running of the tide the fish escaped all to about 12 hhds. There is still great bodies of fish seen on our coast.

13 November (RCG) On Tuesday 3rd inst., the Court of the Right Hon. Anne Lady Grenville was held at Boconnoc House,....on which occasion the Hon. Geo. Fortescue as the representative of her ladyship presided. The tenantry assembled on the occasion were numerous and highly respectable. After partaking of a plentiful supply of good old English fare, on the removal of the cloth the Chairman gave the "King", which was drunk standing amid the cheers of the assemblage of true hearted Cornishmen, who like their fore-fathers are staunch supporters of the Constitution in Church and State. The health of "Lady Grenville" was next given and drunk in rapturous applause. The Chairman rose and begged to return thanks in behalf of his noble relative - he stated that it was her Ladyship's request that he should make known to the tenantry how much she felt from so long an absence from them, which was unavoidable on her part. She had now endeavoured to remedy this by requesting him (the Chairman) to reside at Boconnoc to administer to the comforts of the neighbourhood and her numerous Cornish Tenantry....no one could be found more anxious to promote the comfort and happiness of the tenantry. He had taken this as the first opportunity of meeting them, ...and he trusted that whatever was wanting on the estate would be made known to him, so that whatever could be done for their comfort should instantly be accomplished, knowing that the interest of both landlord and tenant are closely attached, and that which is for the interest of the one is for the welfare of the other. He next alluded to the Game around the domain, which he trusted would be preserved for his enjoyment, and begged to say that the farmers residing at a distance were at liberty to kill for their own enjoyment and use.... Many other appropriate toasts were drunk during the evening; and upon the whole (says our correspondent) a more comfortable day could not be spent. The old Yeomen were full of glee; and the thoughts of old customs and by-gone days were depicted on their countenance over which hung their silvery locks, and many a tale was told of the happy hours spent within the walls of that mansion, which has borne the noble families of "Mohun", "Pitt", and "Grenville", and which has now.... a descendant of the noble house of "Fortescue".

1836

11 March (RCG) About nine a.m., during a heavy gale from the Southward, the sloop *"VENUS"*, of this port, Warn, Master, from Exeter, laden with sand, bound to Parr, was capsized off Pencarrow-head, about two miles to the Eastward of Fowey Harbour, she immediately sank and the crew consisting of the Master, one seaman and one boy were drowned. - The schooner *"PROVIDENCE"*, of Plymouth, Bate, Master, saw her go down, but was unable to render any assistance. As soon as it was known here that a vessel had sunk, the pilot gig of Polruan, manned by Richard Johns, a branch pilot and a crew of six men, put out at the risk of their lives in the hope of rescuing the crew, but without success. The greatest praise is due to them for their manly promptitude and activity.

17 June (RCG) On the 9th inst, about one o'clock in the morning, Matthew Johns, fisherman of Polruan, in this port, whilst fishing at anchor in his open boat at sea, about five leagues south of Fowey Harbour, was run down by the brig *"Acorn,"* of Yarmouth, bound from Jersey to Wales. Johns was alone in the boat, and fortunately succeeded in saving himself by springing to the bow of the brig, and getting on board by the chain cable, shortly after which the boat sank. The master of the brig was not on deck when the accident occurred, but from Johns' statement no proper look out could have been kept, for he had a light, and hailed repeatedly, directing the brig to alter her course so as to go clear of him. By this accident the poor man has been deprived of the means of supporting himself and family.

9 September (RCG) The return match between the Fowey and St. Austle Cricket Clubs was played at Fowey on Monday the 5th September, 1836, when the former Club again came off victorious, by beating their opponents 44 runs.-The contest was a very spirited one. The field was numerously attended with ladies and gentlemen, who felt great interest in the result. At the commencement of the game the weather was exceedingly boisterous and very heavy rain, and as the Fowey Club had the first innings it was a great disadvantage to them, the ground being saturated with water, the players had great difficulty in running or standing at their wickets. During the remainder of the day's sport the weather was fine, when the playing in the second innings of the Fowey Club was very superior, and much admired....

A booth was erected in the field where refreshments were provided for the players, and at the close of the first innings they partook of the same. - At the conclusion of the game the cricketers adjourned to the Ship inn where they were provided with a dinner served in Mrs. Borlase's best style. Upwards of 40 gentlemen sat down to partake of the same. The evening was spent in the greatest conviviality....

14 October (RCG) An inquest was held at Fowey on Wednesday last,....on the body of Richard Mallet, aged 22 years, a hatmaker in that place, who hanged himself in his own shop, and from the evidence given, the jury returned a verdict of insanity.

1837

17 February (RCG) BANKRUPT'S ESTATE AND EFFECTS FOR SALE....BY PUBLIC AUCTION, by order of the Assignees of WILLIAM GEACH the Elder, WILLIAM GEACH the Younger, Bankrupts, at the undermentioned times and places respectively, viz; at the SHIP INN, Fowey on Monday the 20th of February inst....

1/16 Part or Share in the Schooner *"SPECULATION"*, Register 70 Ton, James Geach, Master.

1/16 Shares in the Sloops *"CORNISH TRADER"*, 40 Ton, Jacob Beer, Master;.... *"LIVELY"*, James Geach, Master;.... *"SPRING"*, 60 Ton, Richard Scantlebury, Master;.... *"GLORY"*, 60 Ton, William Salt, Master;.... *"FOUR FRIENDS"*, 80 Tons, Thomas Scantlebury, Master;.... *"FANNY"*, 70 Tons, Philip Pill, Master;.... *"FLOWER"*, 60 Tons, James Tippett, Master;.... *"NEWHOUSE"*, 90 Tons, Peter Tadd, Master;.... *"ROSE"*, 60 Tons, Benjamin Brokenshaw, Master.

1/16 and 1/32 in the Sloop *"CHARLOTTE ANN"*, 76 Tons, Robert Pearne, Master.

3/15 and 1/32 in the Sloop *"ELIZABETH AND ANN"*, 66 tons, Charles Hodge, Master.

All the above vessels belong to the Port of Fowey, are substantially built, and well found in stores of all descriptions and all at Sea, and expected in Port daily.

At the SHIPWRIGHT'S YARDS in *Polruan*, on Tuesday the 21st, precisely at One o'Clock, several hundred feet of Oak, Elm, and Bulk Timber, quantity of Oak Plank, several dozen Spars, five very good Pilchard drift Nets, several Boats, Shipwright's Tools, Steamers, Boilers, some Thousand Trenails, Vessel Mounlds, Fire Wood, &c.

At the DWELLING HOUSE and STORE ROOMS in *Polruan*, on Wednesday the 22nd and following days, precisely at One, a quantity of Groceries, Drapery, Hardware, Drugs, Oils, various Paints, Nails, Pitch, Tar, Salt, Coals, Ovens, Bricks, Carpentry tools, and all the HOUSEHOLD FURNITURE, comprising Mahogany and other Tables and Chairs, Sofa, Mahogany Chest of Drawers, an excellent eight day Clock, China, Glass and all other articles of Household Furniture. The above Property which is well worth the Public attention, will be SOLD in convenient Lots to the best Bidder....

17 February (RCG) The Beacon on the Gribbon Head at the entrance of the harbour of Fowey was much injured on Monday morning by the severe thunder and lightning storm; many weighty stones are removed, but the extent of the damage is not as yet ascertained.

17 February (RCG) The influenza has been raging badly at Fowey during the past month, there being scarcely a family that has not been afflicted with the disease, leaving great debility - the aged and young have suffered most, but few deaths have taken place.

17 March (RCG) On Wednesday evening the 8th instant, a vocal and instrumental concert, was held in the long room at the Ship Inn, which was numerously and very fashionably attended.- The overtures were played in excellent style and the glees and songs received the greatest applause. This is the first entertainment of the kind that has taken place for many years at Fowey, and as it has given general satisfaction, it will in future be regularly continued.

12 May (RCG) A friendly game of cricket took place at Polruan, near Fowey, on the 27th ult., between Polruan and Fowey Clubs, in consequence of a challenge from the former club; the following was the result of the game: - Fowey 1st innings 101, Polruan 1st innings 50. 2nd innings 20 - 70. Fowey beating the Polruan Club in 1 innings, 31.

At the close of the game, both Clubs adjourned to the Lugger Inn, where an excellent dinner was provided by Mr. Hicks. The greatest harmony and conviviality prevailed during the evening.

26 May (RCG) TO LABOURERS. WANTED, for the BRAZILS, a Number of LABOURERS, from 25 to 40 years of age, with their Families..... None need apply who cannot produce the most satisfactory testimonials as to character.

8 September (RCG) The Amity seine of Fowey, Mr. Geo. Nickels, took in St Austle bay, on Saturday night last, 35 hhds. of pilchards, which were landed the following morning at Fowey; and from the great demand, the whole was sold to the inhabitants of the town and neighbourhood in a few hours.

13 October (RCG) We did hope that the fine weather which has prevailed for a week or more, would have brought the Pilchards to our shores; but....this has not happened, and we fear the season will close unsuccessfully. It is some satisfaction, however, to find that the Fishermen take a few herrings and mackerel; and rather because these branches of the Fishery are wholly in the hands of poor men.

20 October (RCG) The Amity seine, Mr. Geo. Nickels, was shot in Lanlivet bay, on the night of the 16th instant, and took up ten hogsheads of pilchards, which were sold to the inhabitants at Fowey on the following morning. - Several hundreds of pilchards have been taken in small seines in the harbour of Fowey; and should the fine weather continue, great hopes are entertained of good catches. Large shoals of fish are seen on the coast.

10 November Fowey.- (RCG) The pilchards have again made their appearance on this coast.... and the drift boats had large catches of very fine fish. Should the weather continue favourable, hopes are entertained of the seiners making a good year. Up to this time so unsuccessful a season was never known on this coast.

10 November (RCG) The annual court of the Right Hon. Lady Grenville for the Manors of Boconnoc....was held at Boconnoc....on Thursday last.... The dinner, which consisted of good old English fare, with venison and hare pies, and such like, was served up on two tables in the spacious hall. About 80 yeomen sat down to dinner, the Hon. G.M. Fortescue presiding. After the cloth was removed, and the "flowing bowl" substituted....the Hon. Gentleman rose and said...I beg to assure those who....voted in opposition to me, that they shall never find any difference in my conduct towards them. (Hear.) I respect every man's opinion, and I wish a man to use his franchise conscientiously.... Last year, I brought before your notice some of the public acts....among them was the Poor Law Bill. I have incurred some unpopularity ....as a resident country gentleman, I lent my aid to do justice to the rate-payer as well as the receiver. Notwithstanding the opposition to the bill in its present shape, I do believe after the cry against it ceases, and after it has undergone....modifications....it will be of considerable value to the aged poor. In this union, a workhouse is erecting, and the money borrowed from the Government.... The Tythe Commutation Bill, which has become the law of the land, has come into operation in many parts of the county. It will be of great advantage to the farmer; and though its operation may be laborious and costly, it will be valuable to improvement; for when you have once commuted your tythes, your improvement will not be subject to any further charges.... I shall be happy to give you....information of any new acts that may be passed touching your interests....

He could assure them that Lady Louisa (Fortescue) was influenced by the purest motives, and he was happy in being able to refer to one of her latest acts, which was the establishment of two clubs - one to raise a fund, to which the labourer might contribute two-pence per week amounting, in the year, to 8s. 8d., to which Lady Louisa added 5s.,....the other was precisely on the same principle; only the money was to be applied in clothing. He mentioned this, hoping it would be an example to many present, to contribute in their own parishes to funds of the same description. It would be of considerable service to the labouring poor, particularly as *no out-door* relief can be granted under the existing law to the able-bodied poor.... The hon. gentleman assured the company, that whatever might be done for the comfort of the poor; they would find Lady Louisa ready to assist in; and he hoped, forward in every work of charity and benevolence.

1838

5 January (RCG) FOWEY - MR. GOODBEAR'S SCHOOL. - On Thursday evening, the 21st of December, the young gentleman of this school recited in the town-hall, Hannah More's Sacred Drama of "Daniel", and several select pieces, before a crowded assemblage of the most respectable inhabitants of the town, who were highly delighted at the distinct and correct manner in which each boy delivered the part assigned to him;.... After the recitals, all the young gentlemen drank tea together in the hall. Before and after tea, they sang grace; and after a liberal distribution of apples and oranges, the proceedings of the evening were appropriately closed by singing "Praise God from whom all blessings flow." (We readily insert this, because we are always willing to cheer and encourage the labours of the many deserving men, engaged everywhere in....education; often without the gratitude to which they are so largely entitled, and sometimes, we fear, without an adequate recompense for the wearisome and responsible duties which they are called upon to perform.)

23 March (RCG) FOWEY.- The *One and All* and the *Boconnoc* were launched from the building yard of Messrs. Marks and Rendle, after having been lengthened

11 feet each. These vessels, with another called the *Place,* had previously been employed as trawlers out of this harbour; but having been very unsuccessful were sold by the late owners.... Messrs. Carkeet and Lake, of Fowey....intend to employ them in the Foreign trade. They will burthen about 70 tons each, are rigged as schooners, and are expected to sail very fast.

6 July (RCG) FOWEY - The festivities of the coronation opened at this place with the firing of a royal salute, at the Custom House, at eight o'clock; when the whole of the merchant vessels in the harbour, with the Revenue cruisers *Repulse* and *Eliza* exhibited a beautiful and splendid display of flags. The Fowey amateur band assembled and played some national airs in the morning, and then paraded through the streets; but at noon they left the town and proceeded to Menabilly, where a dinner was provided by W. Rashleigh, Esq. for his tenantry on the occasion of his eldest son's having attained the age of 21 years, and in celebration of the great public event of the day. At one o'clock a royal salute was fired from the "Repulse" cutter; and at intervals during the day, some merry peals were rung on bells. There was a public tea drinking in the streets, where some of the oldest inhabitants greatly enjoyed themselves. At sun-set another Royal salute was fired from the *Repulse*, and at night that vessel was beautifully illuminated, for which much credit is due to the officers. The villages of Polruan and Bodenick were also illuminated, and torches blazed on the hills surrounding the harbour, which had a most brilliant and striking effect. In the evening, the band returned, and again played some national airs.- A display of fireworks on board the *Repulse* cutter, followed the illumination, and a balloon ascended from the shore, which closed the day's amusements.

27 July (RCG) FOWEY REGATTA - The aquatic sports which have given so much celebrity to this ancient town for many years, took place on Tuesday the 17th inst. At an early hour all was bustle and activity. Triumphal arches were erected in the different streets, decorated with evergreens, intertwined with oak and the gayest flowers of the season. That on the town-quay displayed considerable taste, having a platform on the top, surmounted with four flags. Gay flags were also displayed from flag-staffs, and from the vessels in the harbour, which were arranged in line, and had a fine effect. At eight o'clock, the amateur band played through the town their most popular tunes, and many merry peals were rung on the bells. As the day advanced, the rapid arrival of persons of both sexes was beyond precedent, and at the commencement of the race the booths erected on the sides of the harbour, and in fact every spot which commanded a view of the boats, teemed with well-dressed spectators, including a brilliant assemblage of beauty and fashion. The arrival of the *Sir Francis Drake* steam-packet from Plymouth, with 170 passengers and an excellent band of music, tended much to enliven the scene; and the numerous pleasure-boats plying about the harbour in every direction, decorated with flags, and filled with ladies and gentlemen of the first respectability, produced a most delightful effect. At twelve o'clock the racing commenced.... Second match - First class two-oared boats.- First prize 1*l*. 5*s*. to the *Goldfinch* belonging to Mr J Brown of Fowey.

Second, 15s. to the *Linnet*, belonging to Mr Brokenshaw of Fowey. This was a very interesting race and was nobly contested. The winning boats are both splendid models, and were built by two of our most experienced ship-builders for the occasion.... A SAILING MATCH for small boats not exceeding 15 feet in length, round the Cannis-rock, a distance of three miles from the Harbour's mouth. - The wind very much increased during this race, and there was much sea outside the Harbour. Four boats started; the *Victoria* of Fowey took the lead, followed closely by the *Jane* of Polruan, until within a short distance of the rock, when the *Victoria* unfortunately shipped a heavy sea and shifted her ballast, which caused her to return. The *Mary Kitty* also returned in consequence of the weather, leaving the contest to two boats only. The first prize 1*l.* was awarded to the *Johanna* of Gorran, beating the *Jane* about a minute and half.... The Gig and Pram Race followed. This was a truly ludicrous contest, and afforded much amusement to all present; the gig winning in 12 minutes - prize 15s. All the matches were contested with great spirit, and drew forth the plaudits of the spectators. At the close of the races, the committee landed at the extremity of the town, and walked in procession, headed by the Fowey Amateur band, to the Ship Inn, where the prizes were awarded. At ten o'clock there was a splendid display of fireworks on the Town-quay, including vertical wheels, large and small sky-rockets, and a variety of others. Two fire-balloons were also sent up in beautiful style. Near the town-hall, on the Quay, the word VICTORIA was formed with lamps, kindly given for the occasion by Wm. Rashleigh, jun, Esq, of Menabilly. These had a most beautiful appearance.- The whole went off much to the satisfaction of every one.... We should add that, for the further gratification of our numerous visitors, admittance was kindly granted by J.T. Treffry, Esq., the High Sheriff, to all who applied to see the interior of his noble mansion; and the number of Ladies and Gentlemen who visited it, is almost incredible. Everyone expressed his admiration at the beauty of the apartments , and the chaste and tasteful style of the....painting and sculpture....

17 August (RCG) Fowey.- During the assizes, Mr. Baron Parke, with several barristers, and other gentlemen, visited Fowey Consols Copper Mine, where they were received by the High Sheriff, J.T. Treffry, Esq.- They all expressed their admiration at the great improvement in the works - the wonderful power and good condition of the machinery, and the excellent arrangement by which this extensive mine is carried on. After making their observations on the mine, they accompanied the High Sheriff to his residence at Fowey; on entering which their admiration was raised to the highest pitch by the beautiful painting and carving, especially of the drawing-room. All the gentlemen said this was one of the most superb rooms they had ever seen; and most probably, was not excelled by any in England - nor, perhaps, in Europe. - We may add here a description of this noble mansion, which appeared in the *West Briton*.- This building, the seat of the ancient family of Treffry, which held a prominent place in the events of our country in the feudal days, and sent forth more than one mailed warrior to the fields of the Edwards and the Henries, is now rendered doubly interesting by being entirely renewed in the richest style of the old Gothic.... The front of the building exhibits a profusion of ornament, worked in freestone, and at the end a granite tower "rears its tall summit." This tower, for its chasteness and simplicity of design, affords a contrast to the more florid style of the other parts of the building, which relieves and captivates the eye. The interior is principally fitted up with beautiful old oak, and in no part has the original style been lost sight of. - It will be sufficient, at present, to glance at the Drawing-room, just completed. This room represents a building of polished granite, with a ceiling of figured oak; it was painted by Mr. Whale, who has been engaged in decorating the mansions of many of the Cornish nobility and gentry, and exhibits on the sides the astonishing number of nearly *five hundred* variations of granite, all selected by Mr. Treffry himself, and which the artist has so nicely imitated, that it is only by very close examination the deception is perceived. This room is also fitted with a massive but elegant mantel-piece, formed out of red porphyry, discovered by Mr. Treffry, reposing on green-stone, and which is said to resemble but to surpass in beauty the famous ancient Egyptian porphyry. The working of this material would have proved almost an impossibility, but for the application of some of the powerful machinery on the Fowey Consols Mines. In proof of its hardness it may be stated that with this powerful auxiliary the sawing of the stone progressed barely three quarters of an inch in twenty-four hours. It may enhance the interest of this room to Cornishmen, to mention that every specimen, both of the granite and oak, is a native of this county; and also that the proprietor readily allows all visitors to inspect it. The approach to this building is by a road, nearly finished, on the side of the hill running parallel with the town, from which there is a fine view of the whole harbour and the English Channel. This road is beautifully decorated with evergreens and fragrant shrubs, and by being liberally thrown open to the inhabitants, forms a delightful promenade, and may be considered as fine a carriage-road as any in England. On the whole, the proprietor deserves great credit for having preserved to this castellated mansion the appellation bestowed on it ages ago - "The glorye of the towne of Fowey".

1839

11 January (RCG) CORNWALL EPIPHANY SESSIONS.- *William Eveleigh*, 38, charged with having stolen at Lanteglos near Fowey, one duck the property of Geo. Hicks, and a bag of wheat the property of Mr. John Hicks.... *William Glanville.* Witness and William Yeo watched the prisoner's house; and on the night of the 1st December saw two men going towards it. About 12 o'clock, two persons came out of the house of one Collins, which is under the same roof as prisoner's; and about four hours after they returned.... They had each a bag on his shoulder. Witness let them go a little way and then fired a gun, calling out "halloa, what have you got there." One of the men said "Nothing but a little cork." Witness knew the voice: it was Collins's. The other man ran off: cannot swear it was the prisoner. *William Yeo*, who watched with the last witness, knows the prisoner; he was one of the men, and carried a long bushel-bag to his own house; the man who ran away was Collins. - Witness in his *cross-examination* said that the first witness knew the prisoner as well as he did, and could see him as plainly: it was a bright moonlight night. *Re-examined.* Glanville could not, where he stood, see prisoner enter his house. *Richard Hicks* is a constable at Lanteglos. On the morning of the 2nd December, went to the prisoner's house, and being denied admittance, burst open the door. He saw a large fire, and wheat burning in it. He stirred up the wheat, and out came a duck and two fowls. He found prisoner sitting on the side of the bed with his wife, and both were crying. Prisoner was the only man in the house. Witness said to him "This is a bad job;" and prisoner replied "It is a bad job;" and turning to his wife, said "My dear Lydia, I shall never see you any more.".... *Mrs. Hicks*, wife of the prosecutor, on the Saturday before the 3rd of December, marked two ducks, by cutting off some feathers above the joint of the legs: they were drakes. On the 2nd day of December she lost those ducks. She saw one of them afterwards at her brother's house. She saw the prisoner at Lynn's house; when he said he took two ducks from Triggibrown - the name of the place where her husband lived. He is the only housekeeper there. She had no doubt that the legs produced in Court belonged to one of the ducks she had marked. - The prisoner's confession was confirmed by another witness. *Guilty. Twelve months' hard labour.*

The prisoner was then tried on a second indictment for stealing 16 gallons of wheat, property of Mr. John Hicks. *Richard Hicks* swore to the burning of some wheat in the prisoner's house, and produced a sample of which he took from the fire. - *W. Yeo* corroborated this. *Wm. Wenmouth*, prosecutor's hind, on the 2d Dec. found some wheat wanting from a heap in his master's barn.... There was an alteration in the heap. He did not measure it, but could see some was gone. Mr. *John Hicks*, a farmer and corn-dealer in Lanteglos, had taken a sample from a heap of wheat in his barn, and on comparing with it the sample taken by the constable from prisoner's fire, no doubt was his property. Richard Hicks, the constable, recalled. Took the prisoner to Bodmin Gaol; and on the road he admitted taking the wheat from the prosecutor's barn. - *Guilty.*

11 January *(RCG) Wm. Curtis*, 25, charged with stealing a pair of oars, the property of the East Cornwall Shipping Company. *Robt. Hill*, a boy belonging to the *Ann and Elizabeth*, on the 25th Nov. obtained leave to go to Bodinnick to see his parents, in the ship's boat, which he left on the beach with a pair of new oars on board her. When he returned, he discovered that the new oars had been taken away, and an old pair of paddles substituted for them. -*Cross-examined.* Knew the prisoner very well: had never had any quarrel with him. *William Hill*, the father of the last witness, watched for the prisoner on the following day, and saw him in Fowey Harbour on board the *Hero*; there was a boat near, and a new pair of oars in the *Hero*. He asked the prisoner whether that was the boat he came in from Lerrin the evening before; the prisoner said it was. He said these are not your oars; they belong to the *Anne and Elizabeth*, and I shall take them to her. Prisoner did not object to this, but said he found the oars the evening before in the *Hydra*'s boat. Witness then took them to the vessel. The mate of the *Anne and Elizabeth* was called, and identified the oars. It was stated in behalf of the prisoner that he took the oars, to use instead of his own paddles, which were useless on account of the violence of the wind; that he intended to return them, and had left the paddles in their place, that it might be known who had taken them. This, it was contended, took away all appearance of a felonious intention. Verdict: *Not Guilty*.

12 July (RCG) MIDSUMMER QUARTER SESSIONS. *Thomas Eade*, 30, was charged with unlawfully obtaining a certain quantity of Foreign corn, from John Martin, at Lanteglos.... John Martin, miller at Lanteglos....had two sets of mills, about two gunshots apart. In April, he had a considerable quantity of Foreign wheat. Prisoner was employed as a porter, carrying this wheat from the vessel to the mill, and was occasionally employed as a labourer about the mill. Witness found some of this Foreign wheat gone in April. Had a sample of that wheat in his possession now. There was no other wheat of the same description sold in the neighbourhood.- William Henry Collins was servant to Mr. Thos. Parsons, a miller. In April last went to Eade's house, and took away a grist of wheat to his master's mill. - .... Thos. Parsons, miller, on the 12th of April ground some wheat brought him by last witness (Collins). It was of a very coarse brown quality, particularly mixed with a good deal of *eaver*.- Robt. Parsons, a boy, had taken flour in April from his father's to Thomas Eade's.- John Martin jun. knew the bran and flour. It was like his father's foreign wheat. Witness went to Parson's mill, and found wheat there, and pointed it out to Parsons.- Thos. Parsons.... stated that at the time this was pointed out, Eade's was the last grist in.- Martha Martin had asked Thos. Eade where he got the corn he had ground at Parson's; but he would not tell.- *Cross-examined.* Eade's wife shewed witness the flour. She knew it was Foreign flour by the smell. The flour from the foreign corn had been sold to customers all round the neighbourhood..... John Martin, the elder, was recalled, and produced a sample of the corn, which was shewn to the Jury.- *Cross-examined.* Bought the corn of Mr. Butt, of Jersey, and imported it at Charlestown.... Did not call it bad quality. There was a smell of the *tar-peas.-*.... Other millers had sold foreign wheat in his neighbourhood, but none of this quality with *tar-peas* in it.- John Martin, jun. produced a sample which he took from Thomas Parson's mill, and had compared with his father's foreign wheat, and believed it to be the same. The smell of foreign wheat with tar-peas differed from that of other foreign corn.- Thomas Parsons called again. The sample now produced was of the same kind as that shewn him on 12th April by John Martin, the younger.- Wm. Henry Collins recalled.... Did not examine the corn in Eade's bag that he brought to the mill; could not say it was wheat or barley.- The Court, after hearing all the evidence with great patience.... directed a verdict of *Acquittal*.

James Swift, 30, was charged with stealing a waistcoat from Robert Colenso, of Lanteglos by Fowey. The waistcoat had been hung out to dry, and was stolen by the prisoner, who seemed to have gained his living as a strolling plunder. Verdict, *Guilty.-* Two months' hard labour.

26 July (RCG) SHIPLAUNCH AT FOWEY.- A fine schooner, of about 190 tons, called the *Gallant,* belonging to J.T. Treffry, Esq. of Place-house, and destined for the coasting trade at Par, was launched last week at Fowey. She glided into the water in fine style, in the presence of a great concourse of spectators, and amid loud and hearty cheers. The name which this vessel has received has reference to the following historical event. About the year 1466, the inhabitants of Fowey, proud of their pre-eminence in naval affairs, chanced to sail near Rye and Winchilsea and refused to vail their bonnets on the summons of these towns; "which contempt," says Carew "caused the Ripiers to go out with might and main against them.... The Fowey-men gave them so rough entertainment at their welcome, that they were glad to forsake patch, without bidding them farewell. The merit of which exploit afterwards entitled them, *"the Gallants of Fowey."*

26 July (RCG) FOWEY REGATTA.... The preparations, it appears, were conducted with all the spirit and good taste for which the inhabitants of this pleasant little town are remarkable. Numerous flags were hoisted along the quays;....the streets were decorated with arches of evergreens and flowers; and even trees were planted in favourable situations, the effect of which was very novel and striking....and the water was covered with yachts and boats of all descriptions, filled with well-dressed company; among which the *Sir Francis Drake* steamer, from Plymouth, crowded with passengers, and having on board an excellent band of music, formed a conspicuous and very interesting object. Early in the forenoon the shores and quays were lined with spectators, all apparently in the highest spirits.... At ten o'clock, the Fowey Amateur Band....began to play the national air; and all was bustle and preparation until eleven, when the sports commenced. The contests were of the most interesting character, exhibiting the finest specimens of skilful seamanship and manly exertion, and affording a gratifying treat to all who beheld them.... *First Match,* for four-oared Gigs, not exceeding 25 feet. First prize 2l. 2s. to the Polruan Coast-guard boat.... *Second Match,* First-class two-oared Boats.... This race excited great attention, and was well contested. The two first were built by experienced ship-builders for the occasion at Fowey, and rowed by *Fowey men;* the third boat, and a fourth, were built by the celebrated Mr. Waterman, and rowed by *Saltash men.* Never was there a better match, but the meed of victory is due to the Fowey lads, who gallantly met their well-known opponents, and triumphed over them by dint of earnest and persevering exertion, joined to practiced skill and determined courage....

In the evening there was a brilliant display of fire-works on the quay; and a beautiful fire-balloon was let off, which ascended to a great height, and excited much admiration. The word VICTORIA was tastefully displayed in lamps, provided for the occasion by W. Rashleigh, junr. Esq. the effect of which was extremely splendid. The amusements of the day ended in the most perfect harmony, and without the slightest accident.... (We think, by the way, that a Ball would have been an appropriate finish. The ladies are never quite content upon these occasions without a dance; and their wishes should always be gratified to the fullest possible extent.)

6 September (RCG) From those who have thrashed new corn we find that the 'yield' is good;....we may conclude that the deficiency will not be so great as had been anticipated. We rejoice at this, because every bushel of corn we grow will serve to keep the value of that bushel in England, and thus save poor old John Bull from a second course of the cruel depletion which he has recently undergone - not through the operation of the Corn Laws, but through their temporary and partial abeyance. For this, in effect, was the state of things, when from the granaries of half the world a vast quantity of corn was poured in upon us at a nominal duty....

The prices of cattle and corn are much the same.... There is very little doing in wool. Old oats are exceedingly scarce and dear. Potatoes promise an abundant crop.

27 September (RCG) On Wednesday, the smack *Farmer's Friend*,.....put into this port with the loss of her bowsprit and jib, with her stem split, and otherwise damaged from having been run foul of by a smack, name unknown, off the Deadman.... The smack offered no assistance to the injured vessel, but proceeded on her voyage. The *Farmer's Friend* is found to have made much water;.... and the ground tier is covered. If the cargo be flour, which we suppose it to be....it must have suffered much injury.

20 December (RCG).... It necessarily follows from the deficiency in the quantity of whale-oil, that fish oil of all kinds must be in great demand during the winter; particularly as it appears, that the old stock is exhausted.... The old stocks were exhausted both last year and this, prior to the new importations.

CHAPTER 5
1840-1849

1840

17 January (RCG) ASPHALTE ROOFING. - This is one of the numerous and ingenious inventions which every day challenge the notice of the public. It is a substitute for slate, zinc, copper and the other materials usually employed for covering buildings, and is recommended by its cheapness and durability, but chiefly by its lightness; a quality so remarkable, that it is expected to lead to a great saving of wood, the most costly of all building materials. It is applicable to walls as well as roofs; a matter of no small importance in this humid climate, where the best built houses of brick and stone, if exposed to the South or West can scarcely ever be kept thoroughly dry. It is also an excellent material for lining vats, troughs, and reservoirs; and in fact there are few purposes for which slate, zinc, tiles, or Roman cement have been usually employed, to which this substance may not be advantageously applied.

14 February (RCG) Fowey.- On Monday morning, the harbour exhibited a beautiful appearance, from the display of flags of every description on board the *Fox* revenue-cutter, and the merchant-ships then lying in front of the town, in honour of the Queen's nuptials. The firing of guns and the ringing of bells were unfortunately prevented by the serious illness of a young gentleman, whose medical attendants were of the opinion that the noise would be fatal to him. This circumstance caused much disappointment, and considerably checked that appearance of rejoicing which this ancient and loyal town would otherwise have exhibited. The inhabitants, however, regaled 117 poor women with tea and cake in the Town-hall; and the ladies kindly waited on them and did every thing to promote their comfort and enjoyment. At seven o'clock, they separated in great good humour, after singing the National Anthem, to the accompaniment of a band of music. - A public dinner, served in a style that did great credit to the worthy host, was given at the Sailor's Return Inn, kept by Mr. Hanson; at which a large party of gentlemen sat down. On the removal of the cloth, the Chairman gave the 'Health of her Majesty the Queen,' which was drunk with all the honours and followed by an appropriate song. - The 'Health of Prince Albert' was also drunk amid much cheering; and was followed by various other toasts, including the 'Queen Dowager and the rest of the Royal Family' 'The Navy and Army' 'The Ladies of Fowey' 'The Mercantile Interest,' and 'Prosperity to the Country.' - Some excellent songs were sung; and the Fowey Amateur Band played several popular airs in their usual good style. The company, which did not separate till a late hour, concluded their festivities by singing "God save the Queen."

21 February (RCG) CORONER'S INQUESTS.- On Wednesday the 12th inst. an inquest was held by J. Hamley, Esq., at Polruan, on the body of Capt. James Wyatt, who disappeared from his lodgings at that place on the morning of the 16th Jan., and had not subsequently been heard of. On Monday, the body was found entangled in the nets of a trawl-boat off the harbour of Fowey, and brought on shore. It was greatly decomposed; and there being no evidence of the manner in which the deceased came by his death, the jury, under the directions of the worthy Coroner, returned a verdict of *Found Drowned*.

3 April (RCG) CORNWALL LENT ASSIZES. - *Catherine Ley*, was charged with stealing, in the parish of Fowey, one cotton gown-piece, one flannel petticoat, and one shawl, the property of Eliza Williams. - Joseph Paine, who is a carpenter, saw the prisoner wearing a shawl of the description which Mrs. Williams had lost; and on giving information, the prosecutrix went to the house of the prisoner's step-mother, where she resided, and asked for her things which she had missed; her property was immediately restored to her. No further evidence being given to fix the theft on the prisoner, she was declared *Not Guilty*.

10 April (RCG) CORNWALL EASTER SESSIONS. *John Searle*, 17, was charged with having stolen a duck from Mr. Sweet, of Tywardreath, on the 16th of March. The prisoner, who had been an apprentice with the prosecutor was allowed to keep a duck with those of his master. On the prisoner's being ill, he received from his master, a mallard, instead of a duck. Afterwards leaving his master's service, he took his master's duck, twisted its neck, and tossed it over the quay at Fowey. Verdict, *Guilty*.... A fortnight's hard labour.

19 June (RCG) FOWEY.- On Friday week, Thomas Netherton, a rope-maker, while engaged in laying a hawser in the rope-walk of Mr. E. Thomas, was unfortunately struck by the handle of the winch, which fractured his skull. The poor man lingered until Sunday last, when he died.

One day last week, another serious accident occurred here, through the sudden fall of a cob wall, which a man called William Brenton, of Tywardreath, was employed in taking down. The man was greatly injured, but is likely to recover.

3 July (RCG) TO BE SOLD BY AUCTION, at the LUGGER INN, in Polruan....the undermentioned Valuable PROPERTY, *Situate at Polruan*....

Lot 1.- All that very excellent SHIPWRIGHT'S YARD with the STORE-HOUSES and MOULDING LOFT therein, which are about 50 feet long by 20 feet wide, together with two newly-erected DWELLING-HOUSES, about 40 feet long by 15 feet wide, nearly finished, enclosed in the said Yard, and commanding a full view of the same, situated at the southern extremity of Polruan, near the entrance of Fowey Harbour, with an excellent Well of Water therein.

The above Yard is now held by Messrs. Marks and Rendle, for a Term of 5 Years from Christmas last, at the low Yearly Rent of £17; an extensive Business has been conducted therein for a great number of years past, and it possesses every accommodation for building and launching Vessel of large burthen, having upwards of 16 feet of water in the Spring Tides.

Lot 2.- All that extensive CELLAR, with STORE LOFTS over the same, adjoining the said Yard, being about 50 feet. long by 14 wide, lately held by the Revenue

Officers, at the Yearly Rent of £10, capable of being converted into Dwelling-houses at a moderate expense.

Lot 3.- A handsome newly-built DWELLING-HOUSE, adjoining the said Yard, being about 22 feet long by 20 wide, containing 6 good Rooms, with Cellar below the same, now tenanted by Mr Hockin, of the Revenue Service. (Out West St., area of Vaughan's Yard).

Lot 4.- A very excellent DWELLING-HOUSE, with an IRONMONGER'S SHOP, having a frontage of about 21 feet, fitted Gardens behind, well stocked with choice Fruit Trees, and screened with an Iron Rail in front, situated in the Old Street, in Polruan aforesaid, commanding beautiful and extensive views of Fowey Town and Harbour, and now in the occupation of Mr. W. Geach Jun. Ironmonger and Colourman. (East St. - Penhaven, perhaps?).

Lot 5.- A very excellent DWELLING-HOUSE, adjoining the last, having the like frontage, comprising Seven Rooms, with Store-houses, Wash-houses, and Walled Gardens behind, also fitted up in a very neat style, for the residence of a genteel family, now in the occupation of Capt. John Geach; together with a newly-built DWELLING-HOUSE adjoining thereto, in the occupation of William Wyatt.

Lot 6.- Either together or separately.... all those FOUR substantial and very excellent DWELLING-HOUSES, newly erected, and Cellar underneath the same, with an excellent Well of Water therein and Coal-houses at the end thereof, situated in Old Street aforesaid, having a frontage of about 57 feet, now in the occupations of Mrs. James Geach, Capt. Thomas Verran, Capt. John Bunt, and others. (East. St. from corner of Quay Hill?).

Lot 7.- Either together or separately, all those TWO very excellent newly-erected DWELLING-HOUSES near the Quay at Polruan aforesaid, having a frontage of about 22 feet 6 inches, with the Cellar below the same, in the occupation of Capts. John Dyer and Joseph Searle.

Lot 8.- Either together or separately, all those FOUR very excellent DWELLING-HOUSES on the Quay, at Polruan aforesaid, which were built, and for many years resided in, by the late Capt. Henry Jane, R.N. having a frontage of about 65 feet, containing altogether 14 rooms; and also the Cellar below, and Yard behind the same, being about 65 by 50 feet, having a landing place from the Harbour, and being a remarkably good situation for a Merchant or Tradesman; now in the occupation of Mrs. Rowe, and others. (Perhaps the houses that used to be on the Wharf?).

Lot 9.- All that large and commodious DWELLING-HOUSE, with the Garden belonging to the same, situate at Polruan aforesaid, now in the occupation of Mr. W. Rendle, shipwright, consisting of two large Parlours, Kitchen, five good Bed-rooms, with Wash-house, Dairy, and Pantry, and delightfully situated, having a commanding view of the Harbour of Fowey, and well adapted for the residence of a large family. (Could this be Dolphins, West St. or Hockens Lane?).

The above Property will be found such a desirable Investment for Capital, as is seldom to be met with; nearly the whole of which was built by and under the inspection of, the late Capt. James Geach, deceased, in the most beautiful situations the town of Polruan would afford, and sparing no expense in procuring the very best Materials of every description.

For viewing the Property, apply to Mr. JOHN JACOBS, Carpenter, Polruan....

4 December (RCG) CURE FOR TOOTHE ACHE.-...Wash your feet in warm water, taking care after you have wiped them very dry, with a clean towel, well aired before you use it, to put on a pair of woolen socks, also well aired. Then go to bed, the bed being first warmed, taking something to throw you into a perspiration, and rubbing the teeth and gums with tincture of myrrh, which under these circumstances will give immediate relief....

1841

8 January (RCG) DEATH OF CHILDREN BY BURNING. - Benevolent advice ....has been frequently offered in our columns to the friends of poor labourers and their families, to endeavour to impress on them the necessity of adopting a different kind of clothing from that which is now commonly in use among the rural poor. Of 23 inquests held by Mr. Hamley during the last quarter, no less than 12 were on the bodies of children burned to death. In none of these areas has any neglect except in regard to the manner of clothing their children, been imitable to the parents. The absence of the mother had in most cases been only for a few minutes, and in one case, the mother and another grown up person were present. Mr. Hamley however, has kindly endeavoured to impress on the parents who have been brought before him, the fact that the light cotton dresses in which it is the foolish custom to dress poor children, in preference to thicker and warmer stuff, become as the children stand before the fire, as inflammable as tinder, and are besides very easily drawn into the fire....

16 April (RCG) FOWEY.- On the morning of Thursday last, at an early hour, it was discovered that the sloop *John*, of Plymouth, Pascoe master, had taken fire. The workmen from Mr. Marks's building-yard immediately went on board her, and after using great exertions succeeded`in extinguishing the flames, when, to prevent further mischief, they hauled her on the beach and scuttled her. On examination it was found that the cabin only was burnt; but we exceedingly regret to add that the mate, a person called John Hocking, who resided at Polruan, and formerly commanded a vessel out of this port, perished in it. He had been left on board on the preceding night, smoking; and it is supposed that he must have fallen asleep, and that a spark from the pipe set fire either to his clothes or his bedding. He appeared to have been dead some hours.- It will be remembered that an accident almost precisely similar to this, happened a few months since at Guernsey; and there too, the mate was burnt to death in the cabin. Those who have the charge of vessels, therefore, ought to be very careful to use every proper precaution against fire; and this`is the more necessary on coming in from a voyage, when the crew are commonly much fatigued and disposed to fall asleep the moment they get into their berths.

30 April (RCG) DIED. On Thursday last, at Fowey, John, son of the late Wm. Pearce, aged 4 1/2 years. About three weeks since, when deceased and his brother were going to bed, he unfortunately caught his night clothes on fire with the candle, and was so dreadfully burnt as to cause his death.

28 May (RCG) PEREMPTORY SALE....*eligibly situated for Business - adjoining the high-road from Fowey to Looe....* TO BE SOLD BY AUCTION....on Thursday the 3rd day of June....at the New Inn, kept by Mr. Edward Roberts, in the Parish of St Veep; all that newly erected DWELLING-HOUSE, *With the Blacksmith's Carpenters Shop, and Garden adjoining,* Situate at Highway, in the said Parish of Lanteglos by Fowey; Held under a Lease for 99 years determinable on the deaths of three healthy lives, aged respectively, 42, 26, and 14 years, late in the occupation of Joseph Whitting. A good Blacksmith's Trade has been carried on on the Premises for a number of years.... Conventionary Rent of 18s. per annum....For a view,.... application....to Mr. John Hicks of Hall.

19 November (RCG) Lostwithiel, Nov. 15.- The usual fair was held here this day. There was a good show of cattle, but very few buyers. As usual it was attended by a gang of thimble rig gentry and pickpockets. A highly respectable farmer was eased of his purse, containing 65 sovereigns and some silver, while viewing some horses. - A woman also had her pocket picked, containing 10*l*. and some odd shillings, while listening to the eloquence of a man commonly known by the name of "Cheap John".... (Thimble rig was a gambling game).

3 December (RCG) LISKEARD BOARD OF EDUCATION. The new school-room at Lanteglos is also completed and the school making rapid progress under the charge of an intelligent mistress....

1842

14 January (RCG) CORNWALL EPIPHANY SESSIONS. *John Hill*, 30, *John Eliot*, 21, and *Richard Taylor*, 18 were charged with stealing a number of articles from a vessel at Fowey, belonging to Richard Pill.... The prosecution....called John Barry.- I am a seaman on board the *Good Intent*. She was at Pont Pill, Fowey, on the 16th of December.... I slept on board that night in the forecastle. While I was there two men came forward. I got up through the hatchway. They said they wanted to have a place to sleep in; I told them they should sleep there because there was no one on board. They asked for meat, I told them I had nothing to give them. Those men were Eliot & Taylor, & they sail on board the *Betsy* which was then lying in Fowey harbour. I then saw another man come from aft; I don't know who he was. That man went in the boat, and the two men followed. This was about twelve at night. I got upon deck and saw three men in it, and something white. The same night I saw that the sky-light was broken open. The next morning I told the captain, and he went down to the ship to see what had been taken. - Richard Pill examined. I am master of the *Good Intent*, of Fowey. On the 17th of December, I went on board my vessel; and found various things missing. I had lost a hat, gun, jar of rum, a pillow, pair of trowsers, sea boots, powder flask and shot belt, spy glass and looking glass, a parallel rule, which is ships property. The companion was locked, and I found two panes of glass and the skylight broken. When I got down into the cabin, I saw tinder lying about. I then missed the rum, which is a ship's store. I went away directly to look for a constable, and in half an hour I went on board the *Betsy*. The constable was there searching. I found my hat, gun, great coat, frock coat, blanket, pair of sea boots, and the other things before mentioned. These things were taken into custody by the constables. I had seen them about mid-day.

John Pearne examined, constable of Fowey, produced the articles in question. In the berth places of Eliot and Taylor, and in the hull of the ship, he found a great number of the articles in question. Took Eliot and Taylor into custody. Eliot said there was another person; he would not split, and that person gave them rum to drink. Witness searched Hill's cabin; in consequence of a discovery, Hill said "I see I am in for it, I may as well confess the whole." He said that he had robbed the vessel with the others, and that it was from want, as he had lost all his things three or four times. He then gave a looking-glass and said it belonged to Richard Pill. After he was ashore, one of the prosecutors (there were several robberies) said he had not all his things; and Hill said they were all on board. Captain Pill was re-called, and identified his own and the articles belonging to the ship. The mate, when called on for his defence, said he was drunk, and he might have done it. The other prisoners said that the mate had brought the things on board, late at night, and had given them a lot of rum, so as to make them drunk, and had then coaxed them away. The witness, Barry, was then re-called by the Court, and he stated that Eliot and Taylor were drunk when he saw them on board his ship. The prisoners were all found *Guilty* of stealing from a ship in a navigable river; but the jury recommended the younger prisoner to mercy.

There were two other indictments against the same prisoners of a similar nature, in which Captains Abraham, Ellery, and Samuel Climo, were the prosecutors, but on these the prisoners were not tried.... SENTENCES. - John Eliot and Robert Taylor....Three months hard labour. John Hill....Twelve months hard labour.

18 February (RCG) LYING AT FOWEY, *And to Sail fourth of April,* 1842, FOR QUEBEC The well-known, fast-sailing, Copper-bolted BARQUE, *ROYAL ADELAIDE, of* 600 *Tons Burthen.* The *Royal Adelaide* is fitted up in the most convenient and comfortable style for the conveyance of Passengers. She is a remarkably *fast sailer* - is a constant Trader to Quebec, and offers a desirable opportunity to Persons wishing to emigrate.... For....particulars, apply to Mr. J Hicks, Merchant, Hall; Captain on board; at Fowey to Mr. Bate, Postmaster.

25 February (RCG) TO SAIL The 5th of April, 1842 FOR QUEBEC, The fine fast-sailing, British-built, Copper-bolted BARQUE *VITTORIA, A Regular Trader,* 800 *Tons Burthen*, MOSEY SIMPSON, Commander, lying at Fowey; has very superior accommodation for Steerage and Cabin passengers, having 7ft. height between decks. The Commander having been many years in the North American Trade, can give much valuable information regarding the Colonies, to any that may feel disposed to take a passage in this strong and splendid Ship, where every accommodation and comfort will be strictly observed.-Families will be taken on moderate Terms. - ....many Berths are already engaged.

11 March (RCG) Accident at Pinnock near Fowey.- On Tuesday last, whilst Mr. Jenkins, of that Farm, was in the act of taking some corn out of the mow, it gave way and falling on him, killed him on the spot. His age was 79 years.

18 March (RCG) On Monday an Inquest was held....at Lanteglos by Fowey, on the body of John Giddy, a lad about 10 years old, servant to Mr. Lambe. It appeared, that on the preceding day after dinner, the deceased and two other boys about the same age were at play; when the deceased got on a water wheel to ride by way of amusement. One of his playmates, unfortunately, turned the water in upon the wheel, which, of course immediately went partly round, carrying the poor boy about half way round, and then crushed him instantly to death between the wheel and the wall. The two other boys ran to the master, Mr. Lambe, in great fright, and a medical gentleman was sent for. But it was found on Mr. Lambe's coming out that poor Giddy was quite dead, and indeed so closely jammed against the wall, that it was found necessary to cut away part of the wheel in order to take out the body. Verdict *Accidental Death.* (Dorset Farm).

17 June (RCG) Prevention of Smoke.... A public meeting was held at Manchester on the 26th ult....that the loss arising from excess of smoke in that distract, in the wear and tear of clothing from the additional washing, injury to furniture & shopkeepers' stocks, greater frequency of painting required &c, was not less than 100,000*l*. a year.... Our steam-engines in Cornwall burn nearly all their smoke, and a smoke consuming apparatus has been lately adopted in steam vessels in the Navy which is said to have succeeded completely. Why then are our manufacturing towns stifled by it?

1 July (RCG) EXCURSION TO FOWEY. The Public are respectfully informed that on Monday next the 4th July, at Ten in the Forenoon, the POWERFUL STEAM VESSEL *Lord Beresford*, John Gundry, Commander, Will (weather permitting) leave Falmouth on an Excursion to FOWEY, and return in the Evening, *calling off Mevagissey to land and receive Passengers each way. The* lovers of the picturesque are invited to visit FOWEY, seated on the banks of a lovely river, environed by lofty hills, each commanding a rich variety of scene - wood and water, ancient towers, and ruined forts combining to form a picture of romantic beauty. PLACE, the richly decorated mansion of J. T. TREFFRY, Esq., is a noble object from the harbour, and claims the attention of every person of taste. It is intended for the "*LORD BERESFORD*" to leave Fowey sufficiently early for parties to return from Falmouth to the neighbouring towns the same Evening. *Refreshments Provided on Board at Moderate Prices.* FARES

Falmouth to Fowey and back...............2s. 6d.
Falmouth to Mevagissey and back.....2s.
Mevagissey to Fowey and back..........1s. 6d.   Children half-price.

8 July (RCG) FOWEY EMIGRATION.- The *Royal Adelaide* which sailed from Fowey in April last with 100 passengers, arrived safe at Quebec on the 29th May, where the passengers all landed in good health and spirits.

22 July (RCG) Fowey.- During the past week great quantities of Salmon Peel have been taken in our river, averaging 3/4 lb. weight. They have been sold at 3d. per lb. and still continue very plentiful.

7 October (RCG) The FISHERY.- Fowey - The pilchard seans are all laid up, and the prospects of fish this season are anything but satisfactory. Great quantities of fine salmon have been taken in the harbour, which have met a ready sale at 4 1/2d. and 5d. per lb.

1843

10 February (RCG) MELANCHOLY OCCURRENCE.- On the evening of Monday last, while Mr. N. Hewett, was returning from the *Caroline*, where he had been taking leave of his nephew, the master of that vessel which was sailing for Venice with a cargo of fish, he was seized with a fit and died in a few hours. He was aged 56 years.

10 February (RCG) Fowey has been styled the montpelier of England, and as proof of it, at the same time shewing the mildness of season, *twenty* Asparagus, of full size, and excellent flavour, grown in the open air were cut in Place Garden on the 3rd instant.

5 May (RCG) FOWEY.- The handsome new sloop *United Friends*, built for Capt. Cornish, of this place, was launched on Monday from the building yard of Mr. Mark. The Lostwithiel band was in attendance, and a large concourse of spectators were assembled. She went off in a very beautiful manner, and a large company afterwards met at the Ferry House Inn, where excellent fare was provided, and the evening was spent in conviviality.

23 June (RCG) EMIGRATION TO QUEBEC. PERSONS desirous of availing themselves of the advantages of settling in Canada under the encouraging prospects of the *new law* for reducing the duties on Colonial Corn and Flour, may avail themselves of a very safe and superior opportunity in the Barque *GOOD INTENT*, WHITBURN, Master, which will sail direct to Quebec from the harbour of Fowey the latter end of July next. This vessel is *quite new* and has very superior accommodation, stands A1 at Lloyd's, is coppered, copper-fastened and strongly secured by an unusual number of iron knees, and is 7 feet high betwixt decks, carries 1000 tons dead weight, sails remarkably fast, and is commanded by an old experienced master. - The charge for passage will be as usual, and applications may be made to Mr. Jno. Hicks, Fowey.... (In Jul 21st issue; Reduced prices- Adults 30s. each. Children under 14 years old. 15s. each. Children under 7 years old. 10s. Prices include head money payable at Quebec.

7 July (RCG) On Tuesday, the 27th ult., was launched from the building-yard of Mr. G. Nickels, the barque *Royal Adelaide*, which splendid vessel has been nearly rebuilt, and is considered one of the strongest and finest vessels of her class. She is intended to sail for Quebec in a few days, with about 80 emigrants on board.

18 August (RCG) Fowey. - THE FISHERY- There has been a very good prospect of pilchards here. All the seaners were put in pay on Monday, went out on the sands and shot all their seans immediately. The *Albion* took up about 40 hogsheads of fine fish, but the *Amity* and another were unsuccessful. The drift boats bring in from 5 to 10 thousand every morning. There are a great many porpoises sculling about our shore, which are not welcome visitors at this season.

6 October (RCG) Wednesday last....being the day fixed for the marriage of the Hon. Mrs. Rashleigh's brother, Lord Blantyre, to Lady Evelyn Gower, second daughter of the Duke and Duchess of Sutherland, at Trenthan, in Staffordshire, the grounds of Menabilly were decorated with flags during the day, and at night a large bonfire, consisting of upwards of 30 tar barrels, &c., was made on the high land of the Gribbon head in commemoration of the happy event.

1844

5 April (WB) NARROW ESCAPE.- On Monday afternoon last, at about two thirds high water, a gentleman, going to Looe, had to cross Fowey ferry, and when on the slip at Fowey, not carefully minding his horse and gig, they went over into the water. The horse took towards Bodinnock, and swam about a third of the width, when it disappeared. At this instant, a boat, with M.S. Nickels, shipwright, in the bow arrived, and rescued the sinking horse from a watery grave. With the assistance of other boats, the horse, (a young and pretty creature), and gig were brought on shore.

3 May (RCG) An inquest was held at the Union House, St. Austell, on the 20th ult.,....of a full grown male child, found on the previous evening in a cow house, near the town, by the side of the new Bodmin road, belonging to Samuel Hawke. It appeared, that Samuel Hawke having gone to the cow house on the Friday evening, to give the cows some meal, while in the act of removing the stale fodder, discovered concealed amongst it a new born male child, quite dead, with a string tied tightly around its neck. He immediately conveyed it to the Union House, where it was taken in charge by....one of the relieving officers. Suspicion having fallen on a young woman,....a native of Polruan, near Fowey, but who has been living in this neighbourhood for nearly a twelvemonth, and who had repeatedly been charged by her landlady and several others with being in a family way, which she always denied, even on the very night of her delivery, she was taken into custody at her lodgings near Carveth, and removed to the *General Wolfe Inn*, in this town, where she still remains. While going from her lodgings to the Inn, she confessed she had given birth to the child alone in a field about 120 yards from the cow house, and had laid it by the side of the hedge, slightly covered over with grass; that the next morning she came over to J. Hawke, and said she would go a milking for him that morning, when she removed the child to the place where it was found. T.Vawdry, surgeon, who had made a *post mortem* examination of the child, proved to the satisfaction of the Jury that the child was born alive, but died from being strangled. The mother not being in a fit state for the jury to see, the inquest was adjourned to the General Wolfe Inn, on Friday the 26th ult., when....a verdict was returned that the child was born alive, but died of strangulation....by.... his mother.

5 July (RCG) CORNWALL MIDSUMMER SESSIONS. *Michael Gill*, 42, was indicted for embezzling the sum of 4*l*.7s. 6 1/2d., the property of his master, Joseph Thomas Treffry, Esq.... It appears that prisoner had been in Mr. Treffry's employ, for upwards of two years, first as shepherd, and then also acting in the capacity of hind. In the latter capacity, he sold cattle, & received the money, for which he was accustomed to account to his master. In March and April last, he sold 9 sheep to a butcher called William Hicks, of Fowey, which were delivered, three at a time, in three following weeks. On the 13th of April, Hicks paid prisoner for the nine sheep, 13*l*.2s.7 1/2d., and was about entering the whole sheep in one bill, but prisoner requested him to put the sheep in three bills - three in a bill, as they had been delivered, observing that his master was very particular, and wished to have a bill each week for the sheep delivered. Mr. Hicks did so, paying him the whole amount. On the evening of the same day, prisoner went to Mr. Treffry's, and handed to a female servant *two* bills only, and the sum of £8 15s.1d., the amount of those two, telling the servant, that those two bills were for *three* weeks' sheep, two each week; but as he had received the money at *two* different times there were only two bills. On being particularly questioned by Mr. Treffry, he persisted in the same story, till Mr Treffry said to prisoner, I have inquired of Mr. Hicks, who tells me that he gave you *three* bills, three sheep in each; and you have withheld one bill and the money;" when prisoner replied that he had received three bills, but had lost one; but he had the money.- The evidence of the prosecutor, Mr. Hicks, Mary Barnicoat, the prosecutor's servant, and Mr. Jas. Whitford, was then taken; after which, Mr. Stokes made an able defence for prisoner, in an address to the Jury. Verdict, *Guilty.* (Sentence, 15 months hard labour.)

26 July (RCG) FOWEY. The drift boats here bring in from 1 to 2000 fine pilchards every day, and the prospect for a good season is very encouraging.

30 August (RCG) FOWEY.- *Smuggling.*- On the 27th inst, was found concealed in an orchard, at Coombe, near Fowey, 95 kegs of Spirits of Brandy. On the Coast Guard approaching the place of deposit, a man was observed to run off. He was pursued, but succeeded in making his escape into the plantation of Wm. Rashleigh, Esq. of Menabilly. The goods are quite fresh, and considered not to have been landed but a few hours.

18 October (RCG) FOWEY.- *Shipwreck.*- On Thursday morning, the wreck of a vessel and her boat were washed ashore at Lantic beach, about two miles east of this harbour. The boat was marked *Elijah Jewell*, the vessel's name *Comet* of Southampton. Her cargo was flour and hoops, and the sacks were marked W. and J. Clark, Botley mill, of which about 100 are washed in by the surf, the flour destroyed by the salt water. The crew are all drowned. On Tuesday afternoon they were observed from the hills floating in Lantic Bay, and a boat put out from Polruan to pick them up.

1 November NOCTURNAL DEPREDATIONS.- On Monday night last, at Fowey, some villains not supposed to belong to that place, threw Mr. William Frost's beer cart over the quay, into the tide, and broke it, - pulled down a window shutter, and broke a pane of glass at the "Commercial" Inn, and pulled down the sign at the "Sailors Return" Inn. It is hoped they will yet be discovered, and punished as they deserve.

1845

8 August (RCG) AFFRAY WITH SMUGGLERS. On Friday night last, as Piper, one of the coast guard men belonging to the Fowey station, under the command of Lieut. Hooper, R.N., was on duty on the beaches near the Harbour's mouth, he observed a party of smugglers landing a cargo of contraband goods, and made signal, by firing his pistol, for assistance. He immediately received a severe blow on the head from a large stone, which completely stunned him for the moment. As soon as he recovered his senses, he found himself surrounded by a host of smugglers, some of whom were binding him with cords, whilst others were holding a consultation as to whether they should beat out his brains or drown him. After binding him hand and foot, they drew him to the water's edge, when fortunately some of the boat's crew arrived and discharged their arms at the smugglers, who decamped with great haste, leaving their booty behind. Had not assistance arrived in a short space after Piper was dragged to the beach, he would in all probability have been drowned. The poor fellow resisted most gallantly, and cried aloud for someone to *cut him adrift..* His pistols and cutlass were found the next day nearly at low water where they were flung by the smugglers, after he had made signal of alarm. Ninety two tubs of spirits and a large boat, were secured. - We are sorry to say that Piper has been confined to his bed ever since the affray. Such gallant conduct on the part of a Coast Guard man deserves the highest commendation, and we doubt not that the poor fellow will receive the reward he so justly merits from the proper quarter.

19 September (RCG) DEATH FROM BURNING. On Thursday last, an inquest was held....at Lanteglos by Fowey, on the body of John Welch. It appeared that the mother and father of deceased went to work in a harvest field, at six in the morning, leaving home three children, the eldest only six years old. They went to school as usual, and in the evening they were seen, leading each other, going towards their home. The mother returned about 8 o'clock in the evening, when she discovered her little boy burnt in a most dreadful way at her door, and quite dead. The little girl said she was lighting the fire to boil the kettle for tea, when the youngest child, 18 months old, pushed her little brother who was helping to light the fire. Immediately his apron caught fire, and the poor little fellow ran to the door, enveloped in flames. His sister said she poured a pint of water over, and then cried herself asleep. Verdict, 'Accidental death.'

111

19 September (RCG) Wanted a Master and Mistress *For the NATIONAL SCHOOL recently built at POLRUAN, in Lanteglos by Fowey.* At present, and for the next three years, a Salary of £25 a year is payable to the Instructors, over and above the payments from the Children, which from the population of this Village will probably amount to a considerable sum. Applications to be made to the Rev. J. Kendall, vicar of Lanteglos.

17 October (RCG) Apple stealing - On the 11th inst. Jenifer Jago, 71, Jenifer Climo, her daughter, Grace Hosken, Hannah Collins, and Elizabeth Netherton, all married women, were committed by the Rev. J. Kempe to Bodmin gaol for two months, for stealing apples from J.T.Treffry, Esq. of Place, their employer. This proceeding and punishment of the parties, it is hoped will operate as a caution to all persons similarly employed. - The five had been cautioned, but repeated the offence of stealing from their master, and are committed accordingly.

21 November (RCG) On the 16th inst., the *Good Intent* Warburton master, which sailed from this port about six weeks since for St. Johns, New Brunswick, and was 1800 miles on her voyage, returned to this port, having met with a hurricane, in which she shipped a sea which broke over the mast head of the ship, carried away foremast with all the rigging and sails, sprung main mast and boom sprit, carried away the boats, broke five beams, and knocked the ship on her beam ends. Very great praise is due both the master and his crew, for their construction of jury masts and other necessary tackle, and for their united efforts in bringing the ship to land.

21 November (RCG) POTATO BREAD. The Royal Agricultural Improvement Society of Ireland have published directions for making wholesome food from diseased potatoes.... The potatoes are to be well washed, and then grated down....into a tub half full of water. When the pulp has settled completely down, the dirty reddish water is to be poured off, and fresh water poured on. The pulp is to be well stirred up again, allowed to settle, and the liquor again poured off. If the water is still discoloured, a third washing is to be used, but two will generally suffice. The wet pulp, containing all the starch, is now taken out, and freed from water by draining and pressing it. A third of its weight of oatmeal is then to be added, with sufficient salt for flavour, and the mass being rolled into a thin cake, is to be baked in an oven, or on a griddle, till it is dry and slightly burned. The cake will keep a long time without souring or spoiling if kept dry. A good plan is to string them, and hang them from the ceiling near the fire. Or the pulp may be dried without the oatmeal and without letting it brown, and the pure potato meal, thus obtained, will keep, if preserved from damp, and may be used in making broth or soup....

12 December (RCG) On Tuesday the 8th inst., Thos. Roach, a young man, and one of the crew of the *Richard Carnall* of Fowey, Dungey master, on her voyage from Wales, when off St. Ives, went out to hand the jib, when the vessel lurched, and threw him off his feet into the sea. Notwithstanding every effort was made to save him, he was drowned. This young man was of good disposition, and very kind to his mother, who is a widow. (Roach was from Fowey).

1846

9 January (RCG) FOWEY.- The schooner *Mary Pope* of Waterford, Barnes master, with a cargo of guano from Ichaboe, arrived here on the 1st inst. in a most distressed state: her crew completely worn out by sickness and fatigue, having been more than four months on her passage - her sails all split, indeed the whole concern in a most deplorable condition. She was boarded the previous night off the Deadman in the most noble manner, in a heavy gale of wind, by the pilots from Mevagissey, and but for this timely assistance she must have been lost. From the worn out condition of her crew, hope had completely left them, one man being laid up with a fractured arm and reduced to a skeleton by scurvy. We trust that the pilots will be well rewarded for their gallant conduct, not only as relates to their boarding her in a gale of wind, but also for their moral courage in venturing their lives when sickness was on board, not knowing but that the disease might be infectious, the yellow flag being hoisted. This vessel left Newcastle in August 1844, with a cargo for Carthagena, manned with ten hands. There she lost one by the upsetting of her boat; at Ichaboe, three more by a similar accident, *two of them sons of the master;* one died of scurvy on the passage home. The master speaks of the great kindness he experienced from the masters of various vessels he met with, who liberally supplied him with vegetables, and such fresh provisions as they had got, and had it not been for these timely supplies, the whole of the crew in all probability, would have died. To such a deplorable pass had it come, that one man actually devoured more than the half of a cabbage raw, cut up into small pieces, because his mouth was so very sore - his desire after it being so great that he could not wait for its being cooked. They all speak with surprise at the rapidity of their improvement, when they got a supply of vegetables. - The return of this vessel is quite a matter of surprise, for Mr Lowry, master of the *Eliza*, of Fowey, told his owner on his arrival at Liverpool of the distressed state of the vessel, and said he did not expect anything else than that she would be lost,- The master of the *Mary Pope* says, that Mr Lowry strove all he could in a most heavy gale of wind, to get to them to render assistance, and only left them when there was no hope of doing so. Mr Lowry's vessel arrived at Liverpool some weeks ago.

- On Sunday last, the captain, his mate, and his crew, assembled themselves with the dense congregation of our church, to present their praises and thanksgivings to Almighty God, for delivering them from their great distress, even when they had given up all for lost; .... and for now anchoring them in a port of safety.

23 January (RCG) FOWEY.-ACCIDENT.- On Sunday, the 18th instant, Samuel Bickle, an apprentice to the owner of the barque *Good Intent*, and three of his companions, named Jolly, Puckey, and Cullis, went up the river in a sailing-boat, and on their return, just below Golant, the boat with a sudden wind capsized. Puckey and Cullis clung to the boat; Jolly swam to the shore; and melancholy to state, Bickle, a young man about 19, was drowned. His body has not yet been found.

30 January (RCG) ICHABOE GUANO. TO BE SOLD BY AUCTION, on Thursday the 5th February next, at 12 o'Clock, at Mr. Lowry's Stores, Fowey, a Prime Cargo of GUANO. About 200 Tons, direct from Ichaboe, and now landing from the Schooner *Mary Pope*, J.C. Barnes, master. *To be Sold in Lots of 25 Tons.* This Cargo is of very excellent quality, and may be seen at any time on application....

6 February (RCG) FOWEY.- On Sunday morning, the smack *William Amelia*, of Fowey, was discovered on the rocks at the eastern end of Whitsand Bay, but how she came there is not known. The crew consisting of three persons, perished. The vessel, which was laden with limestone, is a total wreck.(Fowey masters, Lanteglos and St. Veep owners)

3 April (RCG) ACCIDENT.- On the 30th ult. the *Adelaide*, Harris master, from Plymouth with a general cargo, while working into Fowey harbour, struck on a rock, by which she filled, and a considerable part of her cargo became damaged.

22 May (RCG) FOWEY.- The experimental squadron has been cruising up and down channel during the week. On Thursday the ships were within 3 or 4 miles of the shore, and presented a grand sight in the bay, being an unusual scene on this part of the coast.

26 June (RCG) FOWEY. - FATAL ACCIDENT. - On Thursday, as Robert Jamieson, servant to Mr. Illingworth, surgeon, was putting the horse in a gig at the higher part of the town, near the Commercial Inn, before he had time to get hold of the reins, the horse started down the hill with great speed, till it came in contact with a house at the corner leading to the rope-walk, with tremendous crash, knocking the gig to pieces, and by the sudden and violent concussion, caused poor Jamieson's death on Sunday.

3 July (RCG) Thomasine Mutton, 40, was charged with having stolen on the 30th of May, a quarter of a pound of loaf sugar from the shop of Mr David Couch, grocer, of Fowey. - Guilty, but recommended to mercy by the prosecutor and jury. Sentence 1 month hard labour.

17 July (RCG) FOWEY REGATTA. - On Tuesday last, day appointed for this annual fete, the town of Fowey presented a scene of unusual gaiety. The town and harbour were decorated with colours to a great extent; the weather was uncommonly fine. At an early hour might be seen groups of pedestrians, carriages, and vehicles of all descriptions, proceeding towards the scene of the appointed festivities. At eleven o'clock, the race commenced between several rowing boats, and it was remarked by an old and experienced seaman, that he never saw such strength and activity as were displayed by some young men of the port. There were several yachts from Plymouth and the neighbouring places all dressed in colors; and the number of visitors was greater than on any former occasion. The *Drake* steamer from Plymouth was crowded with passengers. There was an excellent brass band on board, which continued to enliven the company throughout the day. The *Dart* steamer was also present with passengers from Truro and its neighbourhood. She was saluted on her arrival by a gun from the *Drake*, which was answered from the town. A gig and punt chase closed the amusements, and all appeared delighted with the proceedings of the day.

7 August (RCG) THUNDER STORM. - A heavy thunder storm visited Fowey, and its neighbourhood, on the morning of the 30th ult., when a fine Colt was killed by lightning, in a field belonging to Mr. Rogers, of Trenant; the animal was worth 30 Guineas.

14 August (RCG) FOWEY. - Fire and Caution. - On Monday, a hay-rick containing nearly 100 tons of excellent hay, the property of J.T. Treffry, Esq, took fire from spontaneous heating, and was entirely destroyed. A similar rick, standing near the burning one, was taken away to an adjoining field by the exertions of the men, women, and children present. The destruction of this rick affords a valuable caution. Good hay always heats, and if the rick be large, there is danger of its taking fire; but this danger is effectively and easily prevented by the simple expedient of making one or two chimneys in the rick, by which the excessive heat is carried off. Mr. Treffry had been in the practice of using this precaution (the chimneys being easily made with a few faggots of wood) and the hay had always turned out well. Unfortunately, at the last haymaking season, he was too ill to see that his orders were attended to; and though he gave his hind positive directions to use the accustomed precautions, the man neglected to do so, and afterwards turned a deaf ear to every warning of the consequence which has now taken place.

14 August (RCG) THE FISHERY. FOWEY. - On Monday, two of our seans shot at large shoals of fish. The *Albion* has taken up 200 hogsheads, the *Valletort*, only 50; for unfortunately, a vessel, the *Stephen Knight*, put out of the harbour, ran into the sean, and parted the head rope, by which a quantity of fish, estimated at from 400 to 500 hogsheads, escaped.

11 September (RCG) EXCURSION OF THE ROYAL PARTY TO FOWEY.... At eight o'clock on Tuesday morning, the Royal Squadron took their departure from Falmouth, and at half-past ten entered the harbour of Fowey. To speak of the exultation and cheers of the multitudes is only to repeat the tale whenever the Queen of England appears. The barge was immediately manned, and her Majesty and the Prince landed at the Broad Slip, which was tastefully decorated with evergreens, and richly carpetted. A royal carriage had been previously landed from the *Garland*, and her Majesty and the Prince drove off, attended by William Rashleigh, Esq., of Menabilly, J.T. Treffry, Esq., of Place, with other gentlemen of the neighborhood, in their respective carriages, to the glorious and far renowned ruin of Restormel Castle....The Royal Party afterwards visited the valuable iron mines on the Duchy property in the neighborhood. Her Majesty, and Prince Albert, with one of her ladies, and three gentlemen, went underground in a tram wagon which was lined with straw, and covered with green baize. They went into the Mine about 270 fathoms. Her Majesty and the Prince got out of the wagon to inspect the workings on the lode, and the Prince himself broke some ore with a pick....So greatly were the Royal party interested that not till 3 o'clock did they return to Fowey, when they drove through

Place Walk to the beautiful and unique mansion of Mr. Treffry. Not so much on account of its architecture, though this for its character and finish might well deserve even Royal notice, but on a consideration of far more interest to a Lord Warden, and a guardian of the Duke of Cornwall, would this mansion repay the attention of its illustrious visitors. Its intelligent and energetic proprietor and restorer, in the spirit of a true-hearted Cornishman, has formed its ornaments from the productions of his native County, proving that our own quarries will afford as rich materials as the most costly importations from foreign lands. The Royal Party remained for some time inspecting the magnificent building, both within and without, and both her Majesty & the Prince were delighted with the Porphyry, Jasper, and different polished Granites. The Prince especially admired the Porphyry hall. The stone, which fully equals, both in color and polish, the best specimens from Egypt, was raised among the rocks of the County, and wrought certainly not without much labor, at a mill upon Mr. Treffry's mine, the Fowey Consols.

The following address from the inhabitants of Fowey was presented by Mr. Treffry, and generously received:- *To the Queen's Most Excellent Majesty.* We, the Inhabitants of the ancient Borough of Fowey and its vicinity, humbly approach your Majesty with our sincere congratulations on your Majesty's arrival in "faithful Cornwall," and with the warm expressions of our dutiful attachment to your Majesty's person and government.

Five hundred years ago, the gallant ships of Foy conveyed an armament to the siege of Calais, under the command of their brave townsman Frisart Bagga, more numerous and formidable than the grand harbour of Plymouth could then supply.

Though time and circumstances have since reduced our ability and importance, we still beg to assure your Majesty that the loyal inhabitants of Fowey and its vicinity will always be ready to support the mild and maternal government of your Majesty with zealous and affectionate fidelity.

And we entreat the Giver of all power and pre-eminence among men, by whom alone Queens reign and Princes decree justice, to bless your Majesty and your Royal Consort with long life and prosperity, and to establish your royal progeny upon the throne of these realms to the latest generation."

From Place House, the Royal party returned down the lawn leading to the churchyard, and through the town to the Broadslip, where they re-embarked; and amidst the ringing of bells, music, and huzzas from the voices of thousands, took leave for the present of their ancient Duchy, the loyal and 'faithful Cornwall'.

2 October (RCG) FOWEY. - Tuesday last was a day of general rejoicing on account of the celebration of the royal visit to this town. Crowds of all classes assembled together, and in an orderly manner paraded the principal streets of the town, preceded by Emidy's Band. At the Broadslip they halted, for the purpose of new naming that place - the landing place of the Queen and Royal party on the 8th ult. It was with due form and ceremony named "Victoria steps" and "Albert quay." At the town hall, all the poorer inhabitants were plentifully regaled with good tea and cake, and about 100 of the inhabitants, chiefly trades people, dined at Sparnall's Ship Inn, where every provision for the festive occasion was served in Sparnall's excellent style, and all faces appeared happy; the town, the hall and dining room were elegantly decorated with evergreens gathered from the plantation of Wm. Rashleigh, Esq. of Menabilly. The usual loyal toasts were heartily drunk by "One and All" the faithful Cornishmen present.- We understand it is proposed to erect by subscription among the inhabitants, a suitable memorial of Her Majesty's visit.

1847

22 January (RCG) From this time, till the Spring vegetables shall begin to come in abundantly, there will and must be severe suffering. Even persons with moderate incomes feel the pressure, since the chief necessities of life are so greatly advanced in price, and the inferior substitutes are not to be obtained. How great, then, the sufferings of the Poor.... In past seasons, the industrious Cottager or Miner could rely on his potato crop in aid of his wages. With store of potatoes, the pig fed with the refuse of the crop, and a few hundreds of fish salted by in the Autumn, his winter comforts were secured; but his crops have failed, and he has nothing but his wages to rely on, with bread nearly double its usual price. The conduct of the poor in Cornwall under their present sufferings has been most admirable.... Reading the Calendar for the late Quarter Sessions....there was not a theft which appeared to have been caused by want.... Nothing is to be expected from Lord Russell and his party; and our County Lunatic Asylum would accommodate all who would yet place confidence in Peel....

22 January (RCG) Last week, it was discovered that delegates from other mines had visited Par Consols, and very soon there was a rumour abroad that all the miners from Fowey Consols and Par Consols, intended to proceed to Par, with a view of preventing a vessel from leaving the harbour, which was laden with corn. The news, however, having reached the ears of J.T. Treffry, Esq., the principal proprietor of the said mines, he immediately adopted such measures as to secure the ship being put to seas without being at all molested; but on Saturday morning, Mr. Treffry learned that none of the miners at Par Consols had gone underground....he immediately proceeded there....and enquired what grievance they had to complain of, at the same time stating to them his regret that their wages at present were very low considering the high price which is asked for corn; but he satisfied them, from the standard being so low, and the mine so deep and expensive, that the adventurers were not realizing one shilling....The Tributers again cheerfully took their pitches and resumed their work....

5 February (RCG) FOWEY. The Lords of the Treasury, in accordance with a memorial from the merchants and ship owners of this port, have granted the privileges of bonding and warehousing foreign goods. Stores are to be erected,....and probably, as most of the timber that will be required for the Cornwall Railway will be landed here, all vessels bound over sea will thus be enabled to be supplied with stores for their voyages on the spot free of duty. The merchants in all the neighbouring towns, no doubt, will be glad to know that the privilege of bonding foreign goods is now brought almost to their doors.

26 February (RCG) On Friday, the 19th inst., an inquest was held....at the Sailor's Return Inn, Fowey, on the body of John Seward, a fine youth, an apprentice on board of the barque *Alicio*, of Plymouth which was lying alongside of the barque *Augusta*, of Bideford. It appeared the *Alicia* was hailed by the master from the shore, near to where the ship was lying, but their boat did not happen to be alongside at the time, when the deceased proceeded to go on board the *Augusta*, for the boat belonging to that ship, and in doing so, he slipped between the two ships, fell into the water, and almost immediately sank. Drags, &c. were immediately used, but the body was not recovered until two hours afterwards. Verdict accordingly....

21 May (RCG) Liskeard- In consequence of rumours concerning assemblages of miners at Callington market, on Wednesday, & at Wadebridge and other places, respecting the high prices of corn, there was not one bushel of wheat or barley in our market, the last market day. The prices at which farmers in the neighbourhood have sold have been: Wheat, 25s. to 27s.-Barley, 13s.- Oats, 11s. per bushel.- Beef, 7d. to 7 1/2d.- Mutton 6 1/2d. to 7d.- Pork, 7 1/2d. to 8d.- Butter 9 1/2d. to 11d.- Potatoes, from 1s. to 16d. per 10 lb.- Eggs, 20 for a shilling.

2 July (RCG) Cornwall Midsummer Sessions. Frances Wetter, 16, was charged with stealing, at Fowey, on the 2nd of June, a pair of stays, shift, pair of drawers, black veil, and piece of ribbon, the property of Elizabeth Moss.... Elizabeth Moss, an assistant in Mr Tregenna's shop, at Fowey....gave evidence.... Other witnesses were also called, and the prisoner was found *guilty*. (Sentenced to six months hard labour)

16 July (RCG) Fowey. - His Royal Highness Prince Albert....has been pleased to patronise the Fowey Regatta advertised for the 20th inst. He has also subscribed 10*l*. to the funds, and with the other subscriptions which have been so liberally given, and which are at the disposal of a well organised committee, it is anticipated that the approaching regatta will be one of the best ever witnessed.

10 December (RCG) CHLOROFORM. This new agent for the prevention of pain, was tried at the Royal Cornwall Infirmary, on Tuesday last, in the presence of almost all the medical practitioners of Truro, with the most satisfactory results. The first patient operated on, was a young woman, from whose arm a tumour was removed, ...without occasioning the slightest pain, nor was she conscious of the stitch inserted afterwards....

1848

18 February (RCG) MELANCHOLY SHIPWRECK.- On the 9th instant, the smack *Louisa*, of Fowey, was wrecked near Bury. The names of those of the crew who were drowned are Richard Salt, of Fowey; R. Simmons and --- Quiller, of Polperro; and a boy named Hosken of Bodinnoc. The master, Mr. Thomas Dyer, who is the principal owner of the vessel, remained at home, in consequence of having injured his shoulder on a previous voyage.

17 March (RCG) FOWEY HARBOUR. The importance of the above harbour or refuge has been exemplified in a striking manner during the late severe gales.... Ships overtaken in the gales which have blown with such violence, have found it secure and offering every facility. From the manner in which the port is laid down in the charts, and referred to in books of instructions, several captains, on a pilot putting off, have, with the greatest difficulty, been persuaded that their lives would be saved, or their ships if they made for the port, and when the persuasions of the pilots has prevailed over the little information with which many masters of vessels are furnished, astonishment has been expressed at the safety and entirely land-locked character of the harbour. In the dreadful gale of Nov. 1824, several were seen in distress between St. Anthony Point and the Ramehead. No pilot could give them any assistance, and it was imagined that no one on board those ships knew any thing of the harbour of Fowey, but one person was acqauinted with it, and his captain gave him in charge. He put before the wind and entered the harbour in safety, when, melancholy to relate, *every one* of the other ships went ashore on the following night with the loss of the greatest part of their crews..... Fowey harbour is one of the finest in Great Britain, equal to any on the south coast. Vessels of large tonnage can lie afloat at low water with a safe anchorage, and even, without an anchor or cable on board, they can be securely ladged.... Vessels....during a heavy southerly gale, may always find safety *by running for this port even without an anchor on board.*

17 March (RCG) FATAL ACCIDENT AT FOWEY.- On Tuesday night, the 7th inst., two young men named John Palmer and Thomas Smith, belonging to the brig *Water Kelpie* of Sunderland, were going on board with 3 others, their shipmates, in a canoe - the kind of boat which they were not accustomed to use, and which was too small to contain so many persons. When about half way from the shore to the vessel, a distance of about 150 yards, she capsized; when Palmer and Smith, two fine young men, were drowned; the other three miraculously saved themselves; one clung to a small rock, another to the canoe, and the other swam on shore. - The bodies of those drowned have not yet been picked up. (Their bodies were picked up two weeks later, and identified by means of their clothes, and buried at Fowey. Palmer was 19, Smith was 21.)

17 March (RCG) On Friday the 18th, a young man called William Rich, in the employ of Mr. Marshall, residing at the mills at Penpoll, was drowned in Penpoll river by the upsetting of a boat in a sudden gust of wind, which was laden with faggot wood. - William Murray, his workfellow, nearly shared the same fate.

9 June (RCG) ACCIDENT.- On the 2nd inst., as Mr. Sparnall and Mr. G. Thomas, of Fowey, were returning from St. Austell in a gig, on passing over the east end of Par bridge, the horse took fright at the sudden appearance of a girl driving a wheel barrow, when one of the wheels of the gig came in contact with a stake or piece of wood that was driven in the ground, by which the gig was upset, and Mr. Sparnall and Mr. Thomas thrown out with considerable force. The former escaped with a slight injury of his wrist, and a few bruises; but in consequence of Mr. Thomas having got his arm entangled with the reins, he was dragged a short distance on the road, and but for the prompt and energetic means used by Mr. Sparnall in bringing the horse to a stand, the accident would in all probability have been fatal.

7 July (RCG) TRECAN BENCH.- Thomas Kendall was....charged by Overseers of Lanteglos, with having neglected to maintain his wife and two children, who had consequently become chargeable to that parish. The prisoner, who was respectably dressed, was formerly assistant overseer of the parish. For the last 12 months he has kept a school in St. Blazey, and besides this is in the receipt of an annuity of 10*l*. a year. He was committed for one month hard labour.

Mr. John Smith, surgeon, of Polruan, appeared to answer the complaint of Mr. S. Langmaid, overseer of Lanteglos, for assaulting him on the 10th June last. It appeared from the witnesses examined, that the parties met in the evening that day, at the Russell Inn, in Polruan. Mr. Smith began to be very abusive, and at length struck Langmaid a hard blow, with a walking stick, and broke in his hat. Smith was fined 8s.6d. and 1*l*. 1s. 6d. costs.

18 August (RCG) SAVING CORN IN DAMP WEATHER.- The following suggestions by Mr. J. Prideaux, the well-known agriculturist....the continued wet weather of the present harvest season, induces us to publish;.... A field of white oats, near this town, was cut wet, and the weather continuing the same, was at last stacked in layers, with dry straw between. On taking abroad the rick, the grain was found in excellent condition, not sprouted or damaged in any way.... In this way thousands of acres might have been saved which have been left to sprout on the ground; and where straw is all used up, other dry stalks, or even shavings, might answer. Where no dry straw, &c. is to be had, it may be dried in sheaf; either by a simple kiln, as in Russia, &c,...or without the risk of fire, by lime, as follows: - If the rick be made hollow, with the grain turned inward, a sufficient quantity of fresh quicklime placed within; and then all closed in from bottom to top, and covered over to exclude the external air, the lime will rapidly dry the air within, which will as rapidly draw moisture from the corn...as quicklime will absorb about one-third its weight of water, a ton of lime will....probably dry 6 or 7 tons of corn and straw. For all this water must come from the corn if the external air is well excluded, and the lime raised from the soil by a bed of stones, gravel, or straw. The lime must not of course touch the corn, and therefore room should be left for it to swell in stacking and for turning it over, to slake all through; and a sort of a doorway must be left on the side of the rick, which can be opened for putting in the lime, and for turning it over; but must be closed up immediately, and kept close, except at those moments.

18 August (RCG) FOWEY.- Good catches of fine pilchards are brought in daily, and sold at 1s.3d. per hundred of 120.

13 October (RCG) FOWEY TOWN-HALL, Oct. 10; before J.T. Treffry, Esq and John Kempe, Clerk.- Mr. Wm. Macpherson appeared to a summons and information charging him with having concealed in his dwelling-house (which he occupies at this place for the accommodation of his daughter Mrs. David Couch) 18 lbs. of foreign tobacco, which was seized by Lieut. Young of the Coast Guard on the 22nd ult. He was convicted in the penalty of 25*l*. with a recommendation by the magistrates to the Hon. Commissioner of her Majesty's Customs that it be mitigated to 5*l*. as they consider that he had not a guilty knowledge of the transaction....

20 October (RCG) RIVER FOWEY. The Rev. R. G. Grylls addressed some queries to Mr. Kendall, as Conservator of the River Fowey, on the subject of the scarcity of salmon in that river, during past years. - Mr. Kendall replied that....the fishery, some years ago, was very valuable; the reason why the fish were now so scarce was from the effect of the mineral waters. There was very little poaching....there were no fish to poach.

27 October (RCG) DIET DURING THE PREVALENCE OF CHOLERA. - (drawn up by a Doctor) *Breakfast.-* Bread baked the previous day, toasted bread, biscuit rusk, with butter; an egg boiled, 3 1/2 minutes; mutton chop; cold chicken. - To drink: tea, coffee, milk, and water. *Dinner.* - Mutton, boiled or roasted; roast beef; eggs, boiled or poached; boiled or roast fowl; tripe; rabbit; minced veal; sago; tapioca; arrowroot; semolina; rice; rice milk; bread; biscuit; light puddings; mealy potatoes. - To drink: weak brandy-and-water; bitter ale; sherry and water; porter; stout. *Tea.* - Bread and butter; dry toast; rusk; plain seed-cake; biscuit. - To drink coffee; black tea. If anything required for luncheon or supper, it may consist of a few oysters or a small mutton chop, with bread. A few glasses of good wine, port, sherry, or madiera, spiced negus, warm brandy, or rum and water may be taken with discretion during the day.... A light meal should be taken every fourth or fifth hour. Much fat should be avoided. Great care should be taken to properly masticate the food, and to rest a certain time after meals.

27 October (RCG)An inquest was held....in the parish of Lanteglos....on the body of a little boy called John Martin, who was the son of a miller, and whilst playing in the upper story of the mill-house fell on one of the wheels and was instantly crushed to death. His father who was in the next floor heard him cry 'father' as he was falling, but before he could get to him his clothes became entangled in the wheel and his head coming in contact with a large board, he was in an instant killed.-Verdict, 'accidental death.' (Trethake).

17 November (RCG) On the 13th inst., an inquest was held by Mr. Hamley at Fowey, on Martha Southern, a girl 16 years old (an idiot). Her mother had left her alone to go into a neighbour's house. She had not been gone long, when she heard a noise in her house, and on going in, with some others, found the room full of smoke. Not seeing the girl, she went up stairs, and there saw her with her clothes burning, and the bed likewise on fire. It is supposed that she must have got to the fire after her mother left, and by some means caught herself on fire, and then ran up stairs and got into bed, which she likewise caught on fire. Luckily the fire was soon got under, but the poor girl was so burnt, that she died the next day. Verdict "Accidental death."

1 December (RCG) FOWEY - SMUGGLING - Cornelius Pill, mate, and Edward Jones, a seaman, of the smack *Lavinia* of Fowey, from Guernsey, appeared before the magistrates at Fowey, on Tuesday, 28th Nov., the former to answer to a charge of having concealed two bottles of spirits with intent to defraud the revenue, and the latter with having stuffed a pair of bellows, with tea and cigars, for the same unlawful purpose.... Lieut. Wise, of H.M. cutter *Fox*, deposed to having boarded the *Lavinia* on Sunday last, immediately on her entering the harbour, and ordered his crew to rummage the vessel, when they discovered the spirit produced, which was owned by the mate Pill. - Mr. Peach, tide-surveyor and searcher at the port of Fowey, proved having received, as found, the bellows with contents as produced. The magistrate convicted Pill in the mitigated penalty of 25s. and costs, and Jones in 20s. and costs.- Patrick Bulgar, a seaman of the barque *Royal Adelaide* arrived from Quebec, was convicted on the previous day in the mitigated penalty of 20s. and costs for having smuggled tobacco. - Two apprentices belonging to the same vessel were remanded until Monday next on a charge of smuggling 15 lbs of tobacco. (*Lavinia* had Fowey Masters and was Fowey owned).

8 December (RCG) The apprentices belonging to the *Royal Adelaide*, William Hill and Richard Collings, who were remanded last week on a charge of smuggling tobacco, were on Monday last convicted in the penalty of £100, and in default of payment were committed to the County gaol for six months. It appears that the law makes every person guilty of smuggling who is found on board a ship in which goods liable to duty are concealed.--On Thursday, the 30th ult., the barque *Good Intent* arrived here from Quebec, soon after which the whole of the crew were taken into custody, for having 200 lbs. of tobacco concealed in the different parts of the ship. On the next day they were brought before the magistrates, and were remanded until Friday the 8th inst., when further proceedings will be taken against them.

8 December (RCG) ROBBERY.- On Sunday evening, the 4th inst., while Mr. and Mrs. Salt, of Fowey, were at chapel, some felon entered their dwelling-house, and stole therefrom £30 in sovereigns and half-sovereigns. From the manner in which the robbery was effected, it is supposed that some one well acquainted with the premises is the thief.

15 December (RCG) On Friday last, the crew of the barque *Good Intent*, who, on the 2nd inst., were remanded, were again brought before the magistrates at the Town Hall.... They all admitted having been on board at the time; were convicted in the penalty of 100*l*. and in default of payment they were all, 19 in number, committed to gaol for six months, notwithstanding that one of the crew owned most of the tobacco found, and pleaded guilty of having concealed the same. Memorials praying for the immediate release of the innocent parties, have been forwarded to the Secretary of State, and to the Honourable the Commissioners of H.M. Customs. The names of the crew are, John Warburton, master; John Thomas, mate; John Roberts, 2nd mate; William Richards, steward; Thomas Couch, carpenter; Martin Ridmore, Thomas Bottle, Charles Beard, William Bray, John Pinnock, Richard Davies, Henry Longmaid, John Lamerton, William and Thomas Fookes, Frank Marr, Thomas Hicks, Joseph Willington, the 4 last mentioned being apprentices.

22 December (RCG) Capt. Warburton, who was recently convicted in the penalty of £100 by the magistrates, for being on board the barque *Good Intent*,....and paid the penalty in full to prevent his being sent to prison, with 18 of his crew, including his apprentices, has had that sum refunded to him, by order of the Hon. Commissioners of H.M. Customs....the 4 apprentices, have also been ordered to be immediately released and taken out of prison. (Captain Warburton was local).

29 December (RCG).... 9 of the crew of the barque *Good Intent*, who were committed on the 9th inst., by the magistrates, to prison for 6 months, for being on board the said vessel, when 224 lbs. of tobacco were found, were released and taken out of prison early on Christmas day, in a vehicle drawn by two horses. They returned to Fowey about one o'clock, just in time to partake of their Christmas dinner, which was kindly donated by Mr. W. Hicks, merchant, and which was served up in Mr. Sparnal's usual style at the Ship Inn. William Hill and Richard Collins, the two apprentices belonging to the *Royal Adelaide*, who were committed for concealing about 15 lbs. tobacco, and three pints of brandy on board that ship, were also released from prison the same day, and all were released by order of the Hon. Commissioners of Her Majesty's Customs, upon the recommendation of the Collector and Comptroller at this port.

1849

5 January (RCG) On Saturday a fine fat bullock and a large quantity of bread were distributed at Menabilly, to upwards of one hundred and sixty poor families residing in the parishes of Tywardreath, Fowey, and Saint Sampsons. And one guinea and a suit of warm clothing and bedding to each of twenty poor widows, inmates of the Rashleigh Alms-houses in Fowey and Tywardreath.

5 January (RCG) CORNWALL EPIPHANY SESSIONS.
MARY ANN HOSKEN, 18, charged with stealing on the 18th of December, at Fowey, nine sovereigns and one half sovereign the property of Thomas Hill. The prosecutor was an old man, nearly 80, a tide waiter, and lodged with a Mrs. Hosken, aunt of the prisoner, who occasionally worked at the house, and sometimes made prosecutor's bed and cleaned his room, thereby having the means of knowing that he kept his money, about 34*l*., in a box under his bed.- The evidence against the prisoner, as concerning the act of robbery itself, was given by the prosecutor, by Mrs. Hosken with whom he lodged, and by Warburton who lived opposite. It was also shown by several witnesses that she had changed sovereigns on the day the money was missed by the prosecutor, although she had but six-pence a week wages. For the defence, the prisoner's mother stated that she gave her a sovereign that day to fetch cream. It was shown, however, that her mother had been formerly convicted of felony - Verdict, *guilty*. Sentence. *Six months hard labour.*

SOPHIA KENDALL, 16, was found GUILTY of stealing, on the 26th of July, about 28s. 6d. in silver and copper coin, various articles of dress and clothing, a gold pin, key, padlock, cigars, &c., the property of Samuel Longmaid, shopkeeper at

Polruan in the parish of Lanteglos by Fowey. The prisoner had been in the prosecutor's service, and when the robbery was detected, and she was charged with the crime, she said "the devil must have been in her;" that she was saving money to go to Guernsey, and that the sweetmeats were for her sister, and the cigars for her father. (Sentence. *Six months hard labour.*

23 February (RCG) A CAUTION TO OVERSEERS - On Tuesday afternoon, a gang of nine Irish mendicants applied to one of the overseers of Fowey, for relief, saying they were starving, and without money. The overseer, not believing all their "blarney," told them to go to a lodging-house, and then went and procured a constable; and judging from their looks that they were far from starvation, he searched the party, and found on them provisions enough for three or four days, and some money besides.

2 March (RCG) Fowey. - THE NAVIGATION LAWS.- On Friday, a meeting, convened by J.T. Treffry, Esq., was held here, to consider the propriety of petitioning both Houses of Parliament against the repeal of the Navigation Laws. Capt. Davis, R.M., presided; and in a very able and lucid speech, showed the effect the repeal of those laws would have on our shipping interests and on commerce, and also the danger in case of invasion, if we had not our own wooden bulwarks manned by our own brave seamen, for our protection .... Captains Smith and Warburton, who were asked for their opinions as experienced men in the foreign trade, stated their belief that the repeal of the Navigation Laws would ruin our commerce, cripple our navy (as our best men are reared in the merchant service), and eventually ruin our country. Resolutions....were unanimously passed by a crowded assemblage of merchants, shipowners, mariners, and others;....petitions are already numerously signed, and will be sent to the Earl of Falmouth and W.H.P. Carew, Esq., for presentation.

23 March (RCG) FAITH IN FORTUNE TELLERS.- At West Looe, on Thursday last, a woman named Mary Vincent, died at an advanced age. This woman had for a great many years carried on a very lucrative business in that town, in "telling fortunes." Great numbers have been in the habit of applying to this imposter, believing she could tell their future destinies, and also to get rid of supposed witchcraft. On the day the old woman died, two young ladies from the neighbourhood of Fowey, called at her house to have their fortunes told; and....left the house sadly disappointed, on finding they were too late.

15 June (RCG) Inquest on the 12th inst., on John Adams, at Fowey, a tide waiter. Mr. Peach, the surveyor of her Majesty's Customs at Fowey, stated that on Sunday morning, about 7 o'clock, he put the deceased on board a vessel called the *Pilot*, Massey master, from Roscou, in charge of her. There were horses and a number of casks on board. He went again about 10 o'clock when he found all was right. He told Adams to assist in getting the horses out, when he (Mr. Peach) left. Mr. Peach went alongside about eleven o'clock at night to make his nightly inspection. He hailed the vessel, but got no answer; on hailing a second time, the master said, "'who's there?" He told him, and asked if Adams was on board. The captain said he did not know.

Mr. Peach then sent Richard Webber, one of his men, on board to see for him, and went himself, when a light was got, and every part of the vessel searched, but he could not be found. On looking into the cabin, Mr. Peach saw his hat. The captain said the last time he saw him, he went on deck, and he heard him walking there; this was after it was dark. All the crew at this time were asleep. He awoke them, and questioned them, when he found that Adams had gone ashore several times during the day, and the master said the last time he came on board he had drunk too much. Every search was made for him in the different public houses in the town, but he could not be found. It appeared now certain that he had fallen overboard and was drowned. On Monday evening, a man called Wellington, who was creeping for the body, pulled him up near where the vessel lay, and brought him ashore. --Several witnesses were examined, who proved to his having been on shore during the day, and that he had drunk rather freely. It was generally supposed that when he was last seen by the captain, he went on deck for a particular purpose, and had fallen overboard. It was clearly proved that he had been on friendly terms with all the crew during the day. There were no marks of violence on the body, and nothing was missing from his person. As there was no direct evidence to show how the accident happened, and the Jury being satisfied that he had not met his death by any illegal or violent means, they returned a verdict of "Found Drowned."

22 June (RCG) We lament to find unmistakable evidence of the reappearance of the Potato Blight, at a much earlier period than in former years, and we fear we must add, in all its malignity....The peculiar character of the Season has doubtless told severely on the enfeebled plant. After a winter of almost unprecedented mildness in the winter months, we had a winter of more than common severity in the spring.... Since that time, we have had extreme and rapid alternations of temperature and weather, most trying to feeble constitutions, whether of man, or of vegetables. Hence probably the earlier appearance of the blight.... A whole field may be diseased weeks before an unpracticed eye would detect other than healthy promise.... And thus the plant may exist, till an extraordinary call is made upon its vital powers, either by the process of blossoming, or some atmospheric change....- barely supporting itself before, it yields to the hurtful impression, and the whole crop goes down at once.

3 August (RCG) FOWEY.-THE FISHERY.- The drift boats bring in good catches of fine pilchards every morning; the prospect is good for the season.

10 August (RCG) TRECAN GATE PETTY SESSIONS. - *Anthony Tucker* of Polruan was fined 2s. 6d. and costs for assaulting Joseph Pearn, shoemaker, on the 9th July.

17 August (WB) Fowey has thus far escaped the scourge which has affected her sister port.(Mevagissey). The place is quite healthy, and a few respectable inhabitants forming a committee....have pursued vigorous measures, and caused the town (though not before dirty) to be rid of any unwholesome place that was found in it, as well as the sewers to be scoured. A fishing boat from unfortunate Mevagissey, landed a man on Fowey Quay,....who had been poorly in his bowels for three or four days previously. Because he was unwell, and from Mevagissey, no one would take him in. He was, however,....taken from the quay, and put on board a boat, some reed, &c., being provided to accommodate him, and persons in another boat were employed to render him assistance as he might require. In the course of the night he died, and was on Sunday sent to Mevagissey for interment. On Tuesday night it was discovered by the populace that the same fishing boat which had landed this man was some where up the river. The people went with boats, and finding it to be so, the boat, with three persons on board, was towed down to the harbour's mouth, and ordered off, with a direction not to come again on pain of being fired on. The committee, however, had no cognizance of this outrage. (Bad outbreak of cholera in Mevagissey that year)

21 September (RCG) The *Chronometer*, Furse master, from London for Trieste, put in here in consequence of the 2nd mate being ill with cholera, of which he died; and a healthy young man, one of the crew, who assisted in doing the last for him, was taken ill and died; and both were committed to the deep. The vessel has since been fumigated, and the remaining portion of the crew, as well as our own town and neighborhood, are in a very healthy condition....

5 October (RCG) FOWEY.- Thursday, the 27th ult., was set apart at Fowey as a day of humiliation and supplication to Almighty God, to remove the pestilence which at present rages in the country. The shops were closed, and business of every kind suspended. At church, the sermon of the morning was preached by the Rev. Mr. Bampfield, (assistant curate) to a large congregation.... The sermon had especial reference to the existence of the cholera, and mentioned many examples of the visitation of sin, by the divine vengence. It also pointed out, in an impressive manner, the efficacy of prayer, repentance, and humiliation, as a means of removing the wrath of the Almighty, and the heavy afflictions consequent upon it. After the sermon, the sacrament was administered to upwards of 70 communicants. In the evening, the Rev. Mr. Ross, of St. Veep, preached.... The dissenting places of worship were well attended and it may be truly said that the day was kept with more then usual solemnity by all classes of the community.

CHAPTER 6
1850-1859

1850

4 January (RCG) FOWEY.- The Christmas charities of J.T. Treffry Esq., which that gentleman has been accustomed to give for more than 30 years past to poor labourers not receiving parish relief, were distributed this year, as usual - the proceeds of six Imperial bushels of wheat made into bread, and an ox cut up into pieces according to the number of the different families.

8 March (RCG) TRECAN GATE PETTY SESSION. - *M--- ---- v J--- ----*. This defendant was brought up in the custody of Mr. Hicks, constable, of Lanteglos, for not obeying an order of justices, which required him to contribute 2s. a week towards the maintenance of complainant's child. The case being proved, and ---- having admitted he had no goods whereon to levy, a warrant was made out for his committal to Bodmin for one month.

15 March (RCG) LOSTWITHIEL FAIR.- At this fair on Tuesday, there was a great number bullocks, but sales were very heavy. Good beef was scarce fetching from 42s. to 44s. per cwt. There were a number of plough oxen and steers, but very little sale. Fat sheep sold at 5 1/2 per lb.

15 March (RCG) PROLIFIC EWES.-Mr. Williams, of Lawhire, in the parish of Fowey....had three ewes which gave birth to ten lambs, 4 from one, and 3 from each of other two - and all are likely to live.

15 March (RCG) TIMBER IN CORNWALL. FOR SALE. - PRIME TIMBER suitable for Naval purposes, consisting of 54 Lots of OAK and 29 Lots of other descriptions, now standing on the lands of RESTORMEL, near Lostwithiel, and about a mile from the navigable port of the Fowey River. (Auction 3rd April, Talbot Inn, Lostwithiel).

12 April (RCG) On the 5th inst., the *Abel*, Hicks, master, arrived here from Savannah, having on board Mr. G. Bullock, a railway defaulter, for whose apprehension a reward of 5,000 dollars has been offered. On reaching the harbour she was boarded by Pearne, an active constable of this place, who had been instructed by Mr. A.O. Butman, an officer who came from Savannah in pursuit of him, and by whom he was recognised and taken into custody. - The prisoner was much affected at his being taken, but offered no resistance. The property found in his possession was trifling, when compared with the very large amount it is said he decamped with.

12 April (RCG) The....*Royal Adelaide*, this favourite passenger ship, sailed for Quebec on the 8th, having on board about 100 passengers, but in consequence of a gale springing up from the S.W, was obliged to put back about 6 hours afterwards. The passengers were delighted, as if they had returned from a pleasure trip.

17 May (RCG) CUSTOMS. - The port of Fowey has been reduced from the 5th to the 6th class. James Brown, Esq., collector, is super-annuated, and William Wreford, Esq., comptroller, is appointed collector.

14 June (RCG) FARMS IN FOWEY....TO BE LET BY TENDER, from Michaelmas next, in one Farm, the several LANDS AND TENEMENTS of *Polvellan, Higher and Lower Penventinue, Higher and Lower Hillhay, and Liscrows,*....and comprising 425 Acres of very superior Orchard, Meadow, Pasture and Arable Land, with the Agricultural Buildings and Several Labourers' Cottages thereon.... immediately adjoining the town of Fowey, and for many years were farmed by the late proprietor J.T. Treffry, Esq. deceased, who expended a considerable sum in bringing the Farm into the highest state of cultivation. Manure of every description may be obtained at Fowey; and, connected with the Estate of HILLHAY, the Tenant will have the advantage of the use of the Drawing Machine there, for conveying Manure from the water side to the centre of the Farm.- For conveniency of shipment of Produce and other advantages resulting from proximity to the water, the Premises are unsurpassed. With the Farm will be let, if desired, the very commodious DWELLING HOUSE situate at the western end of the town, formerly occupied by Admiral Peard, and contiguous to the Estate - and also the Dairy and Dairy House at the rear of Place, with the large and convenient Cow Yard and Sheds adjoining. The Dairy is fitted up with every requisite and is the most complete in the County.

21 June (RCG) The *Royal Adelaide*, which sailed from this port on the 12th April last, was the first passenger ship that arrived at Quebec the spring voyage. The number of passengers she took out was about 100, who were all much pleased with the sailing of the ship, and with the accommodation and other arrangements on board; and the kindness received from and the attention paid to the passengers during the voyage by Capt. Smith....

5 July (RCG) NOTICE. TO BUILDERS. PERSONS willing to Contract for the ERECTION of certain FARM BUILDINGS at CARNEGGAN, in the parish of Lanteglos,....may inspect the Plans and   Specifications at....Truro. TENDERS will be received until the 14th day of July.... Further particulars may be obtained....of Mr HENWOOD, Carneggan.

19 July (RCG) TO SCHOOLMASTERS. WANTED at Michaelmas next, or sooner if practicable, a SCHOOLMASTER and his WIFE, for THE NATIONAL SCHOOLS at *Polruan*.... Salary £15 per annum, with House rent free, and about £26 per annum from the children. The Master must be competent to instruct two Pupil Teachers in the third year of their apprenticeship, for which he will receive £10 per annum in addition to the above. Address to the Rev. JAMES KENDALL, Lanteglos Vicarage, Fowey.

26 July (RCG) Arrived, *Royal Adelaide*, Smith, from Quebec. She left Fowey on the 12th April last, with passengers, and was only 3 months and 10 days from Fowey to Quebec and thence to Fowey with cargo of timber.

23 August (RCG) FOWEY.- A servant girl, called Jane Ivey, has been discharged from the service of Mr. White, surgeon, for feloniously destroying a letter, containing one half of a bank note, which she said she had posted; but circumstances led to the confession of her own guilt.

23 August (RCG) FOWEY. The drift boats here continue to bring in good catches of pilchards, which are sold at 1s. per 120.

13 September (RCG) ST. AUSTELL COUNTY COURT. - *Rogers v. Rogers.* Plaintiff is a farmer residing near Fowey, and defendant a dealer in cattle residing near Bodmin. It appears that defendant bought some lambs of plaintiff, and paid part of the money, and took away part of the lambs. After this a disease made its appearance in the lambs, and he refused to take the remainder.... Several witnesses proved the custom, that after a bargain is made, the purchaser bears the risk of all loss, a verdict was given for plaintiff for £10 with costs.

20 September (RCG) TO be LET by TENDER, for a term of 7 or 14 years, from Michaelmas, that very compact and desirable FARM called TRIGGABROWNE, In the parish of Lanteglos by Fowey, now in the occupation of Mr George Hicks; Consisting of a good DWELLING HOUSE with convenient Farm Buildings, a Thrashing Machine, and 243 a. 2 r. 11 p., of good Arable, Meadow, and Pasture land....for particulars....by which the rent will be made to depend upon the prices of Wheat, apply to Mr. Pease, Stewardry, Boconnoc.... Tenders....received until the 23rd

18 October (RCG) EMIGRATION. Her Majesty's Colonial Land and Emigration Commissioners, are prepared to receive....applications from a limited number of Miners, Agricultural Labourers, Shepherds, Herdsmen, Female Domestics, Farm Servants, and a few rough Country Mechanics, who may be desirous of obtaining passages in their Ships to Adelaide, Sydney, Port Philip, and the Cape of Good Hope. A few Tailors and Shoemakers may obtain passages to the Cape. A considerable demand exists for the services of the above classes,....who are absolutely free on arrival ....

22 November (RCG) FOWEY. - A meeting was held at the Town-hall, by the church wardens of this parish.... The meeting was very fully attended; and it was resolved that an address be forwarded to her Majesty, expressive of indignation and scorn at the late aggression of the Pope upon our Protestantism, and of a desire to restrain the unworthy sons of the Church of England from leaning towards the Romish doctrines and practices.

22 November (RCG) SHIPWRECK.- The schooner *Richard Hicks*, of Fowey, was on her passage from Pentewan to Runcorn, laden with china clay, when, within seven miles of Holyhead, the crew saw a large barque running before the wind approaching them. They hailed her several times, but received no answer, and there appeared to be no look-out kept. She shortly afterwards struck the schooner about the fore-chains, and in ten minutes she went down. The crew had just time to get on board the barque, the name of which they found to be the *Leonora Thompson*, of and from Liverpool, bound to Demerara. Next day, the crew were put aboard the *Margaret and Rachel*, from Glasgow, bound to Rye, and were landed at Milford. The schooner was the property of Mr. John Hicks, merchant, of Hall, near Fowey. The cargo belongs to Mr. Elias Martyn, clay merchant, St. Austell - all uninsured.

1851

9 May (RCG) Coroners Inquest. On the 29th ult., at the parish of Liskeard, on the body of Elizabeth Treleaven. It appeared that she had been staying with her daughter at Looe, and was going from that place to Fowey in a van. On coming to Bodinnick Passage she got out to walk down the hill, when a bullock that was driven down the hill for the purpose of being taken across the ferry ran at her, and gored and injured her so much that she was taken back to Looe and from thence to her home, where she died in consequence of the injuries she received from the bullock. There did not appear to be any blame to any one, as the bullock was frightened by the people endeavoring to get him into the boat. Verdict accordingly.

5 September (RCG) *To Ship Builders, Timber Merchants, and others.* TO be LET by PRIVATE TREATY, with immediate possession, the very commodious YARD, *Building Slip, Sheds, Quays, and Premises,* Situate at Caffa Mill Pill in Fowey,....for several years in the occupation of Mr. George Nickels as Tenant. The above Premises are most conveniently situated on the margin of Fowey River, and possess a good depth of Water in front, and other unequalled advantages for carrying on an extensive and highly profitable trade. To view,....apply to Mr. James Whitford at Fowey....

26 September (RCG) An inquest was held at Bodinnoe, near Fowey, on the 23rd instant, on the body of Robert John Hicks, son of Mr. Hicks, Master of the *Abel*, of the port of Fowey, who accidently fell into the water at the slip there, and was soon after picked up floating on the water, drowned. Verdict accordingly. (aged 22 mos.)

17October (RCG) On the 11th inst., an Inquest was held on the body of Thomas Lee, an old inhabitant of Fowey, who was found drowned in the water closet, on Albert Quay. Verdict accordingly.

28 November (RCG) FALL OF A HOUSE. - On Thursday morning, about 4 o'clock, the inmates of a house occupied by Mr. Hawken, blacksmith, at Polruan by Fowey, were alarmed by a rumbling noise, accompanied by a shaking of the premises, and they had scarcely time to recover from their surprise when the corner of the house gave way and fell into the sea below. On examining the spot at daylight it was found that the damage was much more extensive. By the side of the dwelling was a capacious shop used by Mr. Hawken, and it was found that this had entirely fallen, carrying with it the implements of his trade, together with a quantity of iron. The wall on which the shop was built had given way, carrying all the erection above with it, and a part of the dwelling-house. There were persons in bed at the time in the rooms, now partially destroyed, but they providentially escaped uninjured. The property belongs to Mr. Carnall, of Fowey. (John Hawken, at Vaughan's yard or Waterfront).

12 December (RCG) FOWEY. - *Gun Accident.* - On Saturday last, Mr H. Searle, blacksmith, put a cap on the nipple of a fowling piece and snapped it, but the cap did not go off. He then cleared the nipple by pricking it, and put on another cap; John Jago, a journeyman who had worked a long time with Mr. Searle, then held his right hand a short distance from the muzzle of the gun to feel the force of air it would send, when a full charge of shot carried away two of his fingers and otherwise shattered his hand to pieces. He is going on favorably under the surgical treatment of Mr. Illingworth, and hopes are entertained that his hand will not have to be amputated.

1852

2 January (RCG) John Cornish, one of the crew of the barque *Good Intent*, of this port, Warburton master, deserted that ship at Quebec in June last, and was not seen or heard of, until he made his appearance at Fowey in the Christmas week, when the owners caused him to be apprehended.... He acknowledged his guilt, and was committed to the House of Correction for 6 weeks. - It is hoped that this will act as a caution to seamen, who are well paid and well fed for what they have to do, not to desert their ships after signing articles for the voyage.

9 January (RCG) On Monday evening, the 5th inst., Capt. Warburton, of the *Good Intent*, of this port, with two young men, named Hicks and Buckingham, went out a sailing in their ship's boat, and when tacking across the harbour near Mandy Rock, she missed stays, and was immediately thrown broadside against a rock which upset the boat, throwing Warburton and the two young men into the breaking sea. Buckingham was saved by clinging to the boat from which he was washed several times, and Hicks was saved by swimming to an adjacent rock, from which he was afterwards hauled to the shore by rope fastened to his body; but Warburton is supposed to have received a blow in his head against the rock when he was thrown out of the boat, which stunned him and he was drowned. He was picked up in about an hour by the light of the moon after the accident occurred, by a boat's crew from Polruan, who heard their distressing calls for help. Every means was used to restore life, but alas, too late, the vital spark had fled. Capt. Warburton was beloved in his life, and much regretted in his death.

19 March (RCG) TREVICKA & LANTEGLOS HIGHWAY, NEAR FOWEY ....TO be SOLD at PUBLIC AUCTION.... Lot 2.- All that Dwelling-House & Shoemaker's Shop with the Garden and Outbuildings attached, situate at *Highway,....* now in the occupation of Mr. William Roberts. These Premises are well situated for Trade and a good Business has for many years been carried on thereon by the present occupier.

Lot 3. - All that excellent Dwelling House, for many years used as a beer-house, consisting of a Kitchen, Parlour, Cellar, and Dairy, with good Bed-rooms over, and an extensive Garden, and Piggeries in the rear, situate at *Highway,....*and now in the occupation of Mr. William Thomas. These Premises are admirably adapted....for an

Inn, being immediately adjoining the high road from Fowey to Pelynt and Looe, and in the centre of a populous district.

23 April (RCG) ACCIDENT BY DROWNING AT POLRUAN. - Hart and Piper, two men belonging to the Coast Guard station there, at midnight, on the 15th inst., were engaged on duty, and when in the act of hauling a boat off by the frape, the lashing, parted to which the block was attached, and both men were precipitated into the water. Hart, who was much respected in the service, was drowned, and Piper narrowly escaped the same fate.

14 May (RCG) PILCHARD ADVENTURE FOR SALE....by PUBLIC AUCTION at the COMMERCIAL INN, Fowey,.... "THE VALLETORT" *Pilchard Adventure*, consisting of Stop and Tuck Seines, Boats Warps, Grapnels, Bucklers, Press Stones, Trap Poles, and every other requisite....for catching and curing. Also, several Tons of prime French SALT. To view, apply to Mr. JAMES WHITFORD.

16 July (RCG) CORONER'S INQUEST July 8th, at Fowey, on Thomas Remfree. It appeared that the deceased was a wholesale and retail boot and shoemaker of Truro, and that he had been at Fowey on business. A woman named Dunn deposed, that she was in the road about half a mile from Fowey, when deceased passed her in his gig at a slow pace. There was a turn in the road, where she lost sight of him, but on coming round the corner, she saw him on his knees by the side of his gig, holding up his hands and crying for help. She went up to him, when he said his leg was broken. Being near a farm-house, assistance was immediately had, and he was removed into the house. Mr. Illingworth, the surgeon, of Fowey, was at hand, and found that there was a compound fracture of the leg, and the only chance was to amputate; but the patient never rallied sufficiently to have the operation performed; he died in about four hours. It was supposed that the horse being tormented with the flies, kicked in the splash-board and broke deceased's leg; and that in jumping out of the gig, he pitched on the same leg, which produced the compound fracture....

16 July (RCG) On Wednesday, the 12th instant, James Serle, a waterman, was brought before T.G. Graham, Esq., charged by Wm. Wreford, Esq., Collector of Customs, with having concealed about his person about 3lbs. of manufactured tobacco, which he took from the *Royal Adelaide* from Quebec. He was fined in the penalty of £2 and discharged.

30 July (RCG) CORONERS' INQUESTS. July 15th, at Fowey, on James Wellington, a boy, who was drowned by falling over the slip. He was seen playing on the slip with a flag in his hand, and soon after, the flag was seen floating on the water, and on looking over the slip his body was seen at the bottom. He was soon got out but was quite dead. As no one saw the accident, the jury returned a verdict of "Found drowned."

3 December (RCG) On the 25th ult., was brought in here the barque *Platina*, of London, Watson master, from Cardiff for Portsmouth, laden with coals, picked up abandoned off Scilly, by the *Happy Return*, of Falmouth. - Also was brought in the schooner *Urd*, of Dram, Allum master, by Robert Johns, a Trinity pilot, belonging to this port, having her sails blown away, and her cargo (railway iron) shifted; from Grangemouth for Barcelona.

10 December (RCG) Coroner's Inquest. - On Friday last....at Fowey on the body of a fine young man only 20 years of age, who was one of a crew which escaped the fury of the late storms, the vessel having been towed into Fowey with two other vessels almost wrecks, and yet melancholy to relate he fell from the mast of his vessel and was killed instantaneously. He has been buried in a land of strangers, for they were all Germans, and had just crossed from America....

1853

18 February (RCG) EXETER DISTRICT COURT OF BANKRUPTCY. Re WILLIAM SKELTON, junr. - This bankrupt carried on business as a black-smith at Fowey;....on his name being called by the usher of a court he did not appear; and he was duly out-lawed.... It was rumoured in the court that the bankrupt had emigrated to Australia. If this be true there will be little work for the officers of the court. Similar cases have been of rather frequent occurrence in this country....

24 June (RCG) ACCIDENT. - John Roberts, a shipwright of good character, fell over the steps leading to Mr. Slade's building yard, at Polruan on the 20th, by which he was so much injured as to cause his death.

14 October (RCG) RIVER FOWEY NAVIGATION. - During the past six weeks persons have been making surveys and sections of the river with a view of improving the navigation between Fowey and Lostwithiel. The engineer employed is Mr. Bampton.

9 December (RCG) FATAL ACCIDENT. - A son of Captain John Lobb, of Fowey, master of the barque *Platina*, was killed at Cardiff, having had his head crushed by a tram waggon.

1854

27 January (RCG) FOWEY.- On Sunday evening last, the dwelling-house of Mrs. Ham was entered by means of a skeleton key, during the hours of divine worship at church, but the burglars being disturbed, decamped without plunder.

17 February (RCG) TRECAN GATE PETTY SESSIONS. - An Order of Justices was made for widening a highway situate between Highway and Whitecross in Lanteglos.

23 June (RCG) NEWS FOR THE FRIENDS OF EMIGRANTS. - The barque *Good Intent*, of Fowey, Captain Gill, arrived at Quebec (with her passengers) in safety on the 3rd instant. She rescued 74 individuals from the wreck of the *Black Hawke*, of Liverpool, and took them on to Quebec.

7 July (RCG) Cornwall Midsummer Sessions. JAMES HARVEY, 49, labourer, had been committed on the 17th May, for want of sureties in a breach of the peace towards Joseph Soady, at Fowey, on the 15th September, 1853.- Soady appeared, and stated that the reason of the long lapse of time between the assault and committal was, that Harvey absconded. He said that he did not wish to prosecute Harvey any further, but only to be protected against his insults. - On the other hand, Harvey, in a humble, and apparently sincere manner, said he had not the slightest animosity towards Soady: it was entirely through drink; there was not a quieter person than he was, except when in liquor, and then he did not know what he was about. - Soady also said he believed it was wholly through liquor; that he had never done Harvey any harm, and did not know that Harvey owed him any grudge. - Under these circumstances, the Chairman, after remarking, as he frequently does with great earnestness, on the many and serious crimes due to drunkenness, ordered that Harvey be discharged, on entering into recognizances to keep the peace. It was understood that he would get work west of St. Austell, and not return to Fowey.

4 August (RCG) TRECAN GATE PETTY SESSIONS. - The only case which occupied the Bench was an application made by Mr. Samuel Langmaid, of Polruan, to have Mrs. Susan Climo, his wife's sister, bound over in recognizance to keep the peace towards him. The case was dismissed; but a summons for an assault was issued....

15 September (RCG) A REMARKABLE FACT. - Tuesday....was the day for the quarterly meeting of the Fowey Friendly society, at which there was only one bill for one week's sick pay presented for the quarter from upwards of 110 members, many of whom are very aged. This fact will show that Fowey and its neighbourhood have been very healthy during the summer.

15 September (RCG) Three seamen, named John Morris, Stephen Davies, and John Smith were sent to the house of correction for 6 weeks hard labour, for deserting from, and refusing to return to their duty, on board the brig *Christiana Carnall* Brokenshaw master, bound from London to the Persian Gulf.

1855

16 February (RCG) FOWEY. -*New Organ.* - On Sunday last, the new organ in the parish church at Fowey was played on for the first time by the organist, Mr. Betty, professor of music, and although not yet quite finished (having two octaves of German pedals to be added to it) it was found sufficiently powerful to fill the fine old church, one of the largest in the county. The singers were those belonging to the church, and although they had but one practice evening with the organist, they acquitted themselves with great credit....

16 February (RCG) *Reward for Saving Life.* - Mr. Edward Thomas,....Rope Manufacturer, has received the honorary "Silver Medal," of the Royal Humane Society awarded at a general court, held the 10th Jan. last, for his courage and humanity at Fowey, on the 22nd September 1854, in having plunged into the sea, at dark night, with all his clothes on, to the relief of an old sailor called Joseph Pearn, who had accidently fallen from the quay, and whose life he saved.

6 April (RCG) Cornwall Easter Sessions. - SAMUEL POLSUE, committed on the 7th of March, for want of sureties in a breach of the peace towards his father, Joseph Polsue, of Polglaze, Fowey. The father appeared, and....made several statements concerning his son's idleness and violence, and....swore that he was still in bodily fear of him. The prisoner being still without sureties for his peaceable behaviour, he was ordered to be remanded. The CHAIRMAN, however, admonished the father that it was his duty, before the next sessions, seriously to consider whether something could not be done to settle the differences between him and his son.

4 May (RCG) Exeter District Court of Bankruptcy. *Re* GEORGE HAWKE, dealer in Hardware, Polruan.... The circumstances of the case....are somewhat extraordinary, the bankrupt having absconded, and his wife had the goods sold by Mr. Richard Davey, auctioneer, after he had heard that Hawke was a bankrupt.... Richard Davey of Lanreath).... produced an account of the sale of the bankrupt's property;....witness knew the bankrupt, who lived about six miles from him, but he was not aware when he went from Polruan. Witness saw him about a fortnight before he left, at Polruan.... When he saw him at Polruan he met him in the street, and did not go to his shop. He went there on business, but he received no instructions from Hawke as to a sale. His reason for believing that the bankrupt had gone away for a clandestine marriage was because it was generally understood so by the inhabitants of Polruan. Mrs. Hawke gave him the instructions to sell the goods. It was said that the bankrupt had gone to Portsmouth, where he was seen by a native of Polruan and that he had embarked on a vessel for America.... *Witness.-* Mrs. Hawkes sent for me on Good Friday and arranged a sale the next day.... No bills were printed; it is not the custom to have bills unless it is a very large sale; the crier usually goes round, which obtains a sufficient attendance. The population of Polruan is between 600 and 700. I sent to the crier, and the sale was announced for 11 o'clock on Saturday morning . I did not however reach Polruan till 3 o'clock in the afternoon....I begun the sale as soon as I came....The goods that were sold were to be removed at once. There is no doubt some purchasers went away without paying.... I saw the goods on the Friday. *Mr. Elmsworthy - What was the value of them?*.... I should think about £50 or £60.... earthenware, china, glass, and clocks....6 or 7, all of which I sold. I continued selling until 10,.... *The Commissioner-* What was the whole amount realised? - *Witness-* I believe it was 24l. 10s....there was a great deal left when I went. One clock went for 19s. 6d.,....the regular price only 15s. 6d. in a shop. *Commissioner-* What became of the money you received? - *Witness -* I only received part of it, and that I handed over to Mrs. Hawke, but I can't tell the exact sum....some parties paid Mrs. Hawke herself. I employed the clerk; his name is Samuel Langmaid, tailor.... I paid over some of the money to Mrs. Hawke on the following Monday.... I sent the money to Mrs. Hawke, at a neighbour's house in Polruan. Mrs. Hawke....told him that some men entered her house on the Thursday night previously, at 11o'clock, and she thought they were robbers.... *Mr Elmworthy-* Did you not know that two creditors, and one of my clerks, were at Polruan on the Thursday night.... *Witness -* Yes....but Mrs. Hawke said she did not owe more than 40*l.* (Richard Davey was instructed to hand over the value of the goods .)

8 June (RCG) Easter Court of Bankruptcy *Re* HAWKE, HARDWAREMAN, Polruan.... The whole of the proceeds of the sale have since, by order of the court, been paid over to the assignee for the benefit of the general body of creditors.... The report of Hawkes absconding....seems to be confirmed by the act of his non-appearance at the Court to-day....according to the usual form, the Commissioner ordered him to be outlawed.

22 June (RCG) CLASSICAL AND MATHEMATICAL SCHOOL FOWEY. Conducted by Mr. Wheeler, of Trinity College, Dublin. The Course of instruction comprehends: - The Greek and Latin Classics; the French Language; Mathematics, as preparatory for the Universities, and for the Military and Naval Colleges; All the essentials of English and Commercial education, to which subjects particular attention is devoted. Several of Mr Wheeler's Pupils have obtained University Honours; and some of them have acquitted themselves with distinguished success at the Naval College as Candidates for Commissions in the Royal Marine Corps. References can be given to shew that domestic arrangements for Boarders have given peculiar satisfaction. It is needless to suggest the advantages of Fowey as a locality favourable to health, and from its retirement, conducive to studious application and moral purity. The number of Boarders is limited to six. Notice of removal is not required. School duties recommence July 9, 1855.

13 July (RCG) Cornwall Midsummer Sessions. SAMUEL POLSUE, 33, was remanded at the last sessions, for want of sureties in a breach of the peace towards his father, Joseph Polsue, of Fowey. The father now appeared against him, and said he was still afraid of him. Mr Everest said it was his opinion the man was insane, and if he were again remanded he should take steps to get him removed to the asylum, where, under the act of parliament, his father would have to maintain him. The CHAIRMAN said that was the better course to be adopted. - The prisoner was then remanded.

28 September (RCG) THE "FORAGER" STEAMER, Thomas Cornish, Master, *Having been supplied with a New Boiler, and the Vessel and Machinery thoroughly refitted, and put into complete order,* Will recommence running between Fowey and Plymouth, with Goods and Passengers (with liberty to tow) on Monday the 24th inst .... Leaving Fowey for Plymouth on Mondays and Thursdays, at 9 o'clock in the morning; and Plymouth for Fowey on Tuesdays and Fridays at 12 o'clock at noon. Goods for Lostwithiel and Bodmin to be delivered at Fowey on her return from Plymouth for St. Austle, St. Blazey, Tywardreath and Neighbourhood, at Par, on Wednesdays, and Saturdays. FARES Fowey to or from Plymouth. Best Cabin 4s. Fore Cabin 2s. 6d.

26 October (RCG) Cornwall Michaelmas Sessions. - SAMUEL POLSUE, 33, had been remanded to prison at the Easter Sessions, and also at the last sessions, for want of sureties in a breach of the peace towards his father, Joseph Polsue, of Polglaze,

Fowey. The father now appeared, and said he was not afraid his son would injure him, but he complained that he was idle; and that he was quiet enough as long as he was let alone, and allowed to eat, drink, sleep, and do nothing. The CHAIRMAN said idleness was not a sufficient reason for keeping his son in prison. He then cautioned the prisoner to conduct himself properly in future towards his father, and ordered him to be discharged.

1856

4 January (RCG) FOWEY.- An order has been issued by the Home Office for closing the churchyard by the first of June next. A vestry was therefore called, and a burial board has been promptly appointed, who have set to work vigorously to have a new burying ground ready by the time appointed. A suitable site has been fixed on.

7 March (RCG) TRECAN GATE PETTY SESSIONS. - Joseph Dove v. Hannah Congdon.... The prisoner, recently married, was brought from Bodmin Gaol, ...charged with stealing from the dwelling house of Dove, at Polruan, on the 31st January, two pieces of India matting.... Joseph Dove is at sea, - Mrs. Dove in December last, locked up her house in Polruan, and went to reside at Devonport. In the latter part of January the back door of the house was broken open and nearly cleared out of the furniture that was in it; and notwithstanding that some half dozen search warrants have been issued, the prisoner is the only one in whose possession any of the stolen property has been found.- Richard Johns, a pilot, proved to having seen the prisoner come from the house with a large bundle on the 31st January; and Susanna Burnett and Ann Bray, sisters of Mrs. Dove, saw the prisoner and her mother burning India matting, which they identified as the prosecutor's, on the 2nd February. The prisoner's mother said that her daughter took two mats, and as she thought there would be a rig about it she was determined to burn them. As the prisoner was not shown to have been concerned in stealing any of the other articles, and as she had already having been in prison a month, she was sentenced to....hard labour for 14 days....

25 April (RCG) Tywardreath. - Porcupine Petty Sessions. - *Criminal Justice.* - *Robert Trewartha*, of Fowey, was brought up in custody, charged with stealing sundry shoemaker's implements, the property of his master, Henry Hooper. Mr Carlyon appeared on behalf of the prosecution; the prisoner was undefended. This was the first case under the act tried at these petty sessions. After the charge had been read to the prisoner, and his consent to be tried by their worships, they thereupon adjudicated and dismissed the charge.

16 May (RCG) THE WRECK OF THE *"ENDEAVOUR"*, NEAR FOWEY.- *Gallant Conduct-....* On the 6th inst., blowing a heavy gale from S.S.E., it was reported to Commander Norcock that a wreck had taken place close to the Gribbon, but that the crew were safe. Commander Norcock immediately gave directions for the assembling of the crews of two stations under the guidance of their officers, to render every assistance, and hastened to the spot. On reaching it he beheld a lamentable sight; the vessel dashed to pieces! and far worse, three out of four of the crew had perished - one falling into the hold of the vessel when she struck, two drowned in their hurried attempt to swim from a rock upon which they had gained a footing, and the fourth and last clinging to it without any apparent chance of being saved. Commander Norcock proceeded to the immediate object of saving the man.... A boat and hawser had been, by the praiseworthy exertions and foresight of Mr. Geach (Mr. Rashleigh's steward) brought on a waggon to the most favourable spot for lowering, near the scene of the wreck (for it was impossible to launch a boat from the new Coast-Guard Station at Polkerris), and Commander Norcock conducted its descent over and down a cliff near 200 feet in height! an act requiring the utmost care, for if injured ere it reached the bottom, all hope of saving the man would be gone. This was fortunately accomplished, and she then was conveyed on the shoulders of the crew of the Coastguard, over high and craggy rocks, to the most suitable spot whence an attempt should be made to reach the poor fellow. The utmost caution and daring were required, to launch the boat, and take her safely to the rock, through heavy seas and rollers, in which two good swimmers had just perished. Commander Norcock having taken off his shoes and upper garments, called for volunteers to go with him, and two Coast-guard men, William Pappin and Charles Henwood, came forward; but the former not being a swimmer, and the risk being very great that so small a boat might be swamped in such a sea, he was not permitted to go, and another volunteer was found in a young man named Johns, son of a Fowey pilot. Watching for a lull in the rollers, Commander Norcock and his brave companions dashed off to the rock, secured the man, and returned amidst the cheers of the beholders and the cordial greetings of those near. The poor fellow, who had kept his spirits up to the time of being taken off the rock, appeared like a corpse when brought to the shore. The ill-fated vessel could not have fallen on a more dangerous or fated spot - rocks high and pointed, over which the waves beat awfully, and between which they rushed like a torrent. Had the little boat being capsized, Commander Norcock and his brave companions would almost surely have met a similar fate as those poor fellows whose bodies were close to them. Great activity was shewn by the lieutenants of the Coast Guard (Cornish and Kinsmen) and their crews, who had acted under the orders of their Inspecting Commander; and great praise is due to Mr Geach for his indefatigable exertions throughout the whole affair. It was by his judgement that the boat and hawser were on the spot; and he evidently felt that he was called on to take a decided and leading part, not only from the promptings of his personal humanity, but also, as the representative of Mr. Rashleigh, to mitigate as far as possible the horrors of a fatal calamity which had occurred on his employer's property. We cannot doubt that the Lords of the Admiralty and the Comptroller General of the Coast Guard, will take the very gallant act of Commander Norcock and his two brave fellows into their consideration, and reward it as it deserves. (June 16 issue - Henwood promoted to Chief Boatman, Pappen to be Commissioned Boatman. £10 to Henwood and Johns, £5 to Pappen, Commander Norcock appointment extended from 5 to 10 years and presentation of a sword from Board of Trade and silver medal from Lloyds. June 20th issue - Royal National Life Boat Institution awarded their silver medal to Capt. Norcock, also to Henwood and Johns for gallant conduct, and special thanks, inscribed on vellum to Mr. W.E. Geach).

11 July (RCG) CAUTION TO PERSONS HAVING POST HORSE LICENCES.- A case of considerable importance was heard at a special petty sessions held at the Porcupine Inn, in Tywardreath, on Monday last, before Richard Foster, Esq., and the Rev. E.J. Treffry. The defendant, Mr. John Sparnall, of the Ship Inn, Fowey, was summoned for having, on the 13th March last, let to hire a certain horse to a Mrs. Giles, which was not included in his licence, and for which he paid no duty, thereby defrauding the internal revenue.... Witnesses were called on both sides, but the evidence was rather of a conflicting nature. Mr. Bishop....on behalf of the defendant ....addressed the Bench at some length....contending that he had not acted in any way unlawful in the matter, and that the charge against him was not sufficiently made out to warrant a conviction. Their worships adjourned to consider the case, and on their return said that the prosecution had failed, and they should therefore dismiss the charge.- There was another summons against the same defendant which charged him with having let to hire three horses more than he paid license for, viz, one horse to a person named William Hillman Stephens, and two others to John Whitehead Peard, Esq., on the 27th day of March last. In this case witnesses were examined on both sides, which occupied some time, and their worships held that the defendant had been guilty of the charge...., and fined him in the mitigated penalty of £25....

15 August (RCG) GALLANT CONDUCT. - On the 6th inst.,a boy named Mann, twelve years of age, while sculling a boat in Fowey Harbour lost his balance and fell into the water. The accident was observed from Polruan, and immediately caused the greatest excitement, as it was known the boy could not swim. Richard Johns and his son, pilots, both noted swimmers, who happened fortunately to be at home at the time, rushed out of their house on hearing cries for help, and not knowing exactly where their aid was required, ran for different points on the shore. Johns went to the rocks below the old castle, and his son to the coastguard landing-place. The latter position was nearest to the sinking boy, and young Johns immediately plunged into the water, with all his clothes on, except his woollen frock, which he had pulled off whilst running, swam out, seized the boy and brought him to the shore in safety. It is supposed that if a very few seconds more had elapsed the boy would have sunk. When Johns took hold of him he had been four minutes in the water, and nothing was visible but his hands. Johns is only 21 years old; and he has received for previous heroic conduct the medal of the Shipwrecked Fishermen's and Mariner's Society, and that granted by Lloyds' for saving life; and has been rewarded by the Lords of the Admiralty, and the Board of Trade, for having signalized himself under the Inspecting Commander of the coastguard at the wreck of the *"Endeavour,"* of Ipswich on the Gribbon Point,....in the month of May last. He has saved six lives at the risk of his own.

5 September (RCG) TO be LET, with immediate possession, all that WATER GRIST MILL,....within half a mile of the town of Fowey; called CAFFA MILL, Together with two MEADOWS of Land, containing about 4 a. 3 r. 8 p. and one acre of ORCHARD, the whole of which is near or adjoining the said Mill, and lately in the occupation of Mr. Joseph Lawry. There has very recently been an entire New Water Wheel, with Iron Axle erected, and the whole Mill (including a New Stone) been put in thorough repair. The Mill has a good supply of water, and is situated in a Locality where an extensive business can be carried on. For viewing....apply to THOS. KINSMAN, House Agent....Fowey.

1857

6 February (RCG) Trecan Gate Petty Sessions....- *Samuel Pooley*, of Bodinnick, Lanteglos, was charged with stealing on the 16th January at Looe roads, in the harbour of Fowey, two battens, the property of Mr. James Bishop, of Looe....having pleaded guilty, he was sentenced to be imprisoned....for three weeks, one week of which is to be hard labour.

6 February (RCG) A numerously attended meeting of the master boot and shoe makers of Lostwithiel, Bodmin, St. Blazey, Tywardreath, Fowey, St. Veep and places adjoining, was held at the King's Arms Inn, on Tuesday,....for the purpose of adopting such measures as the present extraordinary high price of leather reders necessary.... Mr. Hooper, of Fowey, said all were painfully aware of the disadvantages with which the trade at present had to contend; for two years past he had served on a rather extensive business without fair remuneration, but with the present prices it was at a positive loss. The masters were willing to bear a portion of the burden, but the public must share....by submitting to an advanced price. Mr. Cole, of St. Veep, said he had paid minute attention to the cost of material, and in many instances had found it fully equal to the price charged when made up.... Mr. Hooper then proposed an advance of from 20 to 25 per cent., and it was seconded....

5 June (RCG) WANTED at Midsummer, a Mistress for the National School at BODINNICK, in *Lanteglos by Fowey*. Salary £15. School Pence about £10 per annum. £3 allowed for house rent. A knowledge of singing required. Address, the Rev. J. Kendall.

12 June (WB) WRECK AT FOWEY. The schooner *Exile*, 30 tons N.M. of and from Jersey and for Charlestown, in ballast, Laming, master, in working out of Fowey harbour on Wed the 3rd June, about 6 am when nearly clear of the harbour missed stays. The captain let go of the bower anchor, which caught in the rock, and by the sudden jerk parted the cable. Before the other anchor could be let go, the vessel drifted on to the rocks at the back of Pontius Cross. Every effort was made by Mr. Richard Johns and his sons, pilots of this port, who immediately proceeded to the stranded vessel, assisted by the coastguards and Captains Tadd and Shadwell, but it being ebb tide at the time, they were unsuccessful and before the flood tide was of any assistance she filled, and is now fast breaking up. The Sails, rigging, masts, and stores, under the able direction of Mr. Richard Johns, senr., were saved, and the crew were taken care of by the agent of the Shipwrecked Mariners society, and forwarded to their homes, except the master and his son, who still continue to save at Fowey what they can from the wreck as she breaks up....

21 August. (RCG) TO ENGINEERS AND SHIPWRIGHTS. PREMIUM OF £20. PERSONS are invited to prepare PLANS for improving the FERRY between Fowey and Bodinnick and send the same to Mr. PEASE, at the Stewardry, *Boconnoc*, on or before the 1st of October next. The Person whose Plan is deemed the best, shall, if such Plan be adopted, receive the above Premium. The Drawings and Specification must exhibit in detail the proposed Plan; and an estimate of the cost, including any alterations to the Landing Slips, must accompany the Drawings; and if the Proprietor should require it, the successful competitor must be prepared to execute the work at the amount of such estimate. The object is to have the Ferry worked in the easiest mode, combined with efficiency and economy, without the aid of steam.

11 September (RCG) LOSTWITHIEL FEAST. This ancient feast, so many years celebrated for its Ringing and Wrestling matches, has of late years been kept up by a Regatta and other amusements, and the tides not fitting on the 31st ult., it was put off until Thursday the 3rd inst., when there was a beautiful tide, and fine weather. The rivalry is great between the boat builders of Fowey, Polruan, and Lostwithiel, also between the Sailors and river Bargemen, &c....

2 October (RCG) WANTED by the Trustees of the Fowey Charities, a MASTER for the Fowey School. The School has an endowment of £80 per annum with a commodious School House. The Master is at liberty to take Boarders; and it is required that he shall be qualified to teach the Latin and Greek languages and be a Member of the Church of England. Further particulars will be afforded, and Testimonials from Candidates received by ROBERT BISHOP, Clerk and Receiver, Fowey, until the 14th day of October next.

13 November (WB) PLACE WALK BANISHMENT AT FOWEY. "Sir, Without a thought of questioning the perfect right of the Rev. E.J. Treffry "to do what he likes with his own", and debar the public of Fowey from the further continuance of a privilege they and their forefathers have so long enjoyed - God knows how long - still, the announcement by bills....distributed through this town, telling the unsuspecting folks they were no longer to air and recreate themselves in Place Walk,....gave them a shock like unto a bereavement.... Place Walk....has beauties to boast of,....which compensate for its too close proximity to the long undignified margia of chimney-pots surmounting the smoking town it overlooks - while its handiness for an half-an-hour's run, or an hour's promenade, made it what it always has been, a most desirable "Place" for an airing, whether by towns folks, or admiring visitors, to whom and all it has become endeared, the present possessor can perhaps hardly estimate.

"Let us go to Place Walk," "Oh lets have a run in Place Walk." "Oh you must (to the visitor) go and see Place Walk, 'tis one of the lions of Fowey." These short, happy, impulsive invitations, free to all, had become phrases "familiar in their mouths as household words."....the tired shopkeeper who goes for his half hour's run, the gentry promenaders, they have....taken their last walk in Place and....must make a circuit.... without the bounds of this forbidden Place, through the dark, dank, and muddy lanes; or through the long ill-paved, forlorn, dilapidated town.... And what for?.... The Rev. E.J. Treffry complains that "his family has been intruded on at all hours of the day....that much damage has been done to his trees and shrubs....asking his friends and neighbours to....help draw the bolt that shuts them out.... In honour of the famous name the rev. gentleman wears of him, whose public works and walks, will be his noblest monument, whose adorning hand and sylvan taste made Place Walk what it is - I would respectfully ask the Rev E. J. Treffry to be magnanimous....abate the rigour of his harsh decree, and forgive those that trespass against him, and not....punish all for the faults of a few, by shutting out the whole town....(signed) One of the excluded.

11 December (WB) FOWEY. To the Editor. Sir, - I know not whether you have ever seen the town of Fowey? Presuming you take an interest in the well-being of Cornish towns generally, you will, I doubt not,....be grieved to learn it is, in appearance, the most downcast, neglected seaport in the West of England,....I assure you that one evening this last summer I counted fifteen houses in a state of absolute ruin. - How many there are dilapidated, only inhabited by very poor people, I can't tell - besides plots of waste ground, on which houses have once stood, but now laying in unprofitable and blank inutility, with a sort of dog-in-the-manger proprietorship, as owner. When I tell you that the greater number of these houses have no gardens - not even back yards - or those conveniences which civilization and decency demand, your surprise will not exceed your indignation..... When I say....that we have no gas to enlighten us, though we have three church ministers - and no police to look after us - and no water, save what every woman in the place fetches like a Rebecca of old, it completes the list of our destitutions - ....   B.

18 December (WB) LANTEGLOS HIGHWAY. TO BE SOLD BY AUCTION at the Ferry House Inn, Bodinnoc, on Sat. the 19th day of Dec at 3:00.... LOT 2 - For the residue of the like term and determinable as aforesaid, all that Chapel or building for public worship, situate at Highway, for many years used by the Wesleyan Methodist Association. The Chapel is substantially built, and at a slight expense may be rendered fit for immediate use, at a small outlay the building may be converted into 2 good dwelling houses. Yearly conventionary rent on the entirety of the premises 18/, heriot 10p, which may be opportuned. To view apply to the tenant....

1858

1 January (WB) CHARGE AGAINST A RELIEVING OFFICER. At the Porcupine Petty Sessions....Mr. Bishop, on behalf of the overseers of the borough and parish of Fowey, made application for a summons against the relieving officer of the Liskeard union. --- ----, aged 17, had resided in the parish of St. Veep about two years, when finding herself with child, she left her service and came to her father's at

Saw Mills, in Fowey parish, where her father was then, and had resided twelve or fourteen months with his second wife and seven or eight small children. The father's parish is Talland, which with St. Veep is in the Liskeard union. She had resided at her father's about two months, and not having room for the daughter to lie-in, the stepmother and she,.... September last, proceeded to Lerrin to see the relieving officer of the Liskeard union, ... They....made application for the girl to be admitted into the Liskeard union house for the purpose of lying-in, and was refused, and also told that application must be made to the St. Austell union, or to the parish of Fowey, as she had been living there. Upon this refusal,....the step-mother and the girl returned,.... made application to be admitted, and was received into the St. Austell union at the cost and charges of the borough and parish of Fowey. There had been no previous application at Fowey to the application at Lerrin.The bench not being unanimous, the case was deferred.

19 February (RCG) On Friday last,....Fowey was enlivened by the arrival of the *"Forager"* steamer, from Plymouth, having 25 soldiers on board, headed by an officer; they landed on the town quay, and were then quartered in the town. Their mission is to place two guns of large calibre, lately brought from Plymouth, on the battery recently erected on the top of St. Catherine's Hill, at the mouth of Fowey harbour.

12 March (RCG) PROPOSED NEW ROAD AT BODINNOC AND FLOATING FERRY ACROSS THE HARBOUR AT FOWEY. A meeting of the committee....was held at the council room of the Town Hall, Fowey,.... A plan of the new floating bridge, was exhibited by the maker, Mr. Littleton, a smith, of Bodinnoe, and which resembles the steam ferry bridge, at Torpoint, but is intended to be worked by winches and manual labour, instead of by steam. The expense of this bridge, together with the approaches, which will involve together an outlay of at least £200, will be borne by the Hon. G.M. Fortescue, who, on the part of Lady Grenville, the owner of the ferry, has liberally promised a revision and reduction of the present tolls. It appears that about £100 more is required to justify the commencement of the undertaking, which, seeing the great improvement which would be effected, in obtaining a good and easy approach to the ferry in lieu of the present difficult and dangerous one, we trust will soon be raised.

12 March (RCG) TRECAN GATE PETTY SESSIONS. *Christopher Slade*, of Polruan, beershop keeper, for keeping his house open after proper hours, was fined 10s with costs.

14 May (WB) FIRE. At Penventinue farm, Fowey, occupied by Messrs. W. and B. Hicks, a hayrick took fire on Monday last, while the inmates of the house were at dinner. It is supposed to have originated by a spark from the chimney, and about four tons of hay were consumed.

25 June (RCG) BENEVOLENCE.- Fowey has lately been visited with much sickness, whereby many of the lower class of people were plunged into misery and privation; and it is pleasing to state that the Rev. E.J. Treffry, of Place-house, directed the medical men to employ nurses to attend the sick; and also to procure necessaries &&c. for them, at his expense,- so that through his kind and timely aid, relief and comfort have been administered to all those who really stood in need. May his example recommend itself to....all those who have the means of doing good....

25 June (RCG) On Tuesday the 8th of September 1846, it pleased our most gracious Sovereign Lady Queen Victoria, and Prince Albert to visit Fowey. Her Majesty and her Consort walked through the streets unguarded, firmly relying on the loyalty and fidelity of the people, and repaired to Place-House, the splendid mansion of the late Joseph Thomas Treffry, Esq., and now that of the Rev. E.J. Treffry.... When they left Fowey, there was a meeting convened by the principal inhabitants, who unanimously agreed to erect a monument near the spot where Her Majesty landed, to perpetuate the event; and the late J.T. Treffry, Esq. gave for the purpose, (at his own expense) five massive blocks of granite from Luxulian quarry, the largest of which is 17 1/2 feet long by 4 feet 4 inches square at the base, and 2 feet 4 inches square at the top below the peak; they were brought to Fowey and landed on Albert quay, where they lay for many years; but it is pleasing to state, that last week, men were employed under the superintendence of Mr. Turner of Pontsmill, to erect the said monument, to whom and to his men much praise is due, for the able manner in which the immense block, before-mentioned, weighing upwards of 15 tons, was raised to stand perpendicularly on its pedestal. The monument is now complete, and has a monumental inscription, describing for what purpose it was erected; it is 25 feet high, and is a pleasing object. Many energetic men were present at the meeting for its erection, whom we should have liked to have seen at the point of its completion; but they have left the stage to others, and happily there are some who still remain.

(WB) The following is the proposed inscription, - "This monument is erected by voluntary subscription, is commemoratious of the landing of her Majesty Queen Victoria, with her Royal Consort, on this quay on the 8th September, 1846; since which date it has borne the name of "Albert Quay", instead of "Broadslip".

9 July (RCG) Trecan Gate Petty Sessions.- *Jonathan Woon* v *Richard Tregaskes*.- The defendant appeared on two summonses, for two separate assaults, committed on the 12th and 16th June, at Polruan. He admitted the first assault, but denied the second. From the evidence of the witnesses it appeared that the complainant had brought a good deal of the punishment he received on himself, by his uncivil tongue.- The defendant was fined 2s. 6d. and costs.

20 August (RCG) SUBMARINE OPERATION.- About a fortnight since, the schooner *Pendennis*, laden with iron stone, caught on the point of a rock at Bodinnick and sunk off Mr. Nicholl's yard. During the last week a diver from Whitstable has been engaged, remaining under water about one hour at a time. The captains' wearing apparel and articles of value from the cabins have been brought up; but the nature of the cargo prevents its recovery by this means. The vessel will have to be weighed, there being 100 tons of ore on board; otherwise it will be a serious impediment to navigation in that portion of the harbour.

3 September (RCG) TRECAN GATE PETTY SESSIONS. *Samuel Collins,* of Lanteglos, was convicted of keeping open his cider shop until quarter past 11 at night; fined 1s. and 9s.6. costs.

24 September (RCG) POLRUAN. - On the 20th inst., as Sally Menear, a widow, was taking coals from a vessel, which there discharging, she fell and broke her leg. This is a very unfortunate affair, as she is the mother of 9 young children, most of whom reside with her.

24 September (RCG) The harbour of Fowey has never been without large ships this summer, the Lew Roads at times presenting the most lively appearance, the flags of four or five different nations flying there at the same time. Between sixteen and seventeen thousand loads of timber-deals, &c., have been discharged at this port since the 1st June, being more than five times the quantity usually imported in the same period. The excess over former years has been importations for the Cornwall Railway by Messrs. Batchelor Brs., of Cardiff, and Walle and Sons, of Hull. The dispatch given by the officers of customs, although the landing watership was vacant, was highly satisfactory to all parties, and the lumpers of the port showed their usual expertness in discharging time. These importations have given a good deal of employment to the labouring classes, which has been particularly seasonable, considering that the pilchard fishery of this port has up to this time been a complete failure.

1 October (RCG) *To the Editor.* Sir,.... All engineers agree that the only plan for procuring an increased depth in any stream and permanently maintaining it, is by narrowing the channel, a fact no one knew better than the late Mr. Treffry, when he contemplated the erection of a walled esplanade from off the old Quay-head, to be carried upwards for 150 to 200 yards parallel with the town....Of the commercial value of an extended esplanade frontage to the town of Fowey, a signal practical proof has been afforded, by that enterprising gentleman, Mr. West, having found it necessary, in fact compelled to adopt the opposite shore, as the site for his intended new quay and warehouse (on account of its superior depth of water) for the accommodation of the goods and passengers brought by his screw steamer *Albatross,* in her trips to and from Truro and Plymouth, and this, in the face of a hill steep as the roof of a house!....it is....a pleasure, to see the new road, forming by subscription, on the estate of Lady Grenville, far advanced and winding its way by a gentle ascent along the wooded slopes;....outflanking the toilsome, dark, and viewless avenue up from Bodinnik Ferry- a double labour to man and horse. The new Road has already a fine, open, and cheering aspect....as it overlooks the water, and the ships below. LOOKER ON.

15 October (RCG) FOWEY HARBOUR. *To the Editor....* Sir, A "Looker-on," in last week's *Gazette,* offers some comments....on....Fowey Harbour.... There are some things....which demand notice:- 1st. The late Mr. Treffry's proposition to build a wall from the old quay upwards. There was nothing, that I know of, to prevent this, but his multiplied engagements elsewhere; and if it had been done....it would have been rather an ornament than of service,.....*unless* the bed of the harbour near such quay had been deepened.... There is naturally a greater depth of water where Mr. West has fixed on for a quay and warehouse - an excellent spot, available at all times. Yet the Lew Roads above the town would have afforded a spot as eligible, now resorted to by timber vessels;.... How to do what is required? In addition to any sum which might be annually raised from the dues, with the refunding of the amounts received by the corporation of Lostwithiel - say for the last ten years past - a party of convicts might be employed on harbour work, as at Portland and elsewhere; thus thousands of tons of mud might be removed, as also sand, useful for agricultural purposes. There are accommodations for landing at low water, "*hards*", much required. Strangers often at low tide pull up and down not knowing where to land, and in stormy weather great inconvenience occurs....there has been a talk of an extension of the Cornwall Railway to Fowey; this would be about 6 miles, and in carrying it out, not £500 worth of cultivated land would be destroyed, a level all the way. It could be brought down near the town, and a Station formed accessible at all times. This would embrace a scenery unsurpassed in the West of England....   WILLIAM HEWETT.

26 November (RCG) *To the Editor*.... Sir.... The Railroad is now near its completion, and I perceive with pleasure that Falmouth men are not only alive to this fact, but are up and doing, and that docks on a grand and extensive scale are proposed....for the advantage of that important town, and the county at large. Now, Sir, on behalf of Fowey, though I am not going to aspire, for the present, to anything so commercially extensive as docks, piers or the like, I do wish to see a well built, and above all, well conducted Inn or Hotel....with such a commercial room as gentlemen travelling for many important houses may be tempted, not only to go out of the way to, but remain at, and where the man of taste, and lover of scenery, better known as the tourist, may secure apartments for days or weeks, instead of being told, as at present, that "no hotel accommodation is to be met with at Fowey, except of a very inferior description, and at most exorbitant charges." A commodious hotel near the landing place would not only pay, but moreover form an important feature in the general appearance of the town from the anchorage; at the same time it would, I hope, be the means of keeping that portion of the public thoroughfare in a more cleanly state than at present, and the eye and nose of the stranger no longer be offended, as is now the case. Only give encouragement to visitors coming to Fowey, and its own natural beauties and salubrious air will do the rest, for I have no doubt villas would soon be erected on that beautiful public promenade, from the Rope walk to "Ready-money Cove", where Mr Rashleigh has already commenced a Marine Villa at the entrance of the harbour, and from what I hear would be glad to encourage....ornamental dwellings, adjacent to it....   NEPTUNE.

3 December (RCG) *Melancholy Accident.* - An inquest was held at....Plymouth....on....William Pearn, aged 65 years.... Richard Pearn, son of the`deceased, said he was a ship-wright, residing at Polruan....his father was the superannuated commander of the Revenue cutter *Lion*, and also resided at Polruan.

He came to Plymouth on the Friday previous, and took lodgings at the White Lion Inn,.... Stonehouse. Witness arrived there on Wednesday, and saw his father at his lodgings at about half-past nine o'clock, p.m. He was then sober; witness drank a glass of ale with the deceased, and then left him there. He did not see him alive afterwards.-Mary Ann Foot, a resident at 46,....stated that at about 12 o'clock on Wednesday night, she....saw something lying across the wall....about ten minutes afterwards, when she was coming home with her husband; they then found it was the deceased, lying there quite dead.... The height of the wall, against which the deceased was lying, was about two feet; there was a flight of steps....but she thought a stranger could mistake the way, and walk over the....wall.... There were no marks of violence on the body; blood was flowing from the left nostril and the right ear, but that appeared as if occasioned by a fall.... The night was dark. There was not the least trace of a struggle around the spot.... The deceased must have been going....to Bell's-lane, and being a stranger, got out of the road and stumbled over the two loose stones, knocking them over and falling himself into the road.

1859

7 January (RCG) CORNWALL EPIPHANY SESSIONS. - JENNIFER HOSKIN, otherwise JANE HOSKIN, 48 was charged with stealing an umbrella, a waterproof umbrella case, a table cover, a decanter, and three pictures, the property of William Sweet....at....Fowey on the 10th of August last.... Prisoner was undefended.- *Mary Ann Sweet*, wife of prosecutor, stated that her husband was a blacksmith and also kept the Sailor's Return Inn; in July last the prisoner was employed there as charwoman; the prosecutor at the same time occupying the King of Prussia Inn, from which he moved to the Sailor's Return. Shortly after the prisoner left the service, just before August, Mrs. Sweet lost several articles, and in November, seeing a pair of pattens of her property on the feet of the prisoner's child, she got a search warrant, and prisoner's house was searched. - *Thomas Carlyon*, police officer, searched the premises in November last, and now produced the articles mentioned in the indictment, and which were identified by Mrs. Sweet. - *Elizabeth Moss*, formerly an assistant in the shop of Mr. Tregenna at Fowey, proved that in October 1857, she sold Mrs. Sweet an umbrella similar to the one now produced; and also that she had given her the decanter. Verdict GUILTY. Mr Bishop recommended the prisoner to the merciful consideration of the court, on the pleas that she had been a long time in prison, and had a long family. (14 days hard labour.)

14 January (RCG) RICHARD COSSENTINE, HENRY CURTIS, CHARLES HAWKEN, AND WILLIAM THOMAS BURNETT were indicted for unlawfully assaulting and beating W. Strike, a Police Constable, in the execution of his duty, at Lanteglos by Fowey on 24th December.... The case as deposed to by the prosecutor was as follows; - He belonged to the County Police force, and was stationed at Polruan. On the night of the 24th December, he was sent to quell a disturbance at the Lugger public-house, but on his arrival there he found that the quarrel was over and that the company were quiet. Amongst those who were drinking were the defendants, and as several of the company appeared to be intoxicated, he told the landlord that he thought he had better supply no more liquor. Prosecutor then left the house, and soon after Cossentine, Curtis, Hawken,and Burnett amongst others, came out. Cossentine commenced shouting and singing, and on prosecutor advising him to go home he refused, saying that he had been in many towns before and no police had made him move on, and no 'Peelers' should order him away. Prosecutor took hold of him by the collar to remove him from the wall against which he was standing, and he admitted that when he got him away from that, he gave him a push, which threw him down. Cossentine immediately jumped up, and struck prosecutor a blow on the eye. Prosecutor drew his staff and knocked Cossentine down, and while on the ground he attempted to handcuff him; but at this moment the other three defendants came to the rescue; one seized him by the breast, another by the hair of his head, struck and kicked him violently, threw him down, wrenched his staff from him, and beat him to such a degree that he became insensible. His coat was torn to rags, and a holland frock which he wore inside his coat, was covered with blood. When consciousness returned, he managed to crawl to the public-house, when assistance was rendered him.- Mr Smith, surgeon, Polruan, deposed that he was sent for to attend Strike about twelve o'clock on the night of the 24th, and found him faint and exhausted. There were only a few slight abrasions of the skin on the head. Witness administered a little brandy to him internally, and attended to his bruises, and in a short time he came round. The injuries....were of a superficial character; and all that he required was a little rest. Corroborative evidence was given by *Wm. Todd*, the master of a vessel, and others.... *Henry Tregoning*....swore that....Charles Hawken never interfered with the officer. *George Jacobs* corroborated this evidence and said it was Moss or 'Captain Joe' who took the policeman's staff. Henry Hawken, brother of Charles Hawken, stated that after Cossentine had been struck by prosecutor, he went towards the officer to ascertain why he struck Cossentine, when his brother seized him, and held him back against a door, until the disturbance was over. *Philip Lean, Harriet Lean, and William Richards* spoke to certain statements made by the prosecutor as to the parties he could identify as having taken part in the assault, being at variance with his present evidence, but Mr. Stokes admitted that their characters were good prior to this occurrence..... CHAIRMAN....referred to the discrepancies in the evidence,....left it to the jury to determine....found Cossentine GUILTY of the assault upon the police officer, Curtis and Burnett GUILTY of a common assault, Hawken NOT GUILTY. They recommended the prisoners to the mercy of the Court, on the ground that they considered the police officer had acted hastily.... *Cossentine, 4 months hard labour; Curtis, 4 months hard labour; Burnett, 4 months hard labour.*

11 February (RCG) On Monday morning last, a landslip took place in the new building yard of Messrs. N. and J. Butson at Polruan, near to which was a vessel almost completely in frame, intended to carry about 200 tons. The earth fell against the shores by which the vessel was supported, starting her 3 feet from her original position; and by falling down in the yard the whole structure became disunited, by which the loss to the builders must be very considerable. But in the midst of this misfortune there is still a consolation, for it is generally believed, that if the land slip had taken place an hour or two later, several lives would have been lost, as the workmen were employed near to the spot where it fell.

25 March (RCG) CORNWALL LENT ASSIZES.- PHILIP RUDD, 42, seaman, was charged with having, on the 7th February, on the river between Fowey and Lanteglos by Fowey, stolen, or received on board his vessel knowing the same to have been stolen, one piece of Norway Timber, the property of William Warren Dingle.- The *prosecutor,* a timber merchant at Fowey, stated that he kept his timber, moored, at different parts of the harbour.... On Tuesday morning the 7th February, he was passing up the river in a boat with some other persons and saw a piece of Norway hewn timber on the deck of a vessel - the *"Two Brothers"*- which was being loaded with sawn timber for the Cornwall Railway; and, going on board, he found it was a piece of Norway timber 35 feet long, part of a cargo he had imported in October. - On *cross-examination*, Mr. Dingle stated that in the month of Sept. and Oct. last he had imported about 3000 pieces, of which he had sold about 1000 pieces, including a raft of which this piece formed part; but which raft it appeared had partly broken up, and the piece of timber in question, together with others, had drifted about the harbour. Evidence of the identity of the timber was given by Daniel William Lovell, Custom House Officer at Fowey, from the entries of the cargo in the Custom House book, and from his own marking of the Customs letters and number on the piece of timber in question; the slab containing the marks being produced by Police-Constable Carlyon.- To prove the act of felony charged against the prisoner, *Thomas Powell*, master of a vessel called the *"Two Sisters"* lying near the *"Two Brothers"* was called;....but the evidence being unsatisfactory, and as his lordship considered the property had not been rightly laid in the prosecutor, the further progress of the case was stopped, and his Lordship directed a verdict of ACQUITTEL.

1 April (WB) ACCIDENT. On Saturday afternoon last, as William Lee, shipwright of Fowey, was returning home from Par, he met with a serious accident by a horse throwing him down and rolling over him. The animal, on which Miss Lamb was riding, shied, and Lee had no time to get out of the way. His shoulder was put out, and the right arm was broken in two places. The young lady was thrown over the head of the horse, with no further injury than a few slight bruises. The accident becomes more serious as Lee is an aged labouring man, with a wife and family dependent on him.

6 May (WB) COMMERCIAL INN, FOWEY. J. Martyn, Proprietor. The above Inn conveniently situated at the entrance of the Town, having been recently rebuilt, will now be found replete with every comfort and convenience for Families and Gentlemen. Commercial Gentlemen will also find a commodious and pleasant room entirely set apart for their accommodation. Good Stabling and Lock-up Coach House. Omnibus to and from the Par Railway Station.

27 May (RCG) LIFE-BOAT FOR FOWEY. - William Rashleigh Esq., of Menabilly, has addressed a letter to the National Life-Boat Institution,....- "I shall be happy to place the sum of fifty pounds at the disposal of the Royal National Lifeboat Institution, provided an adequate sum is subscribed within the space of 12 months from this date, for the purchase of a Life-Boat for the Port of Fowey....I should also gladly further the carrying out the project, by granting a suitable spot for the erection of a Boat-house, together with the stone necessary for the erection. There are three convenient beaches to the westward of the Port of Fowey, where good landing in most weathers can be had."....a Life-Boat has long been required at Fowey, where some dreadful shipwrecks have occurred.... Considering how many Life-Boats are still required on the dangerous coast of Cornwall, and that a Life-Boat establishment costs between £300 and £400 in addition to an annual expense of about £20, to pay the Coxwain and crew of the boat, we earnestly trust that many will be found to emulate....Mr. Rashleigh in this truly phillanthropic work.

26 August (WB) It has been remarked that from the commencement of the season the fish of the drift boats have rarely been the same size or condition two mornings following;....as if the largest and fattest kept together....in separate schools.... The ravages committed by the dogfish are sadly complained of; the fishermen are obliged to be constantly hauling to save the pilchards that are firmly meshed, which those pests attack by hundreds when the nets are even alongside the boats.

23 September (RCG) On Thursday, the 15th instant, the children of Fowey Church Sunday School, and their teachers, met in the Free- school, and after an address....formed a procession to the Vicarage-house, where, after singing a hymn, three hearty cheers were given in the good old Cornish style of "One and All" for the Vicar, the Rev. J. Kempe, and his family. They then perambulated the town, bearing flags with mottoes, and halted in front of Place-house,....where they sang some hymns, and after giving three enthusiastic cheers, repaired to the Town Hall, where an ample supply of cake and tea was provided for them.... Miss Kempe, and other ladies, the Rev. C. Kempe, and the Rev. J. Hilton, tended greatly to the`enjoyment of all present. The hall was tastefully decorated with evergreens and flowers. At the upper part of the room was a fine spruce fir tree, extending from the floor to the ceiling....studded with articles of all descriptions, wrapped in paper as prizes for the children, and illuminated with a great number of lights. The boys and girls of each class were allowed each to choose a prize, which was immediately cut off, and given to the chooser: this afforded for a long time a fund of amusement; and the rest of the evening was spent in playing at blind man's bluff. About nine o'clock, three hearty cheers were again given for the Vicar and his family, and also for the Rev. E.J. Treffry and his family, and thanks for his gift of the tree....After having sung the evening hymn, an excellent address was given to the teachers and children by the Rev. C. Kempe, on the importance of scriptural education....

30 September (WB) FOWEY CAUTION TO SPORTSMEN. A correspondent calls public attention to a circumstance which might have resulted in fatal consequences to two persons, from the incautious manner in which guns are too often handled. It appears that Mr Abraham called at Mr Crapp's shop on Thursday, the 22nd inst., to be supplied with percussion caps, and placing one on the nipple, fired. The gun was loaded unknown to the owner, (having lain for some time on a rack at home), and the charge went through a partition which separates the shop from the kitchen. About two minutes previously there were two persons engaged in the room, in the direction of the line of fire; but for a Providential interposition in one of the party being called away, and the other moving to perform some household duty, a most fearful accident would in all probability occurred. The warning now given to all, it is to be hoped, will be attended to, as to how they manage such dangerous weapons....specially....at the present time, when the sporting season is onward.

30 September (WB) MUTINY AT SEA. Intelligence has been received from the ship *Blanchmore*, Thomas Nickels, of Fowey, commander, - sailing from Liverpool, that during the voyage out to Calcutta, the men broke into the hold and tapped the beer which formed a portion of the cargo; then rose in mutiny, when the captain in self-defence fired and killed one man and wounded another. The mutineers, on arrival, were arrested and lodged in prison. The vessel is of the first class, having on board, including officers and men, forty-five persons.

11 November (RCG) The Royal National Life Boat Institution has this week sent two lifeboats to Polpear, Lizard, and to Polkerris near Fowey. The life boats are 30 feet long, and row 6 oars. They combine all the latest improvements that have been made in the boats of the institution. They will row fast in a seaway, and if filled by a sea, will clear themselves of water in 20 seconds; they have much stability, requiring the weight of 14 men on one gunwale, without any counteracting weight on other side, to immerse it; and they would instantly self right if upset.... The Fowey lifeboat was brought by Railway to Lostwithiel, the companies having as on previous occasions, given readily free conveyance to the life-boats.

25 November (RCG) MIRACULOUS ESCAPE FROM DROWNING.- On the 15th inst., James Rundle, an industrious and sober man, and his son, aged 15 years, went to Pridmouth Beach, about a mile seaward from the entrance of Fowey Harbour, to load his boat with sea-weed, for manure, and about 5 p.m. they proceeded with their load towards home; but after pulling a short time, and when about half-a-mile from the shore, both Rundle and his son were stunned with the appearance of the boat sinking under them: the son at once stripped himself of his clothes, and jumped into the sea; and his father, who could not swim, was left to struggle with the deep. The son reached the shore, and climbed a cliff, and then ran naked a distance of half-a-mile, until he came to a Limeburner's Cottage, at a Cove called Ready Money, where he was in every way very kindly treated by Dorrington, the limeburner, who immediately after hearing what had happened ran into the town, a distance of nearly another half-a-mile, when he called upon Josiah Phillips, a labourer, who called upon two or three others of his class, and who promptly took a boat and proceeded towards Pridmouth, and found poor Rundle struggling in the sea, with his head just above the water, supported by a small spar and one of the paddles belonging to the sunken boat, almost exhausted,-for he had been in that perilous situation, at night time, for upwards of an hour and a half. And it should again be stated that by the prompt exertion of Phillips and his companions, under Divine Providence, Rundle's life was miraculously saved. - He was soon landed and carried to the "Crown and Anchor", kept by Mr. Collins, where he received the kindest treatment; and the usual appliances having been made for the restoration of life by Dr. Davis, who was soon on the spot, Rundle rallied, was placed in bed, and the next day was able to walk to his own home, where he met his wife and eight children to weep and rejoice over him. (the Royal National Lifeboat Association committee later awarded ten shillings each to the 4 men who went to the assistance of Rundle.

16 December (RCG) FOWEY VOLUNTEER ARTILLERY CORPS. This corps is getting on rapidly with drill; it musters about 70 strong. The members drill four evenings in the week in the Town Hall, which has been placed at their disposal for the purpose. The Rev. E. J. Treffry has subscribed £10 and offered to provide 8 volunteers their uniform dress, and has proposed that the entire corps shall dine together annually, he promising to present them with a bullock. - The ladies of Fowey present colors, and arrangements are in progress for getting up an efficient band.- The "gallants of Fowey" have not lost the ardor and zeal which they inherited from their forefathers.

CHAPTER 7
1860-1869

1860

20 January (RCG) FOWEY. -.... The fishermen have been much annoyed, as the porpoises drive away and devour the salmon; and in order to put a stop to the career of these great and greedy visitors, the fishermen one and all agreed to shoot their four seans across the harbour, so as to arrest their progress seaward - a plan that proved effectual; for as these monsters of the deep were enclosed in the inner net, and closely taken, they would break through, but were again within the compass of the other nets, and being so enclosed, a number of coastguards and others took boats and proceeded to the spot; and as the porpoises, (some of which weighed upwards of 1/2 ton) leaped above the surface of the water to blow and breathe, 8 of them were shot and landed, and others sunk to the bottom by being shot, and will be taken up when the seans are drawn. - These immense fish it is said are very valuable for the oil they produce, by which the fishermen and others it is hoped, will be amply rewarded, both for their labour and skill in capturing them.

23 March (RCG) *Polruan Volunteer Artillery.* - Two long 24 pounder guns have been supplied to this corps. They were landed on the quay on Friday last, and on Monday removed to St. Saviour's for practice. Owing to the steepness of the street, the removing of the guns, which are 50 cwt. each, was a matter of no small difficulty.... The farmers of the neighbourhood lent horses, the volunteers turned out, and so prevalent was the enthusiasm that almost every person in Polruan, whether belonging to the corps or not, assisted. In two hours after the commencement of operations the guns were mounted on their carriages on the highest part of the hill, and their muzzles pointed to sea.

4 May (WB) THE FOWEY CHARITIES AND ENDOWED SCHOOL. The following has been addressed to Mr. H. Sergeant, Head Master....by....one of the Inspectors of the Diocesan Board for Devon;- "In accordance with your request I examined your school, and had much pleasure in doing so; your private scholars, as well as the foundation, went through the ordeal. The subjects of examination were scripture, English history, English and Latin grammar, geography, arithmetic, chronology, parsing, &c., and I found their knowledge of the several subjects accurate, and evidenced by such a readiness and quickness as reflected much credit on your exertions. The outlines of maps drawn by the scholars, and their writing on copy books were very praiseworthy....

3 August (RCG) TRECAN GATE PETTY SESSIONS. - Mr. James Bray, of Polruan was charged by Mr. Smith with laying timber on the highway; Fined 1s., and 12s.6d. costs.

24 August (WB) FOWEY COTTAGE HOSPITAL. A small but valuable institution has been recently established at Fowey, designed for the accommodation of the poor when suffering from sickness or accidents. The establishment consists of a regular nurse, who has residence in the cottage rent free, and is paid when her services are required, and at other times has permission to attend poor women at their own houses during their confinements. Patients are admissible on payment of a fixed weekly sum, depending in amount upon their circumstances, but the medical officer (Dr A.A. Davis) gives his services without fee or reward. The hospital is not designed for the reception of chronic cases, but for such diseases as are likely not to require a very long and expensive course of treatment. Such a provision in a town and port so far removed from a public hospital will probably be of great service....

7 September (RCG) *To the Editor....* Visitors....will be glad to hear, in common with its rejoicing inhabitants, that there is now a probability of the removal of "The Shed" that has so long been suffered to shut out so large a portion of the view of the Harbour.... It is readily conceded by all parties that a Rope Walk with its retrograding rank of spinning artisans, is anything but a pleasant or fitting place for a promenade; and that for well-dressed folks to feel themselves compelled to go through this long dark tunnel, beneath a perspective of gallowses, ranged at intervals in ominous succession over their heads, is a most disagreeable necessity; that whether a person's purpose is business or pleasure,....they have no other alternative but to "run the gauntlet" of its contaminations, to the imminent risk of spoiling their apparel from unctious contact with dirty grease tubs, unconscious tarry attachments, or the fall of promiscuous oil-drippings, as they pass along this difficult passage of the Ropers' Straits, side by side with an extension of twisting rope in process, trailing or travelling machine en suite, accompanied with the whirl and noise of a small maufactory. It will not be wondered at that the generous proposition of the adjoining landed proprietor, W. Rashleigh, Esq., offering the means of remedying this`anomaly has been received with a general joy..... ONE OF THE COMMUNITY.

14 September (WB) A PUBLIC IMPROVEMENT. Mr. W. Rashleigh, of Menabilly, has in course of construction a marine villa on the site of the old battery, at the end of the walk, outside the Ropewalk, commanding a fine sea view. Very recently he has informed the inhabitants of Fowey, by a printed circular, of his intention of bringing a road through the Levere estate to meet the above walk, and of forming on the same a raised footpath which will be an extension of the promenade, diversifying the view in a very pleasing manner. In order, however, that this may be carried out as to have a good roadway to the town of Fowey, Mr Rashleigh has appealed to the inhabitants to combine with him in removing the present ropewalk with all its gear - keeping in view at the same time, that Mr Thomas, the present occupier, shall experience no inconvenience thereby.... A considerable fall of the cliff, close to the roadway, which is through the ropewalk, requiring immediate attention, as persons in passing tread on the edge of a precipice of more than 100 feet descent..... A public meeting was held in the Townhall on Thursday,....to take Mr Rashleigh's proposition into consideration....resolutions accepting the same were passed, and a subscription made to remunerate Mr. Thomas for any expense to which he may be put in removing the shed and other gear.

21 September (WB) PUNISHMENT OF THE STOCKS. On Sunday evening last, a boy employed by Mr Sparnall, of the Ship Inn, Fowey, underwent the punishment of the stocks, in the porch of the church, for the offence of pilfering a ring from a table in the dressing room of the house.

2 November (WB) .... The Railway is intended to be a single line 5 1/4 miles in length, leaving the line of the Cornwall Railway, near the Lostwithiel Station, and following the western shore of the Estuary of the Fowey to a terminus at Caffamill Pill, contiguous to the town of Fowey. The advantages of thus bringing the port of Fowey in direct connexion with all the main lines of railway in the kingdom, and with the chief producing districts of this county, are scarcely capable of exaggeration....

The quantity of china clay and china stone shipped from the district....connected with the proposed line of railway, annually exceeds one hundred thousand tons, more than one third of which goes to Foreign ports. Serious delay and expense is now incurred in the shipment of these articles from tidal harbours; as it often takes a fortnight to discharge and reload a vessel, and it is now impossible to use vessels of large tonnage.... Previous to the opening of the Cornwall Railway, the cost of bringing the clay and stone to Fowey was so great that, with the exception of a small quantity that was brought round from Charlestown and elsewhere in lighters, for re-shipment, nothing was done to turn these advantages to account. On the completion of the proposed line, however,.... there is every reason to believe that the bulk of China Clay and stone will be shipped from ....Fowey in addition to the timber, ore, and other merchandize.

28 December (RCG) Lostwithiel.- At a petty Sessions....*Cornelius Pill*, fisherman, of Polruan, was summoned on the complaint of Inspecting Commander Norcock, for anchoring fishing-nets within the harbour of Fowey....the fishermen were in the habit of obstructing the Channel, and very recently one of H.M. cutters became entangled, and some damage accrued. The penalty incurred for the offence (....admitted by the defendant) was, according to Act of Parliament, ten pounds. Captain Norcock pleaded hard that the penalty might be mitigated and the magistrates....fined....two shillings and sixpence, and twelve shillings costs.

1861

19 April (RCG) COUNTY POLICE.- Samuel Yeo, beerhouse- keeper, of Pont, Lanteglos, appeared....charged with having refused to admit P.C. Cole into his beer-shop, on the afternoon of Good Friday;.... It appeared that....four sets of ringers had met to "try" Lanteglos bells, some of whom, with their friends, put up at defendant's beer-shop. About 4 o'clock, P.C's. Cole and Hyde went to the house, which at that hour should have been closed. The defendant was standing at the front door, and was in the act of closing it as the police approached. P.C. Cole called to him that`he was coming in, but defendant immediately shut the door and locked it, as Cole put his hand on the handle. Cole then went to back door, and met 6 or 7 men rushing out; others seeing Cole, made for front door, unlocked it, and ran against Hyde, who had remained there on Cole leaving. The defendant called witnesses to prove that there had been no drinking within prohibited hours, though both policemen swore they saw a man drinking as they passed the window. There was, however, no defence to charge of refusing to admit the police....justices therefore fined Yeo £1 and costs. Defendant....had been fined twice last year.

24 May (RCG) FOWEY.- At half-past one o'clock p.m. on Whit Tuesday, the Fowey Artillery Volunteers assembled on the Town Quay, where they were put through various evolutions before a large assemblage of people.... Great praise is due to Bombadier Harris, for the way in which he has brought on the corps both at small arms and great gun exercise. From the town quay the company, headed by their officers and music, marched to St. Catherine's battery to fire at a target.... In the afternoon they were joined by the Polruan corps, headed by their officers, and drum and fife band. At 5 o'clock they proceeded to the beautiful Vale, which slopes from Lenhire house, (the residence of Mr. Williams) to the beach, and in that part of the Vale adjoining the rope-walk, 30 tables were prepared for a public tea drink, in aid of Fowey and Polruan Artillery Volunteer Fund, at which about 500 sat down to partake, and it was a pleasing sight to see so many enjoying themselves to their hearts' content. During the repast, the brass, drum, and fife bands alternately livened the scene by their capital style of playing; great praise is due to the ladies who presided, for their condescending kindness and constant endeavours to make all before them happy and comfortable. The rope-walk was literally crowded with spectators, and "One and All" seemed highly pleased with the proceedings of this auspicious day.

31 May (WB) On Tuesday the 21st inst, John Way, accompanied by his wife, was engaged in fishing at Lanivet Bay, to the eastward of the harbour; about six o'clock p.m. they observed a boat under sail off Pencarrow Head, a strong breeze blowing at the time. The sailing boat was observed to suddenly turn over. Mr. Way pulled hard to the rescue and came up in time to save the two coastguardsmen whose craft was overturned. The boat was with some difficulty towed to the beach under the station without damage;.... The case has been represented to Captain Norcock, Inspecting Commander of the Coast Guard, and it is thought that the Humane Society will reward Way for his diligence in such an emergency. John Way is a baker's foreman at Polruan.

28 June (WB) FOWEY COTTAGE HOSPITAL. This institution was opened about 12 months since,....rented from the Rev E.J. Treffry at a nominal rent of 1s per annum.... The hospital has been hitherto self- supporting, although there have been eleven patients in it. All the cases have terminated favourably, with the exception of that of a sailor, who died from typhus fever, and who was in a dying state when brought on shore from his vessel.... There are at present in the hospital three beds, but the cottage will admit of five.

26 July (RCG) POLRUAN 7TH (CORNWALLl) VOLUNTEER ARTILLERY.- Charles Rundle, member of this corps died on the 16th inst., and on Thursday was buried in Lanteglos churchyard.... The friends of the deceased expressed a wish that there should be no firing party, but out of respect to their comrade, about 70 of the Polruan and Fowey Volunteers attended his funeral, accompanied by the brass band of the Fowey battery, which played the "Dead March in Saul" on their way to the churchyard. Rundle was a shipwright, and his death was caused by an accident in a building-yard; he ran a nail through his foot, and for eight or nine days went about and thought lightly of the accident, but on Monday, feeling worse, he for the first time, sought medical advice. Dr. Davis, who attended immediately, pronounced, to the astonishment of Rundle's friends that the poor fellow was beyond the reach of human help. He died of tetanus the following morning.

27 September (WB) BITE OF A VIPER. On Saturday last, the wife of Captain J. Harvey, residing at Military-road, Fowey, had a basket of blackberries brought to her, under which there were cabbage leaves, which she turned out on the table in a dish, returning the cabbage leaves to the basket, when she saw a reptile, which she took in her fingers heedlessly, it being not above two inches in length, and returned it also to the basket. Soon after she felt pain between her thumb and finger, with swelling and discolouring of the part. Dr. Illingworth passing at the time, was shown the part affected; he pronounced it the bite of an adder, and directed Mrs. Harvey to drink milk, which she did, and applied a poultice to the affected part. She was soon relieved but the discolouration remained for two or three days.

27 September (RCG) Fowey. - *Serious Accident.*-As Mary Ann May, the wife of William May, a mariner, of this place, was locking the door of her garden (which is only accessible by a flight of steps), her foot slipped, and she fell backwards over the steps, a height of 12 feet. In lifting her up it was found that she had sustained serious injury; her collar bone being broken, and her skull fractured. Prompt attendance was given by Dr. White, but she remains in a very precarious state.

25 October (RCG) SALMON FISHERY. Fowey.... Notice is hereby given that we....fishermen respectively engaged in the Salmon Fishery in the waters of and at Fowey, and residing at Polruan....do intend....to apply to Her Majesty's Justices of the Peace....for an extension and variation of the present time for taking salmon within such waters.... (Signed) William Curtis, George Climo, William Climo, Christopher Slade, William Salt, William Curtis, junr., Thomas Mark, William H. May, Thomas Harvey, John Salt, Peter Todd, Anthony Tucker.... It had been the practice to take salmon at Polruan and Fowey,....at the mouth of the harbour from the latter part of August or beginning of September to the 31st of December; but the Act of last Session....enacted that no person shall fish for salmon between the 1st of September and the 1st of February, except only....with a rod and line between the 1st of September and the 1st of November....the fish do not usually make their appearance in the waters of Fowey until the latter end of September, and have been usually taken from that time down to the end of December, to which period they have always been considered perfectly good and in season, such fish not being taken up the`river, but at the mouth and entrance of the harbour....Many of the Fishermen....and their families....have embarked their little capital in boats, nets, and gear....and great hardships and loss will be sustained by them if the said Act of Parliament be not remedied.... Your Memorialists would therefore earnestly request....that your Worships....cause the necessary application to be made....to the Home Office for an extension and variation of the time for taking Salmon in the waters at Fowey....from the 1st of September until the 31st of December in every year....

Mr. Bishop proceeded to examine witnesses in support of his application:- *William Salt,* aged 72 years. I have lived at Polruan....ever since I was born, and have known the Fowey fishery about 65 years; I have myself been engaged on it 55 years, and for 19 years was lessee of harbour dues under the Lostwithiel Corporation. In Fowey waters we take the salmon at the mouth of the Harbour, between Punch's Cross and the old Castle- a width of about half a mile. I have gone to fish as early as the latter part of July, but sometimes in August; but our general rule is to go to fish about the first Monday in September, and we go on fishing till Christmas. The largest catches I ever made were in two hauls, one year, between Christmas-day and New Year's day; that was 45 years ago; we took 240 in one haul and 103 in the other; these fish were very good, and the last catch was taken to Plymouth market. During the last ten years we have fished until the first spring tide after Christmas.... The fish go up the river only when tide flows high....we don't go up the river at all. Between December and September we don't put our nets, for there are no salmon... *George Pearn,* also a fisherman of Polruan, aged 87 years, gave similar evidence.... *George Climo,* aged 61, a fisherman of Polruan during the greater part of his life, said....the fish had always been found good until about Christmas.... *Mr. Kendall, M.P.* deposed....that about October or the early part of November, the finest salmon were found at the entrance of Fowey Harbour; but for many years he believed the fish had been taken very improperly, to a much later period -much to the damage of the fishery....the CHAIRMAN stated.... I shall make application to the Home Office to extend the open season, for the Fowey waters, to the 7th November.

25 October (RCG) Porcupine Petty Sessions.- John Sparnall, of Fowey, innkeeper, was summoned for driving a stage carriage, without having a proper licence. The defendant....had, since the opening of the Cornwall Railway, been in the habit of plying a carriage from Par Station to Fowey. He has also conveyed the mails. On the 29th August last, Mr. Sparnall, as usual, proceeded on his journey with his passengers, amongst whom was an Excise officer, who for detective purposes, came all the way from Bristol. Of course, Mr. Sparnall jogged on his way little suspecting the nature of his goods, and on his arriving at the place of destination, the Exciseman's watch was consulted, to shew the time taken, when it was found to be a minute or so less than allowed.... The Bench gave the defendant the benefit, and dismissed the summons, whereupon the Excise appealed.

John Martin, of Fowey, innkeeper, was summoned for the like offence on the 26th August. In this case, the complainant was successful, having proved by his witness that the defendant completed the journey in half-an-hour less than the time allowed him. The Bench fined him £20. (Note, because the narrow wheels dug up the roads, carriages were not supposed to exceed 4 mph.).

20 December (RCG) Porcupine Sessions (Held at the Porcupine Inn) *Card Playing.- John Frost*, the`newly installed innkeeper at the Ship Inn, Fowey, appeared to the charge of suffering card playing in his house on October 7th.... P.C. Charles Riggs....detected the offence from outside the`window at first. Defendant in his attempt to screen himself, contended that the party was a private one, and did not require the surveillance of the complainant; and entangled the names of several respectable gentlemen of the town, some of whom, in vindication of their character, appeared before the bench and received admonitions; but for obvious reasons we refrain from mentioning their names. (WB - same case as above).... Mr. Frost....on the night referred to had an opening supper at his house, at which 50 attended. A few remained behind the others, but he had no idea anyone was playing cards in the house. The chairman said perhaps it was not a case of direct gambling, but no doubt the defendant had committed an infraction of his licence. He was fined 20s and expenses.

1862

17 January (WB) BOAT ACCIDENT. On Thursday, the 9th instant, Mr. Asher Joel, a jeweller, of Stonehouse, with his man, about 2 p.m. engaged Jonathan Tadd, of Polruan, with a small boat, to take him, his man, and his box of jewellery from Fowey to that place. There was what is termed "a little cockle," on the water, and the boatman requested them to sit still; but the spray coming a little over the bow, Mr. Joel was afraid of damage to his ornaments, valued at £2000. When about half-way across, he attempted to move the box aft; and stepping a little from the centre the boat took in some water, and the next step to bring her up turned her over, and all three and the box were in the water. Many saw it, and were at once on the alert to save life. *Fowey* men being expert at the oar, the work was done in a few minutes, and all were saved. Two shillings worth of beer was ordered for the sailors, but, as they considered the prize was worth more, they moderately asked £5, to which there was a demurrer, but it was settled by his worship, Rev. E.J. Treffry and Dr. Davis awarding £3 10s.

17 January (WB) PRACTICE GROUND OF THE VOLUNTEERS. The Fowey Volunteers have chosen a piece of ground for carbine practice,....in a valley, part of the adjacent farm of Coombe, in the occupation of Mrs. Penrose, and distant about a quarter of an hour's march from the town. As the sides of the valley are steep as the roof of a house, with a range in the bottom of 200 yards, the place has all the advantages of a "natural shooting alley," while the target being just over the beach, the missing shots will all go safely and harmlessly to the sea. As the consent to the use of the ground was promptly granted,....it is hoped the idle medley of camp-followers, that too frequently trudge along promiscuously in the rear of troops marching to their "field of action," will not be permitted too much liberty of trespass, and that the crops and hedges will not suffer for the privilege so cheerfully and patriotically accorded.

4 April (WB) A correspondent states there have been many vessels in Fowey harbour waiting (for some weeks), for tide and space to enter Par and Charlestown to load with clay, &c. There is an absolute necessity for having a railway from Lostwithiel to Fowey to accommodate the shipping interest, and especially for the china clay trade. The *Hannah Hicks* lately loaded with china clay brought down from the Cornwall Railway at Lostwithiel, being the first vessel thus loaded with the assistance of the railway. She was chartered to Genoa, and is now on her passage.

23 May (WB) FOWEY BAND OF HOPE. The first anniversary of this society was held on Tuesday last, at two o'clock. The members of the society assembled in the Town-hall, and headed by their fife and drum band, marched to Place,....where....the band played several animated airs; thence they marched through the town to the Town-hall, where they found excellent tea and cake provided for them, of which 400 partook. The fife and drum band....played at intervals many favourite tunes in good style.... After tea, they were marched to that lovely vale which slopes from Lewhire-house (the residence of Mr. Williams) down to the beach. The weather was fine, and here the juveniles enjoyed themselves in all manner of sports, after which they again returned to the Town-hall, which was tastefully decorated with evergreens, beautiful flags, and banners, having mottos on them, relative to the proceedings of the day. In the evening, the meeting was enlivened by melodies, which were well sung, and in which the audience engaged in chorus, and many recitations were given by the boys and girls, on the evils arising from intemperance....

13 June (RCG) 3RD BATTERY (FOWEY) DUKE OF CORNWALL'S ARTILLERY VOLUNTEERS. On Monday, the bugle was heard sounding through the town, at about eleven o'clock a.m., which denoted to the volunteers that they must be up and doing. It being holiday time, a large number were soon in uniform and at the armoury, and received orders to march to Lanreath - a distance of about five miles. Thirteen file formed the company, and were headed by the band, making a total of forty men. The weather was fine, and the march was enjoyed by all. At Mr. Andrew's, Polvethan, they were regaled with cider, cake, &c., and joined by Sergeant Andrew, the host's son, and proceeded to Lanreath, arriving about two o'clock; there various manoeuvrings were gone through, and the men dismissed to partake of refreshments prepared for them, which reflected great credit on Mr. and Mrs. Davey, of the White Horse Inn. The Rev. R. Buller sent an invitation to Capt. Sobey for the corps to parade in his splendid gardens, throwing them open to the corps and the visitors, who mustered between two and three hundred persons. The corps went through various manoeuvrings in the rev. gentleman's grounds, which, with volley firing, were executed in first-rate style. The band played at intervals. The Rev. R. Buller addressed the officers and men in a very complimentary manner, and three cheers were given to the corps, which then returned home, arriving at their armoury at half-past ten o'clock. (WB adds- the manual and platoon exercises by Captain Sobey, afterwards firing 2 volleys, each man being supplied with 5 rounds of blank ammunition, which was gone through admirably.... The volunteers, both on the march out and home, were handsomely treated by the farmers of the neighbourhood; - and, on returning, they met with a similar reception at Mr. Williams', at Trefaul....)

11 July (WB) 7TH BATTERY ARTILLERY VOLUNTEERS, POLRUAN. On Thursday, the 3rd instant. at 11 a.m., the 7th Battery D.C.A.V. assembled at their battery, under the command of the Captain and Officers to compete for prizes offered by the County Volunteer Association. The target was moored about 1400 yards distance from the battery, on the west side of the offing. Some good firing was made,....yet the flag on the target stood the "battle and the breeze". The first prize was awarded to H. Climo, 30s.; the second, 15s., to T. Climo; and third, 10s., to W. Langmaid and J. Kenton, the ties being shared with Cater. Lieut.-Colonel Gilbert made some remarks on the volunteers, their soldier-like appearance, and their smart firing and practical discipline and performance.

11 July (WB) NO. 3 (FOWEY) CORNWALL COUNTY ARTILLERY VOLUNTEERS. On Thursday last, the volunteers assembled at the Castle, at two p.m....to compete for prizes, offered by the Cornwall Volunteer Association. The target was moored at the distance of about 1,450 yards, and some first-rate firing was made.... The first prize of £2 was awarded to Gunner R.B. Williams, whose shot completely smashed the target....In the evening there was a tea in aid of the funds of the battery, which was held in Mr. Thomas' rope walk. The weather being so unfavourable quite put an end to the arrangements which were made for holding it in Lewhire valley, as was at first intended; however, an excellent arrangement was made, and great praise is due to the ladies who presided at the tables.... After tea, arrangements were made for a dance on nature's green carpet, the excellent band of the battery contributing the music.

11 July No 3 (Fowey) D.C.O. Artillery volunteers.... On the 4th instant, there was a second tea. Capt. Sobey treated many poor widows to the tea, held in the rope walk, and others paid their fare and partook of the repast. After tea, many amusements were indulged in amongst the seniors and juniors of the company - viz., "Striking out the Cuckoo", playing at "Aunt Sally," &c. Afterwards they closed with a dance. The band of the 3rd Battery attended.

8 August (WB) FATAL ACCIDENT. On Wednesday morning, John Jago, a labouring man, above sixty years of age, having a family mostly grown up and earning their own living, was in the act of firing a brass cannon belonging to the custom-house of Fowey, when it burst, and a splinter of the gun broke open his skull, and literally knocked his brains out, and scattered them over his person. This sad accident took place shortly before the commencement of the annual regatta. Men are stationed at different places along the race course, on the Fowey side of the harbour, to fire guns at their respective stations, and thus to report, by firing at each place, the progress of the boats. Jago was one of the number thus placed, but the contest of the boats had not begun when he fired. The body was removed to the cottage hospital to await a coroner's inquest.

5 September (WB) EARLY LAMBING. The Rev. E. J. Treffry, of Place House, Fowey, has had for some time a flock of sheep of the Dorset-horn breed - an early sort for lambing. One of the ewes lambed last week, and is doing well.

12 September (WB) On the handsome and lofty church tower of Fowey there was formerly four pinacles, with a vane on each, but the lapse of time and the effect of storms since the erection of the structure in the fourteenth century, caused one of them to fall more than a quarter of a century ago, and the other fell in the winter of 1861. Much credit is due to the vicar, Rev. J. Kempe, and others, who by their liberal efforts have been the means of restoring these ornaments of the tower to their former position.

12 September (WB) THE FISHERY AT FOWEY. The seine belonging to Messrs. G. Nickels and Son, shipbuilders, enclosed thirty-five hogsheads of pilchards ....brought in on Wednesday morning. On the evening of the 9ths instant, pilot Johns caught ten thousand or more in his ground seine at the mouth of the harbour. The drift boats have also caught many thousands of pilchards.

26 September (RCG) VESSEL LOST. The brigantine *Polyxena*, Steele, master, of Fowey, from Poole, was run down by the French brig *Divinity*, of Bordeaux, on the 2nd instant, and sunk. The crew were saved, but lost all their effects. They were taken to Flushing, in Holland, and forwarded thence to England. (Polruan Master, Polruan and Bodinnick owners).

31 October (RCG) MR. RASHLEIGH and his NEIGHBORS AT FOWEY. Mr. Rashleigh, having recently erected a beautiful Marine Villa, at Point Neptune,....the opening of Mr. Rashleigh's new road, and the dedication to public use, of the New Footpath, took place on Tuesday last.... The Fowey Artillery Volunteers attended with their band; and by 2 o'clock,....a large number of persons of all classes, ranks, and ages,....had congregated at and near the northern entrance to the new road; Mr. Rashleigh being seated in an open phaeton, and the Hon. Mrs. Rashleigh and Miss Rashleigh taking warm and active interest in the rural holiday.

At the entrance to the new road was erected a handsome arch bearing the mottoes "Welcome," and "Ships, Colonies, Commerce," wrought in flowers, and surmounted by a banner with the motto "God bless our Queen Victoria."

Before entering the gateway leading to the newly-formed road and causeway, Mr. RASHLEIGH, inaugurating the proceedings with his wonted loyalty, said;- "Ladies and Gentlemen, I trust that I am not asking more than is natural and proper in this great country....if I request you to join me in three times three hearty cheers for Her most Gracious Majesty, Queen Victoria -Queen of Great Britain, Empress of India, and, I am happy to add, mistress of the seas.- (Cheers were given most heartily,.... the band of the Fowey Artillery Volunteers playing "God save the Queen.")

The procession was then formed. It comprised the Band and other members of the Fowey Artillery Volunteers, about 45 in number, under command of Capt. Sobey, Lieut. Short, and Ensign Hicks.- Mr. Rashleigh in an open carriage.- A considerable number of ladies and gentlemen, and other inhabitants, of Fowey and its neighbourhood; and a very much larger number of girls and boys - belonging to the various Sunday schools, bearing banners of various kinds....

At a point which commands a good view of Ready-money Cove and its adjacent scenery, the pathway is considerably widened, and seats are placed there for the accommodation of weary wayfarers or of lovers of the picturesque. Above this spot, was displayed a pendant bearing the word, "Catharine" - the name by which the newly-made footpath is henceforth to be designated, chiefly in compliment to the Hon. Mrs. Rashleigh (who takes an active interest in all that affects the happiness of her neighbours), and partly in reference to the name of one of the olden castles near the entrance of Fowey harbour. At the end of the road and leading to Mr. Rashleigh's new Marine Villa, at "Point Neptune," there was another triumphal arch, bearing floral mottoes, - "Prosperity to the Port of Foy", and "Welcome"; these being surmounted by the motto "God save our Queen Victoria"; and at the Villa, and at various other prominent sites in the vicinity, were abundant displays of flags in great variety; the whole presenting what would have been a scene of considerable beauty and exhilarating influence had the weather been only moderately favourable Unfortunately....there was close and heavy rain. From his carriage Mr. Rashleigh addressed the assemblage around him "....having presented to you this pathway, I claim the right to christen it the "St.Catharine's Parade.".... I have long wished for the prosperity of Fowey; but I see in it a great lack of that go-ahead spirit which our friends the other side of the water used to show us, and without bloodshed. I must say there is in Fowey greater inaction than I ever saw in any other port, although its natural beauties surpass what I have met with elsewhere....you must rouse yourselves and do something for the place; if it is to be a Railway Terminus; it will not do to have a railway terminus among a parcel of tumble-down buildings.... Just look at the Landing-place; I ask if that landing-place is not a disgrace to a port having such a name as yours has. The very name of "Gallants of Foy," inherited from the time of the Edwards, ought to rouse you. At all events, I don't want to see you go below Par (laughter).... I have long wished that my late venerable friend, the greatest employer in this county, instead of taking away the trade of Fowey, had brought his talents, his capital, and his energy to bear on this port; for I believe that in that case, Fowey would have stood next to the port of Falmouth. I say that without the slightest disrespect to the gentleman who now so well represents and manages the Treffry property....we must try to put our shoulders to the wheel. A public company brings you a railroad; a private individual gives you a path-way; but I want to see a little more energy and *esprit de corps* among Fowey people. You have the best anchorage that I know anywhere; you have a most lovely river;.... I have no doubt that with spirit and energy on your parts, you may have villas built there and their occupants spending money among you.... I should certainly like to see villas similar to my own, close at hand here. But all that would not do without a first-class Hotel. You want such a house with suitable rooms where public spirited men may meet and transact business, and with proper commercial rooms....

Hearty cheers were then given....and the band playing suitable music, the party separated; a large and respectable portion accepting Mr. and the Hon. Mrs. Rashleigh's invitation to luncheon at Point Neptune; and a still larger number proceeding to Mr. Thomas's rope manufactory, where upwards of 350 children of various schools were liberally regaled. The luncheon at Point Neptune was a most bounteous and elegant display of substantial and tempting refections and excellent wines, laid out in the large dining hall, commanding an interesting view of the entrance to Fowey Harbour.... Mr RASHLEIGH presided; and....proposed a succession of loyal and other toasts.... He spoke of the freedom in Church and State....which all persons enjoy in this country; one of the great bulwarks....being the established Church of England - the firm support of Protestantism....

Rev. E.J. TREFFRY returned cordial thanks for the kind way in which Mr. Rashleigh had spoken of the Church and her ministers.... He entirely endorsed the opinions uttered by Mr. Rashleigh.... He was for liberty of conscience; but at the same time he felt that the Church of England was one of the bulwarks of the nation, and that it would be an evil day for all classes and sects in this country, if the time should come that the Church should cease to exist in union with the State; and he believed that right-thinking dissenters held the same opinion....

Rev. E.J. Treffry. - Ladies and Gentlemen; I have permission to propose a toast. .... When our friend and neighbour Mr. Rashleigh and his honourable lady came to this County a few years ago, there were none who more sincerely than the people of Fowey....welcomed them to Menabilly.... I should address Mr. Rashleigh....also with reference to some observances which Mr. Rashleigh has made.... I regret, even more than he does, the tumbledown state of many of the houses in Fowey.... We will repair these tumbledown houses as soon as we can see our way clear to have tenants to occupy them. It would be a long story if I were to take you back to the condition of Fowey before it got into Schedule A, on the passing of the Reform Bill....from that time it has been in a gradually declining state. But now we have....a railroad coming close to our doors....Fowey must become the shipping port for the China Clay and China Stone of the neighbourhood...and Fowey must become a prosperous place.... It seems to me that the great rivalry will be between Fowey and Falmouth....

21 November TYWARDREATH PETTY SESSIONS. Christopher Slade, of Polruan, and John Pearn, of Fowey, appeared to a summons charging them with rolling a lighted tar-barrel through the streets of Fowey on the 5th inst. The case was proved by P.C. Parkyn, and defendents were fined 1s. and costs each.

1863

6 February (WB) On Sunday last, W.H. Lee, an apprentice to Mr. Henry Hooper, boot and shoemaker, Fowey, was apprehended by P.C. Parkyn, charged with absconding from his master's employ. He was taken before the Rev. E.J. Treffry on the following day, and committed to the house of correction for two months with hard labour.

13 February (WB) THE VOLUNTARY PRINCIPLE .... The Rev. E.J. Treffry.... has made a conditional offer to his congregation, that if they can guarantee him a certain amount, by means of pew-rents, other small but necessary charges he shall be glad to dispense with altogether; while the contingent hope is added prospectively, of the chance of getting a new organ, to be followed in due time with other improvements....there have been no church-rates....for several years, and as the new proposition involves only the very reasonable charge-of 4s. a head per annum, it has been....happily acquiesced in.

27 February (RCG) COTTAGES FOR AGRICULTURAL LABOURERS.... A cottage should contain....two rooms on ground floor, one larger than the other, for a general living room for the family, and the smaller one fitted up with sink, oven, copper, &c., for washing, cooking, and the work of the house; two bedrooms are positively necessary and in many instances, three, it being highly improper that, when a family is growing up, children of both sexes should sleep in the same room, as is too often the case now-a-days....a small shed should be added at the back of the cottage as a store place for fuel, tools, and such like articles. This....can be in most instances secured for an outlay of from 60*l. to* 80*l.*, yielding a rent of from 3*l.* to 4*l.* per annum, with from 20 to 40 poles of garden ground.

6 March (WB) STEALING ROPE AT FOWEY. On Tuesday last, Samuel Scantlebury was apprehended by P.C.Parkyn for entering seine stores and taking eleven fathoms of new rope, the property of John Langmaid, fisherman, Fowey. Scantlebury was taken before the Rev. E.J. Treffry, when he confessed the robbery, and implicated Charles Johns, of Polruan, aged 18, as his accomplice. They will be summoned to appear at the next petty sessions at Tywardreath.

13 March (WB) On Tuesday, the day of the Royal marriage, the fifes and drums of the Band of Hope were heard early in the morning, and about eight o'clock peals were rung on Fowey fine-toned bells. Shortly after nine, the 3rd D.C. Artillery Volunteers assembled to attend Divine service at the Church. At noon the gunners fired a royal salute of 21 guns, and then marched to the town quay and fired a *feu de joie*, after which they paraded through the town with their band. The day was rather wet and unfavourable to the rejoicings. At one p.m. a dinner was provided by subscription in the school-house for the male and female poor - good substantial fare being supplied by Mr. Martin, of the Commercial Inn. About 150 partook of the dinner, and 30 more dined at Mr. Martin's house. The Rev. E.J. Treffry presided, and various toasts were enthusiastically received, including, of course, the health of the Queen, and health, long life, and happiness to the Prince and Princess of Wales. The band of the 3rd Battery played at intervals, and concluded with the National Anthem. At two p.m. a large concourse of people assembled in the meadow to see the cakes given to the school-children; 400 were given to the children of the schools of different denominations, and to others belonging to no sect; a cake, 1 lb. weight, and an orange were given to each boy and girl. At 3 p.m. there was an Ordinary at the Ship Inn.... Loyal and other toasts were heartily drunk, and in the evening the Ship Inn was illuminated. At nine p.m. there was a ball at the residence of Capt. Sobey, the band of the 3rd Battery being in attendance. The bells rang merrily during the day.

27 March. (WB) FOWEY ENDOWED SCHOOL. Mr. Henry Sergeant, who has conducted the duties of the above school for the last five years, has left Fowey for Scilly....to the curacy of St. Agnes.... Mr Tonkin, of Redruth....has succeeded Mr. Sergeant in the mastership of the Fowey Endowed School.... Credit is due to Mr. Sergeant for the very efficient manner in which he conducted the duties of his school; the behaviour of the boys when at Church, in particular, was apparent to everyone; his general discipline was morally good. On the 20th instant, the Rev. E.J. Treffry, M.A.,....gave the boys an examination, after which he distributed twelve medals to the most deserving. Mr. Sergeant's boys have exhibited maps and etchings lately, and for plain useful Writing, no school in the west exceeds his.... Mr. Sergeant also boarded young gentlemen, and fundamentally instructed them in the classics and mathematics,....English, French, Latin and Greek.

29 May (WB) NEW BATTERY. The Naval Reserve, having increased in numbers, the Fowey one-gun battery used by that force and the Coast Guard, having been found uncommodious, has been dismantled, and a new wooden casemate erected on the opposite side of the river; so that Polruan now has four guns to the Fowey two, which cross-fire with them, the whole six commanding the entrance of the harbour. The new battery, like others for the same purpose, though externally a black and unsightly edifice, "has that within which passeth show", being a *fac simile* of a portion of the "between decks" of a man of war; and as the building has been justly intrusted to....one of Lord Exmouth's Algiers' veterans, resident in the town, a guarantee if felt that the new work is....fitted "with all appliances and means to boot" for the instruction of naval gunnery.

26 June (WB) TYWARDREATH PETTY SESSIONS.... John Vincent, of Fowey, was charged with wilfully damaging a window and carpet, by throwing a bucket of water through the window. It appeared that defendant and others were out practicing the fire-engine at Fowey, and they appeared to have entertained an opinion that while so doing they could do whatever they felt inclined, so that any person who at any time might have displeased them would be likely to receive a quantity of dirty water on their persons or property. Mr. Lowry....withdrew the charge on defendant's paying costs incurred, the Chairman cautioning him as to his future conduct.

24 July (WB) We regret to hear that Scarlatina has been raging among the young of both sexes at Fowey for some time past, and that many children have fallen victim to the disease. (Deaths of two reported July 3 aged 4, infant; three....June 26 aged 6,5,6; three reported 24 July aged 4, 18 mos, 2; two reported 5th June aged 10, 5).

14 August (RCG) DEATH BY DROWNING. POLRUAN.- On Monday, a fine boy aged five years, son of Captain Welsh, of the *Fortune Teller*, of this port, was found by his mother on the beach just below her dwelling-house, dead. He must have fallen overboard unnoticed, and been drowned.

21 August (WB) On Tuesday, an inquest was held by Mr. Hamley, county coroner, on the body of William Powell, a navvy who had been working on the Lostwithiel and Fowey Railway. Last Sunday, Powell and another navvy, named Tuck, gathered a quantity of mussels on the beach of the Fowey river, and after boiling them, Powell partook of three pints of the mussels, and became unwell, swollen much in body, and died before the surgeon, Mr. White, could come to his assistance. It was thought that he had been poisoned by the mussels. The jury, however, returned a verdict "died of heart complaint, coupled with the partaking of mussels."

16 October (RCG) SHOCKING ACCIDENT.- Recently, as Mr. Wills, driving home from Par station, was turning the corner of the road near the entrance to St. Catharine's Parade, he came into collision with a conveyance proceeding to Par station to meet the last up train, driven by a man (WB-Thomas Grenville) in the employ of Mr. Frost, of the Ship Inn. The shaft of the latter vehicle entered the breast of Mr. Will's horse, causing its death. It was very dark at the time of the occurrence. (WB - Nicholas Wills was a Fowey innkeeper).

11 December (WB) On Saturday, as Mr. Charles Treffry, of Place, was returning from hunting, and was crossing in Bodinnick ferry boat, his horse became restive, on which he used his spurs for the purpose, as he thought, of quieting the animal, but instead of being quieted it jumped overboard with its rider, who extricated himself and swam ashore. The horse drifted away with the tide, but was followed by the boatman and eventually rescued.

25 December (WB) On Saturday morning, about 10 o'clock, John Couth, of Par, a labourer, was with a horse and cart descending Lostwithiel-street, Fowey, when the horse started. Couth in attempting to check him slipped his heel and fell, and the cart wheel went over him. He was instantly killed.

1864

22 January (RCG) Letter from John Jeffery, Carharrack, January 15. Sir, - On Friday night the 8th instant, the *"Prince of the Seas,"* from Colombo to London, when five miles off Fowey, came into violent collision with a schooner, which almost instantly sank, and when (as usual in case of forcible clashing,) all hands were lost. Had the *"Prince of the Seas"* put directly into Falmouth instead of first going up channel and afterwards coming back to that out-port, her own serious damage would not have occurred, and the precious souls of the crew of the schooner would probably not have been hurried prematurely into eternity.

Addenda. Were but an order given that the West India steamers should touch at the Westerly Harbour, letters would be delivered 18 hours earlier than now, in London; transatlantic intelligence, instead of being conveyed 200 miles at 8 or 10 knots an hour only, would be flashed along the wires scores of miles a minute....

29 January (RCG) CORNISH RAILWAYS. LOSTWITHIEL AND FOWEY.- There are now upwards of 100 workmen employed on the line, but as soon as the weather improves that number will be trebled. It is considered, however, that the contractors will not have finished their undertaking by Michaelmas next, as was first stated, especially as it is decided to carry the line further towards Fowey Town than was originally intended. There are six cuttings, but the most formidable portion of the whole line is at the "flat-rock", which cutting is 40 feet high through the cliff, and is not far from Bodinnick Passage, Fowey. Twenty men have been from the commencement constantly engaged at this cutting, and many tons of powder have been expended in the necessary excavations on the banks of the upper harbour of Fowey. Upon the whole, these important works are now progressing favourably. "Dobbin" carts are used for removing the rubbish, and as the wheels of these vehicles in wet weather soon become imbedded in the mud, that mode of transit is not so expeditious as the tram- waggon process.

5 February (RCG) FREEMASONRY.- The ceremony of consecrating the New Lodge at Fowey was performed on Tuesday by the R.W.P.G.M. for Cornwall, Aug. Smith, Esq., M.P. The members of the new lodge attended. Divine service at the church at 11 o'clock. At two o'clock, brethren and visitors from other lodges, about 50 in number, assembled in their room at the Ship Hotel.... The ceremony of consecration was impressively performed by the P.G.M. and his officers.... The lodge having been duly closed.... (WB -the Brothers, headed by a band of music, marched in masonic order to Place House, the beautiful residence of the Rev. Br., E.J. Treffry....where a most excellent and ample repast was provided by Br. Frost, of the Ship Hotel, to which the Brethren, about sixty in number, did justice..... Lodge "Fowey" bids fair to be second to none in the province, and other lodges are shortly to be opened in the district.)

5 February (RCG) Penny readings have been commenced at Fowey. A large number of working people attended on the "first night," on Saturday last.

22 April (RCG) GUNPOWDER EXPLOSION. - A serious explosion took place on Sunday, on the works of the Lostwithiel and Fowey Railway - now in course of construction - at Golant. It appears that a man employed by the company as timekeeper invited some villagers to witness a new kind of "safety powder" contained in a shed which is used as a magazine, and is erected in a field near the village. Several men and children remained outside the shed until the timekeeper entered for the purpose of bringing out a specimen for their inspection. Before so doing, however, he placed his lighted pipe just outside the door of the building, and almost immediately after he had got what he required there was a fearful explosion. It is believed that a spark from the pipe fell on a train of powder which in all probability was accidently made by the man when carrying a large handful of powder from the barrel to the door. Happily, there was no sacrifice of life, but....one man had his face severely burnt, whilst another had his hair singed off on one side; another man is burnt a good deal about the hands and back of the neck, and his shoulder bruised by a blow from one of the beams of the shed; and the children are injured, but not dangerously. The quantity of powder in the magazine was about 6 cwt. It is stated that the explosion was not caused by the "safety powder," but is attributed to the fact that a quantity of ordinary powder was in the same shed.

22 April (RCG) FOWEY. CRICKET. - The members of the newly formed and promising cricket club of Fowey met for the first time last week. There was a large attendance of playing members. The ground is pleasantly situated in a field adjoining Lankelly-house.

29 April (WB) .... It was expected that Garibaldi and his suite would embark on board the Duke of Sutherland's yacht, the *Undine*, lying in Fowey harbour, for Caprera. The third Company of the Duke of Cornwall's Volunteer Artillery, under the command of Capt. Sobey, were in waiting to give the General a salute whenever he should take his departure. The inhabitants of Fowey had also decorated their little town with much beauty. In the broad space in which stands an obelisk recording the fact that it was erected....in commemoration of the landing of her Majesty Queen Victoria and his Royal Highness Prince Albert on that quay (Albert Quay), September 8th, 1846, five rows of trees had been placed, and in many parts of the town there were flags and banners erected.... One just painted was put up in the afternoon, on which were inscribed the words - "May health and blessings attend thee! Farewell, Garibaldi!". Two steamers ran from Plymouth to Fowey, to witness the embarkation, but the passengers, of course, found themselves to have been premature. Owing to the boisterous state of the weather, General Garibaldi did not sail that evening.....

Shortly before nine o'clock on Wednesday morning the news was brought to Fowey that General Garibaldi was on his way from Penquite. The intelligence was quickly spread through Fowey, and an exodus immediately took place from the houses to the Albert Quay and the thorough-fares leading thereto.... Captain Brine had his coastguard men on duty,....and a body of the county constabulary were present under the direction of Inspector Grant.

Just before nine the church bells struck up a merry chime, a distant hurrah broke upon the ear, the cheering rapidly increased in volume, and presently Colonel Peard's carriage drove on to the Quay. In a moment the doors were besieged, and there was some difficulty in keeping the crowd back and clearing a space for the General to alight. Colonel Peard assisted out his illustrious guest, and....the cheering redoubled in vigour, and all who were sufficiently near to reach the General endeavoured to catch him by the hands. For some minutes Garibaldi was fully occupied in returning the cordial grips of his admirers.... Mr. Treffry received the General on behalf of the inhabitants of Fowey, and when he arrived opposite the place where the representatives of the metropolitan and local papers were stationed, introduced these gentlemen to him.... Garibaldi who evidently recognised them as having attended on him before, shook their hands heartily, saying, "Thank you, thank you; I am very grateful for what you have done for me." This was his last public act on English soil; he then at once stepped into the gig which was waiting to convey him on board the yacht, and....left the shore. His path from the carriage to the water's edge had been strewed with flowers by the Misses Treffry, Miss Bishop, and Miss Davis. After he had passed, some of these floral offerings to the great man's fame were picked up, doubtless to be treasured as memorials. The general's son and the members of his suite next embarked with the luggage in the coastguard gigs, under the direction of Capt. Brine. Garibaldi was received on board the *Undine* by the Duke of Sutherland, who had placed the best cabin at his disposal, and who, with Lord Sefton, will accompany the General on his voyage.... The yacht was attended in her progress seaward by numerous small craft, and Miss Treffry, Colonel and Capt. Peard and Capt. Brine kept company with her in one of the coastguard boats until they saw her clear of the land. Miss Treffry presented an address in Italian to the General, to which she received a written reply. When the *Undine* arrived abreast of Fowey Castle, the 3rd battery of Fowey Artillery Volunteers, under the command of Lieut. Short, fired a salute of 15 guns, and as she passed Point Neptune the ensign flying there was dipped.

19 August (RCG) On Friday, a destructive fire happened at Highway, about a mile from the Bodinnic-ferry, in the parish of Lanteglos by Fowey. Some children, in the absence of their parents, had procured a candle and matches; in playing with them they set fire to some shavings, and three cottages were in consequence burnt to the ground.

4 November (RCG) It has been resolved at a public meeting, to lay on gas at Fowey, by the 1st of January next. A company is being formed with a capital of £1,000, giving the shareholders five per cent. on outlay. The shares are almost taken up.

1865

11 January (WB) Letter to the Editor. Fowey and Polruan fishermen are called poor though Fowey gets fish from other places, i.e. Polperro and Mevagissey, by boat or overland by cart. Very few in Fowey or Polruan get a livelihood exclusively from fishing. The fishermen of Fowey and Polruan are a miscellanya of individuals - gentlemen amateurs, Customs officers, retired sea captains, sailors, Coastguard, pensioners - who own a little boat and go out in their spare time - equal to those who fish by trade; salmon 3 months, crab and lobster May-Sept. Other places have fishing fleets all year. Fowey remains inert, doesn't compete in the open sea.

20 October (WB) A correspondent writes: It is a common fact, often noticed how easily and cheaply Fowey might obtain an additional supply of good water, having sources both east and west of the town, which, time out of mind, has been allowed to pass unheeded away like a thing of no value. During the late and protracted drought, when the inconvenient fetching and carrying of water had almost become a tiresomely dry subject, never was superabundance on both sides, and absolute want in the middle, more powerfully and ridiculously contrasted; for, while that old purveyor of the public, popularly known as the "town cock", was reduced to the last dribbling extremity of a few drops, scarcely competent to fill a pitcher in half an hour and putting the grumbling and impatient town on short allowance, two ample, yet neglected streams, right and left were pouring their libations forth at each end of it, and literally and laughingly running to waste! To remedy this aqueous anomaly, as far as regards his own household at Point Neptune, Mr. Rashleigh has availed himself of one of his own possessions, and intercepting a spring, at its fountain head, has turned a portion of the westermost stream to good purpose, bringing it along the slope of the hill, by an underground conduit, into his own dwelling, ready for every domestic requirement - an example which might easily be followed for the benefit of all.

1866

11 January (RCG) THE FOUNDERING OF THE *HOUND*, OF FOWEY. - THE CREW SAVED. - The smack *Hound*, Sangwin, master, of Fowey, bound from a French port for Plymouth, with a cargo of hides, was reported to have foundered and all hands lost, during the heavy gale at the end of November last, and the families of the crew who reside at Fowey had mourned for their loss. On Sunday morning, however, a letter was received from New York conveying the joyful intelligence of the safe arrival of the crew at that place. It was true that the vessel foundered, but it appears that when she went down the crew were taken off by a steamer and carried on to New York. Prayers of thanksgiving for the safe deliverance of the crew were offered up during morning prayer at Fowey Church.

25 January (RCG) CRUELTY TO ANIMALS NEAR FOWEY. - James Stick, a colt breaker residing at Castle Door, near Fowey, was....charged by Mr. Tucker, of Lescrow Farm, with cruelty to animals, inasmuch as he did wilfully and maliciously, on the night of the 16th instant, cut off the tails of four horses, and the manes of two others. It appears the prisoner had been seen about the stables at Lescrow during the day in question, but subsequently left. Mr. Pearce, the landlord of the Sailor's Return Inn, Fowey, said the prisoner came into his house on the evening in question, and had two pints of beer and some tobacco. He left the house suddenly, omitting to pay for what he had ordered. Shortly after, Thomas Hambly, a labourer, working for Mr. Tucker, and living on the premises, heard the gate leading to the farmyard closed, and some one entered, which he at first supposed to be his master, but he afterwards found he was mistaken. All was right in the stables at 9 pm. The next morning, on his going into the stable, he found the horses manes and tails cut and jagged, apparently having been done with a knife, and thrown on the ground. On making further search he discovered strange footmarks, and called his wife, who immediately said "I am sure they belong to Jemmy Stick" (the prisoner). Police-constable Philp said the footprints had been traced from Lescrow Farm across several fields in the direction of the prisoner's home. On his apprehending the prisoner he took a knife from him which he (the prisoner) said he always carried with him. He also asked him whether he had been to Lescrow Farm on the previous day, to which he at first replied that he had not, but afterward admitted that he had. He had measured the prisoner's boots with the footprints mentioned by Hambly, and found they fitted exactly. Besides which a nail missing from the toe of one of the boots, and there were twelve nails on one side and thirteen on the other of the remaining boot, and the footprints corresponded precisely with these marks. It is supposed that prisoner's motive for doing this was in revenge for Mr. Tucker's not having employed him to clip his horses this year, as....previously.... Prisoner denied the charge, and was remanded till Friday when he was fined £4, and 16s. expenses or in default two months' imprisonment with hard labour.

1 February (RCG) On Saturday, a horse belonging to Mr. Prynn, of Tredannick, near Fowey, fell into the river on the Fowey side of the Boconnoc ferry just as it was about to get into the ferry boat. The horse, which was drawing a cart containing several bushels of oats, swam into deep water, and was carried away by the tide before assistance could be obtained.

19 July (RCG) TYWARDREATH PETTY SESSIONS. - On Monday before Colonel Peard and Rev. Dr. Treffry, Mary Ann Hockin was summoned for violently assaulting Jane Giles at Newtown, near Fowey, on the 28th ult. Plaintiff stated that on returning home with a Mrs Jury on the morning in question, the defendant met her and threatened to tear her life out; she then took a piece of iron out of her pocket, and struck her over the head, causing her to bleed freely, and said she would kill her. She also stated to a witness the night before that she would take her (the plaintiff's) life the next night. Margaret Jury stated that she accompanied the plaintiff home on the night in question, when, near home, they saw the defendant coming. Defendant on coming up struck at the plaintiff, they then closed, but at witness's request they ceased for a time; the defendant then struck plaintiff over the head with the iron, causing the blood to squirt over her. Defendant was fined £1 and costs, or 14 day's imprisonment. Then came on for hearing an assault case in which Hockin was plaintiff and Giles the defendant, but the magistrates did not see sufficient evidence to grant a conviction.

26 July (RCG) FASHIONABLE MARRIAGE.- A general holiday was observed at Fowey on Tuesday, in celebration of the marriage of Miss Ann Ellen, eldest daughter of the Rev. Dr. E.J. Treffry, of Place House, the much respected vicar of Fowey, to the Rev. H.N. Purcell, B.A., curate of St Kenelms...Worcestershire... The hour appointed for the ceremony was eleven o'clock, but long before that time the church was filled and the approaches thronged with spectators.... The bride was attired in a dress of white satin trimmed with Brussels lace, a shawl of the same material, and a white tulle bonnet ornamented with orange blossoms and jessamine; the wedding bouquet, it was remarked, bore a striking resemblance to that of the Princess Helena at her recent marriage. The dresses of the bridesmaids were of white tarlatane trimmed with pink and cherry lace, and they wore tulle bonnets trimmed with blush roses.... At the conclusion of the ceremony the bridal party proceeded to the residence of Dr. Treffry, and were lustily cheered by a large throng of persons. A wedding breakfast of the choicest rarities was served up in the breakfast-room of the doctor's residence.... The bridal presents were numerous and costly, and included many presents from residents in the town and neighbourhood. The bride and bridegroom left Fowey to proceed by the afternoon express train, and it is understood that the honeymoon will be spent in Scotland. Later in the day....the Sunday School children, to the number of about 200, were regaled with tea and cake in the Market-house, at the expense of Dr. Treffry, who also provided tea in the Townhall for the aged people of the neighbourhood, and a substantial dinner for the men in his employ.

9 August (RCG) FOWEY AND POLRUAN REGATTA. The Fowey and Polruan regatta took place on Monday under very discouraging circumstances.... A sharp south-west gale rendered racing outside the harbour altogether out of the question. Early in the day the committee decided that unless a sufficient number of luggers entered for an extra match, which had been arranged by the committee in anticipation of there being no races for yachts, by twelve o'clock, the regatta should be postponed until Wednesday; but just at this moment the *Wellington* steamer, with a party of excursionists, arrived from Plymouth, and it was then resolved that the races should proceed.... The *Wellington* had encountered very boisterous weather on her passage, her skylights being washed in, and her cabin and engine-room flooded. She landed her passengers in a most pitiable plight, many of them spending the remainder of the day until evening in bed, and nearly all preferring then to return by train rather than risk a repetition of the morning's disasters. A steamboat was advertised to leave Falmouth with a pleasure party, but did not make its appearance.... The first start was effected at 12:55, and was for SAILING BOATS belonging within the harbour of Fowey, not exceeding 16 feet in length....and not carrying more than three sailors. First prize £2.... The course was three times round the harbour, the extreme points.... marked by a boat off St. Catherine's Point, and a boat off Bodinnick. The boats started in half a gale of wind from S.S.W., some of the boatmen having provided themselves with cork lifeboats in case of accident.... Very early in the race some lost masts, and others their bowsprits; and out of the seven that started only five went around the first mark,....and the first three only completed the race....

6 December (RCG) MAUSOLEUM AT FOWEY. - A very handsome mausoleum is being constructed at Fowey for Mr. W. Rashleigh. The work....is situated on the crowning summit of what is known in the vicinity as St. Catherine's Hill, the picturesque sea-side castle terminus of the public walk, and the conspicuous vantage ground of the whole view; which comprises the open expanse of the sea on one side, and the harbour and Point Neptune on the other. The actual site was formerly known as, and is now called, the one-gun battery. A small plateau in the centre of the excavation has been formed by miners. Looking into this shaft-like opening, the spectator sees the underground works so far completed, that the arch of the vault is being turned with white fire-bricks. Whether any superstructure will be built over the sepulchre, to accord with the surrounding scenery, is not known, but, considering the spot selected for this last resting place, it will be perhaps the most unique in the county.

27 December (RCG) FOWEY.- Numbers of wild strawberries, quite ripe and very fine, have been gathered from the hedges in this neighbourhood by school-children during the past week, thus showing the extraordinary mildness of the weather.

1867

4 July (RCG) COUNTY QUARTER SESSIONS. SALMON FISHERY. Mr R.G. Lakes had given notice that he should bring before the Court the injustice....as regards the application of the Salmon Fishery Act, so far as it relates to the fishermen of Fowey and Polruan.....otherwise the fishermen....should be told that they must sell their boats and fishing tackle, as not a single salmon had been caught at Fowey since the passing of the act. Indeed they might as well pass an act to say that sportsmen should shoot woodcocks at Midsummer instead of Christmas....

17 October (RCG) CORNWALL MICHAELMAS SESSIONS. - ELIZABETH MALLETT, 34, a married woman, was charged with breaking into the dwelling house of Thomas Walls, at Colquite, Lanteglos-by-Fowey, and stealing....four sovereigns and one half-sovereign, the property of Thomas Walls, the younger. Mrs. Walls locked her house up on the morning of the 31st August, leaving the money which had been entrusted to her by her son for safe keeping, safe in a purse in a drawer. When she returned the door had been unlocked, and the money was gone. The prisoner, a poor woman, was seen to spend money freely and was apprehended on suspicion. The evidence.... failed to bring home the case.... Prisoner was acquitted.

24 October (RCG) LAMENTABLE SUICIDE OF A YOUNG WOMAN. - On Thursday, an inquest was held at the Globe Hotel, Fowey,....on the body of Ellen Daniel, who committed suicide by drowning herself. Mr. Elias Piper said that he married a sister of the deceased, who came to live with him on the 6th of August last from Leicestershire, having given up her situation..... The deceased's health had been failing for 18 months previously. On Tuesday evening she said she felt a little better.... He came home in the evening a little after six o'clock and found the deceased in the kitchen, when, in a reply to a remark that she was looking very much flushed, she replied that she had had a dreadful headache during the day. Shortly afterwards the deceased passed his bedroom on her way down stairs.... He did not see her again alive.... Witness had heard her say several times that she wished she was dead on account of her ill-health. Witness made every enquiry amongst the deceased's friends, as he was alarmed at her prolonged absence, and on returning home at nine o'clock his wife asked him to go upstairs to see some papers, from the purport of which he was afraid that deceased had destroyed herself. Having obtained assistance, witness searched the surrounding fields and everywhere he could think of, but without success. The dead body was not discovered until the following morning at half-past

174

twelve. He had given the letters found in the deceased's room to Dr. Davis....but some of her relatives have suffered from insanity. A letter was then read by the Coroner, in which the deceased bade farewell to the witness and her sister, saying the Devil was working and tempting her. - Mr. William Martin, of Fowey, said he....saw the deceased pass his shop on Tuesday evening. She was not walking fast, and he did not remark anything particular in her appearance. He searched in every direction with P.C. Rowse, but without success; but he subsequently went to the Polly Foot Cove, where, after searching a considerable time, they found the body in a Cove under the Esplanade. There were marks on the deceased's inside garments as if she had slid down. The cliffs were about 60 feet high, and the deceased must have slid down 30 feet and fallen thence into the water. There were no marks on the body with the exception of light bruises on the cheeks. Dr. A.A. Davis having given medical evidence to the effect that the deceased died in the water, read several letters written by the deceased, addressed to her relatives and friends, making disposition of every article of clothing in her possession, stating also that she should wish to be buried after dark, and as she supposed she should be buried like a dog she did not wish anyone but two of her relatives named to attend the funeral.... The jury returned a verdict, "that the deceased committed suicide by drowning herself, being at the time in an unsound state of mind".

14 November (RCG) FOWEY. SMUGGLING SPIRIT AND TOBACCO.- On Thursday Wm. Climo, Charles Dyer, and Theophilus J. Salt, (all of Polruan), part of the crew of the schooner *Thomas Aylan*, of Fowey, from Rouen for Londonderry, were charged by Mr. Wm. Silley, the chief officer of the Coastguard, before Dr. Treffry, at Fowey, with having about 3 pints of brandy and 4 ounces of tobacco, 1 1/4 gills of perfumed spirits, and one bottle of Geneva (diluted) in the boat belonging to the above-named vessel while landing to see their friends. The case was favourably considered,....and each was convicted in the lowest penalty, namely, William Climo 11s.9d.; Charles Dyer 5s.8d.; and T.J. Salt 3s.10d.;....without costs.

12 December (RCG) TRECAN GATE PETTY SESSIONS. - William Thomas, of the parish of Lanteglos-by-Fowey, who was convicted....on 25th of September last, for unlawfully killing game on the 6th of September,....was now summoned....for not having the proper licence to kill game. The case was proved,....and the defendant was find £5 and 17s. costs.

19 December (RCG) TYWARDREATH PETTY SESSIONS. - Richard Nellow, of Fowey, was charged by Jane Allen with assaulting her at Fowey, on the 19th November. Defendant said he merely gave the complainant a push. Complainant said she was in Mrs. Scantlebury's bakehouse, when defendant came in and used most disgusting language to her, and finally struck her several times, giving her two black eyes and inflicting other damage. The defendant detailed several circumstances which led to the disturbance, and stated that the complainant assaulted him first....but the chairman....considered the case proved,....fined the defendant £1 and costs, or 14 days' imprisonment with hard labour.

1868

23 January (RCG) TYWARDREATH PETTY SESSIONS.- Thomas Phillips, of Fowey, was ordered to pay 5s., amount of poor's- rates due from him. The Rev. Dr. Treffry said he knew defendant had received some "charity" money, and he should then have paid his rates. Defendant said he had no bread in his house at that time. It was remarked that the collector of rates appeared, but one of the overseers, a churchwarden, should also have been present.

23 January (RCG) TYWARDREATH PETTY SESSIONS.- William Sweet jun., butcher, Fowey, was fined £1 and costs for cruelly treating a pig on Christmas day. It appeared the animal was one of many being then discharged from a vessel, and this one was injured in the sling. The police constable said the defendant cut its throat, and then thrust its fore leg into a can of hot water. The pig kicked and would have got away had not some men held it tight. He then put the hinder leg also into hot water, when the animal again struggled.

6 February (RCG) A widow, Mary Toms, aged 82 years, who has worked at Trenant Farm, Fowey, for the last 40 years, still travels daily to Trenant, a mile out of town. She works in the fields, and resides in one of Mr. Rashleigh's widows' houses. She is fond of boasting that she is independent of all aid from the parish.

20 February (RCG) COUNTY COURT ST. AUSTELL.- George Dunn v. Charles White. - This action was brought for the purpose of recovering the sum of £4 5s. for labour done and materials provided by the plaintiff at the defendant's request,....the former being a carpenter, and the latter a farmer belonging to Fowey. From the plaintiff's statement it appeared that on the 29th November last he received an order from the defendant to make a corn-hutch, the dimensions of which should be 12 feet in length and 4 feet in width and depth.... On the 11th of December the defendant called on him to ascertain how he was progressing with the work, and intimated that he would require the hutch to be completed as speedily as possible. A week or ten days afterwards, however, the plaintiff received a message from the defendant stating that as he had been detained so long he would not require the hutch at all, but as the hutch was finished on the same day the plaintiff forwarded it to the defendant who ultimately returned it, positively refusing to keep it. Mr. Wallis, on behalf of the defendant said that....he took it that every tradesman was bound to supply an article ordered of him within a reasonable time;....as the plaintiff had delayed completing the article in question until after the lapse of two months, a breach of contract had been committed.... His Honour said that he was aware that the tradesmen were in the habit of detaining customers very frequently for an unreasonable space of time, and that being so, they were not in a position to recover any losses which they might sustain. In the present case, he was of the opinion that the plaintiff was entitled to some compensation, although not to the amount claimed, and that he had arrived at the conclusion to deduct 10 per cent. from the original price of the article, which he should order to be paid....

19 March (RCG) CORNWALL LENT ASSIZES. JOHN COLLINS, a labourer, was charged with stealing two mats and one sack, the property of Christiana Watty, ... The mats and sack were in the passage of the prosecutrix's house, at Fowey, on the evening of the 15th ult., and during her and her daughter's absence for a short time they were stolen. The same night the prisoner, who is a collector of bones and rags, brought them to the lodging-house at which he was stopping, at Fowey, and said he had bought them from a boy. The jury acquitted the prisoner; but his Lordship....told him that he had had a very narrow escape, and cautioned him to have nothing more to do with mats in the future.

26 March (RCG) FOWEY INQUEST. An inquest was held at the Globe Hotel, Fowey, on Saturday evening....for the purpose of enquiring into the circumstances connected with the death of the infant child of Mr. Parrot, mariner, of Fowey. From the evidence of the mother it appeared that she had been nursing the baby a few minutes previous to its death, on Friday evening, when it appeared to be in good health. Dr. Davis said he had examined the body, and gave it as his opinion that the deceased had died of convulsions, consequent on a sudden influx of water on the chest.

14 May (RCG) A CRUEL MOTHER.- On Monday, at St. Austell,....Elizabeth Kitt, of Fowey, an inmate of the St. Austell workhouse, was charged with threatening to destroy her child, aged 19 months. The evidence went to prove that because the child was restless at night, and so prevented the mother's sleeping, she got out of bed and proceeded to the window (thirty feet from the pavement), and held the child out of window, at the same time threatening to throw it out. The woman in the room at once took the child from her. The magistrate told the woman that as she appeared to be of a violent temper she might one day really do the child an injury; he therefore ordered the master to keep the child from her at night. She then cried bitterly at the idea of having her child taken from her. She has since discharged herself from the workhouse.

13 August (RCG) WATERSPOUT.- On Sunday morning near Fowey a number of people were standing on the town quay....at about nine o'clock a.m., when they noticed what appeared to be a dense column, not unlike in colour the smoke from a steamer, broad at the top and tapering downwards, and scudding over the hills opposite, apparently making for the sea in a south-easterly direction. It swiftly passed away seaward, and ultimately burst on the Pencarrow Rocks, between Polruan and Polperro. It was pronounced by several old mariners to be similar to the waterspouts which frequently take place in the Mediterranean Sea, but are hardly ever seen in this country.

27August (RCG) POLRUAN REGATTA. - A very interesting little regatta was witnessed by a large number of people at Polruan on Tuesday. The arrangements were good, and everything seemed to go on harmoniously. The Polruan rifle band attended and played a nice selection of music. The umpires were Messrs. J.W. Todd and R. Woon. Mr. P. Harvey acted as referee; Capt. Wm. Smith, starter; Sergeant

Denison, treasurer; and Capt. J. Moss, secretary. The regatta was patronised by numerous gentlemen belonging to the Royal West Yacht Club. The course was from the committee vessel, which was moored a little distance off Polruan Quay, to Castle Point, round a mark back to the committee boat, a distance of about two and a half miles. The course for sailing boats was about six miles. The sports commenced about 11.15.... A sculling match and a gig and punt chase closed the proceedings.

10 September (RCG) FOWEY. OUTRAGE ON A FOWEY SCHOONER BY SPANIARDS. It is clear we shall have to do something with Spain before long. Another curious outrage is reported to a British schooner, the *Marie Stuart* of Fowey by the *Gibralter Chronicle* of the 29th ultimo. It seems, according to the statement of the mate and crew (four in number) of the vessel, that when some 20 or 30 miles westward of Carthagena last Wednesday week, two boats were observed approaching the schooner. On coming alongside the crews of these boats, 14 men and a boy, boarded the schooner, and said they wished to exchange fruit for the sulphur which formed part of the schooner's cargo. The captain of the British vessel was ill in his cabin, and the mate, who was in charge, refused to exchange, saying he did not want any fruit. Upon this the Spaniards declared that they would have the sulphur, and took upon themselves to open the hatches. The mate interposed and insisted upon replacing the hatches, and seeing a vessel in sight hoisted the British ensign. The Spaniards, however, forcibly hauled down the flag, and, in so doing, tore it. After this they proceeded to plunder the ship. They took possession, among other articles, of some pork, a pigeon, a pair of trousers belonging to the mate, some matches and two shirts from one of the crew. The mate and crew being outnumbered were in fear of their lives, and could make no resistance. Moreover, the mate was eventually compelled to surrender a little sulphur, in order to satisfy the thieves. The Spaniards remained on board the schooner about three hours, and soon after 8 a.m. left. They again returned later in the day, but by this time the crew of the schooner had been able to make preparation for their reception. There were two old rusty guns on board, which were fished out by the mate and loaded. On the arrival of the Spanish boats within hailing distance the mate ran up the English ensign and said he would fire on them if they tried to board again. On seeing that the crew of the schooner were ready to receive them, the pirates turned and made off as rapidly as they could.... If English shipping is to be thus harassed within a few miles of the coast of a foreign Power, it is time to ask that it should be afforded some protection by cruisers of our own.

3 December (RCG) READING ROOM.- The vicar of Fowey, the Rev. H.N. Purcell, has fitted up and opened in the centre of the town a working man's reading room. There are already nearly 70 members.

1869

1 April (RCG) NEW COTTAGE HOSPITAL.- It is proposed to erect one of those most excellent and useful institutions, a cottage hospital at Fowey, and on Tuesday, a bazaar in aid of the funds was held at Bolton House, which was placed at the disposal of the committee. The bazaar was liberally furnished with useful and ornamental articles, and the stalls were arranged with much taste....There was also a refreshment stall under the care of Dr. Davis and Mr. G. Treffry. Mr. Hinks exhibited a zoetrope, wheel of fortune, galvanic battery, and some interesting optical illusions and stereoscopic slides. The Rev. Dr. Treffry and Mr. W. Wreford, devoted their talents to the getting up of raffles, and "Aunt Sally" also lent her valuable assistance to the funds by bringing in the pennies. Talling's Lostwithiel quadrille band furnished agreeable music during the day. ("Aunt Sallie" was a wooden head on a pole - the player threw a club to knock the nose or.... the pipe stuck in its mouth. sally= shoot at + Aunt= old woman)

24 June (RCG) FOWEY. THE CLAY TRAFFIC. - The brig *Urania*, Capt. Pinkham, has completed loading a cargo of clay which was brought over the Lostwithiel and Fowey Railway. The captain is very much pleased with the arrangements for loading. Vessels drawing 17 feet can lie afloat alongside the jetty at the lowest spring tides, and Fowey harbour is both safe and commodious.

17 July (RCG) The salmon fisheries in this port are reviving. A private company has recently been formed by a few gentlemen of Fowey, under the name of the "Teazer" company, of which Mr. J. Treffry is secretary, and Mr. Wakeham, working manager. The operations so far have not been extensive; but on Saturday morning an unlooked-for catch was made in the shape of a fine sturgeon, weighing about 33 lbs., and upwards of 5 feet in length; in addition to which 10 salmon averaging 7 1/2 lbs each were enclosed. In the evening of the same day, the seine was shot and another sturgeon was caught about 3 1/2 feet long and weighing 14 lbs. The first one was sent to Her Majesty, by the 12 o'clock train from Par, the same day, the other being purchased by Capt. Sobey.

17 July (RCG) NARROW ESCAPE FROM DROWNING. - As a man named Vincent was passing the Albert Quay, on Tuesday morning, he saw something white several feet below the surface of the water, which he at first thought to be a large "blubber" or jelly fish, but on another inspection he thought it resembled some child's clothing. He plunged his boat hook into the water and brought up a little girl. The child was a daughter of Capt. Elias Piper, who had been on the quay looking out for a boat in which was a person she wished to see, and as she was stretching over the quay, she over-balanced herself and fell head-foremost into the water. No one witnessed the accident, and had she not been providentially rescued in the manner described would have been drowned.

24 July (RCG) FISHERIES.- This harbour has been visited by large quantities of fish, consisting principally of mackerel and pollock, during the past week, and several good catches have been made. A monster seining company from Looe secured a goodly number of the finny visitors.

7 August (RCG) DEATH BY DROWNING. - A sailor called John Abbott, a native of Beer, in Devonshire, returned to his ship, the smack *"Lavinia"*, of Fowey, on

Tuesday night, at about eleven o'clock, accompanied by a son of the captain, a little boy called William Langmaid, who was to have slept on board for company with deceased. The boy was undressing, when deceased went on deck for something, and as he did not return as expected, the boy went on deck and could not see him anywhere on board, but on looking over the ship's side he saw deceased struggling in the water. He immediately gave an alarm, but as the vessel was lying at the Pont Pill, some distance from the shore and there being no vessels in close proximity, before assistance could be rendered the deceased was drowned. He is stated by the captain to have been a very steady young man, and was only 22 years of age.

28 August (RCG) FOWEY. OPEN AIR PREACHING. - On Tuesday evening last Lord Cholmondeley preached on board his yacht, lying in this harbour, to a large audience, in fact the vessel was crowded almost to excess by people from both sides of the water. Again on Wednesday evening he preached to a goodly congregation at the Albert quay. The scene at the latter place was both picturesque and impressive, especially when a hymn was sung at the close, all the male portion of the audience took off their hats almost simultaneously, and the expression on the sea of upturned faces was apparently most devout and earnest.

13 November (RCG) A FASHIONABLE SWINDLER. - Under the name of Captain Byce, Royal Naval Reserve, a pleasant and gentlemanly person some time ago disported himself at St. Mawes and Falmouth, obtaining goods to a considerable amount, and free board and lodging, under the assurance that he was possessed of large property....these pretences were backed by cheques, which on presentation were dishonoured.... The place became too hot to hold him, however, and a few days ago he made off. A Mr. Ivey since appeared at Morcom's Hotel at Par, and was believed to be the same individual.... On Saturday afternoon he took a trip to Fowey, putting up at the Ship Hotel, where he soon became eminently popular. But the newspapers had meanwhile arrived at Par, giving an account of Capt. Byce's Falmouth adventures, and Mr. Morcom....communicated with Inspector Greaves, who accompanied Mr. Morcom to Fowey, and on Capt. Byce's - or as he was there called, Mr. Ivey - coming down to breakfast at the Ship, presented his bill, amounting to £3 4s. Mr. Ivey was greatly taken aback by this sudden demand from the landlord of the Par Hotel, and handed over to him all the money he had with him - £2 - on account. Further demands were pressed, and the gallant captain was ultimately taken to lodge in the Tywardreath police-station on a charge of obtaining goods under false pretences. He has....been removed to Falmouth, and....remanded. (sentence -12 months hard labour)

CHAPTER 8
1870-1879

1870

12 March (RCG) LOSTWITHIEL.-At the Petty sessions....Wm. Dingle, Lanteglos,....for cruelly working a horse suffering from wounds, was fined £2, and costs 13s., or one month's imprisonment.

23 April (RCG) POLRUAN. ACCIDENT.- As Mr. Nicholas Butson, of the firm of N. and J. Butson, shipbuilders of Bodinnoc and Polruan, was engaged in working on a new vessel now completing at Brazen Island Yard, he by some means fell off the scaffolding and came with great force to the ground, sustaining a fracture of the skull and compression of the spine, besides other injuries. The unfortunate sufferer, who is under the care of Dr Davies, of Fowey, lies in a precarious state.

23 April (RCG) ACCIDENT. - As Dr. Davis was returning from seeing a patient, when near the head of the hill leading into Fowey on Thursday morning, his horse, which previously had done a similar action, bolted and came into collision with the side of the cutting bounding the road. Dr. Davis and his little boy, who was riding with him, had a very narrow escape with a severe shaking. The conveyance was completely wrecked, and the horse, with the shafts dragging about it, galloped down the hill with great fury and was eventually brought to a standstill by knocking itself against the wall surrounding Mr Moreland's garden with such force as to completely displace the masonry and severely injure himself.

23 April (RCG) The well-known church bells of Fowey, whose thrilling sound has not only contributed towards the festiveness of all joyful events for some generations past in the neighbourhood but has also on divers occasions welcomed royalty itself to the ancient borough of Fowey, are it is hoped to be still further improved by the addition of two new bells, making a complement of eight. It has long been the wish of a certain section of the gentlemen of the town, and in fact not only so but all lovers of campanology in the district, that the peal of bells should be improved....

7 May (RCG) DEATH BY DROWNING. - An inquest was held on Saturday, at Lanteglos by Fowey, before Mr. John Jago, coroner, on the body of a little girl called Jane Roberts Martin, aged one year and seven months, only child of Mr. W. Martin, of the Church Town Farm. It appears on the previous day the deceased had been missed for a few minutes, and on the maid servant going out by the back part of the premises, she saw the child in a tray of water with its head downwards; she immediately took it up and carried it into the house but life was quite extinct. There were about 6 inches of water in the tray. The jury returned a verdict of "Accidently drowned."

1 June (WB) FOWEY. - It has been suggested to put up a town pump in Fowey, to be paid out of the poor rates! A notion as infelicitous as the Chancellor's tax on the lucifer match makers.... It is true the town cock has latterly made a miserable exhibition of itself, being often at its last dribble and a pump much required. Let the trustees of the town get it, other proprietors joining in the expense....But why this pump at all? For both east and west of the town are water resources....running to waste, that need only a few yards of stoneware pipes to supply without stint the wants of....all.

2 June (WB) THE FISHERY. Mr. W. Hewett writes: - "A salmon seine has been seized for rent at Polruan, which, in all likelihood, would not be the case if the operation of a stupid and unnatural law had not caused the property to be unproductive as recent notices of the Fowey Salmon case have fully explained. A rich gentleman may lodge a complaint against persons disturbing the tranquility of the herd of deer in his park, and no long space of time would be allowed to intervene before police officials and others would be on the look out to capture delinquents of such a criminal stamp. Let such persons have the requisite protection; but let not partiality give occasion to the poor to complain. The machinery of law should be irrespective.

23 July (RCG) POLRUAN. - HOUSEBREAKING - Frequent complaints have lately been made to the police by Mrs. Luke, wife of the master of the schooner "*Chase*," of Fowey, that some person was constantly stealing various articles from her pantry. P.C. Brock stationed himself on the premises during Saturday night and remained until five o'clock on Sunday morning, but the thief did not make his appearance. However, during the absence of the constable he again paid a visit to the pantry and committed fresh depredations. While watching again on Monday morning early the policeman heard some one open the pantry door and on looking in discovered John Vallack, a labourer of Polruan, helping himself to a pie, and at the same time secreting a cake under his frock. Brock made Vallack a prisoner, and subsequently brought him before the magistrates, by whom he was committed for trial.

23 July (RCG) On Monday night, twelve salmon were caught in the Fowey River, ranging from 6 lbs to 18 lbs each, but averaging about 12 lbs. They sold on the spot at 1s. a pound, and realised £7 9s. This has been the best take of the season.

27 August (RCG) FOWEY. - Some fine salmon have been caught in Fowey River during the season now drawing to a close. It is still evident, however, that the Salmon Fisheries Act is highly detrimental to the fishermen's interest, and not suitable to the habits of the fish at Fowey.... Mr. JE Climo writes in *Land and Water* The salmon fishery commenced on the 15th August.... It is very unfortunate that the close season is so close upon us, as the fish are just coming to our harbour; they are to be seen jumping at sea, in the estuary, and in the river; and to all appearance will be in abundance during the whole of the natural open season, viz., from September to Christmas.

17 September (RCG) LANTEGLOS-BY-FOWEY. - A harvest thanksgiving was held on Thursday, in the fine old church.... The sermon was preached by Rev. H. N. Purcell vicar of Fowey. The collection at the close amounting to £4 18s.10d.,....to be devoted towards the fund being raised for the relief of the sick and wounded in the Franco-Prussian war. Tea was subsequently served in a field adjoining, kindly lent by Mr. W. R. Martin, of the Churchtown farm, the receipts at which realized £14 3s. 4d. Unfortunately, consequent on the unfavourable state of the weather, the attendance at the tea was not so numerous as was anticipated, but a larger assemblage has never before congregated at one time in the church.... Some fireworks were to have been let off in the evening but the promoters were precluded from doing so by the heavy rain which fell.

31 December (RCG) THE POLRUAN FERRY-BOAT - To the Editor.... Sir, - The dangers and inconvenience attending the passage by the Polruan ferry-boat from Fowey, are exceedingly numerous. In the first place the boat itself is not safe for persons crossing the harbour in rough weather. Secondly, it is too small and very "crank," and latterly has been plied while in a damaged state, to such an extent, that passengers cannot fail to get wet feet while crossing the harbour from Fowey. I would suggest that the proprietor of the ferry be requested to replace the present boat immediately with a new one, in order to prevent loss of life, which must inevitably ensue if the present arrangements are allowed to continue....THOMAS TADD

1871

14 January (RCG) THE POLRUAN FERRY BOAT- To the Editor.... Sir, - A letter appeared in the *Cornwall Gazette,*....signed "Thomas Tadd".... The fact that no accident has ever occurred to the Polruan ferry-boat proves the inaccuracy of Thomas Tadd's statements.... The boat, he says, "is too small and very crank." This is a mistake, for on many occasions as many as 14 persons have been conducted safely across the ferry. It is hardly possible to keep a ferry-boat from leaking, when people are continually passing; but I am prepared to prove that the "Polruan ferry-boat" was not in such a damaged state as Thomas Tadd would....declare it to be.... Yours,.... JAMES TADD

14 January (RCG) To the Editor.... Sir, - My attention has been directed to a letter,....signed "Thomas Tadd.".... I have crossed from Fowey to Polruan in the ferry-boat several times lately, and....I have yet to learn the dangers attending the passage. I think "Thomas Tadd" should be the last person to rush into print, when it is well known he has been strongly opposed to the ferry, so much so as to put a boat in opposition to the ferry. If the letter....had been written to benefit the public, I should have supported it, but I have reason to believe it was written with a selfish motive, and to annoy the lessee of the ferry. I would advise him to mind his own business, and in future to leave other people's alone, which I deem more consistent with those who professes to do good. Yours obediently, NAUTA

21 January (RCG) POLRUAN FERRY BOAT. To the Editor.... Sir, - I thank you for the insertion of my letter respecting the damaged and leaky condition of the Polruan ferry boat. The day after its appearance in your paper the old, crank, and leaky boat was put aside and another boat put in its place. This, although not a leaky craft, is not adapted for a ferry boat, being too barrel-bottomed. Thus, the public have to be content with whatever the lessee may choose to employ for the conveyance of passengers to and from Polruan and Fowey. With regard to....the Polruan ferry boat....let any one examine the boat at the present time and they will find it in a very damaged state and full of water. I deny the assertion of "Nauta," that I had set on a boat in opposition to the lessee of the ferry, and maintain that the present boat is too narrow-bottomed, and consequently unsafe in boisterous weather. Yours truly, THOS. TADD, Sen.

18 February (RCG) A SERIOUS DISASTER. The master and crew of the schooner *Fortune-teller*, of Fowey, have arrived at Polruan. The vessel was driven on the Sperm, at the mouth of the Humber, on the night of the 10th, and the crew, six in number, took to the rigging, and remained there from 11 o'clock on the Friday night until 7 o'clock next morning, when they`were taken off by a lifeboat. The men lost all their clothes and effects.

11 March (RCG) POLRUAN. - CONCERT - A musical entertainment in aid of the blanket fund, for supplying the poor of the parish of Lanteglos by Fowey, was given at the National School-room on Thursday last. The attendance was very large and the receipts highly satisfactory. The performances were received with applause throughout. Mr Jas. Tadd was loudly encored as also were the Misses Barrett and Hocken, the two latter of whom sang the duet "Evening Bells" in a most pleasing manner. Mrs. Charles Hawken also delighted the audience by singing "Call me not back" very creditably. Messrs. Skinner, Bailey, Dean, Keyes and Pearce, and a string band also contributed to the very successful entertainment.

1 April (RCG) DESIRABLE COMPLETION OF WORKS - There is now a prospect of the skeleton houses, which were run up by a London builder and then left by him in all their ugliness to mar the beauty of the scenery on the Esplanade, being completed at an early date. Contracts have been taken by various tradesmen and the premises are to be completed by the 20th of June next. The site commands a comprehensive view of the delightful scenery for which Fowey is noted.

8 April (RCG) FOWEY. WORKING MEN'S INSTITUTION.- At this Institution on Monday evening, a prize was presented by the president (the Rev. H.N. Purcell) to Mr. Henry Simons, for the best essay on the subject - "How best to raise the moral and social condition of the working classes." The paper was ably written, and reflected credit on the writer. There were several competitors.

9 April (WB) POLRUAN. LANTEGLOS CHURCHTOWN.- An entertainment was given in aid of the expenses connected with the choir of Lanteglos church, on tuesday last, at the National school-room. The public tea was well attended, the following ladies being very conspicuous in their assistance. At the first table, the Misses M. , A. , and Mrs. Roberts; the second table, Mrs Ellery, Mrs Barrett, Mrs Grace Tadd, Mrs. Bayley, and Miss H. Smith. Subsequently during the evening, readings and songs were given by the Rev. H. N. Purcell, vicar of Fowey, Rev James Kendall, vicar of Lanteglos, Mrs James Tadd, Mr William Smith, jun, Mr William

Roberts, and the Misses Barrett, Ellery, Dyer, and Messrs Skinner, Bayley, Bunt, L. Dean. Mr James Tadd's performance on the harmonium was very much admired. The attendance was large and the receipts, it is to be hoped, were satisfactory.

15 April (RCG) POLRUAN. METHODIST FREE CHURCH. - The anniversary of the United Methodist Free Church was held on Easter Monday. A procession was formed, and the children and their teachers, after marching round the town, were conducted to the Volunteer drill-room, where tea was partaken of. Subsequently services were held at the Chapel many people being unable to get admitted. The children sang hymns, composed for the occasion, very creditably. A collection was made at the close.

15 April (RCG) ACCIDENT.- Mr. John Reed, of the Commercial Hotel, Fowey, was driving from Par Station to his home on the evening of Good Friday, and when near Menabilly Lodge, in endeavouring to pull back the drag, he overbalanced himself and fell off the conveyance, which was full of passengers, and the vehicle passed over one of his legs in the middle of the calf, breaking both bones.

15 April (RCG) THE CHURCH BELLS.- A concert, in aid of the Fowey Church bells fund, was given at the Town Hall, on Tuesday evening, to a not large, but very appreciative audience. In consequence of the inclement state of the weather, numbers of people were prevented from attending, who undoubtedly would otherwise have done so. The stage was prettily decorated with various exotics, from the Rev. Dr. Treffry's conservatories at Place. The first part commenced with a fantasia on popular airs....The first portion of the entertainment concluded with the quadrille, "Rage of London," by the full band. A peal on the hand bells followed as an interlude...The whole of the performances were greatly applauded....

29 April (RCG) OBSTRUCTING THE HIGHWAY. - At the Tywardreath Petty Sessions, on Monday, William Mellow, of Fowey, was summoned by the Tywardreath Highway board, charged with breaking up and obstructing the highway at Fowey.... Defendant said that owing to the mode in which the board's surveyor had caused the sewage pipes to be placed, the refuse leaked into the house he occupied and spoilt the drinking water, and to prevent this he dug down into the road so as to find the proper drain in order to rectify the nuisance. The defendant was fined 2s. 6d, and costs, rather hard lines under the circumstances, although he did not go the proper way to get the evil remedied.

6 May (RCG) - A FIGHT FOR MAY-POLES. - It appears that there is an old custom in the neighbourhood of Polruan not only for villagers to erect May-poles, but for the inhabitants of one village to carry off the others' pole either by stratagem or force. Accordingly on Monday the "braves'" of the hamlet of Highway sallied forth to carry off a neighbour's pole, trusting to the women of Highway to protect the handsomely decorated pole which they had erected in the centre of their own village. During their absence the gallants of Polruan made an incursion into the Highway territory, and carried off the pole, and though an alarm was sounded and the marauders intercepted on their return, they succeeded in carrying the pole to Polruan where they planted it in the centre of the town and where they still keep it in defiance of the Highway men, policemen and all other opponents. The Highway men have several times renewed their assault upon the Polruan stronghold but have been ignominiously repulsed. Altogether the excitement in the neighbourhood is such as the proverbial "'oldest inhabitant" cannot call to memory.

20 May (RCG) FOWEY. SANITARY MATTERS During the last summer the town suffered much in consequence of an inadequate supply of water.... It was mentioned incidentally that more than half the houses in the town are not drained, and that the streets are disgustingly dirty and ill-paved....the following resolution was carried:- That it is expedient, taking into consideration the amount of property owned by the Treffry estate in Fowey,....that a memorial be presented to the trustees drawing their particular attention to the utter neglect which they shew towards the sanitary arrangements of the town, and also asking them to consider whether the quay and market dues should not be restored to their original purpose." ....remarks from Mr. Lowry, calling attention to the want of a scavenger for the town, as the present one was unable to work through advanced age....

3 June (RCG) FOWEY. The adjourned meeting of a special vestry was held in the Town Hall.... It was proposed "That this meeting consent to the expenditure out of the poor rates of about £12 in procuring a better water supply, by cleaning out and fixing the pumps.... An amendment was moved "that no money be taken from the rates for the repair of the pumps and water supply for the town of Fowey."....carried by 23 to 4. The Rev. Dr. Treffry condemned the selfishness of some of the inhabitants, who, having wells, refused to supply their less fortunate neighbours with water.

29 July (RCG) BODINNICK REGATTA - This waterside village not the least pretty of many within the port of Fowey, was the scene of unusual gaiety on Tuesday afternoon, consequent on the annual regatta. The weather was, until near the close of sports, very fine and the attendance of spectators was large, the pleasure boats being particularly numerous. A steamboat from Falmouth brought up about 120 excursionists. Besides the boat racing the principal amusements were swimming after ducks, and eating loaves and treacle suspended by strings, the competitors....having their hands tied behind them, the first that succeeded in eating his loaf taking the prize....

5 August (RCG) CORNWALL SUMMER ASSIZES. - CHARGE OF RAPE AT POLRUAN..... A rabbit trapper, was indicted for committing a felonious assault upon....a child of 13 years, at Polruan, on the 4th June..... It appeared that the girl went to the prisoner's house to sleep, and whilst in bed with another little girl the prisoner effected his purpose. The jury found a verdict of GUILTY,.... The prisoner was sentenced to TEN YEARS PENAL SERVITUDE. (Remarks of the Judge at the beginning of the Assizes) If the girl in respect to whom the complaint arose had been of mature years, there could be no doubt the bill ought to be thrown out - the offence having been committed on the Thursday, and she made no complaint till the following Sunday. But it seemed that the girl was thirteen years of age, only just a year older than the period at which she would have been absolutely protected by the law.... The age in which young girls were protected in this country against offences of this description was less than it ought to be. It was absurd to say that a girl had arrived at a state of maturity at twelve years of age.... It is unlikely that a girl of that age would be a consenting party....

7 October (RCG) News has been received that Capt. Richard Bate, of Polruan, has been drowned at Dordt. He was engaged in laying down an anchor from his ship, the *Capella* of Fowey, when the boat he was in capsized. He leaves a wife and young family.

21 October (RCG) LISKEARD. DESERTED WIVES- The guardians now refuse relief to all women deserted by their husbands except in the house. The relieving officers have been ordered to bring up a list of all women who have been deserted, in order that their out-door relief may be stopped.

28 October (RCG) Tywardreath Highway Board.... with reference to the alteration of the Fowey streets. Mr Dingle, the waywarden, said he did not approve of the proposed use of coal tar, sand, &c.,but the surveyor....remarked that he had....visited Chesterfield, where a pitch pavement answered satisfactorily. It was resolved that the asphalte method should be adopted, by way of an experiment, in the narrowest portion of the town, to an extent of about one chain in length.

4 November (RCG) Farmers and poor people with small patches of ground (on which they place so much dependence for winter dinners) are great sufferers this year by the potato disease, which has already caused more destruction than for many years past.... In Truro....scores of bushels have been turned out for the pigs.

5 November (WB) THE EDUCATION ACT. FOWEY.- A meeting of the ratepayers of Fowey was held.... to consider the operation of the Education Bill in reference to the parish. The Rev. Dr. Treffry remarked that he thought Fowey was very badly off for school accommodation, particularly as regarded the boys' endowed school, and that the infants' and girls' school consisted of about 106 children .... There were from 130 to 140 children in the town who would not be provided for by the existing establishments.

11 November (RCG) MR. H.M. PRESTON, Surgeon Dentist from London. TEETH on the improved principles of self adhesion; no wires or fastening required. TEETH EXTRACTED, FILLED AND SCALED. All Mechanical Dentistry warranted. CONSULTATION FREE. Teeth extracted gratis from half-past 9 to half-past 10. Mr. Preston or his certified assistant may be consulted at....FOWEY. - The First and Third Saturdays in the month, at Mrs. Wilcocks', Webb- street, from One to Five.

30 November (RCG) FOWEY. The first winter week service was held on Wednesday in the parish Church. The sermon was....by the Rev. Dr. Treffry, rector of Lansallos, who told the congregation that the vicar hoped to apply the collection....to giving a blanket each to twenty-four of their poor neighbours. The congregation contributed funds sufficient to give a blanket to each of twenty-six persons.

16 December (RCG) FOWEY. The drapers of this town have unanimously agreed to close their shops on the 26th inst. in order to give their employes a three days' holiday in the festive season.

16 December (RCG) The sturdy fishers naturally hail the appearance of pilchard with great glee, and when the fish were plentiful the local consumption alone was something like 15 million fish per annum. Every poor family deems it bad times indeed if they are notable to store up for their use a good stock of cured pilchards, to be boiled as they could be afforded, in the same pot with the potatoes when the nipping weather came.

1872

6 January (RCG) An inquest was held at Polruan on Thursday by Mr. John Jagoe on the body of George Henry Minear, a farm-servant....of Mr. Truscott, of Tregabrown, in Lanteglos,....whose death was occasioned by the horse on which he was riding running away, throwing the deceased against a projecting wall, and fracturing his skull. The jury returned a verdict of "Accidental death."

24 February (RCG) POLRUAN.EDUCATIONAL MEETING. - On Friday a public meeting, presided over by the Rev. James Kendall, vicar of the parish, was held in the National Schoolroom. H.M. Inspector of Schools was present, and explained the existing school accommodation, and the number of children in the town and parish between the ages of three and 13. After making all deductions, and taking into account the present school accommodation, it was found there are still about 75 children to be provided for. It was unanimously agreed that the present National Schoolroom be enlarged to meet the necessary equipments, and to adopt the voluntary system.

23 March (RCG) POLRUAN. SUDDEN DEATH. - An inquest was held on Thursday on the body of Charles Draper, aged 14, who, while standing in the shop-door way and speaking to Mr. Clogg, fell down and expired immediately. Evidence was produced showing that deceased had suffered from heart disease since infancy....

23 March (RCG) EMIGRATION. To the Editor.... Sir,- I think all Cornishmen ought to be proud of the accounts lately given....of the prosperity of our county. There appears at present to be a great demand for all kinds of metals, but especially iron and tin, which is found abundantly in our county. Blast furnaces are to be placed at Fowey; coal must therefore be brought to manufacture the iron; railways are to be laid to connect the most important towns with each other, and made available not only for....minerals, but also for passengers. In fact, the hitherto quiet aspect of Cornwall is to be changed to a busy, flourishing, and manufacturing one..... If such be the case why are so many of our fellow countymen bidding adieu to happy and cheerful English homes, and giving up the happy comforts and enjoyments of old England, to live under a foreign sky. They surely are not afraid to face the labour in store for them, for no Cornishman was ever afraid of labour. But the motto of every Cornishman is "Good pay for good work," and because they can not obtain this in

Cornwall, they must go where they can; but probably they will be enabled in the course of a year or two to earn as much in Cornwall as they can at present in America.... then Cornishmen need not emigrate to maintain their motto.

4 May (RCG) FOWEY. ALARMING FIRE. - On Thursday night a fire, from which serious consequences were at one time feared, broke out at Beaumont House, in the occupation of Captain Dyer, R.N., Mr. Ritchings, seed merchant, and others, situate at the entrance of the town. The fire was first discovered by Anna Waters who is in the employ of Captain Dyer. An alarm having been raised, the Fire Brigade, which has recently, together with the engine and gear, been resuscitated, was, under the command of Mr. W.N. Abbott quickly on the spot, after several laborious hours' work, during which very material assistance was rendered by Messrs. G.H. Bate, S. Waters, Slade, Richards, Searle, and others, the fire was got under, but not until considerable damage was done. The premises are insured in the Sun and County offices. The fire is said to have originated from a fall of soot, which became ignited by sparks communicated with the woodwork in Mr. Ritching's store, and thus set the flooring, &c., in a blaze. The matter caused quite a consternation in the town.

27 May (RCG) FOWEY. THE RAILWAY.- In connection with the railway extension at Fowey, surveyors have been busy in that portion of the Treffry estate known as the Carne-fields, bordering the river just above the town; and a house is about to be erected to accommodate one of the contractors, the frame-work of which (wood and iron) is now said to be on its way from London. The style of the new cottage is to be Swiss, and pretty enough in all probability, taken in relation to the site selected, the marginal bit of land bordering the seaside of the Esplanade, and looking immediately down on the old castle, though some people have fears the contemplated erection will impede the view of the harbour, an obstruction which would be much regretted. Should the new comer be a lover of the picturesque, and prove a "friend in need" to the ruined castle, by checking any further decay of its crumbling remnants, he will confer a timely favour on an historic landmark of the place.

3 August (RCG) FOWEY. The shipments of china clay appear to increase. Over 1,100 tons were shipped during the past fortnight.

17 August (RCG) GALLANT CONDUCT OF THE VICAR. - On Friday afternoon a gentleman who has lately become a resident at Fowey, ventured into the sea to have a bathe. The sea running high at the time he was soon overpowered, and would in a few minutes have been drowned, had not the Rev. H. N. Purcell, the vicar of the parish, who was fortunately standing near, jumped into the sea and brought him to the shore. The rev. gentleman was, unfortunately, somewhat bruised by striking against a rock.

17 August (RCG) SUNDAY SCHOOL CHILDREN AT MENABILLY. On Tuesday last the children of the Church Sunday schools of Tywardreath, Fowey, and St. Sampsons, with their teachers, numbering upwards of 400, were most hospitably entertained at Menabilly by Mr. and Mrs. Rashleigh. The juveniles, accompanied by their teachers, arrived at the entrance lodge in procession, and were marched with their gay banners through the park to the avenue on the lawn, under whose stately and shady branches the tables were laid for dinner, which consisted of an abundant supply, including plum pudding. It was a pleasing sight to witness the two rows of parallel tables so laden with creature comforts, and the real enjoyment they appeared to give to the numerous guests assembled. Before commencing the meal, "Praise God from whom all blessings flow" was sung by the children and the visitors present, and also a thanksgiving hymn after the repast. Mr. Rashleigh then addressed the company in the most kind and feeling manner. He said he was glad to see so many happy faces of his neighbour's children around him, and hoped they would enjoy themselves; and....would feel thankful to God for the fine weather, and for His having put it into the hearts of Mrs. Rashleigh and himself to entertain them. He hoped they would show their gratitude in two ways. First, by being punctual and regular in their attendance at the Church Sunday schools, for he felt that pains were taken there to have efficient and intelligent teachers; and secondly, that they would show their gratitude by all of them praying that evening for his eldest son, who is dangerously ill, that his life may be prolonged, and that he may be prepared for whatever may be God's will....

After repeated cheers for their benefactor and benefactress the children dispersed over the beautiful grounds, where various sports were provided for their amusement, and everything that could be done by the family and their visitors at the mansion to add to the enjoyments of the day was most kindly provided for. Before leaving, the children and the other visitors assembled in front of the mansion, and, after singing a hymn, each child was presented with a large cake, after which they were taken to their homes,....their happy countenances expressing their gratitude for so much enjoyment.

24 August (RCG) FOWEY. SERIOUS ACCIDENT. - A serious accident has occurred at the Cornwall Mineral Railway Company's Works. Four men employed in boring No. 2 shaft, near Fowey, had prepared a fuse to remove some rocky substance at the bottom, and, as usual, one man was left to complete the work by exploding the fuse. In the meantime the kibble or raising bucket was ascending to the surface with three men, and when near the top one of the occupants named Wm. Warn, of St. Blazey, in attempting to jump up slipped through and below the kibble, falling a distance of 60 feet, striking the sides twice, and receiving such injuries that his life is despaired of. The man at the bottom of the shaft cut the fuse, which he had just ignited, only in time to prevent a greater catastrophe.

31 August (RCG) FOWEY. - .... A fancy fair and bazaar was held in the beautiful grounds of Place, Fowey, on Tuesday and Wednesday. The work of Church restoration has been going on for several years according as finances have allowed. The first portion....was the re-enclosure of the churchyard, which cost a couple of hundred pounds. More recently the belfry has been put in thorough order, and a couple of new bells added, bringing the number up to eight. This work cost £260; and the peal is now one of the finest in the two counties: the tenor weighs 24 1/2 cwt. To defray the balance due....is one of the aims of the bazaar. A second is the restoration of the church windows - the stonework of which much needs renewal - and the carrying forward of other necessary internal works, which will absorb another £400 or £500. A third object is the....welfare of the cottage hospital which has been so successfully worked under the care of Dr. Davis, of Fowey....it is felt that the hospital should be put upon a lasting foundation, and occupy its own premises. The total cost of the hospital buildings will be about £300.... £150 has yet been raised....

The bazaar was suggested by Miss Treffry.... The Rev Dr. Treffry, ever ready to help on any good cause at Fowey....kindly consented to throw open the romantic grounds of Place;.... On the lawn in front of the grand old house were pitched the tents, beneath which were erected two stalls....loaded with articles including valuable old china and a number of fine examples of modern statuary porcelain. To Mrs Treffry's stall was likewise contributed a fine drawing by Mr. Girardot, and photograph of another painting by that gentleman....we are glad to hear that the affair was altogether a success.

14 September (RCG) THE FATAL BOAT ACCIDENT. - In our last issue we gave a brief telegram, announcing the picking up of the body of a petty officer of her Majesty's Navy, and of a Cutter belonging to *H.M.S. Implacable*, stationed at Plymouth. It turns out that the Cutter left Plymouth on Thursday morning for Falmouth, with....Lieut. Napier, on board. It was very rough when they left, and afterwards the wind increased to a gale. It is thought they endeavoured to make Fowey, but were swamped by the heavy cross-sea.... The body of Lieut. Napier was picked up in Lantic Bay about a mile east of Fowey harbour, on Wednesday. It was devoid of clothing, the unfortunate man having evidently undressed in order to save himself by swimming....

14 September (RCG) FOWEY. - The recent melancholy accident points to the necessity for a life boat at Fowey....

28 September (RCG) The funeral of Michael Adams, drowned in the recent boat accident, late petty officer of the *Implacable*, aged 26, took place on Thursday. The body was buried at Lanteglos by Fowey. Mr. Cullinane and four petty officers from the *Implacable*, with the wife and mother-in-law of deceased, followed as mourners. The Coastguards of several sections in the Fowey Division, under command of Mr. Selley, also attended. The funeral was conducted with military honours; three volleys were fired over the grave. The burial service was impressively read by the Rev. H. V. Purcell, vicar of Fowey. An offer was made by the officers of the *Implacable* to have the body taken to Plymouth....which, however, was thankfully declined by the wife, who preferred its being buried at Fowey.

26 October (RCG) FOWEY COTTAGE HOSPITAL recently built in this town will be ready for the reception of patients in the course of a few weeks. Sir Morton Peto with his usual liberality has given a donation of £58 to pay off the residue of the debt.... The hospital will contain eight beds, and the sanitary and domestic arrangements of the building reflects great credit on Mr. W.E. Geach, of Penellick, who has kindly given his services as the architect.

7 December (RCG) FOWEY BOAT ACCIDENT. - On Friday evening Capt. Johns, of the schooner *William*, with three of the crew, were engaged in carrying away the second anchor, and when in the act of dropping it the buoy rope fouled one of the boat's fenders, causing her to capsize instantly, and throwing the four men into the water. Matthew Johns, pilot, being on board a vessel close at hand, hearing cries of distress, instantly manned his boat, and succeeded in rescuing the men, and placing them on board their ship, apparently none the worse for their immersion.

1873

1 March (RCG) WORKING MEN'S INSTITUTE. - A mechanic's institute until within the past few years was one of those things very little comprehended by the people of Fowey, but owing to the exertions of the founder, the Rev. H.N. Purcell, the vicar, the number of subscribers has rapidly run up to a very respectable total, while the funds in hand (£25) have enabled the committee to acquire a suite of good sized rooms, which they have furnished with nearly all the adjuncts of a respectable club on a small scale. On Tuesday evening the formal opening of the rooms took place.... After a neat and appropriate speech by the president, three times three were given. A vote of thanks was proposed by Mr. H. Simons and seconded by Mr. H. Hooper to the Rev. Dr. Treffry, for his kindness in granting the rooms at a nominal rent.

8 March (RCG) CRUELTY TO A GIRL.- A case of revolting cruelty to a girl,.... under 11 years of age, was investigated by the magistrates at Liskeard on Wednesday. The allegation was that...., a woman of 60, of Triggabrown Farm, Lanteglos-by-Fowey, forced the girl, as a punishment for fouling her bed, to swallow her own excrement. A farm boy .... was the only witness against her, and the magistrates.... appear to have believed his story, and fined the defendant £20, or six months' imprisonment, and intimated that if it had not been for her weak state of health they would have sent her to prison without the option of a fine.

22 March (RCG) GALE IN CORNWALL.- The sea was running mountains high at the entrance of Fowey harbour, and even inside it. At about two p.m., a large steamer was descried off the Gribbin Head, evidently in distress, with her union-jack up at the mainmast-head signalling for a pilot. The chief officer of coastguard at the station at Polruan, Mr. Selley, caused many guns to be fired from the battery, in order to warn the vessel to keep off the shore, as she was fast running towards the rocks to the eastward of Fowey Harbour.... Messrs. Philip Pill and Matthew Johns, two pilots of Polruan, after making almost superhuman efforts, and at great danger to their lives and those of their crews, succeeded in boarding the vessel, and brought her safely into the harbour. The ship whilst coming in fouled with the *Wild Wave*, of Fowey, laying at anchor, and injured her starboard quarter, &c. She subsequently collided with the schooner *Julia*, of Fowey, and a Plymouth trawler, not however doing much damage to the latter. She proved to be the steamer *Rainton*, of Newcastle-on-Tyne, Owners master, 473 tons register, with a cargo of 1,500 tons of maize, lentils, beans, mother of pearl, ivory, &c., 23 days out, from Alexandria, for London. She was short of coals. When first seen the sea was making clean breaches over her. On Saturday morning she had a portion of her bulwarks carried away, her bridge damaged, one boat stove, and the lifeboat washed in on the bridge, carrying away the iron stanchions and rails with it. The *Rainton* is said to be the largest trading steamer that has put into Fowey. Just after the arrival of the steamer a smack, the *Lively Cruiser*, of Portsmouth, with flour, &c., for Plymouth, ran into the harbour, and drifted ashore under Whitehouse Cliff. Owing to the timely assistance rendered by several people who happened to be out in boats, she was got off without receiving any very material injury.

29 March (RCG) NARROW ESCAPE.- Capt. Brooks, formerly of the 14th Light Dragoons, on a visit to Miss Rashleigh, of Point Neptune, had a narrow escape, together with his wife and child on Wednesday, while driving between No. 2 shaft of the Cornwall Mineral Railway works and Castledoor in St. Sampsons. It seems from some unexplained cause, the horse, which is a valuable one, belonging to Miss Rashleigh, ran away, came in collision with the hedge, throwing out the occupants of the trap, and smashing the vehicle to pieces, and then turned about and made towards Fowey, but was eventually stopped at a place called Newton, where it was found very much cut up. Mr. W.N. Abbott, of Fowey, who was driving by,....came up with the party, who he found....shaken, but not seriously hurt, and returned with them to Point Neptune in his conveyance.

5 April (RCG) ACCIDENT TO A VESSEL IN THE RIVER. - The galliott *Solphide*, of Boston, Lincolnshire, while dropping down the river, drifted too close to the shore below Boddinoc, and on her anchor being let go her stern tailed on the rocks. As the tide fell a screw was brought to bear on her, and while her bow was nearly under water she slipped off, fell over on her broadside, and swinging to her anchor sunk in deep water. The vessel and cargo were fully insured.

12 April (RCG) A SUNKEN VESSEL. - The galliott *Sylphille*, which sunk on Thursday last, is now alongside Fowey Quay discharging her cargo of barley, which does not appear to be so much injured as might have been expected. The arrival on Monday afternoon of the Government steamer with the diver, and all the necessary gear caused some little excitement in our usually dull town. The task of slinging the vessel was rendered somewhat difficult from the fact that she was lying on the ribs of a former victim. But these difficulties were overcome by the Admiralty diver, Charles Incledon, with great skill and perseverance. With the rising tide of Tuesday afternoon she was successfully raised and towed into shallow water. No damage has been done to the hull of the vessel. The cargo was sold on Tuesday.

12 April (RCG) A SCHOONER BURNT. - Early on Saturday morning the inhabitants of the eastern part of Fowey were startled by an alarm of fire. It was found that the *Feronia*, of London, but belonging to Looe owners, of which Mr. Taylor is master, from Newport, discharging coals at the jetty, from which she had hauled off, was on fire, her main boom and other gear, and her bulwarks being in flames. Mr. Richard Pomeroy, of Mr. Tremayne's yacht, laying near, was the first to render assistance, and was quickly joined by the master....and crew of the *Pearl*, of Jersey, and Captain W. Creak and crew of the brigantine *Jim Crow*, of Yarmouth, who did their utmost to put out the fire and managed to save a considerable portion of the gear. The crew of the damaged vessel escaped with their clothes. The master was absent. Finding all attempts to arrest the force of the fire useless, it was decided to scuttle the vessel,....and she lies in five fathoms of water, in dangerous proximity to the main channel up the harbour for vessels proceeding to the loading place, and will have to be removed as soon as possible. The fire is thought to have originated through the heating of the cabin stove, which set fire to the woodwork behind it. Signs of fire were observed before the crew retired to rest, and means were taken, as they thought, to prevent any possibility of its recurring.... The vessel....is not insured.

5 July (RCG) FOWEY.- New houses are to be built on the side of the esplanade, thus obstructing a view of the Harbour. This is causing considerable dissatisfaction.

26 July (RCG) POLRUAN.- The Salmon Seine Company had the finest haul for the season in Fowey River, catching upwards of 45 fish, which readily sold at from 10d. to 1s. per lb., the greater portion being dispatched to the London market.

9 August (RCG) DEATH OF INNKEEPER. An inquest was held....at the Ship Inn, on....Mr. L.J. Nurse, the late landlord. The deceased, who had been suffering for some days, awoke soon after midnight on Thursday under the hallucination that robbers were in the house. In endeavouring to escape from the imaginary danger, he fell out of a window on to the street, and died in a few minutes. The verdict was "Temporary insanity."

11 October (RCG) NARROW ESCAPE FROM DROWNING. - Kate Wise, a servant to Mrs. Elford, of Fowey, was at the White House ferry on Monday evening waiting for the passage-boat to go across to Polruan. A man named James Vallack came by and offered her a passage over, which she accepted and got into the boat. There was a heavy swell coming in and just as another man was attempting to get into the boat a heavy wave drove its stern on the rocks, when she heeled over. The occupants of the boat went on the other side to attempt to lighten her, when she filled with water and the young woman fell overboard and drifted away. Fortunately an alarm was immediately given and a Mr. Miles, of Fowey, who was out cruising, and a boat of the schooner *R.T.K.*, of Charlestown, were quickly on the spot, and succeeding in rescuing the poor girl, who was quite insensible. They immediately took her to the Crown and Anchor Inn, where she was duly attended to by two medical gentlemen, Messrs. Daves and Shoebridge, who succeeded in restoring animation, and she is now progressing favourably. The doctors said that if she had been one half-minute longer in the water all attempts to restore life would have been useless. This affords another illustration of the great need of a proper landing place at the ferry, (which is the property of the Hon. G. Fortescue, of Boconnoc), as persons have to land on bare rocks, and when there is any swell on it is exceedingly dangerous.

1874

24 January (RCG) FALLING OVER CLIFF.- On Tuesday, Mr. Clogg, butcher, of Polruan, near Fowey, was bringing his bullock home from Penpoll, when, on arriving at his slaughter house door, the animal started off and made for the cliffs, over which it fell a distance of more than 100 feet, and was instantaneously killed. The carcase was washed ashore at Atlantic Beach, where it was skinned. The animal was valued at £30.

21 February (RCG) FOWEY. HIGHWAY ASSAULT. Col. Peard and Mr. Jonathan Rashleigh, county magistrates, were engaged on Tuesday, in investigating a charge of assaulting Mr. Ritchings of this place, on the high road, Polmear, about half-way between Par Station and Fowey on the 9th inst. It appeared....the complainant....was driving his wagon up Polmear Hill, himself walking and leading the horse towards Fowey, when he was suddenly attacked by two men. A tussle took place, and Captain M. Salt, of Polruan, and a gentleman of Newcastle-on-Tyne....who were riding in the conveyance, came to the rescue, and succeeded in capturing one of the men referred to, named Francis Dawe, of Padstow, mate of a vessel, who was convicted and sentenced to six weeks' imprisonment about a week since. The present prisoner, William Cowling, who has been working on the railway now constructing between Par and Fowey, was apprehended by P.C. Warren, at Fowey, on Saturday last, on his attending at the pay-table for his wages. Prisoner denied his guilt, and the Bench expressed sorrow that a man who had previously borne a good character should have been guilty of the offence....and he would be sent to prison, with hard labour, for six weeks.

23 May (RCG) FOWEY.- Mr Morgan Smith (a coloured man from America) with the assistance of his wife, who is a very superior white woman, gave a grand drawing room entertainment, on Monday last, at the Town Hall. The most forcible illustration was that which shewed how ridiculous a man does make himself while in a state of inebriety,.... Other theatrical representations followed and were much appreciated by the audience which was considerable.

3 October (RCG) FOWEY. - A large quantity of iron ore is now being forwarded from this port, and the most valuable assistance is being afforded by means of the piers, steam cranes, and tipping appliances....erected by the Cornwall Minerals Railway Company.

3 October (RCG) THE POLRUAN FERRY. - In consequence of the many complaints which have been made respecting this ferry, Mr. Pease, the steward of the Hon. George M. Fortescue, who has the right of the ferry, with Mr. N. Kendall and several of the inhabitants of Fowey and Polruan, held a meeting at the Townhall, Fowey.... Mr Pease....stated that Mr. Fortescue himself derived no pecuniary advantage from the ferry, as all the rent was applied for the benefit of the Polruan

School. The subject of the improvement of the landing was then discussed.... Mr Pease announced that.... M. Fortescue....would subscribe three years' rent of the ferry towards the intended improvement.

31 October (RCG) FOWEY.- At the Tywardreath Petty Sessions....Mr. J. Sparnall, of the Ship Hotel, Fowey, was summoned....for neglecting to abate a long-standing nuisance caused by a dung-pit, at the back of his stables. The medical officer of health....stated....that the nuisance in question was injurious to health, and Joseph Pearn asserted that he and his family had suffered much from the nuisance.... Mr. E.S. White, surgeon....admitted that the thing complained of was a nuisance and ought to be removed. The defendant was ordered to remove the nuisance within ten days, and to pay the costs amounting to £2 15s.

14 November (RCG) FOWEY. - By the liberality of Mr. Rashleigh, a reading-room and institute has been established at Polruan for the use of the inhabitants. Mr. Rashleigh has given the necessary furniture and a useful library, and supplies several daily and weekly newspapers.

12 December (RCG) FOWEY. - SUPPOSED LOSS OF A VESSEL. - The smack *Need*, of Fowey, portions of which have been washed ashore near Padstow, sailed from Fowey on Friday, November 27th. She had on board a cargo of barley, and her crew consisted of Tiller (the master), his son, who was mate, and another young man from the neighbourhood. Tiller, if the vessel is really lost, leaves a wife and five children, but fortunately for the bereaved family he was a member of the Order of Foresters. The *Need*....belonged to Mr. James Hayes of Bodinnock, and was uninsured, but the cargo....shipped by Messrs. Parkyn and Sons, of Lerrin, was insured.

1875

16 January (RCG) NARROW ESCAPE OF THREE PERSONS. - As a horse boat, containing the coachman to Mr. Glencross, a woman, and a boy, was crossing the ferry from the Fowey side on Tuesday it was drawn in under the yard of Messrs. Butson, where some men were engaged in hauling up a piece of timber. Just as the boat got under the chain broke, and the timber stove the boat which immediately sank, thus throwing all the occupants into the water. Several boats from the ships near were immediately on the spot, and rescued the three persons; the horse swam ashore. The tide was running down very strong at the time, and they had a narrow escape. The boat has not yet been recovered.

15 May (RCG) FOWEY. THE SANITARY CONDITION. - At a meeting of the St. Austell Board of Guardians,....Mr J. Samble, the inspector, reported that he had again made a careful inspection of the sanitary state of the town of Fowey.... In Lostwithiel-street there was no kind of drain whatever, the street receiving the refuse and other offensive matters from the houses.... He strongly recommended that a main sewer should be laid through the street, and stated that Dr. Treffry (owner of the Fowey property) had refused to proceed with any more sanitary improvements until such main sewers were laid. He also recommended that the whole of the drains should be flushed out in the dry summer months with sea water, which could be easily obtained. Nearly all the houses were without closet accommodation, and even without any place to erect one. Many houses were in a most filthy and unwholesome state, and not fit for habitation.... The Fowey guardians, Messrs. S. Short and Oliver, promised to call a vestry of the parish to consider....laying down a main sewer.

10 July (RCG) FOWEY. FORESTRY. - The members of Court "Treffry"....held their quarterly meeting....at the Court-room, Fowey. The receipts from this meeting from members' subscriptions, &c., were £104 14s. 6d. The Court "Treffry" has now been established about 11 years, during which time it has proved of great advantage to the working classes of this neighbourhood. Its members and their families have received in sick pay, funerals grants, and widow and orphan pensions about £1,800. The Society now numbers 330 members, and the reserve balance.... is £1,200.

2 October (RCG) SANITARY IMPROVEMENTS.- At length the Sanitary Authorities have decided to attempt to make the town of Fowey ordinarily decent. Messrs. W. Smith and Co....the contractors will have at least to burrow to the extent of twenty feet under the level of Trafalgar Square. The inhabitants of Fowey are delighted to hear of these intended improvements, and trust the Inspector, Mr. Samble, will make proper provisions for sluicing purposes. The works are under the immediate superintendence of Mr. E. Crapp.

18 December (RCG) FOWEY. SERIOUS ACCIDENT. - On Monday morning, while several persons were engaged in unloading a truck of timber at the Fowey and Lostwithiel Railway Station for John Stephens, of this place, a serious accident happened to a youth named John Moon. He was on top of the timber in the truck, and whilst engaged in lifting a piece off, the iron stanchions broke, causing the timber to suddenly give way, and throwing the youth down. His leg was caught between two pieces, and the knee of the left leg was very seriously crushed. The poor fellow was promptly removed to the Cottage Hospital....

1876

1 January (RCG) RAPID VOYAGE.- The schooner *Little Beauty* of Fowey, built by John Stephens, and commanded by Capt. E. Coombes, arrived at Cardiff on Tuesday, the 21st inst., from Palermo with fruit, all well. This vessel (the last launched by Mr. Stephens) sailed from Fowey on the 15th October last for Naples with fish, and from thence to Palermo, and back to Cardiff, thus accomplishing the round in that short space of 68 days, including the days of sailing and arriving.

29 April (RCG) SUDDEN DEATH.- On Saturday morning last three men, named respectively Joseph Glanville, John Wyatt, and George Climo, left Polruan early in their boat for the purpose of hauling their trammels and crab-pots outside the harbour. After inspecting the trammel they were about to proceed to the crab-pots, when Joseph Granville, on taking his oar in his hand, was observed by the other two men to fall forward on his face on the next thwart of the boat. They immediately raised him up, but he was quite insensible. They made all speed for the shore, but the poor fellow died without uttering a word in about fifteen minutes after he fell, and before they reached Polruan. Deceased was about 67 years of age.

3 June (RCG) Capt. Koning of the Dutch galliott *Zephyr,* was charged at Fowey, on Wednesday, with throwing overboard some ballast in the harbour during the night of Tuesday. The case was proved and the captain was fined the full penalty of £5. and costs 18s.

17 June (RCG) At a special session at Tywardreath on Tuesday, John Smith, a sailor, belonging to the *Margaret,* of Bideford, was....charged with committing indecent assaults on Jemima Retallick (St. Blazey), Bessie Northcott, and Catherine Brewer..... Bessie Northcott....is a servant at Mr. Robert Michell Trenant's, Fowey; and the prisoner assaulted her on the 9th inst. On the evening of that day the prisoner ran after her as she was going home, and caught her up just as she got to the gate leading into Mrs. Geach's farm, at Penhale. Here he caught hold of her, put his handkerchief over her eyes, and then thrust it in her mouth, causing it to bleed, and attempted the assault he was charged with, but prosecutrix....freed herself from him, and ran into Mrs. Geach's farm, and gave the alarm.... The Magistrates committed him to Bodmin Gaol for three calendar months with hard labour for each.

1 July (RCG) CORNWALL MIDSUMMER SESSIONS THE TREFFRY-MARESCAUX CASE.- The Grand Jury threw out the bill against Capt. Alfred Frederick Marescaux, in command of the coastguard, Fowey, for assaulting George Steele Treffry, at Fowey, with intent to do him grievous bodily harm, but found a true bill for common assault....committed after great provocation.... The prosecutor stated that he lived at 2, Florence-villa, Fowey, and was on friendly terms with the defendant to within six weeks of 31st May last. On that day he went to defendant in his garden, and asked him to speak to him. Defendant said he would, and went into his house for a stick. They then walked into the road in front of the house, and when there he told defendant he had been saying things about him, and that he was an infernal liar. High words ensued, and the defendant hit him over the head with a stick, stunning him. They fell into a potato plot where, when he was on his back, defendant knelt on him, and hit him several times over the head with a stick. He could not say how he got up.

Crossexamined-..Had been in the army, first in the 45th regiment, and changed into the 63rd, which went to India. Afterwards went into the 2nd West India and sold out of that. Was reported for having been drunk, and recommended to leave. Was not quarrelsome, only drunk. It was not the first time. Had been charged twice before for being drunk. Once in the 45th and twice in the West Indian Regiment.

Mr. COLLINS;.... Have you ever been charged with assault? Yes. At Swansea I was summoned for assaulting Mr. Williams. The magistrates thought I was guilty, and fined me £3. I was sober when I committed the assault.

Witness....lived next door to Capt. Marescaux. After being much pressed, the witness admitted that his intention in going to the defendant was to bring him out into the public road and call him an infernal liar. It did not strike him at the time that if defendant struck him, he should strike him again....he said he did so strike him, but that was a mistake owing to his being ill and weak. It did not occur to him that on being called an infernal liar, the defendant would strike him.... Did not remember saying to Captain Marescaux, "You have been telling a damned lot of lies about me,".... Would not swear he did not strike the defendant , but would swear that he did not strike the defendant before the defendant struck him.... Had no recollection of seizing Captain Marescaux by the necktie or holding him by the collar when on the ground, or trying to take his stick from him. Heard Mrs. Marescaux say "You struck my husband first," but made no reply; had no recollection of calling her a liar. Could not remember saying to the boy Wakeham "That rascally fellow does not fight fair." Had had the "gloves" on, but not for some years. Did not remember saying to Mr. Davis, his doctor, "I have had a damned good licking;" still it was natural for him to have said he had had a licking. Had two black eyes and several cuts across the head. .... Was in a semi-conscious state after being hit on the head by the defendant.

Samuel Wakeham, errand boy, Fowey, saw Mr. Treffry and the defendant talking together. The latter hit Mr. Treffry with a stick over the head. He was falling into the potato patch below, when defendant gave him a push, upon which Mr. Treffry caught hold of him by the throat and both fell. On the ground defendant knelt on Mr. Treffry and struck him over the head with a stick. A man named Blight parted them, and after that the defendant went back and struck Mr. Treffry several times with the stick. When he got up Mr. Treffry said "that rascally fellow does not fight fair."

Frances Jane Glasson, who witnessed the affray, never saw Mr. Treffry strike or attempt to strike Captain Marescaux.

Edward Blight said when he saw Mr. Treffry in the potato patch he was lying like a man half dead and bleeding very much. Captain Marescaux then commenced a second attack, and he had no doubt that Mr. Treffry's head was made a little softer by the blows - (laughter).

Edward Gardener, Fowey, said....the defendant came to his lodging with his coat and wrists covered with blood. In reply to witness defendant said, 'I have half-killed George Treffry," adding when asked how the row commenced, "George Treffry called me a liar, I then called him a liar and a blackguard, and shortening my stick gave him a blow over the eye, knocking him over the parapet."

P.C. Davis deposed that when in the lock-up the defendant remarked to him, "If it had not been for one of Dr. Treffry's tenants I should have killed George Treffry on the spot."

Arthur A. Davis, surgeon, Fowey, said he found three wounds on the top of Mr. Treffry's head, a cut on the forehead, and the left eye completely closed. Afterwards he found him suffering from pains in the side and bowels, and vomiting, and, in consequence of the symptoms, he called in Dr. Prance of Plymouth.. Mr. Treffry's life was in danger 24 hours. Kneeling on a man's chest would have caused the symptoms from which Mr. Treffry suffered....

Mr. EDMONDS, in summing up his case, remarked upon the tactics of the defence in not calling any witnesses, contending that this in itself was a sufficient proof that an assault had been committed....

Mr. COLLINS, in defence, asked the jury whether they did not think that the chastisement which Mr. Treffry had received was not richly deserved.... Was Mr. Treffry, who had been previously convicted of an assault, the quiet, unassuming gentleman unlikely to commit an assault? Would any one of the jury have acted differently from Capt. Marescaux if they had been insulted in the way he was? Mr. Treffry, who it was charitable to suppose was very excited, came out of his house with a whip in his hand, called Captain Marescaux, who was sitting quietly in his garden, into the road and grossly insulted him,.... Sometimes it was said that there was one law for the rich and another for the poor, but certainly Captain Marescaux had nothing to congratulate himself on from being a gentleman of position; for he was served far worse than any agricultural labourer would have been. He, an officer in the navy, who was the most unlikely person to leave his home to avoid proceedings before a court of justice, was apprehended like a common felon, and remanded for 24 hours without bail.... Mr. Treffry had said to his medical man that he had had a good hiding, and the jury would no doubt consider that that was the truth. If Mr. Edmonds had been consulted in the first instance, he would not have advised criminal proceedings. The serious results apprehended at one time were not due to the blows of the stick, but to the defendant falling on Mr. Treffry.... The jury....returned a verdict of "not guilty." Many in court applauded thereat,.... When outside the court Captain Marescaux was received with considerable applause....before they had left the court - Captain Marescaux offered his hand and shook hands with Mr. Treffry.

4 November (RCG) FOWEY FIRE. - Between the hours of one and two on Wednesday morning, the premises of Messrs. Bennett and Bennett, grocers, &c., situated on the Town Quay, were discovered to be on fire. An alarm was immediately raised. Mrs. Bennett was aroused by the noise and found her room full of smoke. She at once called her husband, after which she aroused his brother, and then the servant, all of whom were sleeping on the premises. Assistance was promptly at hand, but the inhabitants of the house had to be taken out of the upstairs windows, the smoke becoming so dense that they could not get out of the front door. The fire was found to be in the shop, and to extend across to the bakehouse, which is joined to the premises. The fire was, after some time, got under chiefly by getting water passed along in buckets from the quay. Fortunately the tide was in, so that there was no lack of water. The goods in the shop are completely spoiled, as also are some of the stores in the warehouse adjoining.... The kitchen and furniture, which is over the shop, was greatly damaged by fire and water.... The house, and stock-in-trade, is partially insured in the Sun Fire office, London. The origin of the fire is not yet ascertained.

11 November (RCG) MARRIAGE OF MISS TREFFRY. - On Wednesday morning the marriage of Miss Zoe Treffry, of Place House, Fowey, with Mr. E. Ruffer, of London, took place at the Fowey Parish Church. At the front entrance leading from Place House to the church an arch was erected and dressed with evergreens and flowers, with the inscription "Health and happiness to the bridal pair," and "May your path through life be a smooth one." At the other entrance to Place grounds another arch was erected, bearing the following inscription: "May you be happy and prosperous." Bunting was displayed from the Place tower and from the church tower, and flags (kindly lent by the captain of the *Bernice*) were hung also across the churchyard. The shipping in the harbour also displayed their colours and many houses in the town were decorated. On the arrival of the bride at the church gates she was received by her father, the Rev. Dr. Treffry, who led her into the church, where the marriage ceremony was performed by the Rev. H. N. Purcell, Vicar of Fowey, and brother-in-law of the bride, assisted by the Rev. Mr. Dobre, of Jersey. The bridesmaids were Miss Maria S. Treffry, sister of the bride; Miss Ruffer, sister of the bridegroom; Miss Boucher, Miss Esther Peard, and the Misses Purcell (2). They were dressed in pale blue silk, and each carried in her hand a bouquet of white and pink roses and blue ageratum. The bride was dressed in a white brocaded silk, looped up with orange blossoms. She wore a wreath of orange blossoms on her head, and had a large bridal veil over the whole. The bouquet which she carried was composed of orange blossoms, white roses, and maiden-hair ferns. The boquets were arranged by Mr. S. Gale, gardener to the Rev. Dr. Treffry. A large number of the neighbouring gentry were present.... At 1 p.m. the happy couple left for their bridal tour.

11 November (RCG) GAS EXPLOSION.- On the morning of the 2nd instant, whilst a man called Lewace, who has charge of the gas works in this place, was attempting to repair a leak in the pipes with the hydraulic, an explosion of gas took place, severely injuring him. He has lost nearly all his hair and his eyes are so injured that the doctors fear he will not recover his sight.

1877

19 January (RCG) ACCIDENT. - On Friday whilst Mr. Geo. Dunn, of Newton, near Fowey, was engaged in sawing some timber at Mr. Short's farm, at Lantilly, he passed a piece of wood under the circular saw attached to the steam machine, and in so doing caught his left thumb under the saw, cutting it off close to the second joint.

19 January (RCG) AMATEUR MINSTRELS - This company, which has been recently formed at Fowey, affords quite a novel feature of amusement for the neighbourhood, and has quickly made very satisfactory progress and become very popular with the public. The company consists of Messrs D. Phillips, J. Belletti, R. Gale, F. Dennison, W. Denison, F. Wyatt, F. Morris, J. Netherton, T. Sweet, and Luther Martin. Monday evening a special entertainment consisting of a select variety of sentimental, serio-comic, and character songs was given by the members at the Town Hall, assisted by the hand-bell ringers, Messrs C. Bryant, W. Lovering, and W. Slade to one of the largest audiences that has assembled there for many years. At the close the National anthem was given with great effect.

26 January (RCG) ANOTHER FIRE AT FOWEY. - The inhabitants of Fowey were alarmed at mid night on Tuesday last by the call of "fire," which was found to proceed from a dwelling known as Moorstone House, in the occupation of a person called Morris, situate in the centre of the town. Owing to the prompt attendance of Messrs. Davis, J. King, Batchelor, Hearn, Blowey, Walton, and Banbury, who were well seconded by others, including many women, the flames were soon got under by a liberal use of buckets, which were quickly handed up over several ladders, the supply of water being good, as the tide was pretty well up. The ancient fire-engine was brought down nearly to the scene of the fire, when it was discovered that the hose was useless. The flames were for a short time very fierce, and threatened the adjoining houses, which are principally of lath and plaster connections and used as shops, the street in this part of the town being very narrow, as indeed the whole of the ancient borough streets are. The fire is attributed to a paraffin lamp being upset and broken, and igniting the partition of the sitting and adjoining bedrooms. The contents are insured....A young man named William Harris had a narrow escape during the height of the fire through a ladder breaking and precipitating him to the ground, but although he had a heavy fall, he escaped with a few bruises. The damage is estimated roughly at over £150.

2 February (RCG) FORESTRY. OPENING OF A NEW COURT AT POLRUAN No greater evidence exists of the thrift and industry of Cornishmen than the success of Friendly societies among them, and not least amongst these is the Ancient Order of Foresters, which was introduced into the county in August, 1860.... Since that time 33 other courts have been opened, the whole numbering about 5000 members, with accumulated funds amounting to about £20,000. The last Court opened was that at Polruan, a large and flourishing village near the entrance to Fowey harbour.... The opening ceremony took place on Tuesday, and was ably carried out by Bro. J.H. James, of Truro....one of the first eight initiated in Cornwall.... Twenty-five were initiated, from which the following were....installed as officers: T. Woods, C.R., James Climo, S.C.R., D. Torbock, treasurer, D.Bailey, secretary, A. Shepherd, S.W., N. Paynter, J.W., E. Wyatt, S.B., W. Climo, J.B. D. Torbock was unanimously appointed surgeon to the court, which is very appropriately named "Perseverance," ....the place of meeting is to be the National school....

After the court had been duly and formally closed, the Brethren adjourned to the "Russell Arms," where an excellent repast was provided by Bro. and Host Woods. About 35 sat down.... The Chairman....in eulogistic terms spoke of the valuable aid rendered Polruan by the St. Austell court and district, when brethren nearer home had refused it,.... The Chairman next gave the "Ancient Order of Foresters," eloquently descanting on the advantages of such societies. After expressing the gratification he felt at the establishment of a branch of such an honourable order in their little town, he remarked that he hoped every man in the place who had not joined some such society, and who was properly qualified, would do so at once. This toast was received with much enthusiasm, which, if continued, will bring

"Perseverance" a rich reward....This makes the second Court opened by the St. Austell United district this year, and from the great vitality manifested since the infusion of new blood, about 9 months since, a prosperous future seems before it.

16 February (RCG) PROPOSED FIRE BRIGADE. - A meeting of the inhabitants of Fowey was held in the Townhall....for the purpose of taking into consideration the present state of the fire extinguishing apparatus and of endeavouring to devise some means of procuring a regularly organised fire brigade acting under a committee management. At present Fowey force possesses an engine nearly fifty years old, almost unworkable, without a suction pipe, and with a hose so worn and decayed by age as to be useless.... Mr L.A.E. Shadwell,....in the uniform of the Slough Volunteer Fire Brigade, of which he was captain for over twelve years.... detailed some of his experiences, concluding by tendering his services in the formation and working of a fire brigade. The balance-sheet of the fire-engine account shewed 3d. as the amount in hand, and it was stated that the fund was in debt over £4.- It was resolved that....a committee....take the necessary preliminary steps for forming a brigade.

20 April (RCG) HEAVY GALE. - The *St. Andrews* schooner, of Fowey, Wm. Cooth, master, owned by Mr. S. Moss, of Par, with a cargo of coals, from Porthcawl for Par, was making Fowey Harbour, when she carried away her fore-yard, and, in endeavouring to weather Daniel Point within the entrance of the harbour, she struck the rocks and quickly sank. The steamer *Treffry*, of Par, being at Fowey, went to her assistance, and arrived only about a minute too late. The crew, five in number, were saved by Messrs. Cornish and Handcock in a waterman's boat. The vessel is gradually washing in towards Ready Money Cove, and is expected to become a total wreck. The boat, hatches, and other portions....have washed ashore.

11 May (RCG) SANITARY MATTERS AT FOWEY. -....The St. Austell Sanitary Authority....some time ago....laid a main sewer right through the town, and erected a small reservoir at the head of it; but there is little doubt that this reservoir is much too small to effectually flush and cleanse the sewer, especially in the event of a dry season. Even now there are not wanting complaints that the street traps of this sewer are at times something like a nuisance themselves.

But undoubtedly the great want of Fowey at the present moment is some proper system for the removal of refuse, and of proper privy accommodation and house drainage....The "Treffry Estate" trustees....the principal landowners....were prosecuted at the Tywardreath Petty Sessions, and fined for not providing proper accommodation for some of their houses; but much still remains to be done.... Broadly,....it is the duty of the owner to provide the property with such structural conveniences as will keep it free from noxious gases; it is the duty of the occupier to make a proper use of these conveniences, and the refuse being focused on the edges of the premises, the Authority should then step in and transport it to a safe distance from human habitations, or otherwise render it innocuous.... For some years a scavenger went around and collected the ashes and other refuse from the houses, but the increasing infirmities of old age precluded his continuing in the office; and his successor, after a little while, gave it up in consequence of the farmers refusing to purchase the stuff from him. The place, too, where the refuse was deposited by the collector was condemned by the sanitary inspector as a nuisance, and very properly so.... The Town Quay is not a place for such a purpose, as could be testified by anyone who had occasion to go near it, and to those living near by it was particularly disagreeable. An order directing its close was....issued; but from that time to this no further provision has been made for the transference of refuse matter from the houses, and no site....selected.... The vestry meeting.... last March....appointed a committee, and empowered them to choose a site and to employ a pony and cart to carry the refuse away. But this committee has done really nothing.... The work....is clearly the duty of the properly constituted Sanitary Authority.... At present no one does it....the people...are positively obliged to accumulate refuse in the courts and back places of their houses, and to resort to the expedient of placing it just outside the old ashpit on the Town Quay, in some cases almost under the feet of the passers-by, or else throw it over the quays into the harbour, a method which would appear to have been adopted by their forefathers many generations back. This....was scarcely likely to suit the Harbour Commissioners....one day last week they sent around the town crier to give notice that any person throwing refuse into the harbour would be prosecuted....by this means the inhabitants are deprived of the only safe outlet they at present have for noxious matter, and are thus constrained still further to pile up abominations on their premises, which, if not speedily disposed of, will produce....seeds of disease....

1 June (RCG) CHURCH RENOVATION. - A bazaar in aid of the funds of the interesting old church of St. Lanty, the parish church of Lanteglos-by-Fowey, which....has a population of over 1,400, was held last week. The pretty summerhouse of Mr. John Hicks was fitted up as a refreshment and resting saloon, and wood and canvas sheds were erected, containing fancy goods of a gorgeous and miscellaneous character....the wares vended were of great variety, ranging from useful farm stock and cottage implements to ornaments sacred to the boudoir. Mr. Andrew, of Polvethian, Mr. John Thomas, of Yeat, and Mr. Henwood, of Carneggan, gave some live pigs, and Mr. Richard Hicks, two lambs. An unfortunate donkey intended for raffling fell over the cliffs, broke its neck, and was washed out to sea. A very handsome new boat, worth about £10, was, however, raffled for. The Band of the Fowey Volunteer Artillery enlivened the bazaar,....there was a very large attendance of visitors....the receipts were greatly in excess of expectation....

1 June (RCG) An old trick, which was thought to have died out at Fowey, and which a great many years since was associated with the doings of some erratic individuals, known then as "the old pair," was revived last night (Thursday), by some person stealing a horse from a field belonging to Mr. Henry Lamb, in getting after which a gate was broken open and other damage done. It is hoped the depredator will be discovered and punished.

4 June (WB). READY-MONEY, FOWEY. The beach, the scene of the late wreck, has now become, every recurring low water, a shipbreakers' yard, the proprietors of the hull (the Messrs. Lovering, of Fowey, who purchased it at the recent sale) being busily engaged daily in taking it to pieces. It is somewhat singular that the locality - Ready Money - now a hamlet of small cottages, was, years ago, occupied as a fish cellar and a shipbuilder's yard, where was launched the schooner *St. Catharine,* the new vessel going triumphant over the very ground where now lie the last sad remnants of the wrecked schooner, the *St. Andrews.*

8 June (RCG) The Cornish coast did not escape the effects of the gale. Among the injured vessels that have arrived at Fowey are the schooner *William Martyn*, of Padstow, Crocker master, from Swansea, with a cargo of coals for Fowey, with topsail yard and boom jib carried away;....*Kingaloch*, of Fowey, Elger master, from Runcorn, with salt, for Newcastle, topsail and jibboom split; and *Silver Stream*, of Fowey, Tadd master, from Smyrna, with a cargo of volonia, for orders, foretopsail and forestaysail blown away....

8 June (RCG) A CORNISH FERRYMAN. - The death took place last week at Polruan, near Fowey, of a local celebrity, Thomas Hill, a ferryman, who plied between these places. The deceased was known as "Tommy." He was formerly the regular boatman of an ancient ferry claimed by the representatives of the late Hon. G.M. Fortescue,....but was discharged many years since by the lessee, and set up in business for himself. Tommy was thereupon served with a writ, to which he paid no attention, and was consequently sent to Bodmin Gaol for contempt of court. Being liberated on promising not to offend again, Tommy, on his return to Polruan, obtained a boat at once, and set to work, for which he was served with a second writ, his case....being taken up by a local solicitor, the late W.T.Sobey, at the suggestion of, and assisted by some of the inhabitants of Polruan, who considered he had a right to ply.... At Bodmin Assiz....a verdict was entered against Tommy for 40s., and an order was made to restrain him from infringing on ferry rights. Tommy obstinately persisted in his disobedience, and was summoned to appear at Chambers. The bearer of the document, Mr Pease junr., of Lostwithiel, was received in far from a conciliatory spirit, and Tommy tore it up in Mr. Pease's face, and threw it overboard, using very strong language. Tommy, after unceasing exertions by his solicitor, who still stood by him, faithfully promised not to offend again, which he kept to the time of his death, with the exception of about a dozen infringements a week, but he has not since been interfered with, and now will probably be carried over more dry land in one day than ever he walked in his lifetime, excepting his special journeys to Bodmin. Tommy persistently refused to do duty on Sundays, but otherwise never failed in his attendance. Let the weather be what it might, he sturdily stuck to his post until two days before his death. His father and himself had worked the ferry for upwards of sixty years.

17 August (RCG) At the Police Court, Fowey, a lad named Ivanhoe Jones, aged 12 years, was brought before the Rev. Dr. Treffry....on suspicion of breaking open the box in the bagatelle room of the Fowey Working-men's Reading-room.... The Rev. H.N. Purcell said his attention was called by the secretary (R. Hellar, senr.), to the box on the 4th of August, and he saw that it had been broken open by some person or persons.- Mr. Samuel Gale, treasurer of the room, said that the money taken out of the box for the corresponding quarter last year was £4 11s. When the box was found broken open it contained only 19s. 11 1/2d.- William Martin proved seeing defendant in the room alone.- William Bersey, a lad, said that whilst bathing at "Whitehouse," the week before Fowey regatta, Jones took out his purse and counted out 15s in silver and coppers. Afterwards Jones showed him a sovereign. Witness asked him where he got the money, and he said he had got it from the captain of the *Ann Beer*.- The case was remanded until the Petty Sessions....on the 27th inst.

14 September (RCG) A baker named Anthony Tucker, residing at Polruan, near Fowey, committed suicide by cutting his throat on Saturday. It was observed that he did not open his shop as usual, and his landlord, Mr. Rundle, who lives next door, spoke to him through a window at the back of the deceased's house. Deceased stated that he was not feeling very well, and intended to lie down for some little while. Between twelve and one a police-constable named Ridge, on duty at Polruan, heard loud groans, and getting over the roof of an adjoining house, and thence through a window, he found Mr. Tucker lying on the floor with his throat cut. The policeman quickly brought Messrs. A.P. Davis, of Fowey, and Torbock, of Polruan, surgeons, but the sufferer ceased to live within a very short time after their arrival. The deceased had completely divided his windpipe and the large arteries of his neck.

21 September (RCG) POLRUAN ANNUAL REGATTA. - The little town of Polruan, situated on the banks of the river Fowey, held its annual regatta on Tuesday, but although the weather was lovely, the prize list tempting, and the various events well contested throughout, little interest was manifested in the proceedings. This is probably to be accounted for by the fact that during the present year no less than five regattas have been held in the river, and the people of the district have thus had quite sufficient of this particular kind of amusement....

19 October (RCG) TERRIBLE HURRICANE.- The streets of Fowey were covered with broken slates, bricks, and *debris* of sundry subscriptions - many houses being more than half unroofed. Vessels dragged their anchors in all directions, and within the harbour the schooner *Hilda*, of Runcorn, narrowly escaped going on the rocks at Bodinnoc. The three-masted schooner *Kocheto*, of New York, drove from her moorings, over a quarter of a mile up the harbour, and fouled the *Calenick*, of Fowey, carrying away her cathead, and damaging the bulwarks and gear of both vessels. At daylight a large number of boats were found floating bottom upwards, and many others were washed away from both Polruan and Fowey sides of the harbour, and sunk in different places. The dolphins used at the Cornwall Minerals Railway stages for mooring vessels were dragged out of their places and sunk. Broken windows and wrecked chimneys are very numerous both at Polruan and Fowey. Some heavy branches blown from a beech tree in the churchyard at Fowey crashed through the roof of an adjoining house, in the occupation of Mr. Richard Hellar, jun., and considerably frightened the inmates. A summer-house in the occupation of Mr. Wellington, chemist, was turned completely round by the action of the wind. During the height of the gale a seaman on board a French vessel *Leons Caline*, who was engaged aloft fell from the foreyard. He was placed in the Fowey Cottage Hospital, and attended by Dr. Percy Davis, who found that he had broken no bones, but had received severe contusions. A chimney fell from Dr. A.A. Davis's house on to the Custom-house roof next door, doing considerable damage. A cowshed at Polruan, belonging to Capt. Smith, was blown upwards of 200 yards, and driven with such violence against the front of a cottage in which Captain W. Sanders lived as to break in the windows and roof, causing the place to be uninhabitable.

26 October (RCG) ACCIDENT AT BODINNIC. - A horse belonging to Mr. D. Venning, brewer, of Liskeard, was drowned at Bodinnic Ferry, last week. It appears that the horse, which some time since cost £60, was harnessed to a dray loaded with casks of ale, and whilst endeavouring to enter the ferry bridge for passage across to Fowey, the bridge, as soon as the horse got his fore feet on it, went off, and the poor animal endeavoured to get a footing the faster the bridge receded. Thus the horse, dray, beer, and all went into the harbour, and the horse was drowned. Had the bridge been properly made fast, there is no doubt the accident would not have occurred. There is no blame whatever attached to the driver (John Mallatt). The ale has all been recovered.

2 November (RCG) IMPORTANT SERVICES ILL-REQUITED. - During the late gale on Sunday, the 14th, among the several vessels which broke from their mooring was the *Isabella,* of Fowey, Capt. Dyer. The watchman, knowing that the crew were natives of Polruan and all absent from the vessel, and perceiving the great damage likely to accrue to her and to the other vessels against which she was chafing, called some men to his aid, who eased her bowchain, put out fenders, made her fast to the quay, and thus prevented serious damage. Five men were thus engaged for the space of three hours; and the captain, deeply grateful for the assistance so promptly rendered, handed them the liberal sum of two shillings, of 4 3/4d. each! alleging that he was a poor man. Not to be beaten in liberality, the plucky men handed back the generous gift, making the captain a present of it.

16 November (RCG) THE LATE REV. J. KENDALL. - The funeral of the late Rev. James Kendall, vicar of Lanteglos-by-Fowey, took place on Friday, and it is very seldom that there is witnessed in Cornwall so spontaneous and sincere a manifestation of respect and regret as there was on this occasion. All classes felt that the strong and faithful attachments which endeared the devoted minister to his parishioners were sundered for ever and that his kindly counsel and tender solicitude of forty years duration were henceforth only memories. Not only from the people of Lanteglos, of all sects and conditions, were respect and sorrow manifested, but from the neighbouring parishes and from places remote hundreds of persons had arrived before the time fixed for the interment. The coffin, on which were laid wreaths of flowers, and which had the simple inscription - "James Kendall, died November 4th, 1877, aged 66 years," was borne to its resting place by the principal yeomen and farmers of the parish.... In the church and at the grave the choir, attired in mourning, sang favourite hymns of the deceased gentleman, and the solemnity of the occasion was further increased by the intermittent tolls of the muffled bells.

23 November (RCG) LANTEGLOS. CONCEALMENT OF BIRTH. - .... (A girl), late a servant with Mr. Harris, of Trethake Farm, Lanteglos, was charged with concealing the birth of a female child.... The prisoner had been living in the situation for about six months, and slept with a girl called Hambly. Just before daylight on Sunday, the 11th, Hambly saw (her) take a light and go to the further end of the room where her box stood. Hambly made a complaint, and on Miss Harris telling (her) that she must have been confined and had concealed the child in her box, the girl went to unlock it, but was so overcome that she was unable to do so. On the box being unlocked, under some things the dead body of an infant was discovered. A *post-mortem* examination was held by Mr. Davies,....surgeon, who gave it as his opinion that the child was not born alive.... (She) was committed to take her trial at Bodmin.

1878

15 February. (RCG) CAPTAIN DROWNED. Information has been received from Portishead of the death of Capt. John Greet, Fowey, by drowning. The deceased had been on shore to take tea with some friends on Thursday evening, when on returning to his ship a little after 8 p.m. he slipped his foot, struck against a pillar on the pier, and falling into the water sank. The body has been recovered, and conveyed to Fowey for interment. The deceased, who was a teetotaler was greatly respected at Fowey and its vicinity, and great sympathy is felt for his wife and child.

15 February (RCG) FOWEY. - The remains of Capt. Greet, whose death by drowning is reported in another column, were brought from Bristol on Wednesday, and interred in the Cemetery the same day. Deceased was a Freemason, and there was a desire, we believe, expressed to bury him with Masonic honours, but there was no time to get the necessary dispensation from Prov. Grand Master, the Earl of Mt. Edgcumbe. The W.M. (Mr. H. W.W. Durant), and Mr. Tonkin, the secretary, and a large number of the brethren of Fowey Lodge, however, attended in black wearing white crepe badges on their left arms and some of their number carried the coffin, on which was a large white wreath. Most of the shops were partially closed out of respect for the deceased. The Rev. H.N. Purcell, vicar,....conducted the funeral service, and numbers of people followed in the procession. (master of the schooner *Julia,* of Fowey, aged 47)

22 March (RCG) *ORDER empowering the Fowey Waterworks Company, Limited, to supply Water to the town and parish of Fowey....* (They) may....make and maintain.... 1) a storage reservoir....on land....of the estate of the late Joseph Thomas Treffry, deceased, being a portion of the farm called Penventinue, at or near the south-west corner of a field known by the name of "Under Town:" 2) an aqueduct, conduit, or pipes commencing at....Fowey, at a spring rising at or near the east corner of the yard adjoining the dwelling-house of Penventinue Farm and immediately to the north of a field ....called "The Wastrel," and terminating at the said reservoir.

3) An aqueduct, conduit, or line of pipes, commencing at the reservoir....and on the east side thereof, and terminating in the town of Fowey, at or near the entrance to the Fowey Gasworks....

At the request of the owner or occupier any dwelling-house....entitled....to demand a supply of water for domestic purposes.

10 May (RCG) FOWEY. NEW BOARD SCHOOLS. - The new Board School for boys was opened on Tuesday morning. At nine o'clock the boys assembled at their temporary schoolroom in the Townhall, whence, having "fallen in", they marched through the town, headed by the band of the Fowey Artillery Volunteers, who played them up to their new and beautiful school on the hill overlooking the town and harbour. Many of the inhabitants joined in the procession en route. Arrived at the school, the boys were formed up into their various classes by the head-master, Mr. Symms, after which the business of the day was begun in the usual way with prayer.- The Chairman of the School Board (the Rev. H.N. Purcell)....then earnestly spoke to the boys....calling on them to be an honour and credit to their town and country by using with diligence all their privileges. Having told them how their fathers would have prized such educational advantages as they possessed, and how they should make the best use of their time to fit themselves for taking in their turn the places of those who were now bearing the burden and heat of the day,....the Rev. gentleman concluded by announcing that the Board gave the school a holiday in honour of the occasion. After the assembled school had sung in a creditable manner a selection of songs, beginning with "and shall Trelawny die," and ending with "God save the Queen,"....vociferous cheers were given....

31 May (RCG) THE FOWEY HARBOUR COMMISSIONERS. TENDERS are invited for the BLOWING UP FOWEY ROCK, and to REMOVE the DEBRIS....

7 June (RCG) A fatal fight took place on Friday night at Fowey causing great excitement in that usually quiet town. It appears from the evidence....at an inquest....on Monday, that about 9 o'clock on Friday night, a woman named Courteney living at Lostwithiel was outside the Commercial Hotel, Fowey, with a cart, when William Penhaligan a driver in the employ of Messrs. Julian & Sons, builders and cabinet makers, of Truro, asked her what a ton she would give for bones. By his manner she thought he had been drinking, and she told him she thought he had come out of a lunatic asylum. He asked her to give him her hand, but she refused, and went into the hotel where she had a glass of ale. She then went to her cart, and Penhaligan came up to her again, and wanted to put his arm around her waist. She struck him in the mouth, whereupon Penhaligan aimed a blow at her, but struck Richard Netherton, a farm labourer, who was talking to the woman. Netherton returned the blow, and both men fell to the ground. After a time they got on their legs, and fought again, and Penhaligan caught Netherton by the throat. After further fighting, Netherton walked quickly away, but was observed to stop, and on its being found that he was unable to walk any further, he was carried to his house on the back of a man. His son went for a doctor, but before one came Netherton was dead. Mr. E.S. White, surgeon, stated that the deceased was a patient of his some ten years ago. He had made a postmortem examination, and considered that the deceased died from faintness through extreme over-exertion. He might have died at any moment through over-exertion. - Mrs Mary Heller said she saw Penhaligan on the night of the affray, and also saw Netherton, and cautioned him not to fight. Netherton replied that Penhaligan should not strike the woman. Subsequently she heard the prisoner say he would "do"for Netherton before he left Fowey.- After a brief deliberation the jury returned a verdict of manslaughter against Penhaligan, who was present in the custody of the police. The affair has caused considerable excitement in the prisoner's native town. Penhaligan is a married man with a family; and his wife is now in Bodmin Lunatic Asylum. Prisoner was subsequently brought before the Magistrates and committed for trial at the Assizes.

(**2 August** issue- At trial it was said that the woman was roughly insulted by Penhaligan who used bad language. There was a good deal of rough talk on both sides. A kind of wrestle or struggle and some blows undoubtedly. Doctor's evidence was that there were no signs of bruises or cuts on the deceased. His heart was very much enlarged and showed fatty degeneration and was much heavier than it ought to have been. No case to answer.)

21 June (RCG) THE RAISING OF THE *"ARIEL"*.- The brigantine *Ariel,* which caught on Fowey rock some weeks ago and sank,....was on Saturday raised by Mr. Lean, shipbuilder, of Falmouth, and towed by aid of a steamboat and two locomotive engines, on the Cornwall Mineral Railway which adjoins, into Fowey Pill, where she at present is on the mud. To-day attempts will be made to take her further in shore, this being prevented Saturday by the sinking of one of the hulks, a small one placed to support the bows. The operation, luckily a novel one for Fowey, was witnessed by hundreds of inhabitants, and the water around was alive with boats of all sizes, making altogether a very interesting scene, which was photographed by Mr. Mitchell, of St. Austell.

21 June (RCG) ATTRACTIONS OF FOWEY. - (from Western Daily Mercury) "Whenever I visit Fowey," said a recent traveller from London, "I indulge in the hope of one day building a nest here, in which to end my pilgrimage. Apart," said he, " from its improved sanitary condition and the most civil and obliging characteristics of its inhabitants, I take pride in its grand historical associations.... So far back as the 13th century, Fowey was an important port, having a great fleet of ships and a far-famed formidable name in naval annals of that period;...." So much for our London visitor; we hope he may speedily pay us another visit, and then fix on the *locale* whereon to build his "nest." It is contemplated, we understand to invite the well-reputed firm of "Julian and Sons," of Truro, to add to the fine buildings they are now erecting here for educational purposes, several well-situated villas on elevations overlooking the harbour and the entrance from the English Channel, if the land can be obtained on reasonable terms; for why should not the ancient and picturesque port of Fowey participate in the advantages of that great influx of holiday visitors who now crowd from far-off places, for health and repose into the seashore haunts of ancient Cornubia?....

28 June (RCG) FOWEY GRAMMAR SCHOOL. The plans for a new grammar school building at Fowey have just been.... finally approved, and works are to be commenced forthwith. The site belonged to the Fowey Town Charity Trustees, and is one of the most commanding in the neighbourhood....approached by a road recently cut in front of the new Board School,....and is so situated that it cannot be hereafter blocked in with new erections, which are expected to follow when the natural beauties of Fowey become generally known. The buildings will comprise on the ground floor a large main schoolroom with two classrooms opening out from it, and all the necessary lavatories, entrances, cloakroom, etc; a master's residence, containing drawing-room, breakfast parlour, large dining- room, study, kitchen, scullery, hall, and cellars, and on the upper floor six bedrooms, with bath-room, box-room, servants' accommodation two smaller and one large dormitory for the boys, with all necessary accessories, forming....one of the best, if not the best, middle class school building in Cornwall. Accommodation will be provided for a total of eighty scholars, and the Charity Commissioners have been very rigid in exacting the amplest cubical space per boy, with the latest means for ventilation. Externally the building will be Elizabethan style, of red brick, with white brick facings, high pitched roof, and ornamental chimney tops.... The architect....is Mr. Silvanus Trevail, of Tywardreath, and the contractors Messrs. J.N. Julian of Truro. Messrs. Trevail and Julian have just completed the new Board School at Fowey. The cost of the Grammar School is estimated to.... exceed £2000

5 July (RCG) POLRUAN. A CORNISH SEAMAN DROWNED. - A melancholy accident, which cost the life of three persons, including Robt. Stephens, a seaman of Polruan, occurred at Aberystwith. The yacht *Avoset* of R.L.Y.C., and belonging to a Mr. Carne, of Cowbridge, was at anchor in the harbour, and a boat, containing the owner and half-a-dozen men, put off for the shore. In crossing the bar the boat was upset and turned bottom upwards, the whole of the occupants being thrown into the sea. Boats from the vessels in the harbour and from the shore at once put off to the rescue, but only succeeded in saving three; the remaining three - Lieut. Richards, a friend of Mr. Carne's, Charles Jones, the steward, and Stephens, being drowned. At an inquest....a verdict of "Accidental death" was returned. Two other Cornishmen were on board the yacht at the time,....namely - Joseph Dyer, of Fowey, and Robert Smith, of Penarth.

19 July (RCG) Polruan is the little town just opposite Fowey, on the other side of the harbour. About a thousand people live there, in houses, some crowded together towards the Quay and by the water's side, others straggling up the acclivity which rises....to a considerable height. It consists of three principal streets, and a few byeways, all converging to the quay and the water's side. There are one or two roughly constructed sewers -with which, however, very few of the houses have any connection; a gutter, either worn by the action of water, or rudely constructed, runs down the centre of the streets, and into this the neighbours on either side throw most of the slops and household refuse of a general description. The water supply is no better organized than the drainage; and hence the few water closets there are are liable to become a greater nuisance than the old-fashioned privies, though even privies are not very general.

The water supply of Polruan might be made thoroughly efficient at no very great expense. At the present time there are three or four pumps or wells in the town. There is a pump at the bottom of Fore street. The well was dug about 20 years ago....but privies have since been built quite close to it; an open aggregation of filthy water at the present moment stagnates around it....the water....contaminated by the percolation of sewage matter.... The people in....West St....have the still more doubtful advantage of an open well. Houses are all around it, and far above it on St. Saviour's Hill; and as there are no public drains whatever in this part of the town, there is too much probability that besides the ordinary dangers of pollution which open wells always run, this well is terribly liable to contamination from sewage. Then,....at the farther end of East-street....there is another open well; but in this instance the water is good, no nuisance or drain is near, and those who use it take commendable care of it. The well is on the property of Mr. Moss, of Lostwithiel,....who exercises a beneficent supervision over the sanitary condition of his premises. What, however, is looked upon as the grand source of future supply is a natural spring just above the town. The water rises at the top of the meadow belonging to the township of Polruan, and known as Vaffary Meadow, and flows in a perennial stream, part of it to waste and part of it under an ancient stone cross, known as Boundary Cross - from the fact of its marking the boundary of the township of Polruan....- and through a shoot into a large stone trough. This is said to be beautifully pure water, and would probably be sufficient for the whole of the town were it all properly utilised. A reservoir at the highest point would be all....that would be required, as the houses to be supplied are at a lower level, and the natural force of the water would distribute it to any part. With a system of drainage, however, the other wells now contaminated would be rendered much more pure, and the supply from this source might be only needed for Fore-street and its immediate vicinity. At the present time the water from the stone trough comes directly down Fore-street-hill, and clearing the sewage as it goes, it finally empties itself into the sea under the Quay.

.... A covered gutter - the same which carries the overflow from the shoot at the boundary cross - runs all down Fore-street. It is a peculiarly rude structure, varying in depth from one to two feet, with dry walls covered with large pieces of shaly stone. At one or two points it crosses the road from one side to the other; and here and there it is "ventilated" by being broken in, or worn through. Sometimes in the winter it gets choked, and the water then sweeps over the road with such force as to take a good part of it down to the quay. A few - a very few - of the owners of the houses on either side have thought it worth while to connect their house drains - if they have any - with this main sewer. But an even more conspicuous failure....occurs in East-street. About four years ago the sanitary conscience of the town grew very uneasy, and in order to quiet it half the length of East-street was laid with 6-inch pipes.... The drainage of no single house has ever been emptied into them.... The house refuse, where not unblushingly thrown into the street, is in many instances allowed to flow out surreptitiously from little iron gratings, and the noxious effluvia arising in some quarters may be imagined, especially during hot weather.... Proper sewers must be made, and with the sewers house drains must be properly connected.

The great question which remains is....who is to do it? Polruan is a township, governed, for ordinary purposes, by nobody in particular. There is some town property, and a town's meeting is held once a year, at which the work of the whole year is once for all decided on! Some few years ago the Polruanites fought hard against being put on an equal footing with the rest of the parish of Lanteglos-by-Fowey.... They kept their own town property, and have made an effort every now and then to mend their ways; but their whole income from quay, meadow, and house property only amounts to £29 a year; and when a gale has come and damaged the quay, or the houses have been out of repair, they have found a balance on the wrong side. The debt has gradually accumulated until it now reaches £168. This being the case, it can easily be conceived that no improvements would be made unless some higher authority could exercise a compulsory power over the place. This needful power is possessed by the Liskeard Board of Guardians, acting as the Rural Sanitary Authority of the district,.... The parish naturally says that as Polruan made so much of its independence a few years ago it must now bear its own burden entirely.... A few people....have already ventured to settle there. Several new houses are being built, and when it is made a little more inviting the place....will no doubt reap much benefit financially, as well as incalculable good in the shape of increased comfort and improved health.

26 July (RCG) The Rev. H.N. Purcell (announced) it was necessary to order a new clock for the Church Tower.... I trust the clock will be in its place in a very short time. The Tower roof was found to be in so bad a state that a new one has had to be placed on the tower before a valuable clock could be fixed. The cost of clock (which will play quarter chimes), new roof, clock case, &c., will be just about £200. This sum I have already received with the exception of about £17. I trust this sum may be gathered outside the Church....for I cannot think it fair or right that the Church should be called to bear the cost of a clock which though fixed in our tower, is placed there for the public benefit apart from all religious distinctions." We cordially endorse the vicar's opinion. There are a goodly number of Dissenters in Fowey, and they ought to help to pay for the town clock which will be of as much benefit to them as to the Church folks.

13 September (RCG) FOWEY WORKING MEN'S INSTITUTE. A *fete champetre* was held in aid of funds of the new building lately erected upon the town quay.... For the past ten years a room near the site of the new building has been used, but of late the members have so increased that the place was found quite inadequate....the new undertaking....will cost £700. When £300 had been collected the building was commenced, and is now nearly completed. It contains one large hall, upwards of fifty feet long, which will be used for amusements and lectures. On same floor there is a retiring-room and premises for the keeper of the Institute. The reading-room, a spacious one, is situated on the ground floor, and a large billiard-room.... The fete was held in a large field....contiguous to the beautiful grounds at Place, which were kindly thrown open to the public.... The bazaar was held in a tent, about 100 feet long, and the articles....were neatly arranged on several stands. Brisk business was done, and by six o'clock in the evening the stalls were pretty nearly emptied.... The tent set aside for refreshments was well stocked with choice viands.... The public tea was also largely attended....Among the many attractions, perhaps the greatest was the performance of the band and pipers of the 25th (King's Own Borderers) Regiment.... The band of St. Columb Rifle Volunteers also played upon the grounds and that of the 3rd D.C.A. Volunteers.... The *Sir Francis Drake* steamer brought a large party of excursionists....from Plymouth. The athletic sports were efficiently carried out.... The contests were close.... A sack race brought together six competitors, and caused much merriment. The proceedings were brought to a successful close in the evening by a well-attended dance held in the Town-hall.

11 October (RCG) POLRUAN. FATAL ACCIDENT.- An inquest was held....on....William Menear, a lad of ten years, who met his death through falling in the hold of the schooner, *Water Lily*, whilst that vessel was undergoing repairs alongside the Town Quay, at Polruan. After the jury had viewed the body of deceased, William Climo said he was a shipwright living at Polruan, and that on the 21st September, about three o'clock in the afternoon, he was at work on board the *Water Lily*. He found the deceased at the bottom of the ladder of the fore hatchway but did not see him fall. The distance was eight or nine feet. He found him bleeding from the left ear. Witness at once carried him up the ladder, and had the lad removed to his home. James John deposed that he was working in the hold of the vessel on the day mentioned and heard a fall, and looking around saw the lad at the bottom of the vessel. Mr. A.P. Davis, surgeon, of Fowey, stated that there was no external injury, but a very tender spot over the left ear, and also a deal of hemorrhage in the left ear. He considered that the child had received an injury over a portion of the temporal bone, and attributed his death to fracture of the skull.

18 October (RCG) On Wednesday a prize ringing match was held at Lanteglos-by-Fowey. The fittings of the bells have for a considerable time past been in very bad order, but have since been put in a satisfactory state by Mr. Walter Wakeham, of Fowey, and in order to inaugurate the event it was decided to have prize ringing.... Subscriptions towards the funds were at once solicited, Mr. Richard Hicks, of Hall, acting as treasurer. As this was the first ringing match arranged to rake place in this parish for many years great interest was taken by the parishioners.... The Vicar.... afterwards presented each of the ringers with a prayerbook. Twelve sets competed.... Refreshments were provided by Mr. Samuel Yeo,.... Ship Inn, Pont.

18 October (RCG) FOWEY.-The *Rippling Wave*, of Fowey, from Brindisi for Hull, with oil, put in at this port on Monday morning with loss of the master, Capt. Roberts, of Polruan. The mate, Mr. William Toms, reported that on the 10th inst.,....they experienced a very heavy gale from the north-west, with heavy cross seas and ship labouring heavily. About 4:30 a.m. she shipped a sea over the weather quarter, which washed Captain Roberts overboard. They threw the ladder and spars overboard, put the helm down, and backed the topsail. Soon after the vessel shipped another sea, which filled her. They could not manage the boat in such weather, but kept the vessel laying to until seven o'clock. They did not see anything of the captain, and in consequence proceeded on the voyage home. The deceased was part owner of the vessel.

18 October (RCG) Since the restoration of the church at Fowey, a great want has been felt of a clock in the tower. During the past fortnight a new clock and chimes have been erected. The clock was set to work on Monday in last week.

25 October (RCG) POLRUAN. - Capt. William Dingle, master of the *Perseverance*, of Fowey, made an attempt on his life by cutting his throat with a common kitchen knife, on Friday morning about two o'clock. He had been drinking hard for some time past, and had been threatened to be discharged from his vessel, but his friends had no reason to anticipate the rash act until he was discovered in his room bleeding profusely from a wound in his throat. Mr. Percy Davis was soon in attendance, and under his care Captain Dingle is progressing favourably. Dingle was brought before the Liskeard bench....on Saturday, when Mr. Davis said he found a wound 2 1/2 inches long, but not deep, just above the top of the windpipe. The prisoner said he had fallen down on the quay and cut himself, and the wound was a jagged cut that might have been caused by falling on a glass bottle. He knew from hear-say that the prisoner had been drinking, and was much excited.- Captain Hawker spoke strongly to Dingle as to the folly of his conduct, and discharged him.

1 November (RCG) FOWEY - NAUGHTY BOYS AT CHURCH. Many complaints have been made of late....respecting the conduct of boys during Divine service....at length summonses were issued against seven of the worst offenders, who appeared before the Rev. Dr. Treffry, at the Town Hall.... Mr. John Bate, church warden, said he thought the lads ought to be punished, but taking into consideration the position of the parents, he would not press for a conviction. Dr. Treffry hoped that parents would in future take their children under their own care to whatever place of worship they were in the habit of attending themselves, so that they might have them under proper control. The cases would be dismissed on the defendants paying the costs, 8s.

1 November (RCG) POLRUAN MEMORIAL STONE LAYING. A new chapel in connection with the United Methodist Free Church is in the course of erection at Polruan, and on Monday....six stones were laid as follows;- Rev. T. Lee Circuit Minister, Congregational stone; Mrs. E. Hocken of Lizzen, Sunday-School stone; Mr. T. Clunes, of Fowey, memorial stone; and a memorial stone by each of the following (all of whom reside at Polruan): - Capt. T. Tadd senr., Mr. R. Barrett, and Mr. N. Penter. Considering the unfavourable weather, the attendance at the ceremony was good. Liberal contributions were placed upon the stones by those who were requested to lay them, and also by the Sunday scholars, visitors and friends - amounting together to £50 3s. 2d. The speeches were very brief owing to the rain. After the ceremony about 200 sat down to tea.... The report stated that the old building, which had been used both for chapel and Sunday-School for over seventy years would still be retained for school purposes, and that the new chapel, including land would cost over £900, towards which they had realized in cash and promises (exclusive of that day) £242....

29 November (RCG) A remarkably expeditious loading of a vessel took place at Fowey on Friday. The steamer *Sappho*, of Bristol, 889 tons register, arrived at Fowey at ten a.m., was loaded with 300 tons of clay from the Cornwall Mineral Railway jetties, and left at three p.m. on the same day for Antwerp.

1879

7 March (RCG) INSOLVENCY OF A FOWEY SHIPBUILDER. John Stephens, shipowner and shipwright, of Fowey,....filed a petition for liquidation a short time since, and....made no mention of large number of Fowey and other creditors,.... Mr A. Dingle, who is a creditor for £148 11s., filed a petition in bankruptcy against Stephens.... If they allowed the estate to go into bankruptcy they would not get more than 2d. in the £,..... The workmen employed at debtor's yard were entitled to two months' wages, due up to the time of the debtor filing his petition.

The statement of accounts shewed liabilities amounting to £2533.... Debtor....had given a bill of sale for £150 on his household furniture.... A ship in the course of building at Fowey was mortgaged for £600.... Samuel Moss, of Par, held mortgages....upon the schooners *Racer*, the *Pride of the Channel*, and....the *Jane*. Mr. John Geldard, of St. Austell, held a mortgage of £65 *upon* .the leasehold yard....in Fowey, estimated to be worth £200....

He had carried on business at Fowey for five years, and prior to that he was in business at Charlestown. He denied that when leaving Charlestown he owed.... £4000 on shipping accounts alone. Since he had been at Fowey he had paid off £500 of the money he had borrowed.... He knew that he was "astern" in his affairs,.... He had proved that he had been hardworking,....and had done all he could to meet his creditors.... The debtor agreed to pay 4s. in the £.

11 April (RCG) LANTEGLOS BY FOWEY SCHOOL BOARD At a meeting ....held at the School Board office, Polruan.... Her Majesty's Inspector's report for the past year was read....: Boys School, of which Mr. Thos. M. Sennett is master; - The discipline is good, and the instruction has greatly improved under the new master, and is now highly efficient in all respects. The classes passed well in grammar and geography. Two boys....obtained honour certificates, and the mean percentage of passes was 93. Mixed school, under Miss E.A. Soddy - "Miss Soddy maintains good order. The attainment of the children, considering that the school had only been opened six months are very fair. The classes passed very fair in grammar and needlework. The infants are, under the circumstances, fairly proficient; but instruction in numbers requires attention."

2 May (RCG) PAR, TYWARDREATH, ST. BLAZEY. The material with which the roads are mended in this district comes chiefly out of old mines, and is poisonous; so that the scrapings, which in most parts command a monetary value, are here worse than useless, as they flow into and poison good land. At a trifling cost good granite metal may be obtained and the scrapings be made valuable.

29 August (RCG) The Rev. H.N. Purcell, Vicar of Fowey, gave his annual outing on Thursday....to the members of the Church Choir and Sunday School teachers. The party started from Fowey about nine a.m. and crossed the ferry to Bodinnoc, where sundry conveyances from the Ship and Commercial Hotels, Fowey, and from Looe, were awaiting to convey them to their destination (Looe).... At Pelynt a halt was made and the fine old church was inspected by the party, and hymns and chants were sung, the accompaniment being played on the old organ by Mr. G.H. Bate, organist of Fowey. The party returned home about nine p.m., all having thoroughly enjoyed their day's excursion.

29 August (RCG)The Fowey Congregational Sunday School had their annual tea and trip on Friday last. Instead of going up the river, a trip to Luxulion by rail was arranged. About 120 friends and school children journeyed by the mid-day train to Bridges, and, after partaking of luncheon, dispersed, the juveniles to a meadow adjoining the station (kindly lent by the Rev. K. Rashleigh, Vicar of Luxullion), where cricket, football, and other games occupied their time until tea. The remainder of the party went various ways, many to the recently restored church, which is well worth a visit, and a number went to the Treffry Viaduct, about a mile distant, all.... returning in time for tea....and ample justice was done to the repast. At eight p.m. all assembled at the Railway Station ready for the return home by the last train, having spent a very pleasant afternoon.

26 September (RCG) FATAL ACCIDENT.- An accident of a fatal character occurred at Fowey on Saturday last to a little boy called Alfred Stephens, aged 11 years, son of Mr. John Stephens, late shipbuilder, of Fowey. The poor lad was playing with others near St. Catherine's Castle, when he fell over the cliffs on to the rocks. He was picked up in an unconscious state and conveyed to his home, where he was promptly attended to by Dr. Davis, but he died in less than two hours - the back of his skull being fractured, besides other injuries. An inquest was held.... verdict ...."Accidental death"

26 September (RCG) Fowey harbour appears to be getting well known and appreciated by yachting men. Several large steamers, as well as sailing yachts, have recently visited Fowey, including the *Juliet*, with Lord Cremorne; the *Bessie* s.s. with the Earl of Harrington on board; the *Queen of Palmyra*, with the Marquis and Marchioness of Exeter, Lord and Lady Burghley, and the Ladies Cecil; the *Diadem*, with the Earl of Loudoun; the *St. Hilda*, belonging to the Hon. G. Duncombe, with General Parker on board,.... Lord Exeter, after visiting Falmouth, returned again in his beautiful steam yacht to Fowey, on Tuesday, the natural charms of the neighbourhood and the good fishing being the attractions.

3 October (RCG)   STRANGE FATALITY IN FOWEY. - A mysterious occurrence is reported from Fowey. On Saturday a respectably dressed elderly man went to the house of Mrs. Northcotte, grocer, and refreshment-house keeper, and engaged a bed.... He informed her that he came from the neighbourhood of Redruth, was about 70,....and had been a widower for twenty years. He also stated that he suffered from heart disease and from severe pains in the head.... On Sunday evening the stranger paid for his lodgings, and he intimated his intention of going to Polruan. This he seems to have done, for at an early hour on Monday a man dressed in black frock coat, vest, and trousers, and a soft felt hat (answering.... Mrs Northcotte's description of her lodger) was seen to land at Polruan Quay. Later on - about eight or nine o'clock - two fishermen named Climo, fishing a mile to the eastward of Fowey Harbour, came across the dead body of a man answering to the description of the stranger. On the clothes being searched there were found in the pockets a linen collar, a coloured handkerchief, and 1s. 8d. in money, but no papers that would lead to identification. Blood was around the mouth of the deceased.... A pilot picked up a felt hat floating in the water. The body of the deceased is described as that of a tall thin man, 5 feet 11 inches in height, and with slight grey whiskers.

3 October (RCG) An inquiry....was held at Polruan.... Mrs. Northcott....identified the body as that of the person who lodged with her. - William H. Climo, of Polruan, deposed to finding the body floating in the water. It was in a standing position, with the head bowed forward and the shoulders out of the water....about 100 yards from the shore, off a place called Bealeshill..... Messrs. William Thomas and William Slade stated that they saw deceased land from the ferry, and he appeared to be in a "deep study," or desponding state. - William Honey, of Charlestown, identified the deceased as his uncle. Mr. A. P. Davis, M.R.C.S., of Fowey, thought that death was caused by heart disease, and not through drowning. It was very probable that if he fell from the cliff, which was about 200 feet high just where the body was found, death might have taken place before reaching the water.

CHAPTER 9
1880-1889

1880

9 September (WB) GAS EXPLOSION. - An explosion occurred on Thursday evening at Fowey Grammar School. Workmen had been repairing the gas fixtures, and had left one of the burners on. The headmaster (Mr. Coghlan) on coming into the room struck a match, and an explosion followed. The roof of the building was lifted several feet, and the explosion blew some five or six hundred bricks out of the wall. Mr. Morris, a mason, who was standing at the door, had one hand injured, the flesh being torn off the fingers.

7 October (WB) FEVER AT POLRUAN. - The medical officer of health for the Liskeard Union (Mr. Nettle) reported to the meeting of the rural sanitary authority, on Saturday, that since his last report three fresh cases of typhoid fever had occurred at Polruan; they are undoubtedly to be ascribed to the wretched state of the drainage; indeed, it is hardly possible to conceive of conditions more favourable to the spread than those existing at Polruan.

1881

20 October (WB) THE FREEMASONS OF FOWEY, who have long been dissatisfied with the accommodation provided in the present Masonic rooms, are determined to have a hall more fitting for the fraternity. Mr. Charles Treffry, of Place, has offered on reasonable terms, to erect a suitable building, and the plans having been drawn by Mr. A. S. Clunes and approved, the contract of Mr. Smith, of St. Austell, has been accepted, and the work is to be proceeded with at once.

1882

13 January (RCG) OVERDUE VESSELS OF FOWEY. - Grave anxiety is felt for the safety of two vessels, principally manned by Fowey men, which are long overdue at their port of destination. They are the *Silver Stream*, of Fowey, Capt. Tadd, bound from Cadiz to St. Johns (N.F.), and *Hecla*, Ellery master, on a similar passage. Both vessels have been a great number of days over the average length of passage, and as a number of other vessels have been recently lost on the same voyage, it is feared that unless intelligence is shortly forthcoming these two vessels have also succumbed to the terrific gales experienced.

13 January (RCG) NEW YEAR'S FESTIVITIES. A very successful children's fancy dress dance was given at Place Castle, Fowey, the residence of Mr. C.E. Treffry, on the 5th inst. The young guests arrived at 5:30 and after tea in the Porphyry Hall, they adjourned to the ballroom, where dancing was kept up until 9 o'clock, when the children had supper, about which hour the elders began to arrive, also in fancy dress. The children then going home, the ball was kept up with great spirit by the remainder until a late hour. The varied and picturesque dresses of the ladies, and the numerous naval and military uniforms, made the scene an animated and brilliant one. Amongst the ladies were noticed the charming hostess in the most becoming dress of the Gypsy Queen, her sister-in-law, Miss Treffry, as Bettina in "The Mascotte," Miss Graves Sawle (Italian Peasant),....Miss L. Coode (Lorna Doone).... Of the gentlemen the most successful costumes were the host, in hunting dress of the ancient times, and Capt. Prickett, R.A., as Sig. Marius. The prettiest children's dresses were the little Neopolitan Fishwives, Columbine, Little Boy Blue, and a black velvet Court dress of the time of George 1V.

3 February (RCG) A serious accident happened at Bodinnoc,....last (Thursday) evening week. Mr. James Rundle went up some steps into his barn, and, on coming out, attempted to pull the door to. The key, unfortunately, happened to be straight in the hole, and the result was that Mr Rundle fell to the ground, a distance of several feet, breaking his thigh, and sustaining other injuries.

24 February (RCG) LANTEGLOS . - A case of farcy, a peculiarly fatal disease affecting horses, having occurred on Trethake farm, Lanteglos, that was on Saturday declared an infected area, farcy being one of the diseases in the schedule of the Act.

24 February (RCG) NARROW ESCAPE. - Two men and four women at Fowey on Wednesday week borrowed a boat and went outside the harbour. It was blowing a gale, and in trying to put back they had a narrow escape of being washed on the rocks at the end of Furze Park, Polruan. Assistance was rendered and they were eventually landed at Fowey in a very wet and exhausted condition.

3 March (RCG) REPAIR OF THE *'ELIZA ANNIE'*. - The completion of the repairs of the schooner *'Eliza Annie,'* at Messrs. N. and J. Butson's yard, at Polruan, was made an occasion by the owner, Mr. W.W. Dingle, of giving the shipwrights and tradesmen employed a tea in the United Methodist Schoolroom, at which about forty sat down. After tea a social evening was spent in singing and speeches. Satisfaction was expressed by the employer at the diligence of the men, and the manner in which the work had been executed; and thanks were expressed by the employed for having had the work to do in such a dead time of the year.

1 June (WB) ASSAULTING THE POLICE At Tywardreath, on Monday, before Sir C. Rashleigh and Capt. B. Rashleigh, a man named Thomas Ward was brought up in custody, charged with assaulting P.C. Thomas whilst in the execution of his duty, at Fowey, on Saturday evening. The policeman had taken a man named Mornington into custody for drunkenness, when the prisoner came forward and struck him violently. Sir C. Rashleigh expressed his determination to protect the police on all such occasions, and passed a sentence of two months' imprisonment with hard labour.

7 July (RCG) MARRIAGE FESTIVITIES AT FOWEY On Wednesday Miss Maria Stuart Treffry, third daughter of the late Rev. Dr. Treffry, of Place Castle, Fowey, was given in marriage to Captain Prickett, of the Royal Artillery. Fowey was very gay for the occasion, and, fortunately, in a very showery day, the weather remained fine during the ceremony, and a few gleams of sunshine fell upon the bridal party. The turrets of Place Castle look down....upon....the grand old church; and their close proximity enabled the walk from the Castle to the church to be carpeted, and over it the bridal party walked. The surroundings were decorated with flags, and at the entrance to the church yard path there was a pretty arch erected by Mr. Isbell, and containing wishes of "Health and Happiness" on one side, and on the other the words, "May Heaven's light be your guide". The church was well filled, and the choir were there to chant the "Amens" and to sing the Psalm.... The bride was given away by her brother, Mr. Treffry, of Place Castle. The bridesmaids were Miss Lilian Coode, Miss Elizabeth Hext, Miss Bourne Royds, and Miss Haye; and three little train bearers, Miss Treffry, Miss Vanda Treffry, and Miss Violet Carlyon.... At the conclusion of the ceremony the bells rang a merry peal, and the band of the St. Blazey Artillery Volunteers was stationed in Place Grounds.

The bridal party presented a very pretty sight as they proceeded to and from the church along the carpeted way. Both the bridegroom and his best man (his brother, Major Prickett, of the Essex Regiment) and the naval officers present wore their uniforms, which added much to the brightness of the scenes. The bride was dressed was in ivory white satin, with a drapery of satin across one side, and a garland of orange blossoms and myrtle on the other side, most beautifully embroidered with pearls. The dress was trimmed with Brussels point lace, and had a very long train of plain ivory satin, bearing a large spray of orange blossoms and myrtle on one side of it. The bride wore a tulle veil, pinned with a diamond and pearl star. She carried a lovely bouquet, composed of stephanotes, gardinieres, lilies, and orange blossoms. The bridesmaids were dressed in white muslin, handsomely trimmed with Talanciennnes lace, with large yellow silk collars, and yellow watered silk sashes. They wore white straw hats, trimmed with lace and Marechal Niel roses, and their bouquets were composed of water lilies and Marechal Niel roses. Four of them wore brooches composed of a hunting stock with a spur across it, and the three little ones had each a gold bangle, the gift of the bridegroom. Miss Mildred and Miss Winifred Purcell wore dresses of blue nun's cloth, trimmed with drab lace. Mrs. Treffry wore a very elegant dress of white Spanish lace, a French bonnet trimmed with violet pansies, and a bunch of pansies on the left shoulder, and long white mousquetairo gloves. Mrs. Prickett, the bridegroom's mother, wore a pearl grey watered silk; Mrs. John Coode, a very handsome coffee-coloured satin; Mrs. Rashleigh, of Menabilly, a sage green satin, trimmed with old lace; Mrs. Wheeler, a beautiful claret-coloured satin and crepe de chene; Mrs. White, a stone-coloured satin; Mrs. Shilson, handsome coffee-coloured satin, trimmed with Indian muslin and lace, Mrs. Battie Rashleigh, olive green cashmere, trimmed with striped yellow and green watered silk; and Mrs. Haye, black velvet, and bonnet with violet satin strings and trimmed with violets.

Breakfast was laid in the Porphyry Hall of the Castle, and made a very elegant display. It was supplied from home resources. The bride and bridegroom left at three o'clock, and drove to Par Station for Dawlish,.... Among the presents were the followng:...some of the tenantry, a tea service....the servants of Place castle, butter knives; the Avenue servants, inkstand;....Joe (an old coachman who has been in the service of the family since the time of the late Mr. Treffry, and who drove the Queen and Prince of Wales, upon their visit to Fowey), a pair of china candlesticks.

7 July (RCG) POLRUAN INQUEST An inquest was held at Polruan....on the decomposed and putrid remains of a child. Captain John Lamb deposed that he was in his garden with his dog on Monday afternoon. The dog was in the habit of hunting rats at the bottom of his garden, and witness saw it with a bone in its mouth. He took it away, and found it to be something much decomposed. He shouted to two men who came, and sent for....P.C. Couch, who took charge of it, and also for Dr. Tortscor, of Polruan. The remains could not have been placed there long, as the dog went hunting daily. Dr. Tortscor gave it as his opinion that the remains were those of a fully developed child at birth, and that it must have been dead several weeks. The head, he believed, had been smashed in, the hands were cut from the wrists, and the feet from the ankles. From some flesh remaining on one thigh the child might have been from six to nine months old when death took place. P.C. Couch did not know of any child missing in or near Polruan. Mr. Christopher Slade, foreman of the jury, remarked that that would exonerate Polruan from any charge.... (I think the paper misread Tortscor for Torbock)

1883

27 March (RCG) Mr. MOSES DUNN, with his crew of six hands, were outside Fowey Harbour on Tuesday night, in the pilot boat *Ernie*, on the look out for vessels. There being but little wind the sails were lowered, and the boat was allowed to drift about. On Wednesday morning, the wind freshening, the hands were called to make sail, the boat then being about two miles to the eastward of the harbour, and off Pencarrow Point. One of the crew named George Tamblyn, of Polruan, on being called went to put on his oil-skin trousers, and, it is supposed, sat on the rail of the boat, as on one of the crew looking around they saw his feet uppermost, and there is no doubt that the poor fellow fell overboard backwards. Ropes and oars were thrown, and Tamblyn caught one of the latter. The crew then used every exertion to get their boat around to rescue him, but could not succeed, as he shortly sank. Search has been made for the body, but it has not yet been found. Deceased was about sixty-nine years old, and had been a sailor all his life.

21 June (RCG) FOWEY. - The business of Messrs. Willyams, Treffry, and Co., South Cornwall Bank, will in future be conducted in the new and commodious premises in Trafalgar-square, near the Post-office. (Postoffice then was where Julians is now)

10 August (RCG) POLRUAN. About two years since the Wesleyans at Polruan opened their new chapel. They have now completed the interior by placing a beautiful new organ in the orchestra. On Wednesday the instrument was opened by Mr. Howlett, organist, Wesleyan Chapel, St. Austell, whose fine playing thoroughly tested its power and quality. It has been designed and built by Messrs. Brewer and Co., of Truro. At the public meeting in the evening the speakers called particular attention to the appearance of the exterior, which corresponds in every respect with the design of the building.... Mr. Howlett invited Mr. Maddern, of Bodmin, who brought with him Mrs. Maddern, soprano, and Mr. Stephens, bass; Mr. Maddern taking the tenor. The people of Polruan were charmed and delighted. The collections were beyond expectation.

10 August (RCG) A meeting of the Liskeard Rural Sanitary Authority was held.... With regard to Polruan,....the committee had passed a resolution to the following effect:-.... that this Board admits what ought to be done, but could not adopt the plans of water-works and sewerage as laid before them, the fact that the rate would have to be levied on the whole of Lanteglos being the main cause of their inaction; that....the inhabitants had done nothing in the way of surface cleaning, although they had town property;.... The committee....considered the plans too elaborate and impracticable and costly for such a place, the estimated expenditure being nearly £1,500. Nearly all the houses had gardens which were being used or could be used for sanitary purposes, and a great many of the houses had private wells. The committee recommended that more simple and less costly plans be prepared and presented at the next meeting....and with regard to waterworks they considered that they should be left to the inhabitants themselves to provide by means of a....company.

21 September (RCG) CORRESPONDENCE. THE TRUCK SYSTEM IN CORNWALL. SIR,.... It is an acknowledged fact that there are hundreds of women employed in Cornwall in knitting "guernseys," for which they never receive a penny in coin. The employer says, "I can give you work if you take the value in goods." The women gladly do this in summer time as it provides them with drapery, but, if they only thought for one moment, they would "one and all" decline to work on this stipulation.... The only point that I wish to press on the fishing community of Cornwall (is) that....there are many disadvantages.

These "guernseys" I understand have to be a certain weight, and if they are not a deduction is made. Then again when the work is returned, the employer is relieved - not of surplus cash - but his stock.... The drapers of course, can charge what they like for their goods;....and they also have the profit of the "guernsey".... The principle of Free Trade is here reversed, as those who labour -....sell in the cheapest and buy in the dearest market.... The employers, by their arbitrary stipulation, protect themselves from going into a state of bankruptcy at the cost of their employes.... It will be said that the women are not obliged to work under such an arbitrary stipulation, and that they should not do it. But what are they to do;....their husbands and fathers in the winter are weeks without earning a penny, and yet all the labour of the female portion of the family does not add a fraction to the domestic exchequer. Better far for the daughters that they left such homes and either go into service or emigrate at once to the Colonies, where they would be paid honestly and fairly for their labour. We know what a miserable existence these people drag out in the winter; we also know that they have as much as they can do even in their prosperous times to make both ends meet. If we go into the homes of the class who are thus treated what do we see? the cottage barely furnished, the cupboards, if not altogether empty, are nearly so; on the hearth or in the grate we see but a few sparks of fire; parents and children are poorly clad. All this, if it were the outcome of idleness, we should expect; but when we ....find that such is not the case, do we not....ask ourselves "if this is the result of the husband's labour and the wife's economy and industry, what must we expect to find when these characteristics are absent?" The women cannot spend their money as they like, because the employer insist on the goods being purchased in his shop. He cares nothing whether they are benumb with the cold, or whether they are next to a state of starvation, so long as he is getting a large profit.... Such things as these belong rather to the middle age than to the nineteenth century. I hope that the women will "one and all" unite in resisting such gross injustice; that they will insist on being paid in the current coin of the realm,....so that by their industry they may not fear the wolf coming to their door in the winter time as they now do. I trust sir, that some ladies and gentlemen will take this matter in hand with right good earnest.... signed, LISKEARDER.

9 November (RCG) OPENING OF A NEW CHAPEL AT FOWEY.... The members belonging to the Bible Christian Connexion resident in the place have had for the past fifty years to worship in various incommodious and otherwise unsuitable premises. This bad accommodation the congregation lately determined to put up with no longer, and after many fruitless efforts a good site for the proposed new chapel was secured in Fore-street. About five months ago memorial stones were laid. The chapel, which has been erected at a total cost of £750 (of which nearly one-half has been raised) is a Gothic structure about 40 feet long by 24 feet wide, and 21 feet high. The building will be lighted with gas. The congregation feel highly pleased at the way in which the architect, Mr. A.S. Clunes, Fowey, and the builders, Messrs. Isabell and Mitchell, Fowey, have carried out the work entrusted to them.

The proceedings of Wednesday were opened with a prayer meeting at 9:30 a.m., followed by a service at 11 o'clock, when the sermon was preached by the Rev. A.F. Trengrove, of Plymouth (the general chapel secretary of the connection).... An adjournment was made at the close of the service to the Workmen's Institute Hall, where in a large room a capital luncheon was provided.... Later in the afternoon a crowded service was held in the chapel....at 5 p.m., a public tea, to which a very large number of people sat down, was provided in the institute. At 7 p.m. there was a largely-attended public meeting in the chapel.

1884

20 June (RCG) BRAZEN ISLAND SARDINE CO., LIMITED, *POLRUAN, FOWEY, CORNWALL*.- ISSUE OF 100 NEW SHARES OF £25 EACH, - *£5 to be paid on application, and £5 on allotment, and remainder by calls up to £20 per share.* DIRECTORS: R.H.Williams, Cuddra, St.Austell. Albertus Dingle, Fowey. George H. Bate, Fowey. Nathaniel Hockin, Polruan. John E. Hocken, Polruan. This new issue is to furnish capital to extend the Company's Pickling Works, which is a very remunerative department of the business. The original capital was 100 shares of £25 each, on which £20 has been paid up. The new shares will, when paid up to £20 per share, rank with the original shares. An early application will be necessary to secure shares, and must be accompanied with £5 per share deposit. Where no allotment is made the deposit will be returned in full.

11 July (RCG) RECOGNITION OF BRAVERY. - At a public meeting on Saturday evening in the Town-hall, Captain John Jenkins, master of schooner *Lizzie Trenberth*, of Fowey, was presented with a magnificent pair of binocular glasses, awarded him by the King of Sweden and Norway, for saving the crew of the barque *Senior,* of Arundal, in January last. A silver plate on the glasses bears the following inscription; - " Oscar, King of Sweden and Norway, to Captain John Jenkins for a brave and noble deed 1884". Mr. W. Gray, superintendent of the Mercantile Marine, Fowey, made the presentation.

1 August (RCG) FOWEY HORTICULTURAL SOCIETY'S EXHIBITION. - For the first time in its history the pretty little seaport of Fowey last week held an horticultural exhibition of its own.... The exhibition was held in a field adjoining Mr. C.E. Treffry's famous "Place House," overlooking the little harbour, that later in the day, when the sun came out, looked very charming with a miniature fleet of yachts and sailing craft within it. The idea of the exhibition was entertained some years ago, but not until the present year have the committee been able to carry it out, and now it has been practically through the kind assistance of Mr. Treffry, who has undertaken the presidency of the association.... To Mr. Treffry the committee not only owe thanks for the loan of the grounds and the accommodation of a tennis court, where the luncheon was held, but for a very handsome collection of plants sent from Place House, which considerably heightened the attractiveness of the marquee. These were placed in the centre of the tent, and with a collection for which a special prize was given to Mr. Carvell, of Lescrow, Fowey, a very handsome group was made of palms and crotons, the gold Allamanda Hendorsonii, orange plants, and some graceful ferns, all assisting in the general effect. The exhibition itself was very good indeed. It was divided into three classes, the first being for gentlemen's vegetables, fruits, and flowers, the second for cottagers and the third open to the county. The fruit was especially good, and the vegetables very fine; indeed, for a first exhibition the committee had very good reason to be exceedingly pleased with it.... The band of the 4th Battalion L.I. (St.Austell) Volunteers attended....and during the afternoon played a selection of operatic and dance music, including "Iolanthe" and "Patience"....

during the whole day there was a considerable number of visitors, all of whom were well pleased with the show, and some running and other matches held in connection with it. (I think Mr. Carvell should be Mr. Carnall of Lescrow)

1885

2 January (RCG) FUNERAL. - The remains of the late Elizabeth Richards, aged 86 years, were interred in the Cemetery at Fowey on Tuesday week. Elizabeth Richards was a valued servant and friend in the family of the late Major Davis, of Fowey, for 53 years, and although she had never partaken of wine, spirits, beer, or *tea* in her life, she enjoyed uninterrupted good health to within a few days of her death.

20 February (RCG) A fire, which might have proved serious but for the prompt action of the fire brigade, which fortunately happened to be close at hand when it occurred, broke out in the cellar of Dr. A.A. Davis, about four o'clock on Wednesday evening. It was discovered by Mrs. Davis, who on going into the dining-room found it full of smoke. She immediately gave the alarm, and Mr. Henry Paul - who in the absence of Capt. M. Rogers had charge of the brigade - with Fireman Vincent, was quickly on the spot, followed soon afterwards by Firemen W. Lovering, A. Hawken, E. Lovering jun., and F.J. Denison. In a short time the fire was got under. The damage is not serious.

20 March (RCG) FOWEY BUSINESS DISPUTE. - After a trial extending over four days the case of Bray against Miller was concluded....in the Queen's Bench Division on Saturday. It seemed that the plaintiff....formerly carried on business as a saddler and harness-maker at Fowey, but owing to the delicate state of his wife's health he was advised by the doctor to remove to a part of the country where the air was more bracing....he got into communication with the defendant, who conducted a similar business at Upper Norwood....he purchased the business on the strength of the defendant's representation that the returns were £2,000 per annum, and he now.... sought to recover damages on the ground that the representation was fraudulent and untrue. After disposing of the business the defendant went to reside - first near Southmolton, and afterward at Ashfold, near Barnstable, and at the present time his mind was affected. His wife, however, gave evidence, and she positively denied that any representation whatever was made to the plaintiff, the fact being that, although he was told it was believed the returns were about £2,000, he thoroughly examined the books of the concern for himself. She admitted that the books had since been used as waste paper, but she positively asserted that when that was done she did not for a moment suspect they would ever be required again. The jury, after deliberating for two hours and-a-half, were unable to agree, and they were accordingly discharged without returning a verdict.

17 April (RCG) FOWEY PROPOSED CHOLERA HOSPITAL At the meeting of the (Liskeard) Sanitary Authority on Saturday it was announced that the Local Government Board Inspector when in the neighbourhood had said that he was extremely anxious that a deputation from the authority should meet one from the

St. Austell Board with regard to a cholera hospital for the harbour of Fowey. He thought it would be better that the two Boards should unite to provide the hospital, which must be provided. A long discussion took place, in which several members gave expression to the opinion that they should not have to bear the expense, as, although the ships came in and anchored on their side of the Fowey river, all the trade was done on the other side at Fowey itself. The matter was then dropped.

19 June (RCG) On Saturday the steam tug *Gallant*, of Fowey, ran upon the rocks at Charlestown, a little to the west of the pier. The tug had towed in the brig *St. Joseph*, laden with staves, and after casting off - through some error of judgement apparently - got aground. By dint of great exertion the vessel was got off in about an hour and a half, seeming not much the worse, and shortly after steamed away for Fowey.

10 July (RCG) LISKEARD BOARD OF GUARDIANS.... A long discussion arose as to whether sixpence per week was too much for a room in which to distribute relief. This sum was paid for a room at Polruan, but less, it was contended, was paid elsewhere. A suggestion was made that the old chapel could be obtained for the purpose required for almost nothing. - Mr. Tamlyn, relieving officer for Polruan, spoke strongly on the subject. It would not be human, he argued, for the Guardians to send him and those who came for relief down into a chapel situated in a back street and without a fire. After riding many miles, and perhaps getting wet through, it was not a pleasant thing to have to sit in a room for two or three hours without a fire. Besides, 6d. a week was not too much when they considered that over forty came into the house at Polruan, and he had the benefit of a fire....

10 July (RCG) The monthly meeting of the Liskeard Rural Sanitary Authority was held when Mr. E. Mallett, sanitary inspector reported.... I have prepared a plan and estimate for waterworks at Polruan. My recommendation is that a reservoir be constructed near the present source.... about half-a-mile from the bottom of the town, at an elevation of 288 feet above the quay, and of sufficient altitude to reach all the parts of the town by gravitation. The size....is 100 feet by 50 feet, and 10 feet deep, which will contain 306,250 gallons, equal to 34 days' supply, calculating the population of Polruan to be 900, with 10 gallons per day each. From the reservoir to the lower parts of the town lay three-inch cast-iron pipes coated with Smith's solution, with fire cocks, hydrants, and sluice valves....for the sum of £550. In reply....the Inspector said that the cost of the drainage scheme ordered to be proceeded with forthwith at their last meeting was £300, so that to carry out the two would cost £850. It was undoubtedly most essential that the two schemes should go together, for if they made the drainage without the water scheme, where would they get water to flush the drains?- After a long discussion it was decided....to write Captain Nathaniel Hocking, of Polruan, that, if the people of Polruan would undertake to establish a water company to supply the village with water, the Guardians were willing to do the sanitary work.

2 August (RCG) SANITARY AUTHORITY.... The clerk read a letter from Mr. Nathaniel Hocking, of Polruan,....with regard to the water supply and drainage.... Mr. Hocking did not think that a company could be formed in Polruan, as people thought it impossible that the drainage could be carried out by the Sanitary Authority, if the water was brought to the place by a private company, for the reason that the water would be wanted to flush the drains. They thought that the Sanitary Authority might easily provide a water supply by a thirty years' loan from the Loan Commissioners. Mr. Hocking believed that if they had a small storage reservoir they could very well do with the water they had at present. A discussion followed the reading of this communication, and Mr. Rowe having given notice that he should move at the next meeting that the sewerage works be stopped after the pipes had been laid from Tinker's-hill to Fore-street, the matter dropped. A circular was read from the Local Government Board drawing attention to the prevalence of cholera in Spain, and the necessity for adopting sanitary precautions. It was stated that the Joint Committee of the St. Austell and Liskeard Boards had met and had found that an iron hospital could be erected for Fowey harbour for £100. A hulk could not be obtained....

16 October (RCG) SHIP ROBBERY AT FOWEY William King, a coloured seaman, was charged, on Saturday, at the Tywardreath police-court....with stealing a watch, £2, and some clothing from the barque *John*, lying in Fowey Harbour, on the night of the 7th inst. Prisoner was further charged with stealing an oil jacket and vest, the property of Thomas Grase, of Fowey. Prisoner, who came to Fowey on board a vessel called the *Black Prince*, having committed the offences with which he was charged, made for Plymouth by rail, where he was arrested by Detective Mutton in consequence of a telegraphic message which had been forwarded to the Plymouth Police by P.C. Thomas, of Fowey. When arrested, a greater part of the stolen property was in prisoner's possession.

23 October (RCG) CORNWALL MICHAELMAS SESSIONS.... The jury having heard the evidence of the various witnesses, found the prisoner guilty. The Chairman remarked that prisoner had been sentenced previously for similar offences. He seemed to have an unfortunate habit of appropriating other people's property whether he called it stealing or not. The court did call it stealing and were in duty bound to protect the public from such men. - He was sentenced to three months imprisonment.- A further charge of stealing a silver watch and silk albert, a pair of trousers, a purse, two watch keys, a knife and £1.19s.9d., the property of Frank Brodersen of Fowey, on the 7th October, was brought against the prisoner, but in the absence of the prosecutor the proceedings were stayed.

13 November (RCG) FOWEY. THE TOWN LIGHTING At a meeting held on Monday evening, presided over by Mr. A. Dingle, a sum of money was voted for the purpose of public lighting during the ensuing year. An opinion was expressed that the price now charged for gas was excessive, and a resolution was adopted asking the Gas Company to reduce their charges, otherwise oil lamps would be used for the purpose of lighting the town.

1886

8 January (RCG) EMIGRATION TO WESTERN AUSTRALIA WANTED, AGRICULTURAL LABOURERS and SHEPHERDS to whom (with their families) FREE PASSAGES....will be granted early in the year 1886. They must be of good character, recommended by their last employer, in sound health and not more than 45 years of age. Wages in the colony are from 15s to 20s per week, with board &c. Applications....in writing to WEEKS, PHILLIPS & CO,....Plymouth.

WANTED, Domestic servants, such as COOKS, PARLOURMAIDS, HOUSEMAIDS, NURSES, GENERAL SERVANTS, and DAIRYMAIDS, to whom FREE PASSAGES to WESTERN AUSTRALIA will be granted during....1886. Wages....from £16 to £25 year (according to occupation), with board and lodging.- Applicants....must be single women not exceeding 35 years of age, and with good characters from last situation.....

5 February (RCG) CORNWALL WINTER ASSIZES. EXTRAORDINARY SLANDER CASE. DAMAGES £150. EDWARDS AND WIFE V BRAY AND WIFE.-.... The parties to the action were neighbouring farmers on the east side of the Fowey Harbour.... The alleged slander consisted in the Brays propagating a rumour that Mr. Bray was the father of Mrs. Edward's last child. In consequence of these rumours the plaintiffs stated that they had sustained special damages with respect to their business in Fowey market.... The case for the defendant Bray was that the allegation was nothing more than a joke. His learned friend wished them to believe that what was said about Mrs. Edwards was said falsely and maliciously, and that because a man said a thing in joke and in private to his wife to appease her annoyance on his returning home late, they were to give the plaintiff exemplary damages. This was making a mountain out of a mole hill.... Plaintiff demanded an apology in the newspapers, but defendant said "No; if you will send anybody to me, I will tell them it is not true." What did they think the man's home would be like after advertising his wife in the newspapers - especially this woman with a kind of religious mania upon her - and Bray naturally declined to do that....and as to Mrs. Bray, it was unfortunate that the woman was in the state of mind she appeared to be, but that did not constitute malice....as to the question of damages, he argued that the market of the plaintiffs were really not lost, as they sold their goods in other ways. Therefore, he asked them to say that Mr. Bray was not liable at all; that Mrs. Bray spread the rumour there was no doubt; as to her motive the jury must judge; and if the plaintiffs were entitled to any damages let them give such damages only as the occasion warranted.... A question of what a man said to his wife in private ought not to be made a case for the exemplary damages asked for.

His Lordship said he must tell the jury that by English law, however much a woman's fair fame might be assailed, that alone was not actionable....therefore this action,as regards the wife, would not lie, unless evidence was given of special damage - that was of some pecuniary injury, or loss of hospitality.... There was evidence that persons ceased to deal with Mr. and Mrs. Edwards, that their friends would not associate with them, but kept them at a distance, as they said, until the truth of the allegation had been disproved.... He had been concerned as judge and counsel in many frivolous actions for slander, but this was not a frivolous action.... However bad the taste and however wrong it might be for a man to tell his own wife he had been with another married woman, or if he had said it as a joke, so long as it stopped there, it might be allowed to pass.... If when this matter had got abroad, Mr. and Mrs. Bray had either of them, or both, written a letter at once saying there was no truth in the rumour....the probability was that nothing would have been heard of this case, but that was not so. On the part of the wife there was a frequent repetition of the slander, as though it were - to use her own words - "Gods truth".... The evidence against the husband was in the interview with Mr. Edwards, where he admitted saying it to his wife in joke. But why did not the defendant say publicly that the rumour was a joke?.... As to the state of Mrs. Bray's mind....there was no evidence of madness in Mrs. Bray's case, but she seemed to take some pleasure in going about and repeating her husband's misdeeds to other people.... The jury, after about twenty minutes' absence, returned into court with a verdict for the plaintiff, damages £150.

26 March (RCG) FOWEY. RUN OVER AND KILLED - A lad named Frederick Pearn, in the employ of Mr. Richard Rundle, of Lankelly, Fowey, was a few days since entering the farmyard in charge of a horse and cart, when he fell, and the wheel of the cart passed over his chest. He received prompt medical attention, but his injuries were so severe that his recovery was hopeless, and died soon afterwards.

7 May (RCG) POLRUAN. The launch of the new fishing boat *May Queen* took place at the Messrs. Slade's building yard at Polruan on Saturday afternoon. Some difficulty was experienced in getting her off, as the slip was too high at the lower end, and after sliding a short way she stuck fast and could not for some time be again started. She was subsequently towed off by the *Gallant*, steam tug. The boat, which is a good one, is to form a part of the Fowey fishing fleet.

28 May (RCG) POLITICAL - At a meeting of the Liberal committees of Fowey and Polruan, held at the Fowey Institute, the following resolution was unanimously passed:-"That this meeting, believing that a speedy extension of self government to Ireland will result in the reconciliation of the Irish people and promote the strength and unity of the empire, condemns in the strongest way the policy of coercion put forward by Lord Salisbury, expresses its unabated confidence in Mr. Gladstone, and earnestly trusts that the House of Commons will pass the second reading of the Government of Ireland Bill."

20 August (RCG) FOWEY. FATAL FALL - A boy about eight years of age, son of Mr. John Lander got on a wall on Bull-hill, Fowey, on Saturday evening, and fell over into the court behind Miss Palmer's shop, about 30 feet. He received such injuries to his head that he expired a few hours afterwards. An inquest was held....at the Ship Hotel,....when the jury returned a verdict of "Death from concussion of the brain caused by a fall."

20 August (RCG) DROWNED IN THE HARBOUR.- A seaman named James Richard, belonging to the yacht *Leander*, was drowned in Fowey harbour on Thursday morning. Deceased was ordered to go on deck and remove a boat from the yacht's side, and whilst going out over the bowsprit to make the boat's rope fast must have slipped and fallen into the harbour. The crew, who were below at the time, heard cries, and at once went on deck, but the means used to try and save Richard were unavailing, and he was drowned. The body was dragged for, and found after about two hours. Deceased was 19 years of age. His father is mate of the *Leander*, and was on board when his son was drowned....

20 August (RCG) FOWEY HORTICULTURAL SOCIETY. ANNUAL EXHIBITION. Fowey Horticultural Society held its third annual exhibition on Wednesday. Mr. C.E. Treffry, the president of the society, with his usual kindness, very generously placed a field adjoining Place-House and its beautiful grounds at the committee's disposal.... The show was held in the commodious covered tennis court, but the entries were so numerous that some of the exhibits had to be lodged outside.... Mr. Jonathan Rashleigh, Menabilly (gardener, Mr. J. Bennett), had a grand show of palms, and the stand in the centre of the building contained splendid collections of plants from Mr. C.E. Treffry's (gardener, Mr. S. Gale), and Mr. A. Carnall, of Lescrow. In Mr. Treffry's collection was a magnificent specimen of the Eucharis Amazonica, which had no less than thirty-eight spikes of bloom upon it. The collections of Mr. Rashleigh, Mr. Treffry, and Mr. Carnall combined made one of the finest stands of plants that has been seen in the county for a long while. Mr. Henry Hodge, nurseryman and seedsman, St. Austell, made a capital show of cut flowers, consisting chiefly of roses, gladioli, and dahlias. Messrs. S. Smyth and W. Dunn, of St Austell, nurserymen, also exhibited. (There followed lists of judges, and prizes for Gentlemen's classes, Cottagers, and Open to the County)

5 November (RCG) FAT STOCK SHOW. - A successful meeting of farmers and others has been held at the Ship Hotel, Fowey, for the purpose of promoting a fat stock, root, and corn show in Fowey at Christmas, which it was unanimously agreed to hold, and a committee was formed as follows: - Dr. A.A. Davis, president; Mr S. Short, chairman; Mr. A.H. Hern, hon. treasurer; Mr. F.A. Alechin, hon. secretary; and Messrs. Richard Hicks, F.B. Williams, Robert Nichols, Tucker, Best, R. Carnal, White, and Lamb.

12 November (RCG) Fowey branch of the Church of England Temperance Society recently held a most successful soiree. The energetic sub-committee of three appointed for the purpose - Mrs. Lacey, Miss Clunes, and Dr. Deakin - carried out all the arrangements. The institute hall was for the evening turned into a miniature "Colinderies"- objects of art, science, and manufacture from various parts of the world, lent by friends, being displayed most tastefully. The telephone and microphone were in full working order, and afforded much amusement. Songs, quartettes, and recitations filled the intervals of the evening. The vicar presided, and addressed the assembled members (some 170), at the beginning and conclusion of the soiree.

A thoroughly delightful and instructive social evening was brought to an end at ten o'clock.

19 November (RCG) NARROW ESCAPE. - On Monday morning a lad named Joseph Martyn, belonging to the sloop *Lavinia*, at present at Fowey, endeavoured to get into the vessel's boat to come ashore, but fell overboard. His cries were heard, and boats were soon on the spot and picked him up, but he was almost exhausted. He was at once taken to the house of Mr. J. Buckingham, master of the vessel, where every attention was paid him, and he is now recovering.

1887

24 February (WB) Letter to the Editor - A Neglected Parish - Sir; Perhaps your readers will hardly think it credible that a parish like Lanteglos-by-Fowey, with a population, according to the census of 1881, of 1,486, would have been for the past three weeks in succesion without a public Church service of any kind whatever. Yet such is the fact, and this parish comprises within its limits the township of Polruan, which, by the census of 1881, contained a population of 1,109. I don't wish to blame any particular individual or individuals - the vicar is confined to his house, ill - but surely, that such an occurrance should take place in this nineteenth century is enough to make the variest Churchman cry out for disestablishment; for, certainly, a Church which allows such a thing as this to take place cannot be fulfilling the purposes for which it is intended.   Yours, &c., PARISHIONER

3 March (WB) Canon Cornish writes us ; - Will you kindly let me say that steps had been taken before the letter appeared in the *West Briton* on Thursday last on this subject to provide temporarily for the services at Lanteglos-by-Fowey

15 April (RCG) LISKEARD SANITARY AUTHORITY. The clerk read a letter from Mr. Samuel Slade, Clerk to the School Board, stating that the school at Bodinnic was closed on account of an outbreak of measles; also that it had been decided to close the girls' and infants' schools at Polruan for a fortnight. The letter also asked that the services of the medical officer might be obtained in such cases, which was granted.

22 April (RCG) THE QUEEN'S JUBILEE. A meeting was held in the Town Hall, Fowey,....to consider the proposal to build at Fowey a seamen's rest.... The movement originated with Mr. Lightfoot, the missionary of the local branch of the Seamen's Christian Friend Society; Mrs. Rogers, and Mrs. Treffry, of Place. About £100 has already been promised.... Though the building....would cost £500, which would be reared under the auspices of that society, its management would remain in the hands of those who contributed to the fund....a Sailors' Rest is much needed for the benefit of mariners and others frequenting this port. On Sundays the sailors had no place but the public-house to which to resort, and as many of them were now teetotallers, it was advisable that an agreeable place should be provided for them. Some had not good clothes, and so could not go to church or chapel, but in a Sailor's Rest they would feel freer, being among their companions, and would thus be able to attend religious services in their own home. - Mr. H. Hicks, superintendent of Customs, (thought) such a house would form an inducement to sailors to go to a place of protection and comfort. - Mr. Graham said he hoped they would be able to have reading rooms in the house, and places for the sailors to write letters &c. Since such Bethels had been started in various towns, many thousands of pounds had been saved out of the men's wages, owing to their having a place to go to from which to send money home. Meetings would be held from time to time, missionary would still visit the ships, and bed and board would be provided at the Rest, besides various evening amusements or help in writing letters.... Mr. Treffry promised to give ten years' issue of periodicals (Chamber's Journal, &c.) for the reading- room.

29 April (RCG) CO-OPERATIVE PRICES at....Truro.... Phillips' Dandelion coffee....5d., Corned Beef.... 2 lb tin 10 1/2d., Wax Candles per 3 lb. pkt.,1s.-1 1/2d., Cod Liver Oil (tasteless), 16 oz. bot. 1s. 9d.; Castor Oil 16 oz. bot., 1s., CEYLON TEA in lead packages as imported, 2s.6d. and 2s.2d. per lb.

6 May (RCG) RAILWAY STATION ACCOMMODATION AT FOWEY. To the directors of the Great Western and Cornwall Minerals Railway Companies:- "We, the undersigned, being residents in the parish of Fowey....respectfully....memorialise you in connection with the following circumstances: - "That we have for some considerable time past been expecting that a new railway station would be built here. Great disappointment was caused in the parish when it transpired that the building, which was erected for the purpose of a new station, was declared useless.... Fowey has rapidly increased during the last few years both as a fashionable watering- place and as a port.... Great numbers of visitors come here in the summer both by rail and sea, and we consider that every effort to meet their requirements, and to encourage repeated visits, should be made. The approaches to the present station have long been a source of complaint, and representations have been made....but with much regret....we observe   that though enclosures are now....being made, no effort is indicated in the direction of improvement.... We beg most respectfully....that it would be for railway companies' interests, and for the public benefit, that a new railway station should be speedily erected, and that the approaches to such new station should be widened and generally improved."

13 May (RCG) ST. AUSTELL AND FOWEY RURAL SANITARY AUTHORITIES. It was decided to purchase the Fowey Hospital ship for the Rural Sanitary Authorities of Liskeard and St. Austell....

10 June (RCG) THE PILCHARD FISHERY. - In reviewing the pilchard trade of the past season we have to record the largest catch since 1873. During the last 35 years only four seasons have shown a large supply. The total quantity caught was about 23,500 hhds.... The summer fishery was a moderate one of some 3,000 hhds. and brought 43s. to 50s. to curers. In the latter part of October a large body of fish visited the coast,....after that date large drift catches were landed at curing places between Falmouth and Plymouth, the boats carrying on the fishery with success to the end of January.... The large and continuous supply tended to lower prices as the season advanced.... Perhaps never before has the need of more care in curing been so conspicuous. Those fish which were pickled, washed, selected and packed in good casks with proper care....sold at full market value....while many of those that were cured in dry salt, with small and inferior fish not carefully picked out, and which were not bright and large, were neglected in the warehouses at Italian ports until the close of the season, when they were sold at prices hardly enough to cover freight to Italy.... Half hogsheads have rapidly grown in favour, and....in Italy, bring considerably more than the extra cost to curers.

10 June (RCG) FOWEY. - At a public meeting, it was resolved to invite the Royal Cornwall Agricultural Society to visit the town in 1888.... Farmers present undertook to bring all the cattle from Par- Station. A guarantee fund for local purposes was started in the room, and over £70 promised.

1 July (RCG) JUBILEE FESTIVITIES. The Queen's jubilee was celebrated at Fowey with much energy. In the early morning merry peals were rung out on the fine old bells of the church. Service was held at half-past ten, the sermon being preached by the vicar, the Rev. H. N. Purcell. The dinner, which was held in the Tennis Court-house in the Place Grounds, kindly placed at the disposal of the committee by Mr. C.E. Treffry, commenced at 12.30, before which, Mr. Treffry, in a short and effective speech, wished her Majesty health and long life, and confusion to her enemies.... About 700 sat down to dinner;....the fare provided being most substantial and liberal. At 2 p.m. a procession, consisting of volunteers, children, and others, paraded the town, headed by the Band of No. 3 Battery (Fowey) D.C.A.V. Tea was held at 4.30 p.m. for all children in the parish and for those who did not go to dinner. The arrangements by the committee were heartily approved, and too much praise cannot be given them. In the evening sports were held in the cricket field for the senior children, and in the vicarage meadow for the young ones. A carnival took place in the evening at 9.45. The town throughout was handsomely decorated with arches, flags, &c; all the shipping in the harbour displayed bunting. Everything passed off in a highly satisfactory manner.

5 August (RCG) TYWARDREATH PETTY SESSIONS. - John Vanson and Richard and Thomas Northcote, of Fowey, were summoned by Captain H.N. Shore for maliciously damaging an apple tree, and Vanson was fined 5s. and costs, the two boys to be birched. - William Hicks and Adolphus Blowey were fined 5s. for neglecting to send their children to Fowey Board school.

5 August (RCG) The *Spinaway* of Fowey, a fishing boat, got on to the rocks just outside the entrance of the harbour on one evening last week. She was working out of the harbour, but owing to an accident to her mizzen gear, would not stay, and drifted on to the rocks. Every assistance was rendered to get her off, but the efforts failed, and after her nets and sails had been saved, she sunk in three or four fathoms of water.

2 September (RCG) Agricultural depression is now about to assume a severity very much exceeding anything hitherto experienced.... Mr. H. J. Harris, of the

London Corn Exchange,.... is of the opinion that we shall have lower prices for wheat in the coming winter than have been experienced during the past 150 years; and that as hay, straw, roots, and winter food for stock generally are only about two-thirds of what they are in the average of seasons, stock-keeping and the feeding for meat will be very expensive.... He concludes that in the coming winter agricultural depression will reach its climax.... The grain farmers have to sell can only be disposed of at a price which cannot pay the costs of production, whilst the keeping of stock and the manufacture of meat will entail extraordinary outlay.... Straw fodder no less than hay is no doubt much scarcer than usual.... By placing charred earth or some other substitute for straw litter beneath cattle and horses, enough might be saved on the majority of farms throughout the southern half of England to make up for the deficiency in the hay crop.... Large numbers of impecunious farmers....want ready money so badly to meet pressing calls, many....overdue that they must thresh out and sell all the grain they have grown, let the price be what it may, after which it is to be feared they would be utterly unable to....buy....foreign corn to convert store cattle and sheep into meat. Their winter stock-feeding must of necessity, therefore, be limited to the roots, hay, and straw fodder on their farms.... There is....a lower depth of ruin still for those numerous occupants of thin-stapled and light sandy soils, which were so utterly burnt up by drought that scarcely anything has been derived from them fit for sale.

2 September (RCG) RAILWAY DEVELOPMENT. At the half-yearly meeting of the Lostwithiel and Fowey Railway Company....the Chairman (Mr. Wm. Lowry) said.... There was a growing conviction in many quarters that the port of Fowey must be brought in connection....with the rest of the county. The visitors to Fowey, who had much increased of late years, complained that they could not get direct from the main line down to Fowey. As the Fowey Hotel and nearly every lodging-house was full that traffic was worth considering..... The chairman of the Cornwall Railway.... looked forward to a great deal of granite and other traffic being brought over the Cornwall line to be shipped at Fowey from the quay....at Carne Point. And if granite came down over the line they might be sure that a great deal of coal would go up over the line. As harbourmaster at Fowey, he could say there was no better place for shipping than the jetty belonging to the Lostwithiel and Fowey line. The deepest water in the harbour was there, and shipping could come alongside at all states of the tide.... The sooner the Fowey line was opened, and the district given direct access to the port of Fowey, the better.... There was no doubt that the town of Fowey was improving and the inhabitants there, as well as in the district between Fowey and Lostwithiel, were anxious to have the Fowey line opened.... The Chairman said, from his official connection with Fowey Harbour, he could say that the traffic in connection with that harbour had been steadily increasing for years. In 1869 harbour dues were £120; they had gradually increased until last year they were £330....in no single year had the dues decreased.

16 September (RCG) OPENING OF A NEW CHAPEL AT FOWEY. On Wednesday last week the new Congregational Chapel at Fowey was opened. The new premises consists of a chapel...with an end gallery; and seating a congregation of two hundred and sixty. Behind the chapel there is an organ chamber, a lecture-hall, and class-rooms to accommodate a hundred and twenty-five scholars. The walls are built of brick and cemented, the front elevation being of limestone with granite dressings. The general style is Early English Gothic, the windows of the facade possessing some pretty tracery in that style. Over the main entrance rises a quadrangular tower to the height of fifty-five feet. The windows are of cathedral-tinted glass in lead quarries, with margins of geometrical patterns of excellent effect. The rostrum, which is of pitch pine, also adds to the beauty of the interior. The seats are open pitch pine benches. The cost of the work is £1,180....the builder is Mr. Nathanial Penter, of Polruan.

The opening proceedings commenced with a luncheon at the Town-Hall, which was gaily decorated for the occasion, and the luncheon was well attended....

4 November (RCG) Our coasts were on Monday night and Tuesday visited by a gale of extraordinary force and from all directions come reports of damage to property and in too many cases loss of life as well. In Cornwall we do not suppose a single town or village escaped entirely free from damage, but fortunately in most cases the injury was confined to property. Our fishing fleets were able to make port before the gale reached its height and no loss is reported in this quarter. A terrific gale was experienced at Fowey, and great damage was done to houses in the town. Vessels in the harbour drove and several met with damage.... The *Susan Vittery* drove ashore on a point of rock near Mixtow, and is lying in a very bad position. The *Mary Johns* drove on to the rocks below Bodminoc Ferry, and has fallen over on her starboard side; the extent of damage is not yet known. The *Crystalline* has had her bowsprit carried away by the *Ocean Queen* fouling her, and the latter has had her port quarter damaged and stanchions carried away. Several other vessels have sustained minor damages. A large number of boats sank at their moorings, and some went adrift, and it is feared that a few have gone to sea with the tide.

4 November (RCG) The National Lifeboat Institution has just sent new lifeboats to Fowey, Hayle and Port Isaac, to take the place of the present lifeboats on those stations. Each boat is 34 feet long and rows 10 oars. They possess all the latest improvements, including the water-ballast fittings, which consist of a series of tanks amidships, one or more of which can be filled with water or emptied at will in the space of one minute. The object is to increase the ballast and immersion of the boats, and consequently their draught of water and stability, when circumstances admit of so doing, without materially increasing their fixed weight for land carriage or their draught of water when launching, or in very shallow water. The lifeboats have all the other characteristics of the boats of the National Institution in the way of self-righting, self-ejecting water &c. The Fowey and Port Isaac boats, like their predecessors, are named respectively the *Arthur Hill* and the *Richard and Sarah*.

236

2 December (RCG) ORIGINAL CORRESPONDENCE Sir; In this section there are not many Cornishmen, and I hope that no more will emigrate at present to the coal mines of Pennsylvania, as things are in a bad way out there, and they are just as well off at home. To the Cornish farmer who has any capital, and can afford to work and live for 12 months before purchasing a farm, so that he can become familiar with the mode of farming and with the people in general, there is a handsome living to be made near here, and a good farm can be bought within 20 miles of this city for £20 an acre. But he must be willing, as I say, to live 12 months before undertaking to farm it, so as to know just what the land will produce. I know an Englishman within 4 miles of this city, who cleared £500 last year off 42 acres of land after paying all expenses for help, manure, &c. His taxes for the year on this property amounted to just £10, so that there is no necessity for a practical farmer with capital to emigrate to the far west just because the land is cheap at first sight, but let him keep near the large cities where there is a market for his produce right at hand.

Jas. Govett Crewes, Philadelphia

1888

6 January (RCG) POLRUAN. NEW MISSION CHURCH. - Some weeks since it was determined to have a Christmas tree, with sale of useful and fancy articles, for the purpose of augmenting the fund now being raised for building a mission or district church in the little town of Polruan.... Notwithstanding the shortness of the notice all interested worked with so much zeal that on Monday not only was the tree well supplied, but there was also a large stall crowded with goods. From half-past two, when the proceedings formally commenced, until the closing at ten o'clock, the room, in spite of the unfavourable weather, was filled with visitors. The result of the day's sales, including the receipts from a tea and also a refreshment stall....have added at least £35 to the "St Saviour's" building fund. It is proposed to name the church St. Saviours because in the old days a chapel dedicated to St. Saviour, and of which a fragment of wall remains, supplied the spiritual needs of the Polruan people. The thanks of all concerned are due to the School Board, who most kindly lent the boy's school for the occasion.

20 January (RCG) The funeral of Mr. C.E. Hocken, Assistant overseer, Fowey, took place on Friday. The deceased was a young man (about 33 years of age) and was highly respected in the town and neighbourhood. He had led a very useful life,....as a Past Chief Ranger of Court "Treffry", and he'd been a Secretary of the Working Men's Institute for some years.... He was also connected with the Wesleyan body and was an able member of Fowey Band of Hope. The funeral was largely attended, and a great number of Foresters were present, as also were members of the Wesleyan Chapel, Sunday School children, and Band of Hope members. The corpse, which was taken from the deceased's late residence by 6 PCRs of Court Treffry, was carried into church by the Sunday School teachers, and was lowered into the grave by 6 PCRs....the deceased leaves a young widow and 1 child.

27 January (RCG) The Primrose League APL meeting, in connection with the Fowey Habitation, was held on Thursday at Polruan Board schools, and was fairly well attended. An address was given by Mr. Egley on Irish affairs, and short speeches were also made by Mr. E. Rashleigh, Mr. Graham, and Capt Pill, interspersed with songs by Mr. F. Denison and Miss Hutchins. Several names were mentioned for honorary clasps for work done in this, the largest habitation in Cornwall.

10 February (RCG) STRANGE PETITION OF CORNISH TENANT FARMERS ....with reference to the drainage of Polruan,....in accordance with the prayer of a petition forwarded by the inhabitants of Polruan....the Local Government Board on the 1st December last addressed a letter to the authority,....that they will forthwith proceed to execute such works as are necessary.... On this letter being read at meeting a short time ago, Mr. T. Roseveare, of Hall, one of the guardians of Lanteglos-by-Fowey, said the Local Government Board very often held the whip over them, but rarely used it. He would call a vestry meeting to consider the matter.... It was held at the Ship Inn, Pont, where Mr. Roseveare came with the draft petition, which, if approved of, was to be signed by the ratepayers of the parish outside of Polruan, as a counter-blast to the petition from Polruan. The petition read as follows:- "We the undersigned ratepayers of the parish,....feel it a great injustice and cruel hardship to be called upon to spend from one to two thousand pounds in improving the house property belonging to a class of independent gentlemen, we being a poor, depressed class of tenant farmers".

Now it cannot be doubted that there were present at the vestry, a few of these "depressed tenant farmers" who could buy up almost all the people of Polruan, there being few parishes which can produce a richer class of tenant farmers than Lanteglos by Fowey. The chairman (the Rev. H.T. Mugford) seeing the utter absurdity of the proposed petition, asked to be allowed to amend it, which he did, the following being adopted: - "We, the undersigned ratepayers of Lanteglos-by-Fowey, feel it a great injustice and cruel hardship (especially in the present depressed state of agriculture) to be called upon the spend from £1,000-£2,000 in improving the house property of Polruan belonging to a large extent to a class of independent gentlemen." The chairman....intimated that as he believed the petition to be quite useless he should refuse to sign it.

3 May (RCG) FOWEY GRAMMAR SCHOOL. - At the Grammar School a musical entertainment, including a toy symphony and a charade, was given on two evenings last week to raise funds for the erection of a gymnasium. The toy symphony and the charade were warmly applauded, and the entertainment was a thorough success in every way. About £16 has been raised towards the proposed object.

17 May (RCG) POLRUAN LAUNCH.- On Saturday evening a yacht was launched from the yard of Messrs. Slade and Sons, Polruan. She is built for Mr. Richard Foster, of Lanwithan, near Lostwithiel, is a beautiful model, and is to be yawl-rigged....Length of keel, 40 feet....22 tons.... The yacht was christened the *Foam* by Mr. R. Foster, this being the name of his old boat. The launch was quite a success, the craft gliding into the water in good style amid cheers of a large number of spectators.... Mr.. Foster entertained several friends and workmen (over thirty in number) at dinner at Ye Olde Ship Hotel, Fowey, after the launch. A first-class spread was provided by Mr. and Mrs. J.M. Williams, to which ample justice was done by those present. The usual loyal and other toasts were proposed and drunk, and a most pleasant evening was spent, hearty cheers being given for Mr. Foster on his leaving.

2 August (RCG) FOWEY GRAMMAR SCHOOL. Sir Charles Graves Sawle distributed the prizes to the boys of the above school on Thursday. - The Examiner.... stated that there was a marked improvement in all the work since the preceding year. He congratulated the masters and boys upon the report, and considered the school both a privilege and an honour to the town of Fowey. Before distributing the prizes Sir Charles encouraged those boys who were unsuccessful in gaining prizes by stating that often the very boys who were not successful in school examinations were in after life. It was the earnest plodders who won the race. - The Head Master read his report, which said that the numbers had risen from thirty-six to forty. In all eighteen candidates had been presented for public examination, all of whom had been successful. Whilst congratulating the boys,....Mr. Deakin expressed the hope that their past successes would only serve to spur them on to renewed efforts.

20 September (RCG) CORNISH COAST MISSION TO SEAMEN. In aid of the building fund of the Fowey Sailors' Rest, recently established in connection with the Cornwall Coast Mission, a fete and meeting were held on the pleasantly situated grounds of Moorswater Lodge, kindly placed at the disposal of the committee for the occasion by Mrs Sleeman.... A house near Albert Quay has been purchased at a cost of £400, most of which has been subscribed. Part of the property, however, is old and will have to be rebuilt in order to adapt premises to their future use.... Favoured by brilliantly fine weather the fete was largely attended, visitors coming from Liskeard, Looe, and Fowey. For their entertainment sports and other amusements were provided. A party of coastguardsmen from Looe gave an exhibition of fencing with single-sticks, and illustrated the working of the ship's capstan by means of a large model. Boating on the ornamental waters in the grounds and archery were among the other forms of recreation indulged in by the visitors, whose enjoyment was further enhanced by the band of the Liskeard volunteer detachment. Tea was also provided on the slope outside the house, and a large number partook of it.

The meeting....was delayed for an hour and a half, awaiting the arrival of the Fowey contingent, among whom were the Rev. G.J. and Mrs. Hill, whose steamer did not arrive at Looe in time to catch the train intended. Brief addresses were delivered, and were interspersed by hymns, sung by the choir of Looe Congregational Church.

The Rev. H.N. Purcell, vicar of Fowey, presided, and explained that two years ago the Cornish Coast Mission began its work in the port of Fowey.... The society's missionary, Mr. Lightfoot, went from ship to ship holding services, which were joyfully welcomed by the crews of the various vessels. On shore recently a Sailors'

Rest had been established, and....several hundred pounds more were required to carry out needed alterations, and to provide reading-rooms for the men who frequented the institution. In every port in which these missions to seamen had been established abundant proof was given that the sailors valued the religious privileges conferred on them, and he invited their sympathy and co-operation.... The Rev. G.J. Hill, secretary to the Seamen's Christian Friend Society, of which the Cornish Coast Mission is a branch, said the work amongst the sailors was commenced in Cornwall by the Rev. G.C. Smith, of Penzance, who afterwards went to London and started the first mariner's church, but....that although the movement originated in Cornwall it was only two years since that the mission was started on their own coast....

11 October (RCG) FOWEY. DROWNED.- On Thursday afternoon a sailor named Harrison, belonging to the schooner *Hematite*, lying in Fowey Harbour, went ashore for letters. On returning to his vessel he stood on the thwarts of the boat and commenced to scull, and after getting a little distance from Passage slipped the oar out of the scull hole, fell overboard and was drowned. After some difficulty the body was recovered.

18 October (RCG) CORNISH FISHERIES. There has been considerable activity among the fisheries this week, Mevagissey has been greatly excited, immense shoals of pilchards having been brought in, amounting to about 2,000 hogsheads. The buyers engaged steamers to tow the vessels to and from the seines, and....the Cornish Sardine Company forwarded large quantities to their stores at Polruan.... Prices-pilchards, 8s. to 14s. per 1,000; mackerel, 15s.6d. to 17s.6d. per score; conger, 9s. to 16s. per cwt....

22 November (RCG) FOWEY. THE BOARD SCHOOLS.- The reports of the inspectors who examined the Board Schools....state that in the boys' school the discipline is excellent, and the instruction highly efficient.... Class subjects are intelligently taught, and singing by note is very good. Grant earned, 20s. 5d. per head. In the girls' school the scholars are in excellent order, and are taught with praiseworthy care and skill. Handwriting and neatness of work on slates and paper deserve special commendation. English and needlework are thoroughly well taught. Grant earned, 20s. per head. In the infants' school the children are in excellent order, and are thoroughly taught. Grant earned, 16s. 8d. per head.

22 November (RCG) POLRUAN. ENTERTAINMENT. - A largely-attended and most successful entertainment....was given in the Board schoolroom, on Friday evening. The first part consisted of Offenbach's operetta, "The Two Blind Beggars," admirably performed by Dr. Boger and Mr. Allchin. The second part consisted of songs, readings, and music.... At the close of the entertainment the Vicar....warmly thanked the ladies and gentlemen who had so kindly come from a distance to amuse his parishioners. The proceeds of the concert will be added to the Building Fund of....St. Saviour's.

1889

7 January (WB) Mr. Edward Stead, son of Mr. Stead of Highway, Lanteglos-by-Fowey, met with a serious accident while out rabbit shooting on Monday. He was in the fields near Pont,and was carrying a muzzle-loading gun in his left hand, when a rabbit started a short distance from him. Before he could get the gun to the shoulder, his fingers, it is supposed, must have touched the trigger; the gun burst, splintering both the barrel and stock to pieces, injuring Mr. Stead's hand, and inflicting a frightful wound in his chest. He managed to walk to the house of Mr. Canning, at Pont, where he was attended by Messrs. Torbock, Tuckey, and Stewart, surgeons, who considered it necessary to amputate the left fore-arm below the wrist. Mr. Stead is in a very precarious condition.

7 February (RCG) POLRUAN. DROWNING OF A CAPTAIN. - One evening in the early part of the past week, William Allen, master of the ketch *Tower*, which is laying at Runcorn, went ashore on business, and not again returning to the vessel, the rest of the crew became alarmed as to his safety. No tidings of his whereabouts could be gleaned until Saturday evening, when Mr. Slade, of Polruan, received a telegram from Messrs. Marwood and Co., Runcorn, stating that Captain Allen had been picked up drowned, and asking him to break the sad news to the widow and give instructions for the burial. No doubt Allen, like many others before him, in the darkness of the night, walked into the canal. Allen was a quiet, inoffensive man, of about 38 years of age, and much respected. He leaves a widow and four children quite unprovided for,....their bereavement adding another to the long list of mariners' widows at Polruan. (Runcorn quay still is very badly lit, the water almost level with the quay with much debris. It is hard to distinguish water and quay at night.)

28 February (RCG) CORNWALL WINTER ASSIZES. CLAIM FOR THE FALL OF A WALL AT POLRUAN. Ede v. Penter.... The plaintiff's case was that as he was passing along a public highway, called Chapel-lane, in Polruan, on October 30th, 1887, a wall which the defendant had built along that highway fell. The plaintiff was buried by the wall, which fell just as he was passing under it, breaking his thigh and permanently injuring his leg, as well as cutting his head and injuring his back. The expenses of his illness were £29 16s. 6d., and damages were laid at £500. The defence was that the wall was well and carefully constructed, with a proper batter or inclination; and that the proximate cause of the fall of the wall was not the way in which it was built, but the pressure, which, by reason of an extraordinary rainfall and flood, was greater than could ever have been anticipated.... Verdict for the defendant.

25 April (RCG) All our local school boards are to be called upon to consider whether they will permit the children and teachers in their schools to be lectured upon the nature and the physical effects of alcohol. The lectures will be under the auspices of the Band of Hope Union, who have raised £10,000 for the purpose.... Opposition may be raised by some....on the ground that the lectures will be merely another form of the teetotal propaganda; but that is hardly true.... The lectures will be of a purely scientific character, and will be made extremely interesting and instructive by means of illustrations and demonstrations..... We can conceive no valid reason why the School Boards should not allow the children to receive some little additional instruction.... We are afraid, however, that the Band of Hope Union will not find the scientific aspect... a very powerful one.

2 May (RCG) The successful Cornish candidates for the Royal Masonic Institution for Girls were Mary Ponsford Gould, daughter of the late Robert George Gould, chemist and druggist, Fowey, with 1,771 votes; and Anita Mary Thorne,....Liskeard, with 1,579 votes.

2 May (RCG) A FOWEY SHIP SUNK. - The brigantine, *Ontario*, 128 tons register, Captain Willcocks, master, Mr. Slades Polruan, owner, struck a sunken rock while rounding Start Point, on Thursday morning. She was in ballast bound for Fowey at the time. The Salcombe coastguards put off to her but found she had sunk about half-a-mile west of Prawle Point. They brought to Salcombe with them the captain, his wife, and child, and the crew of five.

2 May (RCG) HE FELL FROM ALOFT. - Fred Hanson, 22, of Fowey, was drowned off the Lizard on Friday afternoon. He was one of the crew of the Plymouth vessel *Caledonia*. On Friday afternoon Hanson went aloft to take a reef in the mainsail, the wind blowing fresh, with a heavy ground sea, and soon after was he seen in the water. A lifebuoy and two oars were thrown to him, but he did not reach them; and the boat lowered with three hands failed to find him after an hour's search.

2 May (RCG) At Lanteglos-by-Fowey Vestry,..... A new window was ordered to be placed on the north side of the Church.

2 May (RCG) FASHIONS FOR MAY Some of the most startling combinations are observable in the new costumes of the season. Green plays a prominent part both for costumes and millinery; quite the light pale greens are used for the latter, but the shade for dresses much depends on what the contrast is to be. If black - and this is extensively used- the shades of green are of he most vivid description. Terra-cotta and the new pink are also favourite colours. Grey is a much admired colour, and always considered in good taste; this season it promises to be very popular. White is much used as a combination with grey, making the most charmingly cool costumes for summer. Silver braiding and fine silver cord is also prettily used as trimmings for the lighter shades of grey. Grey and blue materials are made up together with very good effect. Quite an old friend in the shape of new materials is to be in favour this season, that is, alpaca. A few costumes made up of this material look exceedingly well; one, a mixture of grey and white, was made with Directoire coat having steel trimmings; the petticoat, of grey and white striped alpaca, was edged with a frayed out ruche of the two colours; an adjustable vest of white was intended to be worn with the coat. Silk dresses will be more fashionably worn this season than for some time. For walking dress the Directoire coat of striped or broche silk is worn. The mantles this season go from one extreme to the other. For elderly ladies the mantle entirely covers the dress. Coats are still considered quite the nicest out-door garment for young girls. There is a decided tendency to wide sleeves, and many of the coat-sleeves are open from the shoulder, and caught together with cord ornaments, this gives room for the full sleeve of the dress. The new bonnets are in decided contrast to those of last season, being quite small and resting flat on the head. Large shapes seem on the increase for hats: these naturally require more trimming- quite a profusion of lace and flowers appears. Small shapes are by no means discarded; these are still in the turban form, with bows of ribbon and spray of flowers set right in the centre of the crown. Quite low-crowned hats have a wide projecting rim turned up at the side, and secured with a bow or fancy ornament.

23 May (RCG) FOWEY. A BRAVE ACT was committed by Mr. Moses Dunn, Trinity Pilot. On Thursday a lad having accidently fallen out of a boat in the harbour, Dunn pulled off his guernsey, dived into the water and fished up the lad, who, by careful treatment, was brought round after his immersion.

13 June (RCG) PRICE LISTS FOR J.C. CRAPP of TRURO.

> new bacon shoulder.... 5d. per lb.
> white moist sugar.... 2 1/2d. per lb.
> best lard....5d. and 6d. per lb.
> cocoa....4 1/2d. per lb.
> best soap....3 1/2 lbs for 8 1/2d.
> matches....1d. and 1 1/2d. per doz.

19 September (RCG) BURIAL DISPUTE. A....vestry meeting was held at the Townhall, Fowey, on Saturday evening, to authorize the Burial Board to raise £250 for the purpose of enlarging the cemetery, enclosing the additional ground, and doing such other work....as may be necessary....there was a numerous attendance, the question of consecration or non-consecration of the new ground having created considerable stir in the parish. Mr Graham, clerk of the Burial Board....said....part of it must be consecrated.... Rev. A.J. King (Congregational)....proposed that the recommendation of the Burial Board, that one-third of the new burial ground be consecrated....be adopted....The Vicar said....that the new ground ought to be fairly divided, one-half to go to those who conscientiously objected to being buried in consecrated ground, and the other half to those who desired it.- (applause)...it was pretty evident that the majority of people desired to be buried under the Church of England.... Rev. A.J. King said personally he esteemed the vicar and good Church people in the town. The only objection he had was one of principle....against public money being spent in favour of any religion denomination whatever. The good people of Fowey had been very serene, but "still waters run deep," and the ripple had been under instead of on the surface - (laughter and applause).... On a matter like that they should speak with freedom and fullness and without fear of being extinguished.... The matter was put to the vote.... The resolution that one-third of the ground be consecrated was carried.

10 October FOWEY CRICKET CLUB being in want of funds a variety entertainment was organized by some ladies and gentlemen, and though the result, from a monetary point of view, might have been better, the performances themselves were worthy of all praise. An overture for violincello and piano having been admirably rendered, "Bluebeard" was illustrated by a series of tableaux vivants. The stage was very prettily arranged with draperies and plants, and the scenes followed eachother smartly. Hoping to swell the exchequer, the entertainment was repeated, but with poor results. Great praise is due to the two ladies mainly instrumental in getting up the entertainment. It was arranged in 5 days.

21 November (RCG) FOWEY WATER SUPPLY. The following letters were read by the Clerk at St. Austell Guardians meeting, from Mr. A.C. Sandoe, the chairman of the Fowey Waterworks Company:- "We are in treaty with Mr. Treffry with reference to the pipe of the stream flowing down the valley from Polglaze.... We have Mr. Treffry's permission to pipe the Polglaze stream, and I will call an early meeting to consider the matter. In the meantime I beg to state that we are not using this water, as it is only an auxiliary source, and our ordinary springs are now sufficient for the demand." - The Clerk said....that the supply was insufficient, and they were constantly trying to increase it....

12 December (RCG) ST. SAVIOURS CHURCH, POLRUAN The foundation stone of a new mission church was laid at Polruan on Wednesday week, the edifice being designed to replace the old chapel of St. Saviour's which existed in the twelfth century. Polruan contains 1,100 people and is a mile and a half from the parish church. The road to it is extremely hilly, and the inconvenience together with inclement weather, at time prevents numbers of worshipers getting to church. During the past two years services have been held at Polruan, which have been constantly attended by as large a congregation as a very inconvenient schoolroom could hold. The estimated cost of the new building is over £1,200 and towards this amount £300 has been secured.... The site chosen is in a meadow in the front street, and has been purchased of Mr. Moss, of Par, for £70. The plans for the church have been prepared by Mr. W. Swift, (Henderson and Sons), Truro, and the contractor is Mr. Penter. The building will be in early English, and will consist of nave, south aisle, and chancel, the dimensions being 80ft. by 30ft. A quarry at the rear of the site will supply the requisite stone....

The proceedings commenced with a service at the parish church, at 11 a.m.... The Vicar having asked Mr. Foster to accept their thanks for his presence and help that day, Mr. Foster replied that he was pleased to know that an effort was being made to supply a building suitable for the services of the Church of England in that portion of Polruan, where they had been under various disadvantages for many years, as their church had been far away from the population. - The Rev. H.N. Purcell, in the course of some remarks, said he....forward to the time when that difficulty would no longer be felt by the people of Polruan, but that they would have their own church in their very midst, where they would be able to worship God as their fathers did before them. The hymn "The Church's one Foundation" was then sung, during which a collection was made....

CHAPTER 10
1890-1898

1890

10 April (WB) COLLAPSE OF A GRAND STAND. At Fowey races, last week, just as the contest for the Torfrey Cup was being concluded, and the excitement on the grand stand was at its height, the whole erection collapsed, and considerably over 100 persons were precipitated to the ground. The highest tier was quite 25 feet high, and those on the lower tiers had to bear the fall of the people above. The excitement was great, and it is remarkable that the accident ended without serious injury to anyone. One woman fainted beneath the weight of several planks and people, but she was not hurt, and soon revived. A man from Falmouth was badly cut behind the right ear, and the wound had to be sewn up by Mr. Sandos, surgeon, of Bodmin, who was luckily on the field. Mr. G.W. Wellington, of Fowey, had the contract for the stand, and in previous years has done similar work for the committee thoroughly well. The only accident on the course occurred in the Fowey Stakes. Mr. J. Sargeny was riding Eclipse (his own horse), and at the first bank was thrown and taken up unconscious. He was conveyed to the Ship Hotel, and Messrs. Davis and Stephens, surgeons, attended. His collarbone was broken.

10 April (WB) FOWEY GRAMMAR SCHOOL. Seven boys from this school were entered in the recent Cambridge Local Examinations. Four took honours - the highest gained by any school in the county - and the other three passed. - In celebration of this success, the boys were, on Saturday, taken by the head-master to Roche for the day. The weather was delightful, and a most enjoyable day was spent.

26 June (WB) On Monday last news was received at Fowey that George Hawken, late mate of the *"Spinaway,"* had died in Harburg from the wounds inflicted on him at that place a few weeks since, when some English sailors were attacked by Germans. Great regret and sorrow is felt at the young man's death. He was much respected, and was of a quiet disposition. Great sympathy is felt with his widow and her young child, only a few weeks old. His old shipmates also express their sorrow at his untimely end, as he was a pleasant companion and a good sailor.

10 July (WB) FATAL ACCIDENT AT FOWEY. A fatal accident befell Mr. Collins, the respected station-master at Fowey, on Thursday. He was standing on the jetty looking over the rail when the steam crane was turned around and the back part of the engine caught him, jamming him on the rail. He was taken to his home in an unconscious state, and at once attended by Messrs. Davis and Boger, but died on Friday.

Mr. E.G. Hamley, county coroner, held an inquest....Saturday.... ARTHUR TRENEREY stated that Thursday morning, between seven and eight o'clock, he saw Mr Collins go on the jetty. The crane was working the opposite way to which it normally did. Deceased stopped at the corner of the jetty, and looked at the crane working.-- ROBERT COTSH, crane driver, said he was working the crane, and saw deceased standing at the corner watching it. Feeling that the crane had been brought up by some obstruction, he at once reversed the slewing gear, and then saw deceased lying on the jetty on his side. Witness at once went to deceased, who said, " I quite forgot you were slewing that way," and asked him to send for the stetcher.-- JOHN MAGOR, who was in the truck slinging casks of clay, said Mr. Collins came on the jetty and spoke to him. The crane at the time was at a standstill. Mr. Collins went and leaned on the rail of the jetty. He saw the crane move and heard a cry, and saw deceased fall back. At once he went to his assistance.-- Dr. A.P. Davis said that he found deceased most seriously injured. Death was due to internal hemorrhage and shock to the system. He asked deceased if anyone was to blame, and he replied, "Oh, no, doctor; purely an accident." - The jury returned a verdict of "Accidental Death," adding as a rider a suggestion that the radius within which the crane moves should be protected.

10 July (WB) The remains of Joseph Atrill Collins, stationmaster and superintendent of Great Western jetties, were interred in cemetery Monday afternoon. He....attended Congregational Chapel,.... He was a deacon of the Chapel and superintendent of Sunday school and a most indefatigable worker in Christian work.... Although the weather was most unfavourable raining in torrents, there were at least 500 persons present to show sympathy.... At the graveside after the service members of Masonic lodges took leave of their departed brother, passing by the side of the grave and each throwing in a sprig of acacia.... During the funeral the bell of the Parish Church tolled out its solemn note, the shops and places of business were closed and flags were flying half mast from various vessels. The sad cause of his death will long be remembered by many, especially by those who worked under him, having lost a true friend and good master.

4 September (WB) THE DECLINE OF THE CORNISH FISHERIES. On Thursday last, Mr. Matthias Dunn, of Mevagissey, read a paper on "The Decline of Fisheries on the Cornish Coast; Its Causes and Cure"....Mr. Dunn....noted the decline of the Cornish summer pilchard and hake fisheries.... In the olden times....every fishing village from Plymouth to the Lands End had had its large pilchard seines, costing thousands of pounds, and each....often securing yearly a thousand or more hogsheads of fish, and giving from three to seven gallons of oil to the hogshead. But within the past 30 years....the fish had dwindled down to a small quantity caught by the drift boats.... Not a seine was to be found on the south coasts of Cornwall looking for pilchards in the months of August and September, the best time for seeking them in the days of our fathers.... When he (Mr Dunn) was a boy, he was often forbidden by the master of the boat to catch hakes, as it was doubtful if a purchaser could be found for them at a penny each.... For the past 20 years the Mevagissey summer boats had not caught an average of one hake per boat. This decline had evidently come from two causes....the present mode of fishing for the great crab lessened the young of these creatures in our seas. These, when in their larval forms, existed on the surface of the sea....the pilchard kept down the number of crabs to the normal quantity. Since the opening of the railways so many of the female crabs are now caught that....the pilchards leave their deep water haunts to come to the coast.... There was another cause....herring, pilchard, mackerel, and scad, are extremely fond of minute crustaceans.... In the Cornish seas....these amphipods, although so fond of the surface of the sea in the spring and summer....lived....in the autumn and winter....near the bottom of the sea in deep water, living in and climbing among the branches of those forests of flexible corals so plentiful at the bottom of the English Channel, illuminating the darkness of night with the scintillating lights.... But no one is afraid of these piskies of the sea now..... Fleets of trawlers root out the corals from the bottom of the sea, thus destroying the winter homes of these creatures, who consequently have to leave or die for want of suitable natural conditions.... Prior to 1860 the haddocks were fairly plentiful on the Cornish coast. He had known a boat catch 200 in one day, and varying from six to twelve pounds in weight.... Between August and December they also had a fishery for conger, hakes, ling, and cod, which maintained at least 100 families between Fowey and Falmouth. Half that number of people were now kept by that fishery....

Mr Dunn....had little to offer as a remedy.... The evil of trawlers destroying the home of the amphipods must be tolerated, as trawl fish is so valuable, and cannot be caught by any other known system of fishing.... He suggested that....the Government should experiment with his brother's (Moses) invention for catching flat fish in deep water....a long revolving cylinder with barbed spikes around it, to be towed over the sea bottom, and by it spearing the flatfish without disturbing the corals or sponges. He would further suggest that a fishing craft be fitted out and manned by practical and scientific men....noting the undeveloped resources around....Great Britain and Ireland, especially reporting on....the seas on the west coast of Ireland. The Armenian Government had vessels of that kind surveying...their extensive coasts. Of the sea bottom they knew nothing. If it was anything like the northwest coast of Cornwall was some four thousand years ago when first touched by.... man, what a mine of wealth was there.

His second case was also a difficult one, seeing the haddock is all but extinct in our waters.... The Fishery Commissioners of the United States before the year 1870 found their seas....impoverished from over-fishing. It was decided to help by artificial means the hatching out into life those millions of eggs which most of the edible fishes were known yearly to produce, turning the results into the sea. In that work they had succeeded beyond the hopes of the most sanguine....

Mr. Dunn stated that for full forty years Mevagissey bay and its neighbourhood supported four trawlers of about 15 tons each for four months in the year. About the year 1881 an extra trawl was set on, and a stray steam trawler or two came into the bay from Fowey and Falmouth. These extra craft over fished their waters, and 1884 saw the bay a failure.... In the summer of 1889 a Plymouth trawler came in and gave a man £2 to show these outer trawl grounds. Soles and brill were found in abundance,

and over £40 worth of these fish were taken to market as the result of this one trawl. Soon other large trawlers, both sail and steam, found out the grounds, and, so far as he could estimate, in three months they took $800 worth of fish out....
(Matthias Dunn was a brother of Moses Dunn, of Polruan)

18 September (WB) A SAILORS REST AT FOWEY. The new Sailors' Rest at Fowey was opened on Thursday last by Mrs. Stopford Sackville. The Rest, which presents a very imposing appearance, has been built from designs prepared by Mr. W. J. Samble, architect, of Fowey. It contains twenty-three rooms, and has on the ground floor, kitchen, study, and coffee room, while another is fitted up in which captains and mates may be able to perform their writing duties. On the second floor there is a very large mission room, which, with the library, offers accommodation for over 250 persons. For this Mrs. Stopford Sackville has kindly given a handsome piano. The library is also on this floor, while the third storey contains cabins for the sailors and apartments for the caretakers. The style of the building is Italian, with an ornamental front. It has been built by Mr. Panter, of Polruan. A paved court is situated at the back. A high mast is fixed at the end of the court, which is at the water's edge, from which flies a large flag, bearing the words "Seamen's Rest" and an appropriate representation of Noah's dove returning to the ark. The home is now started in fair working order. There remains a debt to be cleared, but it is small in comparison with the amount that has already been raised.... The building will now be the headquarters of the Cornish Coast Mission of the Seamen's Christian Friend Society, of which Mr. Spence is the resident missioner....

18 December (RCG) GOOD NEWS. - The people of Polruan received with much joy on Tuesday, the intelligence of the safety of the crew of the Fowey schooner *Waterlily*, who, it was feared, had gone down with the vessel, last heard of a week previously off the Lizard, bound for Fowey with coals. The glad tidings was received by Mr. Hockin, of Polruan, managing owner. The *Waterlily* was run into and sunk at six o'clock on the morning of the 9th inst. off the Lizard by a French fishing barque. The crew was rescued by the Frenchman, but her master, in spite of the entreaties of Climo, refused to land the ship-wrecked crew on this side of the Channel, but took them on to Fecamp, where he was bound. Capt. Climo, his two sons and a nephew, William Lean, the mate, and George Wheeler, the other seaman, all belonged to Polruan.

1891

8 January (RCG) FOWEY. AN EXHIBITION OF TOY YACHTS took place on Tuesday....in the Town-Hall. There were a large number of yachts shown, most of which were built in Fowey. Mr. W.S. Lacey took first and second prize....for two cutters.... *Silver Star* was beautifully finished off, all the fittings being of brass. The *Tartar*....last year took the silver cup. A beautifully made yacht was shewn by Mr. Murray Rogers, but was not for competition. This was his own work and showed how thoroughly he understands the art of yacht building. Mr. Watty (builder) took first prize for a cutter in Class III, and *Valkyrie* took the second prize belonging to Mr. Langman. A beautiful little canoe was exhibited by Mr. Atkinson and the *Allonette*, built by Mr. E. Treffry reflected the greatest credit on him. A very interesting model was that of a steam trawl, shewn by Mr. E. Treffry and built by Mr. Claud Foster. The yacht was beautifully fitted with engines, and was a beautifully finished boat.... Various other yachts were shown, one of polished tin being unique.... Tea was going on during the exhibition.

12 March (RCG) Scarcely ever before in the history of the present generation of Cornishmen has such a severe snowstorm visited the western parts of England as that which commenced on Monday shortly before noon and lasted, almost without intermission, until Wednesday morning.... The sleet was blinding, and backed by a strong gale from the east,.... Heavy as the fall was, the average depth being somewhere about a foot, nothing particularly serious could have been expected, had not the wind increased in violence and caused the snow to drift in blinding clouds.... There was almost an entire blockage of the railway traffic....and telegraphic communication with all parts was cut off.... Large numbers of sheep have been buried....but it is probable that the majority will be recovered alive.

19 March (RCG) FOWEY. LOSS OF HORSES BY THE STORM ￢ Snow fell again heavily on Thursday night and Friday, until after middle day. A thaw then set in again, and has continued ever since. The new road on Sunday presented a curious spectacle, a pathway being cut through the snow, which was in places six to eight feet high. St. Catherine's-parade was impassable except on the hedge in many places, the snow being very deep. Mr. Nicholls, of Trerrant, has lost two valuable horses, and we hear of lambs and ewes being lost in the drifts. Mr. Julyan, cabinet maker, had the side of his new workshop blown in owing to the fury of the gale. There was no damage to the shipping.... In the Lanlivery and Luxulyan district....one farmer.... found on digging for his sheep found one of the hens had made a nest and layed an egg in the snow; the bird was none the worse for being so long buried.

23 April (RCG) The charming short stories which "Q." has contributed to the "Speaker", and which have been an attractive feature of that journal, have just been published in book form.... There are twenty-four stories or sketches in the volume.... "Q," whose real name is Mr. Quiller-Couch....is a young Cornishman - still under thirty. He is just now making a tour of the Cornish coast, and will pick up a few short stories before he returns....

23 April (RCG) FOWEY. UNPLEASANT INCIDENT AT A WEDDING. - On Saturday morning a wedding took place in the parish church, and, after the ceremony, the bride and bridegroom, (a highly respectable couple) walked up Lostwithiel-street, to return to their friends. To the astonishment of those who happened to be in the town, they were followed for some distance by a mob of big schoolboys and girls, who hooted and shouted after them in a most disgraceful manner, which made the passersby wish that Fowey's one policeman could be ubiquitous.

11 June (RCG) FOWEY. Between eleven and twelve o'clock on Saturday night two young men named George Elliot and Wm. Webb Burnett, of Polruan, were crossing from Fowey to Polruan in a punt, the property of Professor Yeo, Fowey. There were no paddles in the boat, and it appears that the two occupants were endeavouring to propel the boat by means of the bottom boards. By some means, however, the boat capsized, and both men were thrown into the water. A noise was heard by the coastguardsman on duty (Commissioned Boatman Cook), who at once put off, as also did the master of the yacht *Foam*, owned by Mr. R. Foster. George Elliot, who was picked up in an exhausted condition, ultimately recovered; but William Webb Burnett was drowned, and his body was not recovered until about mid-day on Sunday. Deceased was about twenty-four years of age, and was a mason by trade....

19 June - (WB) There are very few places a car ought not to be taken, but one is Fowey. Why doesn't an enterprising person buy relatively cheap land on the heights above and put up a garage? Cars ought not to be allowed to descend the steep hill with its right angle turn into town, pass through the narrow main street, 1 mile plus, to get to the only garage.

Last year I was guaranteed I could lock the car if I descended the hill. I was willing if the hotel porter sat beside me as guide. He was reluctant. As we got to the bottom I made a sharp turn by backing the car once. He heaved a sigh of relief and said that in a nursing home further along was someone's motorman who got injured a few weeks ago attempting this - he was still semi-conscious. We went at a walking pace, came to another bend where he said a few weeks ago a car had run into a wall which had resulted in concussion for the chauffeur and other occupants. We ultimately arrived at the garage, a wide open shed into which anyone could stroll at any time. Motor cars are out of place here. The average motorist will be quick to recognise this and welcome the opportunity to leave cars on the hill on coming to Fowey to enjoy its beauties as a pedestrian.

25 June (RCG) FOWEY AND THE AGRICULTURAL SHOW. - Fowey was almost deserted on Tuesday and Wednesday week, Par Agricultural Show being the attraction. It is said that nine hundred left Fowey on Wednesday, five hundred of whom applied for tickets by one train alone.

25 June (RCG) THE ROYAL CORNWALL AGRICULTURAL SHOW. When first the invitation came from the Royal Cornwall Agricultural Association to visit Par, there seemed to be some little doubt as to what the result would be if that place was selected by the Council. The district is not an over-populous one,.... Par with St. Blazey and Tywardreath all thrown together would hardly make a small town.... But....Par itself is the junction of three lines of railway....and being central, offered convenient opportunity to those desiring to exhibit, of easy transit both of animals, poultry, floriculture and implements.... The presence of the Duke of Edinburgh, the delightful summer weather, and a lovely site overlooking the sea, all contributed to the consummation of the desires of all concerned, and the show proved one of the most successful....for several years both in point of numbers attending and finances, a much larger number having entered the yard during the first day at 2s. than for some time.

The Great Western Railway Company had its resources well tried.... The excursions were well patronised, but we cannot say that the arrangements for the booking at Par Station were by any means a success. Instead of the office being open at the proper hour, the office window was closed until a few minutes before the trains reached the station when it was impossible to issue tickets to the crowds desiring them, and many passengers having business at Truro and elsewhere were precluded from taking the ordinary trains in consequence, and had to be subjected to the crowding and crushing of special trains where fifteen or twenty passengers were huddled into a single compartment intended only to contain a dozen....

The arrangements at the showyard, speaking generally, were very satisfactory, though the grand stand proved far too small the first day, for during the jumping hundreds had to be turned away. There was a considerable strain on the water supply at the yard, but....the little Mineral Water Works at Tywardreath , under the care of Mr. Caleb Thomas, of Newhouse, executed an order for 1,000 doz. bottles of aerated water for the occasion, a somewhat severe test for the little factory, which, however, came out of the ordeal with great credit to itself and those concerned.

The local shows were, beyond doubt, as well managed as ever....and the committees are to be congratulated....on the cleanliness everywhere displayed, and the careful supervision exercised. The excellent tents, as well as a great deal of the canvas supplied to other parts of the ground came from the stores of the Cornish Tent Company, whose head offices are at Tywardreath.

The music of the Marine Band, during the first day,....was a thorough treat, and the band stand, during each performance, was thronged with an admiring crowd of visitors....

One of the many things upon which the local committee are to be congratulated, is the success of their carnival on Tuesday evening.... It was really good, and was witnessed by thousands of people....who had stayed in Tywardreath to patronize the fair, which was held in a large meadow at the higher side of the quaint and picturesque old village. When the torches were lighted after dark, the procession, over half a mile long, looked extremely well.... The cattle were shewn in excellent form. Devons were very strong and some of the animals would do justice to any show.... **Mr Nicholls,** of Fowey,....had a splendid bull which was awarded a first prize....

9 July (RCG) POLRUAN WESLEYAN SUNDAY SCHOOL. The anniversary has just been held, and attended with great success, nearly £20 being taken.... On Monday afternoon children paraded the town singing, after which they were regaled with tea..... The secretary's report stated the number of scholars on the books to be 175, and 34 officers and teachers - 209 in all.

9 July (RCG) EXCURSION STEAMERS. Last Thursday the *Sir Richard Grenville*, (the beautiful and commodious pleasure steamer) called to take passengers to the Mevagissey Regatta, on its way from Plymouth. The steamer was crowded when it reached Fowey, but when that haven was reached many of the pleasure seekers were thankful to set foot again on dry land. A large number of passengers were embarked, both at Fowey and Charlestown, though the heavy roll of the sea at the last named made the embarkation somewhat difficult. The return voyage was a rough one, but the steamer behaved splendidly. Many of those who landed at Fowey, in the morning, had returned by train, owing to the heavy sea which was running. It is to be regretted that the Plymouth steamers, when at Fowey for many hours each Thursday, do not utilize the time by running a short excursion for a couple of hours, and thereby reap a considerable harvest from the many visitors, and residents of Fowey, who now have no opportunity of a water excursion of that kind.

16 July (RCG) FOWEY HOTEL. The new addition....is rapidly approaching completion. It consists, among other things, of about 20 new bedrooms, and fine new dining-room, billiard-rooms, and smoke-room. The addition will, in fact, make the hotel more than as large again, and so popular has this become as a holiday resort that already had the new building been ready, it would have been engaged to the full for the present season. The cost....will be about £5,000. Mr. Isbell is the contractor, and the architect is Mr. H.J. Snell, of Plymouth. Mr. Snell has also designed two new villas to be built beyond the hotel towards Point Neptune, one for Mr. Bate and the other for Mr. Grundy.... On Friday evening Fowey hotel was for the first time lighted up by electricity, and the whole of the lights gave entire satisfaction, being a very great improvement on the old gas jets. It is hoped that Fowey will soon be lighted by the electric light, as the price of gas is very high and the quality not of the best.

13 August (RCG) Dr. Mason, medical officer to the St. Austell Union, visited North-street., Fowey and found that three openings in the sea wall for drainage were most offensive, more especially at low water. It was dangerous to health. The openings of the drains should be cut down and piped.... An open closet in a cellar at Fowey was found to be in a most filthy condition, and it was recommended that notice be served on the owner at once.... Sanitary inspector was instructed to meet a committee at Fowey to see if the sewer drains could not be cut down to the water-line, some of them being quite seven or eight feet above at present.

20 August (RCG) FOWEY ROYAL REGATTA.... The naturally pretty harbour was rendered more picturesque than usual by a number of yachts and vessels which displayed bunting. Steamers were also there with excursionists from Plymouth and Falmouth, and with these and other visitors the little town was *en fete* and exceedingly lively.... Shortly after ten o'clock the day's programme commenced. There were altogether seventeen events....the fishing boat race,....a match for sailing boats of the harbour of Fowey....the pulling match between four-oared gigs belonging to her Majesty's service....watched with keen interest. A novel race took place between two national lifeboats, the boats being fully equipped for saving life, and the crew wore their lifebelts and the boats' valves were open. The Fowey and Mevagissey boats competed, and the former won in a very creditable manner.... The Stenalees brass band were stationed on the committee boat, and their selections of popular airs were much appreciated. In the evening a water carnival took place, and a large fleet of illuminated boats went round the harbour, and, together with a brilliant display of fireworks, a grand spectacle was witnessed.... The committee offered substantial prizes for the best illuminated boats....1st, Professor Yeo; 2nd, Coastguard Boat; 3rd, Mr. Mallett; 4th, G.B.Brokenshaw....

Four-oared gigs belonging to H.M.S. for coastguardsmen of the Fowey Division;....about six nautical miles - Much enthusiasm was extended to the race, the stations represented being Fowey (Black Cat), Mevagissey (Flying Fish), Polperro (Aurora), and Polkerris (Fortunate). The Fowey men were hot favourites, and fully justified the confidence reposed in them, as they won by three minutes from Polkerris....

In the evening a water carnival took place. A number of illuminated boats assembled....when prizes were awarded for the best decorated craft. The boats were afterwards formed in procession, and towed around the harbour, the effect being extremely pretty. A highly successful day was brought to a close by a display of fireworks.... A collection was made in the streets for Fowey Cottage Hospital. Bunting was freely displayed from many of the houses.

3 September (RCG) A large quantity of salmon has lately been caught in the Fowey river, and at the mouth of the harbour, and our many visitors, as well as residents in Fowey and Polruan, have had the opportunity of purchasing the "king of fishes" at the comparatively low price of a shilling per lb.

17 September (RCG) FOWEY. THE FAIR.- In days gone by, fairs were very important and much looked forward to by the inhabitants of the "borough", but times are changed and the fairs have become little more than a name, and a sweet stall, by the churchyard gate, exciting the wonder of the strangers, and which did not appear until afternoon, was the only sign of "fair-day" to be seen on Thursday last, though, no doubt, a welcome one to the young people of the place, and as a demand is said to create supply, judging by the varied wares, a very good business must have been done by the stall keeper.

1 October (RCG) It is expected towards the end of October, that St. Saviour's Mission Church, Polruan, will be opened for divine service. The church is almost completed, and a most tasteful, though simple, edifice it is. Internally, it is most neatly finished off, and shows what s l and labour have been bestowed upon it. The Vicar has indeed worked nobly to erect this sorely needed church, and we hope those who have it in their power will aid him to soon exterminate the debt for the building. Seats are the great pressing need, chairs at a cost of 4 s. each are to be supplied, and anyone who will aid the fund for their purchase will....be doing a good work.

8 October (RCG) FOWEY IMPROVEMENTS. - Various alterations are being made in the Fowey streets, some old houses being pulled down and rebuilt, which, when complete, will be a great improvement.

22 October (RCG) THE NEW MISSION CHURCH AT POLRUAN. - A sale of work on behalf of the Chair Fund....was held at Fowey on Saturday afternoon in one of the rooms of Mr. Brokenshaw's new house, now nearly completed. The effort owed its origin to eight little girls, the stall keepers being Miss Carrie Brokenshaw, and the Misses Penrose, Behenna, Rawlings, and Clunes. The room was prettily decorated, and, by the kindness of Mrs. Brokenshaw, an excellent tea was provided, which was presided over by Miss Maud Bolton. There was a good attendance, and the proceeds reached a satisfactory amount.

5 November (RCG) WEDDING AT POLRUAN. A very pretty little wedding took place at the Wesleyan Chapel, Polruan, on Monday morning, the contracting parties being Mr. O.C. Wellington, of Wadebridge, and Miss Katie Cowl, of Polruan. The ceremony was performed by the Rev. A. Newbery, of Wadebridge, in the presence of a crowded congregation, and being the first of its kind that has taken place in this chapel, the trustees, through Mr. Widlake, presented the bride and bridegroom with a beautiful copy of the Scriptures, as a memento of the occasion. A large number of presents were received by the happy couple, who, amid the respect and goodwill of many friends, left for Torquay on their honeymoon. Mr. W.S. Lacey, of Fowey, played the "Wedding March."

3 December (RCG) CORNISH CAPTAIN DROWNED - All hope of the safety of Captain Thomas F. Tippett, of Polruan (of the *ss Rossend Castle*, of Newcastle), and his crew has now been abandoned. The *Rossend Castle* was on a voyage from the Black Sea to Bristol, with grain, and was a steamer of 1,728 tons gross register, and about 3,000 ton burthen.... Captain Tippett was about 27 years of age, and a lieutenant in the Royal Naval Reserve. The vessel left Gibralter on the 7th inst. for Bristol, about two hours previous to the Wear steamship *Galveston*, which in crossing the Bay of Biscay afterwards experienced one of the most terrific gales that any of the crew could remember. They report having sailed through large quantities of grain and barley. Bunker and other hatches were clustered about in the water, while later on, a charthouse, a flagstaff, and several other articles belonging to a steamer were also seen. Two lifeboats, greatly damaged, with the name "Newcastle" alone visible on the stern, were afterwards seen, but no trace of any man whatever could be found. The crew concluded that the wreckage belonged to the steamer *Rossend Castle*, and the official intimation of her being overdue tends to confirm their fears.

1892

7 January (RCG) A CHARMING ENTERTAINMENT was given at Polruan, on December 30th, got up in aid of the fund of St. Saviour's Mission Church, by the Misses Veal and friends. The room was crowded, and so successful was it, that it had to be repeated the next evening. The performance is to be given at Polperro, and we understand it will also be given in Fowey.

14 January (RCG) LANTEGLOS - Owing to the wintery weather, and the distance of the parishioners from their parish church, and its extreme discomfort when reached, the congregation on Sunday morning last dwindled down to one. The services at St. Saviour's Mission Church, Polruan, are well attended, and the inhabitants show their appreciation of the great efforts that have been made to plant a church in their midst.

11 February (RCG) FOWEY WAKING UP. Fowey seems at last waking up to the fact that its beauties might be better known, and the meeting last week for this purpose was well attended. Some suggest that cleaner roads would aid the matter; certainly they would not retard it, for the condition lately of even the roads that are as a rule fairly clean, has been most filthy. It is a pity that the authorities cannot see their way to employ a man and a small mud cart (such as can be seen any day in neighbouring towns no larger than Fowey) daily, and use better material for repairing the roads, and not leave the stones to be trodden into place by the inhabitants, to the injury of their boots, and the enriching of the boot-makers (to say nothing of the torture of this proceeding to those who have corns).

11 February (RCG) FOWEY.- It is satisfactory to note that smoking concerts, which are now so much in vogue in large towns, are being introduced here, and No. 3 Co., 1st C.A.V. are to be congratulated on having taken the initiative in introducing them, for good attendance shows how greatly these concerts, and their excellently rendered programmes, are appreciated. And it is to be hoped that the promoters will find that they continue to attract, and that these pleasant evenings will bring in substantial aid to the funds for their new drill hall.

18 February (RCG) FOWEY Another entertainment was given at the Grammar School, on Monday evening, on behalf of the fund to provide the boys with a library, which ought to be a singularly fine one, judging by the frequency of these entertainments and the large audiences which they attract. The encores were very numerous, the performers being most kind in repeating the various items.

3 March (RCG) FOWEY. A STEP IN THE RIGHT DIRECTION A meeting has lately been held here to take into consideration the advisability of having licensed watermen,.... Of late years so many boats have been hired out to visitors and others, by persons having other occupations, that the interests of those whose livelihood, in a great measure, depends on what they can make by taking people on the water and letting out their boats, have been greatly interfered with, and the harvest which they justly looked for during the summer has fallen far short of what they had a right to expect, and has gone to benefit those less in need of profit from such a source.

3 March (RCG) FOWEY. - We are glad to find that at last our fine old church is to have a surpliced choir- not that we would for a moment be supposed to be ungrateful to those ladies who have so long and so zealously formed part of our choir, but we feel that, in so noble a church, a surpliced choir is more in character than a mixed one. It appears that the change is not to be made until the organ has been greatly enlarged, and otherwise improved, and we understand....that the organ is to be completed about the middle of June. When finished we may feel sure that it will be an instrument worthy of the builders and the sacred edifice for which it is destined. Is it too much to hope that the almost universally used "Hymns, Ancient and Modern" will be introduced with the surpliced choir?

10 March (RCG) MILITARY FUNERAL. - On Sunday afternoon a very large concourse of people assembled at Lanteglos church to witness the funeral of a young man named Tarry, who has been lately invalided home from his regiment on account of consumption from which he died last week at his home at Bodinnick. The Volunteer Artillery Company attended with their band; the unusual sight of a military funeral bringing people from all the immediate neighbourhood. A firing party was in attendance and at the conclusion of the burial service, which was taken by the vicar, the Rev. J.T. Mugford, a volley was fired over the grave.

10 March (RCG) THE MISSION CHURCH of St Saviour's, Polruan, has recently had presented to it a handsome gift of a carpet for the chancel with a solid brass fixing rod, and panels for the pulpit of beautiful brocade of ancient design. These very acceptable and much needed additions to the internal fittings have been provided out of the proceeds of the entertainments, consisting of Tableaux Vivants and music, etc, got up by Miss Maud Bolton, and given at Mr Brokenshaw's new house, St. Catherine's, Fowey, in December last, and supplemented by an entertainment given lately at Polruan.... The carpet, which is of ecclesiatic design in gold on a rich crimson ground, and with a handsome border, was supplied by Messrs. Maple and Co., London, as was also the ancient looking brocade for the pulpit panels, and the brass rod, with "fleur de lis" finials and fittings, was supplied by Mr. Mallett, of Fowey.

7 April (RCG) FOWEY RACES appear to be more popular than ever, judging by the number of people who came into the place on Tuesday. The streets in the afternoon were quite deserted, and apparently everyone who could possibly leave his occupation had done so, and was "on pleasure bent" to the scene of the races. Even Polruan joined in the exodus. Two ferry-boats were plying, and to judge by appearances, quite a harvest of coppers must have been gained. The weather....was much more favourable for standing about than at the last two meetings, when a piercing wind made everyone feel chilled to the bone. The day, though dull, was warm. During the evening the streets were crowded, but the people for the most part were fairly orderly.

14 April (RCG) What might have proved a very serious accident occurred here last week. A little girl of about three years, daughter of Mr. Varcoe, jeweller, fell from the third story of a house, on the pavement below. Luckily the awning over her father's shop broke the force of the fall considerably. When the child was picked up, she was insensible but quickly regained consciousness. The doctor was soon on the spot and ascertained that no bones were broken and no serious injuries sustained.

12 May (RCG) CONTEMPLATED IMPROVEMENTS. - While we hear of various plans for making Fowey more widely known, and that among them is one for the issue of a "Guide," and that steps are to be taken to advertise it by means of photographs, &c., and....a scheme is in hand to alter the approach to it from the station, and to otherwise improve the streets (at the risk, we fear, of not improving their quaint appearance), the improvement of the streets and roads, as regards the comfort of pedestrians, is a matter which, as far as we know, does not seem to be occupying the minds of those who are anxious to bring visitors to Fowey.... After rain it would be difficult to find more muddy streets in any town, and as they are so narrow that footpaths are impossible, it ought to induce....some great effort to....make them a little less unlike those in other seaside resorts....

26 May (RCG) THE LAST OF THE BROAD GAUGE. The great railway event of these parts took place on Saturday and Sunday, when the Cornwall Railway was converted from the old seven foot gauge to the gauge of 5ft.8 1/2in., which is now the guage of the whole railway system of the country. The length of the line to be converted was 160 miles, including the main line from Exeter to Truro and all the broad gauge branches. Between four and five thousand men were employed....from all parts of the country. Traffic west of Exeter ceased on Friday night, and the navies began work in earnest at daybreak on Saturday, and by Sunday evening experimental engines had been run over every section of the line.

FOWEY. On Saturday morning at an early hour, everything tended to show that something a little out of the way was impending, and by a little before seven o'clock, the harbour was alive with small boats, awaiting the arrival of *ss Gazelle*. By that time the road above Whitehouse was a scene of great animation, where coaches and other vehicles were assembled. The beautiful horses in the St. Austell coach (a team of four), were much admired. The crowd soon increased, and by the time the *Gazelle* was inside the harbour, the rocks and approach to the slip were covered with people. Mr. Moses Dunn, of Polruan, was engaged to load and unload the mails, parcel baskets, etc., and a large barge, and a smaller boat were taken to the steamer, and in a wonderfully short time the barge was seen being towed up, with a flag proudly flying and a postal official in charge. The barge, though loaded to a very considerable height, was by no means large enough to contain all the mails, and another boat followed, that also being in charge of an official. These were met at the slip by the staff of the Great Western Railway Company from Fowey Station, and then the scene became most exciting, as the boats were unloaded and the mails and parcel baskets were sorted for the different coaches. There were many helpers, so in a very short time the various vehicles had their passengers and mails, and shortly before eight o'clock they had all set out on their journeys. By five o'clock again the scene became very animated, but there were not so many people as in the morning. The coaches were quickly unloaded and their contents transferred to the boats, and so to the *Gazelle*. On Sunday morning there were not so many mails and parcels, one barge being sufficient. There were a few passengers each day, and the station-master

257

dispersed a fair amount of tickets on the slip. On Sunday afternoon there was a large number of people to witness for the last time the dispatch of the mails by sea. The coaches drove up smartly a little before five and had a good many passengers, who had evidently taken the opportunity of seeing the sight. There were a few passengers for Plymouth. The station-master and porters were again in attendance, and in a very short space of time the coaches were unloaded, and the mails, etc., and luggage were dispatched to the steamer, which swiftly left the harbour at a few minutes past five o'clock.... *Gazelle*....one of the fine steamers belonging to the Great Western Railway Company....had been specially brought to Plymouth for the mail work of Saturday and Sunday. (Cornwall Railway was narrow gauging the Cornish line.... The length of the line to be converted was 160 miles....including Exeter to Truro and all the broad gauge branches. Work began at daybreak Saturday and was complete and tested by Sunday evening.)

30 June (RCG) FOWEY ACCIDENT. - On Saturday, while a young girl was engaged in shaking a mat, the board on which she was standing gave way and she was precipitated into the sea. Luckily, it was high water, and she escaped without injury except a wetting. Had it been low water, she might have had a very serious accident.

28 July (RCG) NOTICE TO MARINERS . ESTABLISHMENT OF A NEW LIGHT IN FOWEY HARBOUR. NOTICE IS HEREBY GIVEN that, on the FIRST DAY OF SEPTEMBER next it is intended to CEASE LIGHTING the present Harbour Light, which is a RED and FIXED LIGHT. A new light has been erected about one hundred and ten feet to the east, and seventy feet to the south of the present light. The light is erected on an iron column and the focal plane is about thirty-five feet above high water spring tides. The height of the column from base to focal plane is twenty feet. This LIGHT will be first used on the evening of THURSDAY, the first day of September next, and will show a flash of WHITE LIGHT of twenty seconds duration every twenty-five seconds. Vessels coming from the west on opening this light will clear the Cannis rock.

28 July (RCG) FOWEY CHURCH NEW ORGAN. There was formerly in the building an organ erected some twenty years ago, but it had recently been found quite inadequate for the services, and the work of restoring it....was placed in the hands of Messrs Hele and Co., Plymouth. Proceeding with their usual good taste, the firm incorporated all that was best in the old instrument with the handsome organ now standing in the Church which is certainly one of the best in the county of Cornwall.... The dedication service was held in the afternoon, when a large congregation assembled.... Chancellor Worlledge, of Truro Cathedral,....described the characteristics of true worship, and said the Church welcomed in worship the thoughtful use of all that was reverent and beautiful.... Nowhere did music, painting, architecture, and sculpture flourish so freely and continuously as where they had been enlisted in the service of Christ. While zealously guarding against the risk of allowing these things to supplant the spirit of true worship, they thought it a noble act to sanctify the arts, to bring gradually and wisely everything that was beautiful into the service of Christ,.... There were two sides to religion, the severe and the beautiful, and they would be sure to swerve from the narrow way, if, while indulging in the beautiful, they forgot the severe.

11 August (RCG) TWENTY-FIVE YEARS VICAR OF FOWEY. PRESENTATION TO THE REV. H.N. PURCELL. There was an overflowing audience assembled at the Institute, Fowey, on Monday evening, to witness a presentation to the vicar....on his completion of his twenty-fifth year of ministry in the town. Mr. Purcell has endeared himself to all classes by his zeal in his sacred office, his geniality and good-fellowship, and his warm espousal of every movement for the social and material welfare of Fowey. The Working Men's Institute, opened in 1878....will stand as a memorial of the excellent work which Mr. Purcell has accomplished during his vicarship.... The proceedings on Monday were exceedingly cordial.... The readiness with which Nonconformists and Church people alike contributed to the presentation quite surprised the collectors, and amongst those present at the ceremony of bestowal were many who were not of the vicar's faith. The gifts consisted of a highly artistic silver bowl in Queen Anne style, bearing the vicar's crest and the arms of Fowey, and on the ebony pedestal a plate with this inscription - "Presented to the Rev. H.N. Purcell by his parishioners as a mark of esteem on completing his 25th year as vicar of Fowey, Trinity, 1892.... Accompanying the piece was a handsome album, bound in whole Morocco, with vellum leaves, on which were inscribed the names and addresses of 454 subscribers.... Mr. E. Rillston said he had been closely associated with the vicar for 14 years.... He thought the people of Fowey had had a good deal to do with shaping their vicar- (laughter)- and they were proud of him -(applause).... The vicar had ever been a good friend to his people, and had always been ready to give them advice on all matters....

The vicar, who was received with hearty applause, said;.... " I feel uplifted in the thought of the multitude of friends who surround me in this parish.... It has been one of the great powers that has upheld me in years gone by, when, as many of you know, I have needed all the help that could be given to one in the midst of sorrow and of difficulty.... One of my friends this evening said I had been shaped by mixing with the people of Fowey. Of course I have....I have learned....that the greatest privilege which belongs to a clergyman is to know more and more of those who need to know him, and who ask, and are good enough to receive, his help in any way.... I think of those many, many, many loved and dear ones to us all who have passed away from our midst.... And as I pass up and down the streets of this parish I often remember with thankfulness, words that they have spoken to me and blessings which they have invoked upon me....

25 August (RCG) FATAL FALL OVER POLRUAN CLIFFS Several children were out on the cliffs at Polruan, on Friday, playing, when one boy named Thomas Henry Tomlin, aged six years, fell over the cliff at a very high place, about 150 feet from the water. Some persons outside in a boat fishing observed something fall, and gave notice to those on the cliff, the wash on the rocks being so that they were afraid to approach the shore. A boat from the coastguard station at once proceeded to the spot and found the boy in a cove under water quite dead.

22 September (RCG) On Sunday evening, there was a harvest festival at St. Saviour's Mission Church, Polruan. The pretty little church was most tastefully decorated with fruit, flowers, corn etc., and did great credit to those ladies who had worked so energetically at this labour of love. The church was crowded, every available place being filled with extra chairs and forms, but....many were unable to find room. The sermon by was preached by the Rev. S. Valentine Baker and was listened to with the greatest attention. He spoke of the pleasure it was....to see such a congregation, and of the joyful time they were celebrating. He also mentioned the early origin of this custom, the "Feast of the Tabernacles" in the Jewish Church being the original "Thanksgiving of first fruits, and of harvest." He also remarked how glad he was to see that all the seats were free, and as in God's eye all are equal, so in church there should not be one seat for the rich and another for the poor.

3 November (RCG) FOWEY SCHOONER DRIVEN ASHORE. - The weather off the Tyne on Thursday was exceedingly stormy. While the schooner *Resolute* of Fowey, from Dunkirk, was attempting to enter Shields Harbour she was driven ashore. The crew of five were with difficulty saved by the rocket apparatus, but were exhausted, having to be dragged through tremendous surf.

10 November (RCG) A few weeks ago an old man was looking about in the rocks on St. Catherine's beach, when he found, wedged in between some of them, an old coin. This he took home, and, after cleaning it, showed it to one or two, who pronounced it to be of value. He eventually sold it, and it turned out to be a doubloon. Some years ago a man discovered a chest somewhere about the rocks at the mouth of the harbour, and he managed to tow it behind his boat, but when near the shore, on the Polruan side, the chest slipped and once again was lost in the sea. This was undoubtedly one of the chests from some Spanish vessel and probably filled with doubloons. The chest has possibly gone to pieces years ago, and some of the coins washed up among the rocks.

1893

5 January (RCG) On Wednesday and Thursday in last week, a very excellent entertainment was given at Polruan in aid of the street lamp fund. The principal performers were the Misses Veale (2), A. Slade, Davis (2), Clemo, and Taylor. The extravaganza 'Cinderella' was the chief feature of the evening. The part of the "Prince" was taken by Miss B. Veale, and "Cinderella" by Miss Annie Slade, who both acted with great spirit and taste. The whole performance reflected the highest credit on those who got it up, and the dancing of the fairies was much admired, as likewise were the very charming costumes of all the performers..... Proceeds amounted to £12 10s.

12 January (RCG) THE WANT OF A LAMP at the Whitehouse landing slip has long been felt, and often spoken of as though no serious accidents have occurred for lack of one, a very great inconvenience and some risk has been incurred by those crossing to and from Polruan after dark, especially in stormy weather. A gas-lamp has very recently been placed on the wall above the slip, which lights it well and now makes embarkation there after dark as easy and comfortable as by day. The approach to the slip has been greatly improved by some steps being put there....

26 January (RCG) THE FUNERAL of Mrs Clegg, wife of Mr. Richard Clegg, butcher, of Polruan, which took place at Lanteglos-by-Fowey on Wednesday last week, was the first ever remembered as exclusively conducted there by Nonconformists. (Should be Clogg)

9 February (RCG) FOWEY NEW WESLEYAN CHAPEL BOUNDARY Mr. Graham, at Friday's meeting of St. Austell Guardians, said there appeared to have been some mistake in regard to the Wesleyan Chapel at Fowey. It was stated when the plans were presented that they complied with the bye-laws, but....he did not think the plans met the demands of the bye-laws. The chapel, it was now stated, would come out to the old line, and leave the street at that spot only seven and a-half feet wide. He believed it was in contemplation to pull down the building opposite, but until that was done he thought the plans of the chapel could not be passed. It was decided to have the matter investigated....

13 April (RCG) FOWEY. - A very successful entertainment was given in the Girls' Board School Room, on Easter Tuesday. After an opening pianoforte duet, by the Misses Mugford and Henwood, the operetta "Cups and saucers" was capitally rendered, Miss Maud Bolton taking the *role* of Mrs Nankeen Worcester, and Dr. Boger that of "General Deelah". The acting left nothing to be desired, and the piece was enthusiastically applauded. "Cups and saucers" was followed by vocal music, in which Miss Henwood, Miss A. Slade, and W.F. Denison, took part. The entertainment concluded with another operetta, entitled "The housebreaker," in which Miss Maud Bolton took the part of Mrs Lascelles Smythe, and Dr. Boger the double part of Mr. Lascelles Smythe; and the gentlemanly housebreaker. In this piece, as in "Cups and saucers" Dr. Boger displayed his skill in "make up", so as to entirely lose his personal identity, while the acting of both the performers was such as to bring home to the audience all the points of the play, keeping them in a state of continual laughter and winning from the performers most enthusiastic applause. Mrs. Bolton accompanied the songs incidental to both pieces, which were rendered with much effect. The entertainment was given in aid of the building fund of St. Saviour's Mission Church, Polruan.

13 April (RCG) Mr. Thomas Gundry, of Torfrey, near Fowey, has made such satisfactory progress, that he has been able this week to get down stairs. Mr. Gundry, who has been very dangerously ill, underwent a very remarkable operation at the hands of Mr. Paul Swain, of Plymouth. Some abscesses having formed on his lungs, it was decided....that these could only be removed by a surgical operation,....the only chance of saving his life. The services of Mr. Paul Swain, who is the most eminent surgeon of the district, were called in, and the operation - which was a most delicate and dangerous one - was successfully performed. Mr. Swain's fee was twenty-five guineas.

20 April (RCG) FOWEY - An Extension of the town quay is being made, which will be a great convenience both to pleasure seekers and those whose business takes them on the water, as it will enable boats to be reached at all states of the tide at the town quay. At present, in low tide, Whitehouse is the only practicable landing place. The alterations there are a very great improvement,....much needed.

4 May (RCG) FOWEY MAY-DAY. The cuckoo was first heard here this year on May-day, and it would have added considerably to the comfort of the inhabitants had its welcome greeting not been followed by other sounds of a very different character. But though (and to their credit be it said) the older youths of Fowey did not disgrace themselves and annoy the inhabitants by the disorderly proceedings which have so often ushered in May morning, in the evening the younger boys of the place, none of whom appeared to be more than ten years of age, behaved in a manner which was simply a disgrace to themselves, their parents, and the place in which they reside. For about two hours in the evening they were rushing backwards and forwards along Fore-St and the Esplanade, dragging a large collection of buckets, tins and saucepans, fastened together with cords, and the noise, dust and confusion they created will not soon be forgotten. Not content with this they rang the bells violently at houses on the Esplanade, in some cases breaking them. In the town itself they broke shutters and did other damage....it was difficult to believe that such proceedings could be permitted in a civilised place, and it shows how much Fowey needs a larger police staff and how unfortunate it is that the frequent efforts of the vicar to procure a second policeman....have not been successful. One man cannot be in two places at once, and while a policeman is wanted at the station end of the town, another is required at the other end, where the boys of the place are a constant nuisance. Stone-throwing, pea-shooting, and other annoyances are constantly taking place.

11 May (RCG) A NARROW ESCAPE. Friday afternoon....the youngest son of Mr. G.B. Brokenshaw, of St. Catherine's House, who is about seven years of age, was climbing up the cliff at Readymoney, when he missed his footing, and fell to the shore, which at that part is composed of large rocks. The child was unable to move or call for assistance, and as the tide was coming in quickly, his position was one of much danger.....a little boy came on the beach, and his attention was caught, and he ran for help, which was speedily on the spot, and the little sufferer was taken to bed, and medical aid quickly called. It was found, that though being severely bruised and shaken, no bones were broken. Had no one come down on the beach, the child would have been swept away, as the tide, a few minutes after he was found, completely covered the scene of the accident.

1 June (RCG) Two serious accidents occurred on Saturday last to children at Polruan. About one o'clock a little girl, daughter of the chief officer at Polruan

Coastguard Station, fell into deep water when playing on the rocks by the old tower on the Polruan side of the harbour. The cries of her companions attracted the notice of Capt. Burns, who was in a boat at a little distance off, and he immediately rowed to the spot, and was, fortunately, just in time to save the child, who, but for his timely aid, must have sunk, but who, happily, was rescued by his promptitude.

Later in the afternoon, a little boy named Nelson, whose mother is a widow, went on the cliffs by the blacksmith's shop to gather some elder blossoms, when he lost his footing, and was precipitated upon the rocks below, and though no bones were broken, he was very seriously injured, and his throat very badly cut, but whether by rocks or some jagged boughs, it was impossible to say. A medical man was speedily on the spot, and the poor child's throat had to be sewn up. It is hoped that he may ultimately recover.

7 September (RCG) THE NEW WESLEYAN CHAPEL, of which the foundation stone was so recently laid, is making good progress, and will be a great improvement to North-street, in which upon the site of the old chapel, it is being erected, though somewhat further back from the road than the old one. We are glad to find that the well, supplied from a spring which rose under the old chapel, will not be interfered with.

7 September (RCG) The Harbour Commissioners have had a notice put on the sea wall at Whitehouse landing slip, warning bathers not to make use of the slip as a bathing place. Throughout the whole summer much annoyance has been experienced both by those living in proximity to it, and those whose business or pleasure makes it necessary for them to make use of the slip, at its being frequented at all times of the day by bathers, children and young men, the latter even adding zest to their bathing delights by making use of the sea wall to dive from. There are many retired places about the rocks, of which bathers could avail themselves..... Should they still persist in a practice that causes so much annoyance, we trust that the magistrates will support the commissioners in their endeavour to suppress a real nuisance, at one of the only two ferries here, and one that is so much frequented.

21 December (RCG) The boys and friends of Fowey Grammar School met on Monday to present the head-master, Mr. A. Newland Deakin (who is leaving Fowey to assume the head-mastership of the Falmouth Grammar School) with a silver tea service and salver, as a mark of their regard for him and their appreciation of his services to the school and town of Fowey. The presentation was made by John Behenna on behalf of the boys. About eight years since Mr. Deakin became head-master, and the period has been one of singular prosperity to the school.... Mr. Deakin spoke briefly and with much feeling, accepting the gift and wishing the Fowey Grammar School a successful career under the new head-master, Mr. Stevens. The meeting broke up with cheers for Mr. Deakin and his assistant-masters who go with him to a larger sphere of work.

1894

29 March (RCG) SAD FATALITY NEAR FOWEY - A trap accident occurred on Good Friday between Tywardreath and Fowey, which resulted in the death of Mrs. Ann Rogers, 74 years of age. The deceased and her husband, Mr. William Rogers, who lives at Keybridge, Blisland, accepted an offer to ride in a neighbour's trap to Menabilly Lodge, near Fowey, where their daughter and son-in-law, Mr. G. Northcott reside. The trap was driven by the owner's wife, Mrs. Govett, who was accompanied by her little son. When they reached Newtown, about one mile from their destination, they met a young man riding a bicycle. Seeing that the horse was frightened, the rider dismounted and stopped while the horse and trap passed. The horse, however, ran away and threw out the occupants, all of whom escaped uninjured except Mrs. Rogers, who in falling caught her leg between the shaft and harness, with her head hanging down. In that way she was carried about 40 yards, her head bumping either against the wheel or on the road. She fell clear when she was just outside her daughter's house. She was then unconscious, with a badly fractured head. Dr. Boucher, of Fowey, was passing, and did all he could for the sufferer, but she never recovered consciousness, and died on Saturday afternoon. (I think they mean Dr. Boger.)

5 April (RCG) POLRUAN has had its share of sorrow in the death of Capt. Toms, of the *Wild Wave*. He had not been well, and it is understood that he was strongly urged to remain at home. Unfortunately he did not realize the importance of rest, and he sailed for Runcorn on the 28th. He became worse, and died early on the 30th. His ship brought him back to Fowey on Sunday evening, and on Monday afternoon his funeral took place at Lanteglos Church. The sight of the procession of boats going up the harbour, and the lovely estuary the coffin covered with a large Union Jack, was as sad as it was picturesque. There were nearly twenty boats containing mourners and friends, and the naval reserve and coastguards attended, accompanied by their chief officer, Mr. Toser. Much sympathy is felt for the daughters of Capt. Toms, who have now lost both parents.

12 April (RCG) FOWEY VOLUNTEERS IN LITIGATION. - An interesting Volunteer case was on Monday adjudicated upon at the St. Austell County Court.... The plaintiffs....were Captain A. Carnall, Battery Sergeant-Major A. Hicks, and Gunner E. Tamblyn, all of No. 3 Battery 1st Cornwall Artillery Volunteers, Fowey, and the defendant is a tailor, named Francis J. Denison, of the same town.... The plaintiffs are members of a committee of the battery formed in 1891 for the purpose of raising money to obtain a new drill hall. Captain Carnall is also the officer for the time being commanding the battery. The committee in 1892 gave several entertainments, and the nett receipts, amounting to £81 13s. 2d., were placed on deposit in a local bank in the names of Captain Carnall and the defendant. About June 1893, Captain Carnall purchased certain premises, with the intent that they should be converted into the required drill hall, and the plaintiffs were desirous that the deposited amount, together with the interest, should be transferred to the name of

Captain Carnall. The defendant, although frequently requested to join Captain Carnall in withdrawing the money or transferring the same into the name of Captain Carnall, had refused to do so, alleging (1) that a certain bill incurred in giving the entertainment referred to was unpaid, (2) that he had incurred solicitor's costs in connection with the money which ought to be satisfied, (3) that the battery should pay him 12s. for a lieutenant's collar, which he alleged was due to him. Captain Carnall had offered to personally disburse the account and solicitor's fees, but had refused to pay the 12s. out of the sum subscribed by the public, and the defendant still refused to join in withdrawing or transferring the said sum.... The Judge....declared the defendant was a constructive trustee....and he ordered him to join with the plaintiffs in withdrawing the said sum, with interest, from the bank and transfer it to the Finance Committee of the corps. Defendant must also pay the costs....

10 May (RCG) DEATH OF DR. TORBOCK. - During Sunday night, Dr. William Hall Torbock, physician and surgeon, of Polruan, passed away. He had been failing in health for nearly twelve months. He held the position of parish doctor and public vaccinator, and earned on special occasions special grants for the success of the latter function. Deceased, who was born in 1844, was interred in the new cemetery near Talland yesterday.

7 June (RCG) Sunday week was the first appearance of an exceedingly handsome altar cloth, frontals, &c., the work of various ladies of Fowey.... It is of rich green colour with various handsome devices. Fowey is now very well off for handsome church altar furniture, all being of the very handsomest material and work....

7 June (RCG) THE NEW WESLEYAN CHAPEL in North-street, Fowey, is to be opened on June 13th. It is a very handsome and commodious building, and adds greatly to the appearance and entrance into Fowey.

5 July (RCG) ANCIENT LIGHTS AT FOWEY - In the Appeal Division of the High Court of Justice, on the 27th ultimo,....the case of Carnall v Knight was heard. Defendant appealed against an order....granting an injunction restraining him from proceeding with certain buildings in Fore-street, Fowey.... Plaintiff is Christina Carnall, a widow, residing in Fore-street, Fowey, and the defendant is John Moyse Knight, of Tywardreath, cattle dealer. Defendant in May last commenced to make additions to his premises in Fore-street, Fowey, on the opposite side of the street to the plaintiff's residence, running up the frontage to such an extent, as alleged by the plaintiff, as to obstruct plaintiff's ancient lights, and to interfere with business.... His lordship granted an injunction restraining defendant from proceeding with the building until trial of the action.... Mr Farwell, QC....for appellant....contended that the only ground of complaint was with respect to an addition of 3 1/2 ft., which left an angle of light of 45 remaining to plaintiff's premises. With such a town as Fowey, where the streets were so narrow, it would be impossible to carry out improvements if such an injunction were allowed to stand.... He agreed, if allowed to complete the building, to pull it down, if the verdict were against him.... Mr Byrne, for respondent, said the additions complained of were proceeded with after notice with extreme haste, and therefore the case was one in which the decision of the Court below should not be interfered with.... The Appeal was dismissed with costs.

12 July (RCG) LAUNCH AT FOWEY - All Fowey and its many visitors seemed afloat on Thursday evening, to witness the launch of a yacht built by Mr. Watty after designs by Mr. Edwin Brett, for Mr. Edward Atkinson, of Rosebank, Fowey. Her principal dimensions are - length....overall, 58 feet.... Her figurehead, an "Airy-mouse", modelled by Mr. Calcott, was cast in gilt bronze by Broad and Sons, London. She was named the "Airy-mouse" by Mrs. H. P. Vuilliamy. As she dipped in the water with a fall of a few feet she shipped a large quantity of water and all on board were swamped. Two pleasure boats got under her stern, but fortunately no accident happened. Fowey Town Band, under Mr. W. Hawken, played selections. Mr. Watty was heartily congratulated on turning out so beautiful a vessel.

26 July *(*RCG) MESSRS. MOON'S NEW DANCE ALBUM. Messrs. Moon and Sons, of Plymouth, have issued a new Album of Dance Music which bids fair to eclipse in popularity their previous productions, excellent though they were. The present publication is in every sense worthy of a place in the home, and the purely nominal price charged for it, viz., sixpence, brings it within reach of all classes. The contents are of such a character as to be specially gratifying to those who love to "trip the light fantastic toe," while those who are not dancers will be pleased with the tuneful music of the various numbers. Of the eight dances comprised in the 48 well-bound pages there are two waltzes by Waldtenfel - "Acclamations" and "Dans Tes Yeux," a waltz "Yours Sincerely" and a polka "Tres Gai" by Coote; a set of Lancers arranged on airs from Lecocq's opera "Incognita"; a waltz "Florentine" and a polka "Farfadet" by Fahrbach; and a waltz "Ever Faithful" by Newcombe. It will be seen then that the book is not merely all that can be desired, but more, and with the remembrances that each piece would, if purchased singly, cost two shillings, the sale of the issue should be very large.

26 July (RCG) SUPPOSED CHILD MURDER AT FOWEY The inhabitants of Fowey and neighbourhood were startled on Saturday morning last to hear that the body of an infant had been picked up on a beach midway between Ready-money and Coombe, commonly known as Johnny May's Church, about a quarter of a mile from the town. Two fishermen, named Joseph Keeble and William Chapman, put into this cove about seven o'clock, when the former, upon alighting, saw what he considered a human form wrapped up in an apron and the chemise of an adult, but declined examining it, whereupon Chapman came ashore, and with a stick moved back the clothes and saw the face of a baby besmeared with blood.

The cliff here is about 120 feet high, and no doubt the perpetrator of the foul deed thought he was throwing it into the sea, but the tide rarely reaches this spot, only at exceptionally high springs or when a strong southerly wind prevails. The body could not have been long there, for it was perfectly dry, and a few hours before there had been floods of rain. They carried it at once to the coastguard watch-house at Polruan, to await an inquest by Mr. A.C.L. Glubb, of Liskeard, coroner. Drs. Boger and Cann held a post-mortem examination on Sunday at noon, when the body was found to weigh about 6 1/2 lb., was terribly bruised about the face and body, no doubt the result of the stupendous fall. The child, a female, had had a separate existance.... It was recently born, and might have been dead seven days, as the body was decomposed.... The matter is being fully investigated by the police.

16 August (RCG) It seems as if there were now no probability of the discovery of the perpetrators of the murder of the infant who was found on the beach near Coombe. The care taken to leave nothing that might be any clue made it most doubtful, from the very first, whether,....the endeavors of the police could be crowned with success.

16 August (RCG).... Some of the seats that were placed about Fowey and on St. Catherine's cliffs in the jubilee year have been tilted, removed, or destroyed. This is a pity, for they were a great convenience, both to residents and the visitors.... The fact of a place having seats put about its roads and cliffs will, of course, not be influential in bringing visitors, but their absence is felt to be a considerable drawback, and visitors wonder why so little is done for their convenience in a place which has so many natural attractions, and where lodging-houses are springing up in every direction.

13 September (RCG) A DELIGHTFUL EXCURSION takes place today when the *Princess Royal* takes passengers from Fowey and also from Charlestown and Looe up the Tamar to the Morwell Rocks. This is the first time that this trip has been arranged, and it is to be hoped that its success will be such as to encourage the Saltash Steam Company to repeat the experiment, and at the very reasonable prices of the present excursion.

23 August (RCG) PERILOUS ADVENTURE OF A GOLANT MAN PICKED UP AT SEA. About mid-day on Monday, as the cutter yacht *Vida* was cruising outside Fowey Harbour to the eastward off "Black Bottle" Rock, about a mile from shore, W. Charles Hunkin, the master, suddenly saw something in the water nearer land. He brought his glasses to bear on the object, which turned out to be a boat, bottom upwards, and at a short distance off he discerned something else. The yacht's head was instantly turned landwards, there being a good deal of wind and sea at the time, and a man lying on his back was soon discovered. The yacht was promptly brought up to the wind, and a life buoy thrown out. The man was then taken on board in a very exhausted condition - in fact, had there not been a medical officer on board the yacht with a supply of whisky, it is very doubtful whether he would have recovered. He was pulseless, and had been in the water over an hour. The *Bangor Castle*, a Plymouth excursion steamer, with a large number of passengers on board, passed quite close to him while he was in the water, but no one appears to have seen him. But for the sharp sight of Mr. W.C. Hunkin, who has been the means of saving many lives at sea, the man could not have been saved. It appears that he had been out sailing in an open boat and had been upset by a sudden squall. On regaining consciousness he wept with gratitude, and offered Mr. Hunkin all the money he had with him. Hunkin replied, "Keep your money, my good man; I did not save you for your money". Hunkin's services deserve notice at the hands of the Royal Humane Society. The man, who proved to be Mr. Philip Blowey, of Golant, gives the following account of the affair;- His boat was struck with a gust of wind and being capsized he got on her bottom. He saw a steamer coming pretty close - the *Bangor Castle* - and waved his handkerchief. But it was not observed, and the sea from the paddles washed him off the boat, which he could not again reach. He then sighted the *Vida* coming towards him, but was then quite exhausted. A rope was thrown to him twice, but he missed it, and sank. On coming to the surface again he felt something strike his face, which proved to be a life-buoy. He remembered nothing more until he was in Fowey Harbour.

27 September (RCG) FOWEY PASSAGE ANNUAL REGATTA....took place in the upper reaches of Fowey Harbour....two sailing races....paddling race for ladies. The race caused great excitement. The Prizes were a silver-mounted umbrella, a lady's handbag, and a silver brooch. Five ladies started....Reseult:-1, Bertie, H.Perry; 2, Annie, A. Copplestone; 3, Sunbeam, A. Lovering. The Cooleen, A. McLellan, was a very close fourth....paddling race for men, swimming race for boys....

18 October (RCG) LARGE CATCHES OF SALMON gladdened the hearts of the Polruan fishermen last week. Eighteen large fish, weighing over 200 lbs., were caught in one haul by Mr. Moses Dunn.

18 October (RCG) GOLF. - Fowey will not be behindhand in golf, at any rate great progress is being made at Coombe, and the links will soon be declared formally opened. A large wooden pavilion is erected with three rooms, and a veranda on one side, which commands a lovely view. Now this popular amusement is started Fowey ought to be able to have its winter season as well as the summer one.

8 November (RCG) THE STREETS OF FOWEY were, on Guy Fawkes day, crowded at places with rough lads, who threw squibs and crackers in all directions with but little regard to passers by. It is a pity that the stringent rules with regard to this dangerous and silly behaviour that are in force in St. Austell and elsewhere are not put into execution here.

29 November (RCG) FOWEY. Some little astonishment and excitement was occasioned by an account of a burglary having taken place at the pavilion, recently erected by the Golf Club. For a short time suspicion rested on persons who afterwards were found to be perfectly innocent, as the burglary turned out to be a so-called "joke," on the part of two members in the club. Had these members received domiciliary visits from the representative of law and order, as did those who were so unjustly suspected of the supposed "burglary," it is just possible that they would have found the "joke"....less amusing.

29 November (RCG) A SCHOONER SUNK OFF THE MANACLES. NARROW ESCAPE OF FOWEY SAILORS. During a heavy fog and half a gale before daybreak on Saturday, the Rye schooner *"Forester"* from Antwerp to Siloth (Scotland) with phosphates, struck the Mannacles Rocks and backing off into deep water sunk bow first almost immediately. Her crew of five just had time to launch the boat, which had a plank stove in through collision with another rock, causing her to leak to such a serious extent that while two hastily rowed her towards Rosemithon three were continuously bailing the water out with their sea boots. Landed without further harm than a thorough soaking, and minus all effects, the unfortunate sailors were for the time well-cared for by a farmer named Francis Eddy, who subsequently sent them on in his trap to Falmouth. Together with his men, Captain Richard Johns, a devout member of Falmouth Bethel of the British and Foreign Sailors' Society, soon found himself before a substantial meal and in possession of dry clothes, provided through the kindness of Missionary J.C. Badger, at the Bethel Institute.... Mr. F.L. Earle rendered further assistance through the Shipwrecked Mariners' Society, enabling Captain Johns and his crew, consisting of Mate Thomas Rundle (Par), James Maber, William Pearce, and Archibald Allen to leave Falmouth by the mail train for Fowey.... The "*Forester*", partly the property of Captain Johns and Mr. J. Bowen, of Rye, was uninsured. Captain Johns had been entrusted with her for 29 years.

1895

28 February (RCG) Lanteglos-by-Fowey Parish Council met in girls' schoolroom, on Friday.... Mr. Moses Dunn's scheme for bringing water into Polruan was presented, and it was thought £76 would cover the whole, and that it could be done in portions at a time so as not to overburden the rates of the town.

11 April (RCG) FOWEY NOTES. The race day was, as is generally the case, fine but very cold, but this in no way deterred those on pleasure bent from attending it, judging by the crowds of people who flocked into the place by rail and sea. The *Princess Royal* was crowded, and the special trains were well patronised. It is a pity that such days should be noted for drunkenness, even young girls being seen in a state of intoxication, though, for the credit of Fowey, it is well to say they were strangers to the place.

18 April (RCG) Much sorrow has been felt since the news reached Fowey that the ship *Dundrennan* had foundered near the Cape of Good Hope. Last May, the elder son of the late Mr. George Bate, of Fowey, sailed in her, his first voyage, and he was expected to return home next month. Only three of the crew, all of them foreigners, were saved. No particulars of the calamity have yet come. George Bate was beloved by all who knew him, and much sympathy is felt for Mrs. Bate and her family in the great and unlooked-for sorrow that has befallen them. On Good Friday....Mr. Purcell spoke in a most touching manner of the death of George Bate, who, up to the time of his going to sea, was the head chorister boy, and always led the choir in and out of the church. He described him, and most truly, as "a dear, bright boy", and one who was esteemed and loved by all.

18 April (RCG) FOWEY. Alterations are being made at the Town-hall which will be a great improvement, for there is no room in Fowey really large enough for entertainments, etc. The Council-room and caretaker's room are all being thrown into the Town-hall, which, when completed, will make it into a room of considerable size.

25 April (RCG) An entertainment, consisting of theatricals, took place at the Institute yesterday week, on behalf of the Choir Fund. The sooner there is a larger room for such entertainments the better, judging by the exceedingly crowded and heated condition of the room, which was packed in a most uncomfortable manner, so much so that one of the audience was ill, and had to be taken out, a feat which was performed with very great difficulty, which made those wonder what would be the fate of the audience in case of a fire occurring. Thanks are due to all those taking part, and especially to Mr. and Mrs. Williams, who organised the entertainment.

20 June (RCG) FOWEY. Through the kindness of Mr Heishmann, the small Roman Catholic communities here and at Polruan are now able to have a weekly service, Mr. Heishmann kindly allowing his photographic studio to be used for the service. The necessary fittings and vestments have been provided by those who attend the services.

4 July (RCG) PATH TO GOLANT. - A joint meeting of Fowey and St. Sampsons have resolved: that the....committee....represents to the St. Austell District Council that the old footpath leading from Fowey to Golant, having been stopped or obstructed by the Cornwall Minerals Railway in construction of the line between Fowey and Par, they urge them, the District Council, to take the necessary steps to open the footpath to the inhabitants of the two parishes concerned, the said footpath having been a footpath from time immemorial."

4 July (RCG) Fowey is very well off now in the matter of steamer trips to places of interest on the south coast. Each week there are several trips advertised. This week the grand doings at Looe, Mevagissey regatta, and a trip to Plymouth make quite a gay time for those on pleasure bent, as steamers are arranged to make trips to all the above-mentioned places.

4 July (RCG) It has been rumoured that the Golf Clubhouse was to be taken down, but, so far, it is still in existence. It is to be hoped that for once "rumour with its many tongues", has made a mistake, as golf would be, without doubt, a very considerable attraction to the visitors who come here.

11 July (RCG) Early on the morning of Thursday, July 4th, Mr. Taylor, grocer, of Polruan, was awakened by a strong smell of burning, and found his room full of smoke. On going to seek the cause he found that his store-room, which was in the house, was on fire, and his daughter in much danger from the burning room. She, happily, was rescued, without sustaining any injury. The neighbours were roused, and soon plentiful help was at hand, and the flames were extinguished, but not until after great damage was done to the interior of the house, and the contents of the store-room, only a portion of which is stated to be covered by insurance. Had not the fire been discovered when it was, the consequences must have been most disastrous, both to Mr. Taylor and his family and to the little town of Polruan, as the house is surrounded by dwelling-houses, many of them very old. (The cafe on the corner of Fore St. and West St.)

18 July (RCG) The arrangements for the re-opening of the old line of railway between Lostwithiel and Fowey are fast approaching completion. Men are now working as long as daylight lasts, Sundays and weekdays alike, so that there is every reason to believe that the line will be re-opened very early in August. When this is accomplished, passengers will be able to travel from Paddington to Fowey without any change of carriage, and the last six miles of their journey, "all along the river" (to quote the title to Miss Braddon's charming novel, which has for its scene Fowey and Lostwithiel) will be one of the most lovely, if not actually the most beautiful little piece of railway in England. It is hoped that the Great Western Railway Company will see their way to having a station at Golant, and also that the beautiful walk to Golant by the side of the railway will not be interfered with when the line is re-opened.

1 August (RCG) FOWEY. - Matters went on in a very orderly and quiet manner on the day of the election, the gloomy weather keeping indoors most of those who were not obliged to go out. But, in spite of the outward calm, the interest felt was great, and anxiety as to the result very greatly increased by the unhappy incident of Mr. Mark Guy's letters. Great was the rejoicing on Friday, when telegrams came announcing the result of the poll, and telling that the Right Hon. Leonard Courtney was again the representative of this division, and that his majority was doubled. The news reached Fowey before half-past one o'clock, and by pre-arrangement it was signalled to Polruan that Mr. Courtney was "in", and Mr. McDougall "out." Ringing cheers went up on Polruan-quay when the signal, the Union Jack, was run up to the mast-head in Dr. Boger's garden, and still louder ones were given when the ferryman had taken the telegram across and the greatly increased majority was made known.

22 August (RCG) Everyone says that never has there been such a regatta as the one of 1895. Not only was the weather superb, but all the arrangements were so well carried out that everything went without a hitch. The fireworks, by Pain, were very good indeed, and the carnival was a big improvement on last year. The various steamers came crowded, and all the events provided for the amusement of those on pleasure bent were well patronised.

A large garden party was given at the Haven by Mrs. Quiller-Couch and the situation, on such an occasion, is an ideal place for such an entertainment with the harbour at one's feet. A portion of the Royal Marine Band delighted the guests by their superb selection of music. Mr. Quiller-Couch let off a good display of fire works later in the evening.

The duchess of Marlborough and Mr. and Lady Sarah Wilson left St. Catherine's House on Thursday last for Newquay. Lady Sarah has greatly benefited by her stay at Fowey, the air having suited her very well. She is now much better, and we are glad to say that the report circulated in a society paper, that her ladyship was dangerously ill, was a great exaggeration.

Fowey is at present crammed with visitors, the majority of whom say that they prefer it to any watering place they have ever visited.

1896

2 January (RCG) FOWEY. Though Fowey is but a small place, not possessing a large population, it has railway and postal facilities which many larger places may well envy. The postal arrangements are singularly good, and include three deliveries of letters and six despatches. The latter during the "Christmas week" were increased, and the post-office officials (fifteen in number) must have had their strength and energies tried to the utmost. By one despatch alone, two days before Christmas, two hundred and fifty parcels were sent away, and those who had occasion to go inside the post-office found it more like a "parcels office" at a railway station, than the post-office of a small country town.

The work at our post-office is now about to be increased by the addition of a telephone between Fowey and Polruan, which will be a great convenience to residents at Polruan, and it is mainly owing to the efforts of Mr. Samuel Slade, of Polruan, that the post-office authorities have consented to arrange the matter. The route by which it will go is a very circuitous one, and will cross the Fowey river at "Wise-man's Stone," about a mile above the Town Quay, going thence above Bodinnick to Point, whence it will go to the Polruan Post-office.

2 January (RCG) A SAILOR STABBED AT FOWEY. An unfortunate occurrence took place on Monday week on board the brigantine *Ada Peard*, lying in Fowey Harbour. Two of the crew, both Bridgwater men, had been ashore drinking heavily, and on coming aboard about 11 o'clock began at once to pick a quarrel with another of the crew, a Russian Finn, who drew his knife in self-defence and inflicted two wounds on one of his assailants. One was rather an ugly wound on right cheek, and the other a small flesh wound in the left breast. The injured man was promptly brought ashore and attended to by Drs. Boger and Carne, by whom he was admitted into the Fowey Cottage Hospital, where he is doing well. The Russian sailor was arrested by P.C. Vicary and conveyed to Tywardreath.

30 January (RCG) FOWEY NOTES. Here, as elsewhere throughout the county, the news of the death of Prince Henry of Battenberg was received with the deepest regret, and with an unwillingness to believe that it was really true. Prince Henry came to Fowey several times, in his yacht the *Sheila*. On the last occasion he remained for about a week, the *Sheila* being anchored off White-house. His utter abstention from all ostentation was the subject of general remark. He was accompanied by some friends, and while his guests never went out without a full boat's crew to row the gig, Prince Henry himself hardly ever used any boat except a dinghy rowed by one man. He used to spend a great deal of his time in walking up and down the *Sheila's* decks, and often took a long walk ashore, and alone. It is said that on one occasion, when he landed at Golant, an old woman who lived near the landing place, somehow or other, learnt who he was, and went to the garden gate and accosted him, and finally, to his great amusement, asked him "How dear Beatrice was". No doubt she was not the poorer for her display of nerve, and for her polite and affectionate, though, it is feared, hardly disinterested enquiry. This visit of Prince Henry took place nearly four years ago, and was his last to Fowey.

13 February (RCG) A very sad accident occurred on Sunday morning near the Gribben-head. Two young men, William Grose and Archibald Watty, were in a punt shooting birds, when the boat overturned. Watty managed to swim to a rock; Grose, being unable to swim, clung to the boat, but Watty lost sight of it as it passed round some rocks. Coastguards rescued Watty, who was brought to Fowey in an exhausted condition, and though a large number of boats went quickly to the scene of the disaster, no sign of the poor young man was found. Much sympathy is felt for his family, as this is the third son who has been drowned in the last two or three years.

Early on Monday morning the body of William Grose was found, having been washed up on a beach by the tide.

19 March (RCG) On Sunday last a confirmation was held at the parish church Fowey by the Lord Bishop of Truro.... Long before that the church was crowded in every part. The dedication of the screen (in memory of the vicar's eldest daughter) was held before the confirmation, the choir and clergy going into the south transept instead of as usual into the chancel. The Bishop then dedicated the memorial, and the choir passed under it into the chancel.... The screen, which has been put up in memory of Miss Purcell, is the gift of relations and friends, Sunday-school children, and church workers. It is of oak, very beautifully carved, and has been made by Mr. Henry Hems. It is a very great and costly ornament to that part of the church in which it has been erected, and it is understood that the memorial has taken the form of a screen, on account of a wish expressed by Miss Purcell a few days before she passed away.

19 March (RCG) On Friday last a fisherman named May went out in his large sailing boat. A stiff breeze was blowing from the westward, and May, who had gone eastwards, was not only unable to return, but was blown some miles out to sea. His perilous position was observed from the pilot's look-out, on Polruan cliffs, and notice was quickly sent to Fowey, and the steam tug, *Gallant*, was soon out of the harbour steaming fast to the rescue. Just as she neared Polperro the fishing boat was seen being towed in by one of the Polperro fishing boats, which had, fortunately, been returning and seen May's unfortunate position, so that the prompt services of the *Gallant* were not required.

19 March (RCG) The consecration of about half-an-acre of ground adjoining the Lanteglos-by-Fowey churchyard, presented by Mr. Bevil Fortescue, of Boconnoc, was effected on Monday week by the Bishop of Truro in the presence of a large gathering. A service in the parish church preceded the ceremony.... A brass cross for the use of the surpliced choir of St. Saviour's Church, Polruan, was dedicated by the Bishop.

26 March (RCG) FIRE AT FOWEY. The Royal Hotel, Fowey was found to be on fire at half-past six on Friday morning. The proprietor, Mr. Beer, on proceeding to the bar, discovered that it was burning furiously. Assistance being summoned, and ladders brought, the barmaid was rescued through the window by a sailor. After considerable trouble the fire was extinguished. Mr. Beer, coming down hurriedly and bare footed, cut his feet severely with the broken pieces of glass, etc. It is to be regretted that there is no efficient fire brigade at Fowey. If it had not been for the prompt assistance of some neighbours and the ready access to some ladders, the place would have been completely gutted, with probably loss of life.

7 May (RCG) A SHARK AT POLRUAN. - A shark of considerable dimensions was close to the shore at Polruan on Sunday afternoon. It was first observed about one o'clock from a lookout at the higher part of the town, and for about three hours it continued to move about in a comparatively small radius. During the afternoon two small boats kept pretty close to it, and its movements were scanned with eye-glasses from the lookout. It is most unusual for a fish of this description to come so near the coast, and especially in this locality.

2 July (RCG) CORNISH SHIPPING IN 1895. Fowey stands next to Plymouth in the importance of foreign trade. For the most part the trade....is connected with the exports, for while only 39 entered, no fewer than 560 vessels cleared with cargoes for foreign ports. The larger portion cleared for Belgium, France, Germany, Holland, Spain, Italy, Russia, and the United States. Of vessels engaged in the coastal trade only 7 came from and one cleared for Ireland. There are 123 vessels of an aggregate of 12,384 tons on the resister at Fowey, the largest being under 300 tons. There are 190 fishing boats registered at the port.

2 July (RCG) OUR WAYZGOOSE - To St. Austell and Fowey. In accordance with custom for many years, the last Saturday in June was observed by the staff of the *Royal Cornwall Gazette* as a holiday - the day of our annual wayzgoose. By general consent we had resolved upon an excursion to Fowey by road, and an extremely pleasant trip it proved to be....we arrived about one o'clock....at this charming little watering place. Several of us took occasion to visit the old church which....is one of the finest in the county; others inspected what else there was of interest in the town, or lounged about the cliffs overlooking the harbour and the channel. Not a few ferried it to Polruan, and spent a very pleasant hour upon the heights there, while others were rowed up to the quaint little village of Golant nestling amid its orchards and gardens on the banks of the river. The wooded banks for a considerable distance, like those of the Fal, slope almost to the water's edge except that on the Fowey side the Lostwithiel and Fowey Railway runs and winds with the winding course of the stream. The opening of this railway with its jetties running out into the tidal waters has given to Fowey added importance, and we are told that already Charlestown, Par, and other small ports, especially those used for the exportation of china clay or the importation of coal along this portion of the coast, have begun to realize the effects. Time would not allow us to tarry long here, and when we had retraced our course to Market-strand, the time had almost come for the commencement of the homeward journey. We never paid for a boating trip with better grace or considered ourselves better served than when we handed Boatman Lean his money on the quay, and thanked him for the courtesy with which he had treated us. If all the Fowey boatmen are as good as he, they deserve the patronage they receive.

1 October (RCG) AGRICULTURAL DEMONSTRATION AT TYWARDREATH. Under the management of the Fowey-Lanreath Technical Instruction Committee demonstrations in agricultural handicrafts and horse-shoeing were held at Pinhale Farm, Tywardreath. The number of competitors was slightly behind that at Lanreath last year, when the committee made their first attempt at anything of the kind.... The 16 acred field placed at the disposal of the committee by Messrs. Geach was well adapted for the ploughing competitions and "cut up" fairly well considering the recent drought. The stone-hedging and spear-making took place in the meadows adjoining and the horse-shoeing on the ground at portable forges, kindly lent....by the Great Western Railway Company....

Generally the work turned out shewed an improvement on that at Lanreath last year, in the stone-hedging especially....(Prizes included Men stone-hedging - 3, C. Pearce Lanteglos, highly commended, W. Bunt and R. Pearce Lanteglos.... Men spearmaking- 2, C Pearce Lanteglos

1897

7 January (RCG) Endeavours have been made by one of the Falmouth oyster merchants to utilise part of the Fowey river as oyster beds. A bed was laid down on the Polruan side of Pont, but someone has been clever enough to steal the oysters, and so far to have avoided detection. Possibly the reward for his discovery was hardly large enough to bring about the desired result.

4 February (RCG) OPENING A NEW RESERVOIR The formal opening of the smaller of the two water reservoirs at Fowey was witnessed by a large and influential gathering of ratepayers,.... Mr. T.H. Andrew, C.E., of Liskeard,....having courteously explained the mechanism of the plant, and the reservoir having been inspected, the Rev. H.N. Purcell, was invited to turn on the valve. - Mr. Purcell , in doing so, congratulated the inhabitants on having seen this part of the work accomplished. He had no doubt as to an adequate supply of water, with two to hold 300,000 and 400,000 gallons respectively. The reservoir is 75 by 60 feet wide, 11 feet 6 inches high, and is supported by strong and numerous pillars. The reservoir at Windmill Field will be completed by the end of April next, when Fowey will have a supply equal to, if not better than, any other town in proportion to the number of inhabitants. The latter reservoir, being more centrally situated, will, when completed, be the occasion of a large demonstration, many persons, owing to the weather, not being able to be present at this gathering.

18 February (RCG) Last week there was an unusually large number of Naval Reserve men up for drill at Polruan, 160 being there, which is the largest number ever known to be up at one time.

18 February (RCG) There is a report that the Naval authorities are thinking of making Fowey a torpedo-station. Whether this idea will be eventually carried out is somewhat problematical, owing to the smallness of the available room in the harbour.

18 February (RCG) WRECK OF A FOWEY SCHOONER - TERRIBLE TALE OF SUFFERING. DEATH OF THE CAPTAIN - The fatal wreck of the schooner *Little Minnie* of Fowey, briefly reported by cablegram from St. John's, Newfoundland was one of the saddest marine disasters on this coast for many years. The *Little Minnie* (Captain Charles Jago) left Trapani on November 5th, with one hundred and ten tons of salt for St. John's, and carried a crew of five all told. From the start she met tempestuous weather. She was time and again swept by the seas, and at frequent intervals during forty days oil bags had to be hung over her sides to break the force of the waves. Sails were blown away, and for a whole month she drifted north, till caught by the ice floe. When two months out the provisions and water ran short, and all hands were placed on an allowance which intensified their sufferings. She made Cape Race, and tried to harbour in Trepassey, as the coast north to St. John's shewed thick broken ice. But the wind not serving, she had to make for here, and slowly work her way through the ice-covered sea. She was off Renews, when the wind veered and blew landward, and within an hour it was seen the vessel was doomed, the ice closing round her and hurrying her to destruction on the rocks. Two anchors and chains were let out, but failed to hold, and she struck on Renews Rock. The next sea threw her over and flooded the decks with small ice, filling the boat and rendering it useless. The captain ran to his cabin for his papers, but just then she was thrown on her beam ends, immense volumes of water swept over her, and the captain was never seen to emerge again. The four survivors scrambled over her side and on to the ice, remaining awhile in the hope of the captain appearing; but when this seemed in vain they started on the desperate attempt of reaching the land. It was just daylight when they touched the shore, and then they had to climb a steep cliff, fifty feet high, an almost impossible task. They were sheltered under the hospitable roof of a Renews fisherman, and when recovered came on to St. John's. The vessel broke up within a few hours, and no trace of the captain's body was seen. The survivors saved nothing but the clothes they wore. Their names are John Treverton (mate), Cornwall; (the other 3 from Liverpool, Newfoundland, E. Africa.)

25 February (RCG) An excellent theatrical entertainment took place in the Sunday-schools, Polruan, on Thursday last, on behalf of St. Saviour's Church Fund. The programme began with an overture by Miss Carrie Brokenshaw, and was followed by an original and farcical sketch, entitled "Stage Fever," which was written expressly for this entertainment by Mr. Wallace Wedlake and Miss Maud Bolton, who respectively took the parts of Professor Footlights and Miss Gerty Giggles. The farce was a complete success, and created roars of laughter, and at its conclusion the authors received a call. Mr. F. Denison's song, "Queen of the Earth" was very successful, and was followed by a piano-forte solo, "Mazeppa," by Miss Ivy Mugford. Miss Maud Bolton was well applauded for "The amorous goldfish," and Mr. Wallace

Wedlake received a tremendous encore for his finished rendering of "The Toreador's song," and very kindly gave "Alcala" in response. Mr. W.G. Lacey's Glee Party sang "Hark, the convent bells" with much finish and expression. Miss Carrie Brokenshaw received a well-merited encore for the piquant way in which she sang, "I don't want to play in your yard," which she sang in character. Mr. H. Gale's violin solo was a great treat, being the favourite air from "Cloches de Corneville." Master Hunkin also is a promising young performer, and was encored for his violin solo. Captain Bullock sang "Beauty's eyes" in a very happy style, and was much applauded.... Miss Annie Slade was loudly applauded for her song, "Thady O'Flyn,".... Mr. Allchin sang "Giles on politics," (in character) in his usual inimitable manner and he most good-naturedly responded to the vociferous encore.

The second part opened with an overture brilliantly played (as a duett) by Messrs. W.S. and R. Lacey, which was followed by Offenbach's amusing operetta, "The Rose d'Auvergne." Fleuresse was brightly acted by Miss Maud Bolton, who took the part in capital style; Mr. F. Denison, as Alphonse, acted the part of the trembling but devoted cobbler in a most amusing way. Mr. Wallace Wedlake (of Daly's Company, New York, &c., &c.), as Pierre, the blacksmith, shewed very great experience and resource, for while his comedy was intensely funny, it was, at the same time, characterised by complete refinement....

At the conclusion Miss Maud Bolton was presented with a beautiful bouquet of lilies. Many thanks are due to all the performers, but especially to Mr. Wallace Wedlake, for the very kind and able way in which he stage-managed the entertainment; to Miss Annie Slade, for the admirable manner in which she accompanied both the operetta and songs; and also for lending her piano; and to Mr. W.S. Lacey, who kindly helped with the musical part of the programme. The entertainment was entirely got up by Miss Maud Bolton, and a substantial sum will be handed over to the fund. There was a large and appreciative audience, and money had to be turned away owing to lack of room. Among those present were Mr. and Mrs. Quiller Couch, Miss Purcell, Mr. Edward Treffry and party, Miss Allchin, Mrs. Cooper, Miss Carthew, &c., &c.

11 March (RCG) In spite of the severe gales during the past week, Fowey escaped unhurt. At Polruan one old building lost its roof, and a few slates came off some of the houses.

Much sympathy is felt for those families in Fowey and Polruan who are so sadly bereaved by the loss of the *Pride of the Channnel* during the late gale.... The three-masted schooner *Pride of the Channel*, belonging to Fowey, from Martinique with rum for Bordeaux, was driven ashore near Naujat, in the Bay of Biscay, and six of the crew were drowned, one only being saved. The vessel was commanded by Capt. Hallow, and had on board 762 barrels of rum at the time of the disaster.

15 April (RCG) FOWEY NOTES.... Our Harbour Commissioners seem to be setting seriously to work to deepen our harbour, and to increase the facilities for vessels of large draught coming here for china clay. On Saturday a large "dredge" arrived, which has previously been in use in connection with the harbour works at Mevagissey, so that we may see the work speedily begun. Some of us are still wondering whether Fowey is to be made a minor torpedo-boat station, and those who enjoy boating on the lovely "Pont River" hope that this is one of the things that will not come to pass.

6 May (RCG) The ship *Dundee*, of Dundee, has lately sailed from Fowey for Philadelphia. She is a splendid vessel, with four masts, and of 2,000 tons burden, and is the largest that has ever been loaded at Fowey.

20 May (RCG) FOWEY On Sunday evening, before the sermon, the vicar, the Rev. H.N. Purcell, spoke very seriously on the subject of those members of the congregation who habitually occupied the appropriated sittings of the parishioners. It was at the request of the churchwardens that he spoke, and he pointed out the fact, that there were three pews marked "Free" at the back of the church, and he hoped in future those who had not sittings would use these pews; or, if they preferred it, there were, in various parts, seats to which the sidesmen (two of whom were in attendance sometime before service) would shew them, and thus the seats, which are appropriated would be at the disposal of those to whom they belonged.

3 June (RCG) A FOWEY BRIGANTINE AMID ICEBERGS Intelligence has just come to hand from St. John's, Newfoundland, dated May 15th, concerning the brigantine *Samuel Moss*, of Fowey, Captain T.J. Mably, and owned by Mr. S. Truscott, Charlestown, which sailed from Britonferry on April 23rd with coals for St. John's. Up to the 27th she experienced excellent weather, followed by high winds up to May 7th, when a dense fog settled down, and the next day icebergs were seen looming. Suddenly a tremendous gale sprung up with high cross seas, into which the ship rolled rails under. Tacking eastward in the hope of escaping damage, disappointment was met with. When about 220 miles E.S.E. of Cape Race she suddenly sailed into a terrible sea, the water pouring over her bulwarks on every side. Hands were instantly summoned on deck, the captain feeling certain something serious would happen. In a short time the ship collided with an enormous iceberg scarcely visible for fog. The iceberg towered high over her masts and carried away her jiboom bowsprit, and all forward tackle, and also her figurehead, with a portion of her cutwater. The bulwarks, port staunchions, and mainsail were swept away, the ship striking three times before being carried off by the tide. For half an hour she lay like a log, the sea breaking over her, filling the cabin, and forecastle, besides washing away every moveable article from the deck. The lifeboat was got ready, and up to his neck, Capt Mably secured some provisions from the cabin, all on board expecting the brigantine would founder. At the same time every effort was put forth to save her. The fore yard was used as a jiboom, and after the most strenuous efforts the crew succeeded in reaching port in safety, thankful for a remarkable escape, for at one time no one expected to live through the storm.

3 June (RCG) THE CRAB BY-LAW. Cornwall Sea Fisheries District Committee, at Truro was attended by Messrs. J. Tremayne, R. Foster, W.M. Grylls, M. Dunn....

The by-laws as to crabs, confirmed by the Board of Trade on the 26th Mar, 1896, reads.... No person shall remove from a fishery any male edible crab which measures less than six inches across the broadest part of the back, or any female edible crab which measures less than five inches across.... Penalty not exceeding for any one offence the sum of £20, and in the case of a continuing offence the additional sum of £10 for every day during which the offence continues....

Mr. Dunn stated that the destruction of five-inch crabs prevented breeding.... Mr. Grylls: Is it an established fact that up to a certain size, they do not breed?- Mr. Dunn said female crabs did not breed up to five inches.... There was a terrible drain on the male crabs now.... There were complaints as to the scarcity of crabs this season, and they ought to maintain the fishery....

It was stated that the present by-law bore hardly on fishermen who were scarcely able to gain a livelihood.... Mr. Tremayne said....he should like evidence as to the age at which female crabs bred....moved that a sub-committee consisting of the chairman, Messrs. Foster and Dunn be appointed to obtain evidence on the scientific aspects of the question.

1 July (RCG) CORNWALL AND THE JUBILEE.

POLRUAN. The celebration was carried out in a hearty manner. Arches, festoons, and other decorations were liberally displayed. Under the leadership of Captain Pelham Bullock a procession, consisting of the committee, children, and adults, marched through the town singing. En route the Jubilee waterworks were opened by Mr. Samuel Slade. On St. Saviour's-hill the children and the old people over 60 years of age had a free tea. Sports were held, and in the evening there was a display of fireworks, and bonfires lit.

LANTEGLOS BY FOWEY. Inhabitants of the rural portion of the parish commemorated the Queen's Diamond Jubilee by a gathering at Whitehouse, close to the new Board School. The greatest enthusiasm was displayed, and two arches decorated with flags marked the spot where the gathering was to be held. There was a free tea on Whitecross Green, during which the Board School children sang a number of patriotic songs. This was followed by sports and games for the children and young people in a field belonging to Hall Farm. With very few exceptions, chiefly persons too old or too infirm to leave their houses, the entire population, to the number of some 300, assembled, and it is probable that there never was in the parish so numerous, so united, and so enthusiastic a gathering before. A bonfire performed a fitting close to the day's proceedings.

FOWEY. Starting The Water Supply. The streets were gaily decorated with trees, flags, and lanterns, the whole of the inhabitants having decorated the exterior of their houses. The day's proceedings opened with the ringing of bells, after which a procession of Naval Reserves, Volunteers, Foresters, Oddfellows, and Sunday-School children, the latter gaily decorated with medals, marched through the town to witness the formal opening of the supply of water to the town from the 400,000 gallon reservoir. Miss Purcell, daughter of the Rev. H.N. Purcell (the vicar of Fowey), performed the ceremony of turning on the water. - The vicar having addressed the meeting, the procession went through the town by another route to the Town Quay, where the Volunteers fired a feu de joie, and the National Anthem was sung. A free public luncheon to all inhabitants over sixteen years of age was provided on a site overlooking the harbour, the vicar and Mr. A.T. Quiller Couch addressing the meeting. A special committee catered for the sailors in port, a free tea being laid for them in the Sailor's Rest. Boat races were included in their programme. A free public tea was provided for all children and adults unable to be present at the luncheon. Sports were held in the cricket field, and a grand fancy dress carnival took place in the evening. The proceedings concluded with a fancy dress ball in the Institute Hall and Town Hall.

22 July (RCG) NOVEL SUNDAY SCHOOL TREAT. - Fowey Church Sunday Schools at their annual festival was marked by a new departure. The teachers formed themselves into a committee, and arranged for an outing to Golant by water. About 230 children started from the church, headed by the Artillery Volunteer band, and embarked in large barges and boats, which were towed up the river by the steam launches, the *Winnie* and the *Rosie*. After landing at Golant the procession was re-formed, and paraded through Penquite grounds to an adjoining field, beautifully situated overlooking the river, and well shaded by trees. About 500, including visitors, partook of tea. The return journey was made about eight p.m., the party disembarking at Whitehouse.

29 July (RCG) Fowey Model Yacht Club - The race for the monthly challenge cup took place on Saturday in a strong southerly breeze and heavy sea. The course was from Polruan Castle to a flag-boat outside the harbour, distance two miles, dead to windward. Seven started, passing the flag-boat in the following order; - 1, *Enigma*, Mr. E. Treffry; 2, *Makeshift*, Mr. D. Treffry; 3, *Buttercup*, Mr. A. Slade. This is the second time *Enigma* has won the cup. Great interest was shown in the race, as *Butterfly* is the latest boat, and was designed and built by Mr. Edward Treffry, as were *Enigma* and *Makeshift*, and this is the third race this season that his boats have taken first and second prizes.

5 August (RCG) FOWEY. During the past few weeks, the domestic pets in the immediate vicinity of St. David's and Albert- terrace, have died a sudden and cruel death, no less than three valuable dogs and several pet cats having died suddenly, and by poison. Four cats and two of the dogs were destroyed in seven days. It is to be sincerely hoped that the reward of £10 which has been offered for any information that will lead to conviction may be speedily claimed, and that the cowardly perpetrator of such dastardly actions may be punished as severely as the law permits.

19 August (RCG) After a very stormy night and a doubtful early morning, the 11th August, the day of Fowey's "Royal Regatta," that great annual festival proved to be all that could be desired, the weather being most lovely on land, while there was a very nice breeze for the yachts - those that contended for prizes and the many that cruised about carrying those interested in the races. The harbour was crowded with craft of all kinds, all decked with flags, and mostly "rainbow" fashion. The two steamers from Plymouth and one from Falmouth brought large contingents of visitors, while a vast number of visitors arrived by rail and by road; and in spite of counter-attractions at Plymouth, which prevented the *Channel Queen* from having sufficient passengers to make it worth her while to fulfil her engagement to run to Fowey, there has never been so large a number of persons present nor a more successful regatta. The church bells rang merry peals throughout the day, and the quaint old town was filled with happy faces. As usual, the steam horses on the Town-quay were never without riders, and equestrians of all degrees yielded to their fascinations. Nothing could have looked prettier than the harbour did, both by day and by night, nor could one imagine a gayer scene, the brightness added to by the delightful strains of the band.... The greatest credit is reflected upon those gentlemen who gave so much time and trouble to perfecting the arrangements and to their being so admirably carried out.

Some disappointment was felt that, instead of their being a water carnival after the regatta, the very successful land carnival that took place on the day of the Queen's Diamond Jubilee was not repeated, this latter, and the fancy dress ball that followed it, having been such an unqualified success. However, we must hope that next year this may be arranged, as it would make such an excellent ending to the pleasures of the day....

In the evening there was a grand display of fireworks from a vessel moored in mid harbour, and this, with the water carnival, proved very attractive. The set piece of fireworks was a yawl yacht in full sail, the Cornish coat of arms, and "Good Night." Substantial prizes were offered for the best illuminated yachts and boats, but the prizes for the floral decorated boats did not draw many competitors, J. Hunt securing the first award. W. Bobs won the first prize for the best boys' darky party and the best decorated boat.....

A great attraction during the carnival was the illumination of the steam yacht *Speedy II*, owned by Baron Barreto, who took her round after the termination of the Cowes Week, at the special request of the Fowey Royal Regatta Committee, to which he most cordially responded. She was illuminated with electric lights from stem to stern. On the evening following the regatta the harbour was illuminated by a powerful search-light.

26 August (RCG) LOCAL GOSSIP. Miss Maud Bolton, of Fowey, has been performing with much success in amateur theatricals at Plympton. At the invitation of Mrs. Nicholls, of Galva, Mrs. Bolton assisted at the piano. At the conclusion Miss Maud Bolton received a beautiful bouquet.

30 September (RCG) Bankruptcy of a Polruan Grocer. George Alfred Taylor, grocer and general dealer, of Polruan, met his creditors at Plymouth on Friday. Debtor....estimated his unsecured liabilities at £189.15.9.... He had been in business a quarter of a century, having started with a capital of £30. Five years ago he paid his creditors by arrangement a composition of 4s. in the £. No deed was prepared, and debtor had since paid several of his creditors in full. To pay the composition he borrowed £100, which he had since repaid, with the exception of a balance of £12. Two years ago a fire occurred on his premises. His stock was fully insured...., but he was insured as a grocer and not as a general dealer, and the company ....paid only the value of the groceries damaged, and refused to pay anything for the other goods, which formed the bulk of the stock. He recently sent a circular to his creditors offering to pay 2s. in the £, but as the creditors did not accept he filed his petition. He attributed his insolvency to want of capital, competition....losses in the business, and by the fire....

7 October (RCG) Fowey Congregational Church continued the celebration of its centenary last week.... At a high tea about 150 sat down. At a public meeting in the evening the church was filled to overflowing.... After the choir had sung an anthem the chairman introduced the Rev. Urijah Thomas (of Bristol), who gave his lecture "Church Comradeship". In the course of his remarks, he made reference to the ringing of the bells of the parish church, which were rung through the greater part of the meeting, much to the annoyance of the congregation. The rev. gentleman said "Much of what we call "Church comradeship" oftentimes is as sweet, alas, as the chiming of yonder bells"....

1898

6 January (RCG) "Q" ON WESLEYANISM IN CORNWALL. Mr. A. T. Quiller Couch last week opened a bazaar at Polruan for the reduction of the debt on the United Methodist Free Church there.... Mr. Quiller Couch said:... my grandfather, Dr. Jonathan Couch, of Polperro, was an original member of your Association, as it was called in 1835.... Further, I....always hold that a Cornishman must be....extremely bigoted....who is not willing to take off his hat to the great name of John Wesley.... After 150 years you are still keeping bright the torch which Wesley re-kindled..... Perhaps....the Divine notions of beauty....find less satisfaction in....easy offerings of the rich than in some humble chapel, every stone of which has been set in place and cemented there by the efforts of poor but cheerful hearts.... That is why I count it an honour to have been invited to declare this bazaar open.

20 January (RCG) It is stated, and upon very excellent authority, that a mansion, with all the adjuncts of a gentleman's seat, is about to be erected on land near Fowey reservoir, the entrance being from the Par-road where there is to be a lodge. The gentleman for whom the mansion is to be built is, we understand, a native of Fowey, who left it early in life, and who still retains, like many others, an affection for the home of his youth. A more beautiful situation for such a house could hardly be wished for. (Fowey Hall, perhaps?)

20 January (RCG) FOWEY. We are glad to hear that the gymnasium classes which were started through the kindness of Mr. Hayton, are to be resumed. The classes have not met with such full support, of a pecuniary kind, as is requisite to carry them on satisfactorily, and it was at one time feared that they must be given up for lack of funds. But this difficulty seems likely to be overcome, and we understand that the weekly classes in the Town-hall will be begun again towards the end of this month; and it is hoped that the young men and boys for whose benefit they were begun, will show their appreciation of the opportunity given them for acquiring skill in athletic exercises, and that substantial assistance may be given by others towards the carrying on of what is practically "a good work."

10 February (RCG) Last week we reported that William Tippett, cook of the barquentine *Ocean Spray*, of Fowey, which arrived at Ipswich from the West Indes, was missing. On Jan. 29 he was left on board, apparently quite sober. When the captain returned, the gangway to the shore was upset, and Tippett could not be found. His cap was picked up in the dock. Nothing further discovered until Monday, when the body of Tippett was found at noon entangled in the lock gate machinery. Tippett was a native of Fowey, where he leaves a widow and family.

The inquest was held....on Monday.... Marcus Hamden, mate of the *Ocean Spray,* identified the body as that of William Tippett, steward of the vessel. He last saw deceased at half-past six on the 29th January. Deceased was married, with seven children, living at Fowey. The body was recovered about thirty feet from where the vessel was moored. The crew went ashore by means of a ladder, upon which was fixed a plank and stanchions. The same night about 11:30, when the captain returned to the vessel, he found the ladder collapsed and one of the ropes broken. They surmised, as the deceased did not return the next day, that he had fallen off the gangway.... Deceased ought not to have left vessel that night, as he was in charge with the boy.- Hedley Vicars Blogg, ordinary seaman, of Fowey, and two witnesses spoke to seeing deceased perfectly sober at nine o'clock the same night. He told one of them he was going aboard to prepare the captain's supper. After other evidence the jury returned a verdict of "Found Drowned".

24 February (RCG) The *Spinaway*, of Fowey, Capt Richards, from Cadiz to St. Johns, Newfoundland, with salt, after being at sea 80 days, during which time she has been caught in the ice on the coast of Newfoundland, has been compelled to put back to Fowey, short of provisions.

24 February (RCG) FOWEY HOTEL COMPANY. - The directors having carefully considered the amount of revenue derived in the past from the posting branch of the company's business, decided to dispose of the horses, carriages, &c., used in this branch. The sale was effected, and an agreement providing....for the service of the hotel omnibus, and for the convenience of visitors to the hotel, was entered into between the company and the purchaser, Mr. W.H. Bunt, who now rented the stables and coachhouse....

10 March (RCG) Yachting men visiting Fowey during the coming summer will, no doubt, be glad to avail themselves of the accommodation which the new club house now being built for the members of the Fowey Yacht Club will afford them. We hear there are over 100 members, who own amongst them over 2,000 yacht tons; and it is said so many candidates are coming up for election that it will not be very long before an entrance fee is charged for out-port members, as is now done for residents. Fowey, being what one might term a half-way house between Plymouth and Falmouth, is a very convenient and charming port of call for yachts. Dredging operations will be recommenced almost immediately. There is some talk amongst the members of the club of forming a small boat racing class, after the style of the Teignmouth class. A rumour is also in the air that the Fowey Model Yacht Club intend opening a club house close by, and it is just possible that two days may be devoted to the Royal regatta this year.

24 March (RCG) The outlook for model yacht sailing in the West of England for 1898 is very encouraging. Plymouth, Fowey, and Brixham Model Yacht Clubs have come to a mutual understanding, and are constructing a class of "20 Raters," L.W.L. and S.A., 6,000 Rule, to compete for the West of England Model Yacht Challenge Trophy, to be sailed for at Fowey on May 30th. Brixham and Fowey clubs are very busy, and their boats will soon be under weigh. Fowey Club have acquired a club-room, and are arranging an exhibition and entertainment on Wednesday, the 30th instant. The Plymouth club start their season on the 23rd prox. with the first of five races to select the three 20 Raters to compete at Fowey.

24 March (RCG) The winter session of the Polruan evening continuation classes has now ended. During the season the average attendance has been 35 - Tonic-sol-fa 44, arithmetic 46, and mensuration 15.

24 March (RCG) EXTRAORDINARY CASE AT FOWEY. CHILD BORN IN A TRAIN. An inquest was held....at Fowey last week, relative to the death of the male child of ----_----, of Esplanade-road, Fowey. Charles Langman, 'bus driver, stated that on Friday, (the girl) arrived by the 3.20 p.m. train from Plymouth. She had a parcel wrapped up in her jacket, and was driven to her mother's house in the 'bus. The mother of (the girl) stated that her daughter had been in service at Stoke for several weeks. She had no idea her daughter was in trouble, or she would not have allowed her to go to Stoke. On arriving home on Friday she noticed she was ill and asked her what was the matter. She replied that she had had a child in the train on her way from Plymouth, and that it was in the parcel. She found the child was dead. Her daughter said just after the train started from Saltash she was confined. On Monday her daughter saw the police outside the house, and she called to her sister to take the child to the sexton, and if she could not find him to walk about for a while and bring it back again. Her daughter went out with the parcel, and soon after returned with the police constable.

Inspector Kitto stated that, acting on information received, he stood in the Esplanade-road on Monday. A young woman, going towards the Fowey Hotel, had a parcel wrapped in newspaper; and, as she answered somewhat the description of the woman who had had a child in the train on Friday, he told P.C. Vicary to ascertain who the girl was and what the parcel contained. In a few minutes P.C. Vicary returned with her, and they went to her mother's house. Her daughters ---- and ---- said, "They want to see what's in the parcel." Mrs. ---- said, "There's nothing there to see, unless it may be my work." He pressed them to allow him to examine the parcel, and they refused. He then called Mrs. ---- into another room, and she admitted her daughter....brought home a child last Friday. He then called in ---- who still had the parcel. On opening it he found a male child. (The girl) said," I was confined in the railway carriage, and was so frightened I did not know if the child was living or dead. I took off my skirt and wrapped it up and brought it home. I was afraid to say anything about it in case I should be sent to gaol.

P.C.Vicary said he was ordered by the inspector to follow a young woman whom he suspected. He followed ---- to the bottom of the road leading to the hotel. When she turned going towards her home, he asked if she had found that parcel. She said, " This is some work mother has done." He asked if he could see what the parcel contained. She answered "No; perhaps mother will let you see."

Dr. Boger, who had made a post-mortem examination, said the child was fully developed. There were no marks of violence on it. It had breathed and death was due to hemorrhage.

....The jury found that death was due to insufficient attendance at time of birth, and added that the conduct of Mrs. ---- was most unsatisfactory. The mother of the child is under police supervision at her home, and when sufficiently recovered will be charged with concealment of birth. (**7 April** issue - the Tywardreath bench.... considered the accused had not actually concealed the birth, but had confided in her mother, who did not take steps to immediately report the matter, discharged her.)

7 April (RCG) PRISONER CUTS HIS THROAT. Respecting Richard Taylor, arrested on Sunday night, on a charge of burglary at the residence of Mr. A.T. Quiller Couch, at Fowey, Supt. Matthews reported to the Tywardreath Bench on Thursday that on Wednesday the prisoner attempted suicide by cutting his throat with a razor. Previous to being placed in the cells he was searched, and it is believed he concealed the razor in his boot, and then after being searched about the upper clothing, slipped the razor up his sleeve while stooping to unlace his boots. Eight razors were found on him, in addition to the one with which he attempted suicide. Immediately after he cut his throat he was discovered, and Dr. T.P. Tuckey was sent for. Meanwhile Inspector Kittow was able to apply the knowledge received at the ambulance classes at St. Blazey to stop the excessive bleeding. Dr. Tuckey found the wound, though serious, was not fatal, and promptly sewed it up.... The prisoner will in all probably be removed to the hospital at the county prison, Bodmin. From the determined attempt which the prisoner made to commit suicide it is conjectured that he may possibly be "wanted" elsewhere.

It will be remembered that Mr. Quiller Couch's home at Fowey was entered on Saturday week, and ransacked from top to bottom. The burglar opened drawers and wardrobes, and extracted a quantity of clothing and boots, opera and field glasses, a silver tea caddy, and a gold brooch, the latter belonging to the servant. On Sunday, in company with Inspector Kittow, Mr. Couch made a round of inspection of the ships in the harbour, and later the inspector visited a lodging-house at St. Blazey, where he found the man Taylor and a sack containing some of the stolen articles.

5 May (RCG) FOWEY. May-day having fallen on a Sunday this year, we were spared the saturnalia which usually prevails here on May morning, though on Monday the youths of the place endeavoured to make up for their loss by ringing furiously at door-bells, and, where there were none to ring, knocking violently at doors, thus rousing the sleeping inmates of the houses which they honoured. The procession of small children dragging tins and kettles did not take place, a custom far more blessed in the breach than in the observance. To keep up old customs which are sensible or picturesque is a thing much to be desired, and too many such customs cannot be maintained, but where the fun comes in of breaking bell wires, and dragging old frying pans and kettles through a town, is, to say the least, somewhat mysterious. Owing to the inclement weather, presumably, no children went about with garlands this year.

23 June (RCG) FOWEY. On Monday, the day on which the Queen entered on the sixty-second year of her reign, the handsome flag presented to the parish by Mr. A.T. Quiller Couch floated from the Church tower. The flag was given last year in honour of the Queen's Jubilee, and we hope that, in spite of her advanced age, it may yet be many years before the 20th of June no longer sees this flag on our tower.

30 June (RCG) FOWEY. A very sad accident took place here on Friday afternoon. Captain Hill, of Polruan, was unmooring his boat, which was fastened up at the town quay, and in order to do so was obliged to stand on a heap of loose stones. One of these gave way, and Captain Hill was precipitated upon the beach, it being then nearly low water. He fell partly against his boat, and sustained very serious injuries, his head being hurt, and one shoulder and his collar-bone being broken. He was attended by Dr. Morse, and afterwards by Dr. Boger and Mr. Cann, and was conveyed to the Cottage Hospital, where he lies in a very critical condition. Much sympathy is felt, for the accident is singularly sad, and Capt. Hill is greatly respected.

7 July (RCG) The new club house, belonging to the Fowey Yacht Club, is, we understand, to be opened on the 9th August,.... It is a very pretty building, and it is a pity that the many new houses which have been built here - some of which are not yet quite completed - have not been built in a similar style, as had this style of architecture been adopted it would have added greatly to the picturesqueness of the place.

11 August (RCG) Tuesday last, the first of our two days "Royal Regatta," will long be remembered as the day on which the Yacht Club's new club-house was opened. The building itself is most picturesque. It is close to the present vicarage, and is built on ground where, for a time, a shed for building a yacht stood. The view from the club grounds is very lovely and commands a view of the entrance to the harbour.... It is near to the Post-office, and has a very convenient water entrance. The flag officers and members of the club celebrated the opening of their new club-house by giving a reception on Tuesday afternoon. The weather was all that could be desired; the reception was a brilliant function, and the invitations given by the club resulted in the assembling of about two hundred guests. The band of the Royal Marines was in attendance, and a most eloquent and sumptuous afternoon tea was provided by the hosts.... The tea was held in the fine billiard room, and the club-house itself was thrown open to the guests. A crimson and white awning was erected along the whole length of the building, and seats were placed under it....

In the evening we seemed to have gone back a year, and to be having a repetition of our "Jubilee day", for we again had a carnival and "a feast of lanterns"....a great many houses along the route were illuminated, and the effect was charming. Among the most beautifully decorated was Dr. Boger's, which was not behind in coloured lamps. After the carnival a fancy dress ball took place in the Albert Hall, which has only lately been completed. A brilliant scene was the opening of the ball, when the lovely costumes were able to be seen to good advantage in the long ball room, which was well lighted.

20 October (RCG) The cricket club had its annual dinner at the Commercial Hotel on the 12th, and, as might be expected, there was a goodly attendance, and a very pleasant evening was spent. The secretary, Mr. J. Hannan, reported that the season had been a very successful one, twelve out of the eighteen matches having been won by Fowey. Next year the committee hope to be able to secure a better pitch.

10 November (RCG) FOWEY. Now that one hears so much in the way of wars, and rumours of wars, it is satisfactory to learn that one little port is not forgotten, and that orders have been issued for its defenses to be strengthened by the addition of some more quick-firing guns.

INDEX

289

Belfast	13
Bell Inn	17
Bell's Lane	147
Bell-ringing	141, 214
Belletti	201
Bennet/Bennett	19, 25, 29, 67, 68, 200, 231
Bennett & Bennett	200
Bersey	206
Best	81, 231
Betchelor	202
Bethel Institute, Falmouth	269
Betty	134
Beverly	33
Bible Christians	224
Bickerlegs	58
Bickle	113
Bideford	85, 118, 198
Bishop	139-142, 147, 158
Black Bottle Rock	267, 268
Black Head	81
Blantyre, Lord	109
Blewett	54
Blight	199
Blisland	264
Blizzard of 1891	249
Blogg	283
Blowey	202, 234, 267, 268
Bobs	281
Boconnoc	23, 33, 89, 92, 93, 129, 141, 194, 273
Bodinnick Ferry	130, 141, 143, 145, 167, 168
Bodinnick/Bodinnoc	34, 94, 97, 118, 130, 140, 143, 144, 173, 181, 186, 193, 196, 206, 207, 217, 220, 236, 256, 272
Bodmin	17, 23, 28, 35-37, 40, 56, 58, 60, 62, 67, 79, 81, 100, 129, 140, 222, 245
Bodmin Gaol	35, 45, 78, 79, 97, 112, 127, 137, 198, 205, 285
Bodmin Lunatic Asylum	210
Boger	240, 245, 261, 264, 266, 267, 271, 272, 285-287
Bolton	254, 256, 261, 276, 281
Bolton House	179
Bonaparte, Buonaparte	21, 35, 41
Bone	64
Bordeaux	22, 23, 46, 162
Borlase	61, 69, 82, 90
Boston, Lincolnshire	193
Bottle	122
Boucher	201

Boundary Cross	212
Bowen	269
Braddon	271
Bray	10, 11, 23, 122, 137, 153, 226, 229, 230
Brazil	64
Brazen Is. Sardine Co.	225
Brazen Island	181, 225
Brenton	102
Breslaw	35
Brest	65
Brett	266
Brewer	198
Brewer & Co., Messrs.	222
Brickel	58
Bridges	217
Bridgewater	272
Brine	169, 170
Bristol	216, 282
Brixham	284
Broad & Sons	266
Broadslip	66, 115, 116, 144
Brock, P.C.	182
Brodersen	228
Brokensha	34
Brokenshaw	54, 91, 94, 134, 253, 254, 256, 262, 276, 277
Brooks	193
Brown	12, 14, 19, 24, 25, 94, 128
Browne	82
Brunel	68
Bryant	201
Buchanon	33
Buckingham	131, 232
Buckingham, Duke of	63
Buenos Ayres	25
Building	101, 128, 142, 149, 164, 165, 184, 189, 194, 206, 207, 210, 211, 216, 224, 236, 244, 252-254, 261, 263, 269, 270, 282, 286
Bulgar	122
Bull-hill	230
Buller	88, 160, 161
Bullock	127, 277, 279
Bunt	103, 185, 275, 283
Burghley, Lord	218
Burial Board, Fowey	243
Burnett	137, 147, 148, 250
Burns	263
Burrough	53, 54
Busan	55
Butman	127
Butson	181

Cochrane	21	Couth	167
Cock	22, 23, 33	Cowbridge	211
Coghlan	219	Cowl	254
Cole	140, 155, 156	Cowling	195
Colenso	98	Crago	35
Collins/Collings	19, 37, 82-84, 96, 98, 112,	Crapp	53, 151, 197
	122, 123, 145, 146, 152,	Crawcour, Messrs	79
	177, 198, 200, 245, 246	Creak	194
Collisions	71, 90, 129, 162, 167,	Cremorne, Lord	218
	192, 193, 248, 278	Crew	53
Colliver	62, 79	Crews	57
Collom	12	Crewes	237
Colmer	13, 14, 22, 48, 52, 53	Cricket	84, 85, 88, 90, 92, 169,
Colquite	174		243, 287
Comb	44	Crimes	79, 127, 129, 133-137,
Commercial Inn/Hotel	111, 114, 132, 149, 165,		143, 145, 155, 164, 171,
	185, 209, 217, 287		172, 176, 177, 185, 198,
Communications	168, 228, 249, 272		203, 204, 208, 215, 266
Congdon	63, 65, 137	Crimes, Animal Cruelty	171, 176, 181
Congregational Church	216, 217, 236, 239, 243,	Crimes, Assault	45, 52-54 120, 125, 133,
	246, 282		134-137, 144, 147, 148,
Connelly	28		171, 172, 175, 176, 186,
Conner	38		187, 192, 195, 198, 209,
Constables	53, 78, 79, 82, 97, 106,		210, 220, 245, 272
	127, 147, 155, 156, 159,	Crimes, Desertion	78, 120, 127, 131, 134,
	165, 169, 171, 172, 175,		135, 145, 187
	176, 182, 195, 199, 206,	Crimes, Dispute	264, 265
	220, 222, 228	Crimes, Fraud	59, 61, 80, 124, 139, 180,
Consumption	256		226
Coode	220, 221	Crimes, Licences	10, 57, 139, 143, 145,
Cook	250		155, 156, 158, 159, 175,
Coombe	110, 159, 160, 266, 268		205, 265
Coombs/Coombes	37, 197	Crimes, Murder	35, 36, 37, 109, 110, 266,
Cooper	35, 36, 62, 277		267, 280
Cooth	203	Crimes, Slander	229, 230
Copplestone	268	Crimes, Theft	10, 28, 70, 76, 79, 82, 83,
Cork	62, 78		86, 96-98, 102, 105, 106,
Corn Laws	100		110, 112, 114, 118, 122,
Cornish	108, 131, 136, 138, 203,		123, 124, 129, 133, 137,
	232		140, 147, 149, 155, 165,
Cornish Coast Mission	239, 248		174, 177, 182, 204-206
Cornish Sardine Co.	240		228, 275, 285
Cornish Tent Co.	251	Crimes, Vandalism	111, 128, 166, 215, 234
Coronations	61, 94	Crocker	205
Cory	57	Crough	66
Cossacks	41, 42	Crown and Anchor	42, 152, 194
Cossentine	147, 148	Cullinane	191
Cotsh	246	Cullis	113
Couch	18, 58, 83, 114, 120, 122,	Culm	38
	222, 285	Curtis	97, 98, 147, 148, 157
Couche	85	Customs	13, 21, 43, 45, 58, 65, 68,
Coulem	58		76, 81, 85, 87, 88, 94,
Courteney/Courtney	209, 271		102, 103, 121-123, 128,
Courts	72		132, 145, 146, 149, 170,

Gill	25, 110, 133	Hamley	87, 101, 104, 121, 167, 245, 246
Giradot	191	Hand-bells	201
Givet Prison	37	Handcock	203
Glanville	96, 97	Hanging	37
Glasgow	130	Hannan	287
Glasson	199	Hanson	101, 242
Glencross	196	Harbour	32, 40, 119, 133, 145,
Globe Hotel	174, 175, 177		149, 160, 163, 164, 170,
Glubb	266		179, 201, 204, 206, 209,
Glynn	60		218, 235, 252, 258, 277,
Goins	79		278
Golant	113, 168, 169, 267, 268,	Harbour Commissioners	204, 209, 255, 263, 277
	270-274, 280	Harper	86, 87
Golding	13	Harrington, Earl of	218
Golf	268, 270	Harris	86, 114, 156, 202, 208,
Goodbear	93		234
Goran	95	Harrison	240
Gould	242	Hart	58, 59
Govett	264	Hart Inn	44
Gower	83, 109	Hart?	132
Gragon/Gregon	18, 44, 46,	Harvey	27, 80, 133, 134, 157, 178
Graham	14, 16, 20, 132, 233, 238,	Haven	271
	243, 261	Havre	64
Grain	11, 12, 120, 235	Hawke, Jonathan	86, 109, 135, 136
Granville	33, 197, 198	Hawken	130, 147, 148, 184, 226,
Grase	228		245, 266
Grant	169	Hawker	215
Graves Sawle	220, 239	Hawkes	135
Gray	225	Hawkins	27
Greaves	180	Haye	221
Greet	208	Hayes	78, 196
Grenoak	22	Hayle	236
Grenville	89, 92, 143, 145, 167	Hayton	282, 283
Gribben/Gribbon	77, 81, 91, 109, 137, 139,	Health	134
	192, 273	Hearle/Hearl	21, 26, 67
Grose	273	Hearn	202
Grundy	252	Heath	86
Grylls	121, 278	Heishmann	270
Guadeloupe	46	Hele & Co.	258
Guernsey	14, 58, 104, 121, 124	Hellar/Heller	206, 207, 210
Gundry	107, 261, 262	Helston	55
Gunpowder	168, 169	Hems	273
Guy	271	Hemsworth	76
Guy Fawkes	164, 268	Henderson & Sons	244
Gypsies	69	Henry, Prince of Battenberg	272, 273
Hains	13	Henwood	128, 138, 139, 204, 261
Hall	105, 106, 130, 214, 238	Hern	231
Hall Farm	279	Hewett	49, 108, 146, 182
Hallet	53	Hext	221
Hallow	277	Hicks	28, 83, 85, 92, 96, 97,
Ham	49, 69, 70, 80, 133		105, 106, 108, 110, 122,
Hambly	37, 57, 76, 80, 171, 172,		123, 127, 129, 130, 131,
	208		143, 163, 204, 214, 231,
Hamden	283		

302

SHIPS INDEX